D1027460

INTENTION
and CHOICE:
The Character of Prose

INTENTION

 RANDOM HOUSE *New York*

and CHOICE:
The Character
of Prose 🙰

EDITED BY *Gregory T. Polletta*

BROWN UNIVERSITY

FIRST PRINTING

Preface

THIS IS AN ANTHOLOGY of essays and other works of prose literature of classic stature or, if contemporary, of conspicuous literary merit. Each piece is an instance of artful writing, and taken
together the selections display some of the essential aspects of
the character of prose in English.

The collection does not pretend to comprehend the whole
reach and range of prose, but neither has it been cut to fit some
prescriptive notion as to what kind of style is best for English,
whether familiar or ornate, plain, middle, or high. The selections
have been picked with an eye to the varieties of artful writing,
and they do illustrate some of the major styles which have
shaped the history of English prose, but before every other consideration they have been chosen as examples of outstanding
performances in words.

The single works included here, classic and contemporary
alike, are meant to show the powers of the literary medium of
prose. They are offered as an exhibition of live and practicing
writers, the classic no less so than the contemporary, with each
man demonstrating his craft in turn, and together displaying the
resources of their common art. The format is historical, but the
selections can be taken as a whole; they compose in their medium
what T. S. Eliot called the "simultaneous existence" and the
"simultaneous order" of literature.

The Questions for Study and Topics for Discussion which
accompany the readings are meant to direct students to those
aspects of composition which make for good writing. They reflect and propose a certain way of looking at prose. They seek
to guide the student in the discovery of some of the properties

of language and structure which need to be understood in order to engage and appreciate the literary qualities of works of prose.

Is this book about the art of reading, or is it about the art of writing? Neither one solely—and, in the end, both. It is about the character of prose composition. It tests the common assumption that one learns to write by reading examples of good writing and by imitating their modes of composition and expression. This is not the only way writing can be taught, but it is the method which is most extensively practiced. I happen to believe that the method can work as well as any other, and better than most, but if it is to be effective we must satisfy at least two conditions.

One is that the models for imitation must be genuinely excellent. There is little value in apprenticing a student to works of prose that are slight in their art and thin in their language, however heavy the topic and insistent the issue, however up-to-date their subjects. Not any essay on civil rights, or alienation, or whatever else is agitating our conscience at the moment, will do. If an essay is to serve as a model for imitation, it must show by the power of its language and the excellence of its form a mastery of the expressive possibilities of the subject, for it is the verbal mastery, and not the subject itself, which students should try to imitate. The contemporary pieces included in this anthology treat important issues in human experience, but that alone does not distinguish them from the mass of articles that show the same concern. They have been picked because they realize by the quality of their verbal performance the most complete and interesting expressive possibilities of the experience.

The other condition which must be satisfied if writing is to be learned by reading excellent models is that the student must be given some instruction in *how* to read. He must learn how to analyze the composition of a work of prose. Critical reading and effective writing are thought to be complementary activities, and I agree that they can be, but learning how to read prose well is not a simple matter. Prose is no less demanding than poetry, or the novel, or the drama.

This book starts with the assumption that prose is an expressive and imaginative verbal medium. Understanding that medium is its objective. As much as any other book it is concerned with the significance of content, but it gives equal emphasis to the need for identifying, exploring, and appreciating the formal aspects of prose composition. The analysis of each work selected for study is meant to proceed by considering the sense of the whole work not as some isolable effect or detachable element, but as the product of the performance of the author's intention and the choices in verbal structure and techniques of language by which he fashions what he has to say.

This approach is analytical in mode and appreciative in spirit. Its aim is to enlarge the student's experience of prose, to acquaint him with the craft of its working, and to help him cultivate a delight in the writer's performance. To facilitate critical analysis I have provided some critical terms by which the student may register his perceptions in the experience of reading. The terms have been kept to a minimum, and, except for the terms "intention" and "choice," I have tried to make them unobtrusive. As much as possible I have relied upon terms which are familiar in modern literary criticism, or I have used terms which are traditional in rhetoric and the study of literary style. Even the terms "intention" and "choice" are common, and though I am using them in a sense which may invite controversy, I have not tried to make this book an exercise in polemical criticism.

Neither the method of close reading nor the critical terminology offered here is particularly new; what is unusual, perhaps, is the richness of the material which is placed before the mind of the student, and the depth and scope of the critical inquiry proposed for his study.

All of the selections are challenging; a number of them, especially the classical pieces, are difficult. Works of prose literature are, as I. A. Richards said of poetry, "relatively inexhaustible to meditation." They tax our powers of comprehension and our skills at analysis and interpretation. They put to an exhilarating test our sense of the way words work in literary discourse. But that does not mean that they should be the exclusive property of specialists in English literature. Even the classical works have been enjoyed by generations of readers of all kinds and stations, of all levels of education. They belong to the permanent history of the written and spoken language; they are instances of the living language in exemplary action; they are exacting but splendid models of the expressive capacities of English. And they are accessible to anyone who is prepared to appreciate the play of the mind in language. They are not beyond the grasp of any literate reader. Indeed, they are the best instruments by which literacy may be enlarged and deepened.

Since the Questions for Study and Topics for Discussion seek to probe as deeply as required by the works they accompany, they are necessarily complex and intricate. They are meant to open the works to clear comprehension, of course, but shallow questions and superficial discussion will not inspire genuine understanding. I have tried to make these fundamental questions, of the kind that one never leaves behind, no matter how far one advances in specialized study. They invite a searching response.

This is not too much to ask, even of students who are about to read and think purposefully about prose for the first time. The material in this book grew out of a course I taught to freshmen and sophomores. While I have no way of knowing to what degree they were typical, my students were a mixed bunch—English and non-English majors, bright and mediocre, articulate and awkward—and they all proved to be quite capable of handling the material. They grasped the questions, even if they could not always find satisfactory answers, and that seems to me to be the first necessary step toward understanding.

The questions here are primarily addressed to the student in order to guide him in his own discovery of certain aspects of the particular prose work, but in addition they direct him to certain topics which the teacher might find useful to explore in class discussion. Most of the topics expand upon the general implications of the work, or they treat some precise aspects of the character of prose. While some relations in style and sense among works are suggested, and some excursions into reflection on the ideas and issues of the works are proposed, the focus of the topics is on the composition of the individual work. These topics and questions are points of departure rather than pre-arranged destinations. Even my frequent asides and extended commentaries are meant to open discussion and stimulate inquiry rather than to impose conclusions. As such, the material gives the teacher ample leeway to develop his own notions and interpretations.

The questions are designed to carry the reader through the unfolding of the argument, situation, and experience expressed in the work. They derive from the principle that critical analysis ought to follow the constitutive process of the composition. The reader is asked to think his way through the work, in much the same way as the author himself fashions his thought in the work, rather than to think about certain topics abstracted from the verbal performance.

Hence, the questions for analysis are arranged as a progress of inquiry from the beginning of the work to the end. In some cases I have begun by posing a series of questions about the work as a whole—as points for the student to keep in mind while he makes his way through the details of the composition. As a general procedure, however, I have gone through the work step by step, stopping for reflection upon certain points of form and meaning—a rich word or phrase, a crucial sentence, a weighty paragraph or section, a turn in the argument or narrative—and exploring the significance of each of these units of composition, the questions coming thick and fast until they fill out the critical implications of the particular division, and then moving on to the next portion of the work. This procedure risks seeming cluttered, of course, but its advantage over single questions on discrete topics is to draw the reader into the local units of composition without his losing the sight and feel of the whole work. It catches the sense and effect of the developing shape of content in the whole work.

Each batch of questions contains a substantial amount of explanatory information. I have put this material here rather than in the more conventional headpiece or footnote because I want to show how the biographical and historical material that needs explanation bears directly upon the points in question. I have tried to anticipate the kind of information that the student is not likely to know but must have some notion about if he is to probe the significance of the portion of the work being studied. My aim in this procedure has been to make the act of critical reading a process of continuous inquiry.

Each set of study questions moves from one selection to the next in a loose progression of focus and intensity. One aspect of prose composition or analysis is stressed over others in each set, and the sets are arranged in a series of increasing scope and detail of treatment. The questions on Sidney's *An Apology for Poetry* delve into the composition of the whole work, but with less intensity than is found later in the book. With each succeeding prose piece, the performance of the whole work is kept uppermost, but some aspect of composition is singled out for special attention. Syntax is emphasized in the discussion of Bacon's essays; figurative language in *Death's Duel;* intention in the *Areopagitica;* irony in *A Modest Proposal;* perspective in the selection by Gibbon; and so on throughout the book. With the last essay, Baldwin's "Notes of a Native Son," all of the kinds of questions and topics which have been discussed are brought into full play in a comprehensive inquiry. Each selection and its accompanying exercises can, of course, be taken out of sequence and studied separately, but taking them consecutively will enable the student to proceed by gradations of intensity and scope in a ripening understanding of the character of prose in English.

Acknowledgments

I WISH TO THANK my colleagues Paul B. Taylor, John B. Gardner, Richard L. Francis, and Jeannette Rider for their help in trying many of the ideas in this book on our students. I am especially grateful to Paul B. Taylor for his contributions to the Questions with the Donne selection, and to Jeannette Rider for hers with the Swift essay.

I also wish to express my appreciation for the generous editorial assistance of Charles Muscatine, Mrs. Eve Shapinsky, and David Dushkin. Mr. Muscatine provided valuable critical counsel. Mrs. Shapinsky gave expert help in the preparation of the manuscript for publication. David Dushkin gave me warm encouragement, and, by perceptive editing and criticism, helped me to say what I mean and mean what I say. I am very grateful.

CONTENTS

INTENTION
and CHOICE:
The Character of Prose

INTRODUCTION

ALL OF US USE words to convey information, relate happenings, or communicate ideas and opinions. We express ourselves in words to explain, entertain, and persuade. The writer of literature differs from us in this common use of language not so much because he has other ends in mind as because he has an uncommon way with words and an uncommon sense of the performance of words. He is an artist at verbal composition. He treats words as a craftsman does his wood or stone or whatever his medium, to carve, mold, polish, and plane them into verbal structures expressing what he has to say and creating something instructive, pleasing, and persuasive all at once. Most of us are casual in the art by which we choose to express what we have to say, and fitful in our attentions to the expressive resources of the verbal medium—but the writer of literature habitually chooses and orders his words in a deliberate manner and for artful effect.

This is what Swift meant when he defined literary style as "proper words in proper places," or Coleridge, when he defined poetry as the best words in the best order. Coleridge learned his lesson when he was a schoolboy. His "very stern master," the Rev. James Bowyer, repeatedly stressed the principle that in works of literature "there is a reason assignable, not only for every word, but for the position of every word." The principle is easily stated and seems quite obvious, but no writer ever outgrows it, and if he does not understand and practice it he will never advance beyond the dreary mechanical labor of most schoolroom composition. Whatever else literature may be, it is the expression of proper words in proper places; the choice of the best words in their best order.

But what is it that determines which words are the "best" words? What makes words "proper"? If propriety is the basis of literary style, what kind of propriety is meant? Obviously, it is something more than the fussy niceties of "correct" usage. Nothing is more misleading than to think of style prescriptively and in absolute terms—as a rigid and narrow etiquette which dictates what a writer must or must not do. Correctness is desirable, of course, but not at the expense of liveliness of utterance, exactness of meaning, or authenticity of expression. Propriety is also something more than the facile admonitions of the conventional manual of style. Literature doesn't get made simply by obeying the rules of a handbook. "Write complete sentences." "Use the active voice." "Place the emphatic words of a sentence at the end." "Keep your strong points for the beginning or the close of a paragraph." "Make definite assertions." "Use concrete language." All of these commandments are useful. They represent sound advice. Every good writer observes them. But they are not inviolable, and they will not of themselves guarantee expressive discourse. All they establish is a set of probabilities; in general, they are more likely to result in effective writing than their alternatives. But the writer who knows his craft can, and often does, break them.

Take the first of these rules. A complete sentence is likely to be better than an incomplete one for fairly obvious reasons; but a writer can violate the rule and be quite proper in his expression. D. H. Lawrence, for instance, does so frequently. He begins his *Studies in Classic American Literature* this way: "We like to think of the old-fashioned American classics as children's books. Just childishness, on our part." Lawrence knows how to write a complete sentence. It isn't ignorance that keeps him from writing "That's just childishness, on our part." He has reasons for saying what he does. One is that he wants to catch the flavor of colloquial utterance. Another is that he wants to establish a certain tone. Another, and this is perhaps closest to the point, is that he wants to make his dismissal curt and final; he wants a decisive break (syntactically and substantively) with the position and attitude represented in the sentence preceding his fragment. The construction is perfectly fitting; it is exactly appropriate to his purpose and it comports properly with the rest of the work. The propriety of Lawrence's choice is judged by the way the expression suits the subject, the occasion of the piece, the impression he wants to make on the audience, and his identity as a writer. A sense of what is fitting is indispensable for literary style, but the measure of what is good, proper, and best is before everything else the way the writer makes his expression fit his purpose.

This is to make literary style more a matter of control than the dutiful observance of fixed rules. No discourse—indeed no utterance, written or spoken—is without style. Each mode of statement delivers different implications of meaning; every different way of saying something means something different, implicitly if not explicitly. "This is H_2O" and "This is water" are each different in style. They convey an identical explicit meaning, but different suggestions of meaning. In the first statement the speaker is likely to be talking about chemical composition; in the second, about the same liquid, but, depending on the context or situation of the utterance, any number of things besides its chemical composition. (As instances: "*This* is water"—meaning that the water here is sweeter than that chlorinated stuff in East Providence; "This is . . . *water*"—meaning that the 3.2 beer they serve here is no stronger than H_2O; "This is water!"—meaning that the ceiling is leaking and I'm fed up, or mad, or scared.) If one were to say "Pass the H_2O" at the dinner table, it would raise a smile or a wince. If that is the effect one wanted, the style would be proper; if not, the style would be miscalculated.

A writer cannot choose between using style or leaving it out. We all use style, we all exercise choice, we are all to some degree aware of what is or is not fitting in a certain context, but the writer of literature has by talent and experience acquired the freedom to say more truly and more exactly what he has to say. He has developed certain favored ways of saying what matters to him, he has a stylistic identity, but that identity is only the product of many trials in expressing the things that matter to him. Each of us has a stylistic identity, but with most of us it is incomplete or inconsistent. In the hands of an artist style is the fully controlled, fully formed, and fully liberated expression of what he is committed to saying.

The writer's control of composition begins with his solicitude for single words. He is scrupulous about the literal sense of words —of what they actually name and mean—but he does not stop where most of us do: with the single and dominant sense of a dictionary definition. He fashions definition by the artful control of context. He can make words say what he means, and mean what he says. Words are not, for the writer of literature, fixed and inert counters that mean one thing and one thing only; they are plastic verbal images, rich with expressive opportunities. Most of the words in our language carry several layers of meaning. They are instinct with connotations, suggestions, and associations. Just about every word can assume a sense in one context of discourse that it will not have in another. Placed in conjunction with other words, so that each animates the others, a word can generate many overtones of meaning. The right use of language is *making* sense; it is, as Croce said, "a perpetual creation."

The writer of literature can make a word say something very specific or he can bring its expressive resources into full play. He can contract or expand the senses of a word as his purpose requires—so that, for example, "civil" will mean "courteous" but not "non-military" in one context, but in another will mean "courteous" and carry overtones of "non-military," "civic," and "civilized" as well. He can create an environment in which even the shabbiest words are brought to fresh life. He can make the most common words ring as true and look as bright as new coin.

Many of his words point to concrete details and tangible objects, but he treats all words as if they were themselves tangible and concrete—even those called "abstract" because they represent concepts and qualities as opposed to objects. The writer of prose is more likely to use abstract words than writers in other forms of literature, but his handling of these words is just as creative. Many abstract words originally had a concrete basis and physical sense. The word "concept," for example, derives from "a conceiving," and that in turn from a word signifying the "seizing or grasping" of something. These meanings are usually lost sight of in common usage, but a fresh and sharp look—indeed, any exact use of "concept"—will quickly revive them. The writer of literature will often recover the concrete ground of abstract words, but even when he does not remind us directly of their root sense, he will invest them with graphic precision and concrete immediacy. Observe what the critic R. P. Blackmur finds in the word "performance": "*Perform* is a word of which we forget the singular beauty. Its meaning is: to furnish forth, to complete, to finish, in a sense which is influenced by the ideas clustered in the word *form;* so that *performance* is an enlightening name for one of our richest activities, rich with extra life." The verbal performance of the writer of literature seizes and draws us into just this kind of close inspection. He never neglects the singular beauty of words, whether they are abstract or concrete, and by his control of context he makes each word rich with extra life.

What I have been saying up to now comes to this: the writer of literature has a finer sense of words, a more skillful command of composition, a keener awareness of audience, a truer voice, a more defined stylistic identity, a greater range of choice, and a surer sense of expressive purpose than other men. He has all of these things by exercise and cultivation of the talent he was born with; they were not given to him outright. "From practice," as Wordsworth said, "he has acquired a greater readiness and power in expressing what he thinks and feels." He differs from us in the art of expression not in kind, but in degree—a surpassing degree, to be sure, but still it is degree and not something completely unlike. He does in consistently masterly fashion what we do poorly, or passably fair, or fitfully well. Most of us have known some moment of triumph when our words expressed what we had to say in a clear, forceful, and appealing manner; all of us are capable of artful utterance. This is not to say that we could all become artists if we put our minds to it, for few of us have the talent to match and sustain that excellence, but if we follow the artist's way with words, if we model ourselves after his characteristic performance, then we too can develop in our own writing a greater readiness and power to express what we think and feel.

And that is the reason why works of literature are worth reading and studying. They are models of instruction in verbal excellence. In writing, as in all the other arts, we learn more by doing than by theory. The most productive study in art is imitation. We learn how to sail by sailing, and if we want to improve our skills, we will do better by watching and imitating how a good yachtsman handles his craft than by looking into a treatise on seamanship. If we study the performance of a superb athlete, a master workman, a gifted mind thinking, we are bound to learn something of their way of doing things. With writing, too, we can improve our skills by studying and imitating the verbal mastery of the writer of literature. Imitation is, of course, something more than copying; it is acting as the skilled performer does, following his form, making his moves, absorbing his art.

Reading literature offers other satisfactions as well. It can be sheer pleasure. Wallace Stevens said "poetry is the gaiety (joy) of language." An appreciation of the pure joy of language in a work of literature is one of the ultimate rewards of reading. That kind of enjoyment may be just as useful as any practical study. Indeed, it may be that no work will yield its lessons unless the reader begins with a sense of pleasure in the play of language.

But whether works of literature are to serve as a source of pleasure or as models for imitation, they must be read slowly, carefully, and critically. As Thoreau said: "Books must be read as deliberately and reservedly as they were written." Reading literature becomes something of value only if we learn the artist's way with words. And that requires, first and foremost, a lively appreciation of the singular beauty and sense of words—an alert and accurate understanding of what words actually name and mean. Beyond this, good reading requires an understanding of the ways in which an artist chooses and orders his words to express his intention in a particular composition.

In more specific terms, the approach I am advocating for the critical reading of prose literature is by way of questions such as these: What is the author's purpose in the work at hand? What is its occasion? What are its formal structures and techniques of language? Why does the author choose this word and not some other? Why this turn of phrase? This syntax or mode of address or rhythm or tone? This order of words and not some other? What effects are achieved by the choices made? What other effects would have resulted from different choices? How do the choices shape the reader's response to the content of the work?

These questions comprise a method for engaging the mind with and thoroughly understanding the style and sense of the work of prose literature. The method is perhaps as close as the reader can come to the creative process. In fact, it is the critical equivalent of the creative process since it fosters that sense of the artful selecting and ordering of language which moves the writer in composition. It opens a kind of dialogue between the reader and the writer—a conversation in which the reader observes and himself articulates the process of artful composition.

Let us look at some examples of how intention and choice function in works of prose literature. Consider first, as an illustration of how the writer invests individual words with meaning, the famous statement in Milton's *Areopagitica*: "that which purifies us is trial, and trial is by what is contrary." What do the words actually name and say? What images are expressed? The concrete ground of "trial" is obvious enough if we think about it; the word signifies a "trying or testing," as in a contest or an ordeal. "Purifies" seems more abstract. Its notional meaning is quite clear, but if we are looking only for that, we are likely to miss the image and experience embodied in the word. If we receive it as an abstraction, we will translate its literal sense into a moral concept: "that which makes us good," and various cognates of this, such as "edifies," "ennobles," or "exalts." These are conceptual equivalents rather than exact renderings of meaning. But the word has, in fact, a concrete sense. It refers implicitly to a particular condition and is meant to provoke a vivid, even physical, response. "Purifies" means "cleansed of infection," "freed of pollution," "cured of disease by a catharsis."

Now one might argue that these meanings have dropped from modern consciousness. "Purify" doubtless had a more immediate impact in the seventeenth century when diseases like the plague were very real threats to life; any word in an oration or sermon or essay which evoked the familiar pestilences would have excited a sharp sensation. But even today the word carries a strong affective charge and it ought to be able to communicate its concrete character to the attentive reader—especially since Milton orders many other words conveying the same image and experience into an informing pattern of the *Areopagitica*. If we fail to perceive the word for what it is, that comes from our indifference to the graphic properties of language, not from the erosion of history.

We can see this, I think, if we compare the word "cancerous" in, let us say, the sentence, "He was afflicted with a cancerous pride." We are as much terrified by cancer as Milton's readers were by plague, but the modernity of the disease does not insure attentive reading. If we receive the word "cancerous" as an abstract counter, we will do the same as with "purifies"—substitute normative abstractions: "an evil pride," "a tragic pride," "a terrible pride." We will not receive its concrete meaning, which is "eaten by cancer," "infested by some swelling malignancy."

Understanding the concrete meaning and the graphic quality of "purifies"—the situation, behavior, experience, and thought it *pictures*—is essential to the understanding of the larger design and the plenary sense of the *Areopagitica*. Milton's argument may be said to take this form: Adam's fall condemned man to know good *by* evil. God has given man reason, which is the freedom to choose, "for reason is but choosing," in order that he might be restored to grace and survive his loss of innocence. Experience tries man; his reason is tested. Books are the breath of reason itself, and he who destroys a good book kills reason itself, kills the image of God. Licensing books (by imprimatur) crops discovery and closes the power of choosing. Licensing mutilates man's saving freedom and dooms him to languish in the corruption and infection of his fallen state. Unlicensed printing allows books to flourish and hence enables that exercise of reason by which the state of infection may be purged. Licensed printing works to perpetuate man's original condition.

Behind the turns and motions of Milton's argument is the Christian commonplace expressed in Sidney's *An Apology for Poetry*: "our erected wit maketh us know what perfection is, and yet our infected will keepeth us from reaching unto it." The purging of infection is not a mere decoration in Milton's argument, and the imagery of "purification" the pretty finery that dresses his thought; it *is* the argument. "Purifies" is an artfully chosen word which expresses precisely and capaciously the author's purpose. It is not something we leap over to get to its "idea"; it is meant to arrest our attention and sink the mind into its depths. That is the way artful reflective prose characteristically works, and that is the way such writing must be read.

Consider as another example, this time to show the way in which a writer orders words, the artful opening of Bacon's "Of Revenge":

> Revenge is a kind of wild justice, which the more man's nature runs to, the more ought law to weed it out. For as for the first wrong, it doth but offend the law, but the revenge of that wrong putteth the law out of office.

Why does Bacon order his words this way and not some other? What effects are created by the particular construction? Questions of this kind are applicable to the whole work. They are significant in all phases of the critical analysis of prose, from single words to phrases, sentences, paragraphs, and every larger unit of construction.

Here the most likely response would be to say that the author aimed at "emphasis"; that Bacon's expression orders the thought of the passage in a forceful manner. But this principle would make the structural pattern, the order of an author's words, little more than adornment—impressive and affecting, to be sure, but an ornament merely. And that would be so even if one reads with an exact sense of what the author's words name.

Unwound and made plain, the meaning of Bacon's passage might be expressed as follows: Revenge thrives in nature, but in the garden where justice is sovereign, it is a kind of wild growth which left unweeded by law can become unhealthy and threaten the dominion of justice. The law must therefore arrest the growth of revenge or destroy itself, and thereby its office, which is to serve and care for justice.

This reading shows some appreciation of Bacon's play of meanings on the notions of revenge, wrongdoing, law, and justice, but it does not probe very deeply into the artistic effects achieved by the structure of the passage. Nor does it answer *why* Bacon chose that particular order of words. We are presented with little more than a description of the content, a rephrasing of its thought, however faithful this paraphrase may be to the words and images of its expression.

Let us look at the passage again, this time with an eye to the way the structure of the words shapes its content. The first clause, "Revenge is a kind of wild justice," is stated as an arresting paradox. We are drawn two ways at once, toward the notion that revenge is just and toward the contrary notion that revenge is wild (i.e., reckless, imprudent, erratic, frenzied, unruly—the word is rich in meanings). If we were to make a stop here, we would be left with the possibility that revenge is justifiable, but it is clearly an uneasy balance from the start, and in developing the paradox Bacon throws the contraries which appear to be reconciled into opposition, making us realize that revenge is more wild than just. We are pulled along by the "which" clause to the point (formed in parallelism and ironical in tenor) that man's nature runs to what the law weeds out. Bacon turns the thought of the complete sentence around so that we are left with the notion that the more man's nature runs to this kind of justice, the more ought law to thwart its career. The second sentence revolves first about the wrong which generates revenge, and then, in almost the same motion, thrusts forward to embrace in its censure the greater wrong which is revenge. The sentence divides into two parts formed in antithesis. The antithesis pivots on "but the revenge of that wrong . . ."; it turns the mind first to the incitement mentioned in the first part of the sentence, then to the contraries of the opening statement, and finally to the thought which rounds out the idea of the passage: The wrongdoing which incites revenge offends the law, but unless it is left to the law to punish, then justice itself becomes wild and disordered.

This kind of analysis describes the *motion* of the meaning. It attends to the structure by which the mind is carried from one point to the next, first one way then another, moving forward and backward in poised articulation. It exhibits the forward progress of the idea, but it also catches the turns and surprises in the argument, the way in which the expression turns the thought over in reflection. In this case, it follows the involutions of Bacon's argument and demonstrates the athletic vigor of the discourse. More importantly, it shows how the movement of the form *composes* the sense of the work.

With some understanding of the way a particular structure functions, and some means by which this working may be described, the reader may be able to move to the larger question: Why did the author choose this particular construction? A full appreciation of the effects achieved by the structure is at least approachable.

In the example "Of Revenge" Bacon's object is to cure a distemper and turn a temptation away from a foolhardy act by friendly counsel. In his essay "Of Friendship" he said: "A principal fruit of friendship is the ease and discharge of the fullness and swellings of the heart, which passions of all kind do cause and induce." Bacon says in the same essay:

> Counsel is of two sorts, the one concerning manners, the other concerning business. For the first, the best preservative to keep the mind in health is the faithful admonition of a friend. The calling of a man's self to a strict account is a medicine, sometime too piercing and corrosive. Reading good books of morality is a little flat and dead. Observing our faults in others is sometimes improper for our case. But the best receipt (best, I say, to work, and best to take) is the admonition of a friend.

"Of Revenge" is written as if Bacon were giving just this kind of admonition. In the sentence following the passage quoted he writes: "Certainly in taking revenge, a man is but even with his enemy, but in passing it over, he is superior, for it is a prince's part to pardon." This flattery, though hyperbolic, might momentarily stay the revenger's hand, or its wit amuse and distract his mind. Look here, Bacon is saying, if you do take revenge, you are a vassal to your passion, and as low as your enemy, who has fallen into lawlessness and lost his place. If you forbear and pass the offense by, you rise to a prince's power, and you avoid the prince's wrath and the loss of your own place. Revenge would only double your injury (Bacon loves to play with divisions and sums of moral action), for in redressing the original wrong you commit a wrong which multiplies your distress . . . and so on through the essay, one man of the world talking to another— prudentially, pragmatically, not prescriptively. Bacon could have said "Revenge is wrong because . . ." and given the reasons I have paraphrased. But that form of argument would have failed his object. It would have been less compelling and persuasive an admonition, being less counsel and more denunciation, either too piercing and corrosive or too flat and dead.

The general effect of the order of Bacon's words is to create an impression of a mind actively thinking. The reader has a sense, as Morris Croll said, of the movement "of a mind discovering truth as it goes, thinking while it writes." The form of Bacon's writing expresses the mind in movement, the mind as it engages problems directly before it, rather than a mind at rest or retired, having done its work, and now only declaring its resolves and sentences. Bacon thinks through the topic of revenge. He does not affirm some conventional or traditional notion, and by rhetorical embellishment merely amplify or wittily express what was commonly thought and said in his time. The idea was familiar to his contemporaries, but he gives it a fresh aspect by his choice of expression. Indeed, the order of his words *makes* his argument.

Now, to say that Bacon "chose" this construction to achieve the effects I have described implies, because of the way we customarily use that word, a strictly rational act of deliberation. I think, however, the word has more stretch. An act of selection

in any given work, not on the mind and personality of the author himself. We can only know what was in an author's mind by an analysis of what he has made.

Even if I were to presume that the "idea" described in my interpretation is similar to or identical with what was actually in the author's mind, I would not want to imply that the author holds a pre-existent thought and then hunts for the best language to express it. An artist embodies an idea; he does not simply dress up a pre-conceived thought. "Thought" in literature is not in-dependent of expression. It does not exist as some abstract entity waiting in the wings of the mind for the most striking costume to show it forth. Expression can be an agent of discovery. Ex-pression can generate thought. At the very least, the bodying forth gives the thought its distinctive character and significance. The embodiment delivers the conception. Even when it does not invent the thought, expression gives the thought a sensible and intelligible form, and thereby brings it into being, creates its visible shape.

Furthermore, there are cases where the writer does not start with any definite idea in mind. An artist in words, whether of prose or of some other form of literature, may be as much con-cerned with exploring the possibilities of imagination and lan-guage—with a play of feelings and words—as he is with arguing notions and representing pre-conceived ideas.

But whatever his motive, the writer often will discover what it is that he has to say in the very act of saying it. He will dis-cover his intention in writing. In such instances the writer himself will not know what he had in mind to say until he has said it.

Now, if the author's intention is derived from the work, if it is an inference from the total performance of the actions and meanings of the words in a given work, why attach "intention" to the author at all? Doesn't it invite the obvious fallacy—the "in-tentional fallacy"—of trying to establish what an author *says* by appealing to what he *meant* to say? Doesn't it give an undue weight to the mental processes of the writer, no matter how in-geniously the notion is hedged by qualifications?

The objections implied in these questions have led many modern critics to be suspicious of the term. They have preferred to avoid any consideration of the author's intention and to con-centrate instead on the intent of the work. The work is what matters, they say, and not the man. What was actually in the man's mind is only of accidental significance, and even in those instances where we have original evidence, the direct testimony of the author, that information is valueless if his aims are not realized in the work. And if the aims can be found in the work, the author's testimony is merely corroborative; it is no more authoritative than that of any other witness, and we can do just as well without it.

There is no refuting this appeal to the work as the final arbiter for any interpretation. Still, it is clearly impossible to banish the author, for the work is, after all, a personal creation. To think that the man who conceived the work is not responsible for its meaning and effect is just as misleading as it is to think that its purpose can be judged only by what is presumed to have been in his mind when he composed it. One should be able to talk about intention without falling into the errors of the "intentional fallacy" and at the same time be able to appreciate how an author makes a work a distinctively personal creation.

If we define the author's intention as "the purpose that informs his work," we will keep our focus where it belongs in criticism, on the analysis of what is actually expressed in the work, but without losing the sense of a person expressing himself, and expressed in, the world his words make. The aim or design of the author will be that which is revealed and embodied in the work. The purpose that "informs" his work will be that which "gives form, formative principle, determinative character" to the composition. Purpose will be a shaping principle—not an aim that is imposed upon the formal materials of the work, but one that generates the form of the materials.

Accordingly, "intention" may be taken to describe that design of the author which shapes the content of a particular composition. Intention governs all of the other elements of composition from the beginning to the end, from the "occasion" to the final "sense" of the work. "Occasion" is the specific event, object, situation, person, action, or whatever, that starts an author writing. "Sense" is the whole of what an author is saying—the plenary meaning of the work; the total structure of meanings and effects, sensible and cognitive, which the work creates. If the occasion is what provides the writer with a subject, the intention is what causes him to conceive and form the subject to achieve the sense of a particular work. Intention directs the writer's choice of the best words in their best order.

That still leaves the problem of what to do with the person of the author, how much we ought to know about the man himself, and what role he plays in his work. If the author is so important, the reader may be left wondering, why can't we look into his life and learn all we can about his personality and intellectual make-up? No reason—except that this kind of investigation often turns up nothing but distractions and irrelevancies. We want, of course, to know as much about the author as will help in understanding the structure and sense of what he creates. An experienced critical reader is not likely to mishandle biographical information; he will know how to apply extrinsic information about the author without distorting the inner form of the work. But there are so many risks in this kind of inquiry that the beginning reader would do better to place the author as a person *in the work* rather than prior to it. He should try to comprehend the self which is expressed in the work, and not some personality antecedent to it. He should attend to the sensibility experiencing that which is communicated, and the mind reflecting on the experience and making it intelligible: the feeling and thinking self inside the work.

This does not mean that the mind and sensibility expressed in the work must be dissociated from the actual author. The person of the author in an essay or other work of prose is not ordinarily a fictive *persona,* an imaginary character. The speaking voice faithfully renders the thoughts and feelings of the man who signs his name to the piece. Whatever tricks he may play on the audience, the author of prose does not usually mask or conceal his presence. He wants the reader to know his mind. But the best way for the reader to apprehend the author's intention is to treat him as a character acting in the world made or imaged in the work.

Obviously, I mean this as something more than an expedient for prose analysis. I am assuming that the essay, and any other form of artful prose, is more the expression of a man thinking than the exposition of disembodied thoughts. It is not the thought, the notional content, merely, of a work of artful prose that holds our interest and quickens our pleasure, but the full play of the mind in words and the whole verbal performance—the mind making its meanings, shaping its reflections, composing its way of looking at things. Hence, an understanding of the person who thinks his way through a work, who expresses what he wants to say and *has* to say because of what he *is*, is of supreme importance in apprehending the structure of words that person creates.

AN APOLOGY FOR POETRY

BY *Sir Philip Sidney*

WHEN THE RIGHT VIRTUOUS Edward Wotton and I were at the Emperor's court together, we gave ourselves to learn horsemanship of John Pietro Pugliano, one that with great commendation had the place of an esquire in his stable. And he, according to the fertileness of the Italian wit, did not only afford us the demonstration of his practice, but sought to enrich our minds with the contemplations therein which he thought most precious. But with none I remember mine ears were at any time more loaden, than when (either angered with slow payment, or moved with our learner-like admiration) he exercised his speech in the praise of his faculty. He said soldiers were the noblest estate of mankind, and horsemen the noblest of soldiers. He said they were the masters of war and ornaments of peace, speedy goers and strong abiders, triumphers both in camps and courts. Nay, to so unbelieved a point he proceeded, as that no earthly thing bred such wonder to a prince as to be a good horseman. Skill of government was but a *pedanteria* in comparison. Then would he add certain praises, by telling what a peerless beast the horse was, the only serviceable courtier without flattery, the beast of most beauty, faithfulness, courage, and such more, that if I had not been a piece of a logician before I came to him, I think he would have persuaded me to have wished myself a horse. But thus much at least with his no few words he drave into me, that self-love is better than any gilding to make that seem gorgeous wherein ourselves are parties.

Wherein, if Pugliano's strong affection and weak arguments will not satisfy you, I will give you a nearer example of myself, who (I know not by what mischance) in these my not old years and idlest times having slipped into the title of a poet, am provoked to say something unto you in the defense of that my unelected vocation, which if I handle with more good will than good reasons, bear with me, since the scholar is to be pardoned that followeth the steps of his master. And yet I must say that, as I have just cause to make a pitiful defense of poor poetry, which from almost the highest estimation of learning is fallen to be the laughing-stock of children, so have I need to bring some more available proofs, since the former is by no man barred of his deserved credit, the silly latter hath had even the names of philosophers used to the defacing of it, with great danger of civil war among the Muses.

And first, truly, to all them that, professing learning, inveigh against poetry, may justly be objected that they go very near to ungratefulness to seek to deface that which, in the noblest nations and languages that are known, hath been the first light-giver to ignorance, and first nurse, whose milk by little and little enabled them to feed afterwards of tougher knowledges. And will they now play the hedgehog that, being received into the den, drave out his host? Or rather the vipers, that with their birth kill their parents? Let learned Greece in any of her manifold sciences be able to show me one book before Musaeus, Homer, and Hesiod, all three nothing else but poets. Nay, let any history be brought that can say any writers were there before them, if they were not men of the same skill, as Orpheus, Linus, and some other are named, who, having been the first of that country that made pens deliverers of their knowledge to their posterity, may justly challenge to be called their fathers in learning: for not only in time they had this priority (although in itself antiquity be venerable) but went before them, as causes to draw with their charming sweetness the wild untamed wits to an admiration of knowledge. So as Amphion was said to move stones with his poetry to build Thebes, and Orpheus to be listened to by beasts—indeed stony and beastly people. So among the Romans were Livius Andronicus and Ennius. So in the Italian language the first that made it aspire to be a treasure-house of science were the poets Dante, Boccaccio, and Petrarch. So in our English were Gower

and Chaucer, after whom, encouraged and delighted with their excellent foregoing, others have followed, to beautify our mother tongue, as well in the same kind as in other arts.

This did so notably show itself that the philosophers of Greece durst not a long time appear to the world but under the masks of poets. So Thales, Empedocles, and Parmenides sang their natural philosophy in verses; so did Pythagoras and Phocylides their moral counsels; so did Tyrtaeus in war matters, and Solon in matters of policy: or rather they, being poets, did exercise their delightful vein in those points of highest knowledge, which before them lay hid to the world. For that wise Solon was directly a poet it is manifest, having written in verse the notable fable of the Atlantic Island which was continued by Plato.

And truly, even Plato, whosoever well considereth, shall find that in the body of his work, though the inside and strength were philosophy, the skin as it were and beauty depended most of poetry: for all standeth upon dialogues, wherein he feigneth many honest burgesses of Athens to speak of such matters that, if they had been set on the rack, they would never have confessed them; besides, his poetical describing the circumstances of their meetings, as the well-ordering of a banquet, the delicacy of a walk, with interlacing mere tales, as Gyges' Ring, and others, which who knoweth not to be flowers of poetry did never walk into Apollo's garden.

And even historiographers (although their lips sound of things done, and verity be written in their foreheads) have been glad to borrow both fashion and perchance weight of poets. So Herodotus entitled his history by the name of the nine Muses; and both he and all the rest that followed him either stole or usurped of poetry their passionate describing of passions, the many particularities of battles which no man could affirm, or, if that be denied me, long orations put in the mouths of great kings and captains, which it is certain they never pronounced.

So that truly neither philosopher nor historiographer could at the first have entered into the gates of popular judgments, if they had not taken a great passport of poetry, which in all nations at this day, where learning flourisheth not, is plain to be seen; in all which they have some feeling of poetry.

In Turkey, besides their law-giving divines, they have no other writers but poets. In our neighbor country Ireland, where truly learning goeth very bare, yet are their poets held in a devout reverence. Even among the most barbarous and simple Indians, where no writing is, yet have they their poets, who make and sing songs which they call *areytos,* both of their ancestors' deeds and praises of their gods—a sufficient probability that, if ever learning come among them, it must be by having their hard dull wits softened and sharpened with the sweet delights of poetry; for until they find a pleasure in the exercises of the mind, great promises of much knowledge will little persuade them that know not the fruits of knowledge. In Wales, the true remnant of the ancient Britons, as there are good authorities to show the long time they had poets, which they called *bards,* so through all the conquests of Romans, Saxons, Danes, and Normans, some of whom did seek to ruin all memory of learning from among them, yet do their poets even to this day last; so as it is not more notable in soon beginning than in long continuing.

But since the authors of most of our sciences were the Romans, and before them the Greeks, let us a little stand upon their authorities, but even so far as to see what names they have given unto this now scorned skill.

Among the Romans a poet was called *vates,* which is as much as a diviner, foreseer, or prophet, as by his conjoined words, *vaticinium* and *vaticinari,* is manifest: so heavenly a title did that excellent people bestow upon this heart-ravishing knowledge. And so far were they carried into the admiration thereof that they thought in the chanceable hitting upon any such verses great foretokens of their following fortunes were placed. Whereupon grew the word of *Sortes Virgilianae,* when by sudden opening Virgil's book they lighted upon any verse of his making: whereof the Histories of the Emperors' Lives are full, as of Albinus, the governor of our island, who in his childhood met with this verse,

Arma amens capio nec sat rationis in armis,[1]

and in his age performed it: which, although it were a very vain and godless superstition, as also it was to think that spirits were commanded by such verses—whereupon this word "charms," derived of *carmina,* cometh—so yet serveth it to show the great reverence those wits were held in. And altogether not without

[1] ["Maddened I seize arms, yet little purpose is there in arms." *Aeneid,* II, 314.]

ground, since both the oracles of Delphos and Sibylla's prophecies were wholly delivered in verses. For that same exquisite observing of number and measure in words, and that high flying liberty of conceit proper to the poet, did seem to have some divine force in it.

And may not I presume a little further, to show the reasonableness of this word *vates,* and say that the holy David's Psalms are a divine poem? If I do, I shall not do it without the testimony of great learned men, both ancient and modern. But even the name "psalms" will speak for me, which, being interpreted, is nothing but "songs"; then that it is fully written in meter, as all learned Hebricians agree, although the rules be not yet fully found; lastly and principally, his handling his prophecy, which is merely poetical. For what else is the awaking his musical instruments, the often and free changing of persons, his notable *prosopopoeias,* when he maketh you, as it were, see God coming in his majesty, his telling of the beasts' joyfulness, and hills leaping, but a heavenly poesy, wherein almost he showeth himself a passionate lover of that unspeakable and everlasting beauty to be seen by the eyes of the mind, only cleared by faith? But truly now having named him, I fear me I seem to profane that holy name, applying it to poetry, which is among us thrown down to so ridiculous an estimation. But they that with quiet judgments will look a little deeper into it, shall find the end and working of it such as, being rightly applied, deserveth not to be scourged out of the church of God.

But now let us see how the Greeks named it, and how they deemed of it. The Greeks called him a "poet," which name hath, as the most excellent, gone through other languages. It cometh of this word *poiein,* which is "to make": wherein, I know not whether by luck or wisdom, we Englishmen have met with the Greeks in calling him "a maker": which name, how high and incomparable a title it is, I had rather were known by marking the scope of other sciences than by my partial allegation.

There is no art delivered to mankind that hath not the works of nature for his principal object, without which they could not consist, and on which they so depend, as they become actors and players, as it were, of what nature will have set forth. So doth the astronomer look upon the stars, and, by that he seeth, setteth down what order nature hath taken therein. So do the geometrician and arithmetician in their divers sorts of quantities. So doth the musician in times tell you which by nature agree, which not. The natural philosopher thereon hath his name, and the moral philosopher standeth upon the natural virtues, vices, and passions of man; and "follow nature," saith he, "therein, and thou shalt not err." The lawyer saith what men have determined; the historian what men have done. The grammarian speaketh only of the rules of speech; and the rhetorician and logician, considering what in nature will soonest prove and persuade, thereon give artificial rules, which still are compassed within the circle of a question, according to the proposed matter. The physician weigheth the nature of a man's body, and the nature of things helpful or hurtful unto it. And the metaphysic, though it be in the second and abstract notions, and therefore be counted supernatural, yet doth he indeed build upon the depth of nature. Only the poet, disdaining to be tied to any such subjection, lifted up with the vigor of his own invention, doth grow in effect into another nature, in making things either better than nature bringeth forth, or, quite anew, forms such as never were in nature, as the Heroes, Demigods, Cyclops, Chimeras, Furies, and such like: so as he goeth hand in hand with nature, not enclosed within the narrow warrant of her gifts, but freely ranging only within the zodiac of his own wit.

Nature never set forth the earth in so rich tapestry as divers poets have done; neither with pleasant rivers, fruitful trees, sweet-smelling flowers, nor whatsoever else may make the too-much-loved earth more lovely. Her world is brazen, the poets only deliver a golden. But let those things alone, and go to man—for whom as the other things are, so it seemeth in him her uttermost cunning is employed—and know whether she have brought forth so true a lover as Theagenes, so constant a friend as Pylades, so valiant a man as Orlando, so right a prince as Xenophon's Cyrus, so excellent a man every way as Virgil's Aeneas. Neither let this be jestingly conceived, because the works of the one be essential, the other in imitation or fiction; for any understanding knoweth the skill of the artificer standeth in that idea or fore-conceit of the work, and not in the work itself. And that the poet hath that idea is manifest, by delivering them forth in such excellency as he hath imagined them. Which delivering forth also is not wholly imaginative, as we are wont to say by them that build castles in the air; but so far substantially it worketh, not only to make a Cyrus, which had been but a particular excellency, as nature might have done, but to bestow a Cyrus upon the world to make many Cyruses, if they will learn aright why and how that maker made him.

Neither let it be deemed too saucy a comparison to balance the highest point of man's wit with the efficacy of nature; but rather give right honor to the heavenly Maker of that maker, who, having made man to his own likeness, set him beyond and over all the works of that second nature: which in nothing he showeth so much as in poetry, when with the force of a divine breath he bringeth things forth far surpassing her doings, with no small argument to the incredulous of that first accursed fall of Adam: since our erected wit maketh us know what perfection is, and yet our infected will keepeth us from reaching unto it. But these arguments will by few be understood, and by fewer granted. Thus much (I hope) will be given me, that the Greeks, with some probability of reason, gave him the name above all names of learning.

Now let us go to a more ordinary opening of him, that the truth may be more palpable: and so I hope, though we get not so unmatched a praise as the etymology of his names will grant, yet his very description, which no man will deny, shall not justly be barred from a principal commendation.

Poesy therefore is an art of imitation, for so Aristotle termeth it in his word *mimesis,* that is to say, a representing, counterfeiting, or figuring forth—to speak metaphorically, a speaking picture—with this end, to teach and delight. Of this have been three several kinds.

The chief both in antiquity and excellency were they that did imitate the inconceivable excellencies of God. Such were David in his Psalms; Solomon in his Song of Songs, in his Ecclesiastes and Proverbs; Moses and Deborah in their Hymns; and the writer of Job: which, beside other, the learned Emanuel Tremellius and Franciscus Junius do entitle the poetical part of the Scripture. Against these none will speak that hath the Holy Ghost in due holy reverence. In this kind, though in a full wrong divinity, were Orpheus, Amphion, Homer in his Hymns, and many other, both Greeks and Romans. And this poesy must be used by whosoever will follow St. James's counsel in singing psalms when they are merry, and I know is used with the fruit of comfort by some, when, in sorrowful pangs of their death-bringing sins, they find the consolation of the never-leaving goodness.

The second kind is of them that deal with matters philosophical: either moral, as Tyrtaeus, Phocylides, and Cato; or natural, as Lucretius and Virgil's *Georgics;* or astronomical, as Manilius and Pontanus; or historical, as Lucan: which who mislike, the fault is in their judgments quite out of taste, and not in the sweet food of sweetly uttered knowledge.

But because this second sort is wrapped within the fold of the proposed subject, and takes not the course of his own invention, whether they properly be poets or no let grammarians dispute, and go to the third, indeed right poets, of whom chiefly this question ariseth. Betwixt whom and these second is such a kind of difference as betwixt the meaner sort of painters, who counterfeit only such faces as are set before them, and the more excellent, who having no law but wit, bestow that in colors upon you which is fittest for the eye to see: as the constant though lamenting look of Lucretia, when she punished in herself another's fault; wherein he painteth not Lucretia whom he never saw, but painteth the outward beauty of such a virtue. For these third be they which most properly do imitate to teach and delight, and to imitate borrow nothing of what is, hath been, or shall be; but range, only reined with learned discretion, into the divine consideration of what may be and should be. These be they that, as the first and most noble sort, may justly be termed *vates,* so these are waited on in the excellentest languages and best understandings with the foredescribed name of poets; for these indeed do merely make to imitate, and imitate both to delight and teach: and delight to move men to take that goodness in hand, which without delight they would fly as from a stranger, and teach, to make them know that goodness whereunto they are moved: which being the noblest scope to which ever any learning was directed, yet want there not idle tongues to bark at them.

These be subdivided into sundry more special denominations. The most notable be the heroic, lyric, tragic, comic, satiric, iambic, elegiac, pastoral, and certain others, some of these being termed according to the matter they deal with, some by the sorts of verses they liked best to write in; for indeed the greatest part of poets have appareled their poetical inventions in that numbrous kind of writing which is called verse—indeed but appareled, verse being but an ornament and no cause to poetry, since there have been many most excellent poets that never versified, and now swarm many versifiers that need never answer to the name of poets. For Xenophon, who did imitate so excellently as to give us *effigiem justi imperii,* "the portraiture of a just empire," under the name of Cyrus (as Cicero saith of him), made therein an absolute heroical poem. So did Heliodorus in his sugared invention of that picture of love in Theagenes and Chariclea; and yet both these writ in prose: which I speak to show that it is not rhyming and versing that maketh a poet—no more than a long gown maketh an advocate, who though he pleaded in armor should be an advocate and no soldier. But it is that feigning notable images of virtues, vices, or what else, with that delightful teaching, which must be the right describing note to know a poet by, although indeed the senate of poets hath chosen verse as their fittest raiment, meaning, as in matter they passed all in all, so in manner to go beyond them: not speaking (table talk fashion or like men in a dream) words as they chanceably fall from the mouth, but peizing each syllable of each word by just proportion, according to the dignity of the subject.

Now therefore it shall not be amiss first to weigh this latter sort of poetry by his works, and then by his parts; and if in neither of these anatomies he be condemnable, I hope we shall obtain a more favorable sentence. This purifying of wit, this enriching of memory, enabling of judgment, and enlarging of conceit, which commonly we call learning, under what name soever it come forth, or to what immediate end soever it be directed, the final end is to lead and draw us to as high a perfection as our degenerate souls, made worse by their clayey lodgings, can be capable of. This, according to the inclination of the man, bred many formed impressions. For some that thought this felicity principally to be gotten by knowledge, and no knowledge to be so high or heavenly as acquaintance with the stars, gave themselves to astronomy; others, persuading themselves to be demigods if they knew the causes of things, became natural and supernatural philosophers; some an admirable delight drew to music; and some the certainty of demonstration to the mathematics. But all, one and other, having this scope—to know, and by knowledge to lift up the mind from the dungeon of the body to the enjoying his own divine essence. But when by the balance of experience it was found that the astronomer looking to the stars might fall into a ditch, that the inquiring philosopher might be blind in himself, and the mathematician might draw forth a straight line with a crooked heart; then lo, did proof, the overruler of opinions, make manifest that all these are but serving sciences, which, as they have each a private end in themselves, so yet are they all directed to the highest end of the mistress-knowledge, by the Greeks called *architektonike,* which stands (as I think) in the knowledge of a man's self, in the ethic and politic consideration, with the end of well-doing, and not of well-knowing only: even as the saddler's next end is to make a good saddle, but his farther end to serve a nobler faculty, which is horsemanship; so the horseman's to soldiery, and the soldier not only to have the skill, but to perform the practice of a soldier. So that, the ending end of all earthly learning being virtuous action, those skills that most serve to bring forth that have a most just title to be princes over all the rest.

Wherein if we can, show we the poet's nobleness, by setting him before his other competitors, among whom as principal challengers step forth the moral philosophers, whom, me thinketh, I see coming toward me with a sullen gravity, as though they could not abide vice by daylight, rudely clothed for to witness outwardly their contempt of outward things, with books in their hands against glory, whereto they set their names, sophistically speaking against subtlety, and angry with any man in whom they see the foul fault of anger. These men, casting largess as they go of definitions, divisions, and distinctions, with a scornful interrogative do soberly ask whether it be possible to find any path so ready to lead a man to virtue as that which teacheth what virtue is—and teacheth it not only by delivering forth his very being, his causes and effects, but also by making known his enemy, vice, which must be destroyed, and his cumbersome servant, passion, which must be mastered; by showing the generalities that containeth it, and the specialities that are derived from it; lastly, by plain setting down, how it extendeth itself out of the limits of a man's own little world to the government of families, and maintaining of public societies.

The historian scarcely giveth leisure to the moralist to say so much, but that he, loaden with old mouse-eaten records, authorizing himself (for the most part) upon other histories, whose greatest authorities are built upon the notable foundation of hearsay, having much ado to accord differing writers and to pick truth out of partiality, better acquainted with a thousand years ago than with the present age, and yet better knowing how this world goeth than how his own wit runneth,

curious for antiquities and inquisitive of novelties, a wonder
to young folks and a tyrant in table talk, denieth, in a great
chafe, that any man for teaching of virtue and virtuous actions
is comparable to him. "I am *lux vitae, temporum magistra, vita
memoriae, nuncia vetustatis,* etc." [2]

"The philosopher," saith he, "teacheth a disputative virtue, but
I do an active. His virtue is excellent in the dangerless Academy
of Plato, but mine showeth forth her honorable face in the battles of Marathon, Pharsalia, Poitiers, and Agincourt. He teacheth
virtue by certain abstract considerations, but I only bid you
follow the footing of them that have gone before you. Old-aged
experience goeth beyond the fine-witted philosopher, but I give
the experience of many ages. Lastly, if he make the song-book,
I put the learner's hand to the lute; and if he be the guide, I
am the light."

Then would he allege you innumerable examples, conferring
story by story, how much the wisest senators and princes have
been directed by the credit of history, as Brutus, Alphonsus of
Aragon, and who not, if need be? At length the long line of their
disputation maketh a point in this, that the one giveth the precept, and the other the example.

Now whom shall we find (since the question standeth for the
highest form in the school of learning) to be moderator? Truly,
as me seemeth, the poet; and if not a moderator, even the man
that ought to carry the title from them both, and much more
from all other serving sciences. Therefore compare we the poet
with the historian and with the moral philosopher; and if he
go beyond them both, no other human skill can match him. For
as for the divine, with all reverence it is ever to be excepted,
not only for having his scope as far beyond any of these as
eternity exceedeth a moment, but even for passing each of these
in themselves. And for the lawyer, though *jus* be the daughter
of justice, and justice the chief of virtues, yet because he seeketh
to make men good rather *formidine poenae* than *virtutis amore,*[3]
or, to say righter, doth not endeavor to make men good, but
that their evil hurt not others; having no care, so he be a good
citizen, how bad a man he be: therefore, as our wickedness

[2] ["The light of life, the teacher of the ages, the life of memory, the messenger of antiquity." See Cicero, *De Oratore,* II, ix, 36.]
[3] ["By fear of punishment" rather than "by love of virtue."]

maketh him necessary, and necessity maketh him honorable, so is he not in the deepest truth to stand in rank with these who all endeavor to take naughtiness away and plant goodness even in the secretest cabinet of our souls. And these four are all that any way deal in that consideration of men's manners, which being the supreme knowledge, they that best breed it deserve the best commendation.

The philosopher therefore and the historian are they which would win the goal, the one by precept, the other by example. But both, not having both, do both halt. For the philosopher, setting down with thorny argument the bare rule, is so hard of utterance, and so misty to be conceived, that one that hath no other guide but him shall wade in him till he be old before he shall find sufficient cause to be honest. For his knowledge standeth so upon the abstract and general that happy is that man who may understand him, and more happy that can apply what he doth understand. On the other side, the historian, wanting the precept, is so tied, not to what should be but to what is, to the particular truth of things and not to the general reason of things, that his example draweth no necessary consequence, and therefore a less fruitful doctrine.

Now doth the peerless poet perform both: for whatsoever the philosopher saith should be done, he giveth a perfect picture of it in some one by whom he presupposeth it was done, so as he coupleth the general notion with the particular example. A perfect picture I say, for he yieldeth to the powers of the mind an image of that whereof the philosopher bestoweth but a wordish description, which doth neither strike, pierce, nor possess the sight of the soul so much as that other doth.

For as in outward things, to a man that had never seen an elephant or a rhinoceros, who should tell him most exquisitely all their shapes, color, bigness, and particular marks, or of a gorgeous palace, the architecture, with declaring the full beauties, might well make the hearer able to repeat, as it were by rote, all he had heard, yet should never satisfy his inward conceits with being witness to itself of a true lively knowledge; but the same man, as soon as he might see those beasts well painted, or that house well in model, should straightways grow, without need of any description, to a judicial comprehending of them: so no doubt the philosopher with his learned definition—be it of virtues, vices, matters of public policy or private government —replenisheth the memory with many infallible grounds of wisdom, which, notwithstanding, lie dark before the imaginative and judging power, if they be not illuminated or figured forth by the speaking picture of poesy.

Tully taketh much pains, and many times not without poetical helps, to make us know the force love of our country hath in us. Let us but hear old Anchises speaking in the midst of Troy's flames, or see Ulysses in the fullness of all Calypso's delights bewail his absence from barren and beggarly Ithaca. Anger, the Stoics say, was a short madness: let but Sophocles bring you Ajax on a stage, killing and whipping sheep and oxen, thinking them the army of Greeks, with their chieftains Agamemnon and Menelaus, and tell me if you have not a more familiar insight into anger than finding in the schoolmen his genus and difference. See whether wisdom and temperance in Ulysses and Diomedes, valor in Achilles, friendship in Nisus and Euryalus, even to an ignorant man carry not an apparent shining; and, contrarily, the remorse of conscience in Oedipus, the soon repenting pride of Agamemnon, the self-devouring cruelty in his father Atreus, the violence of ambition in the two Theban brothers, the sour-sweetness of revenge in Medea; and, to fall lower, the Terentian Gnatho and our Chaucer's Pandar so expressed that we now use their names to signify their trades; and finally, all virtues, vices, and passions so in their own natural seats laid to the view that we seem not to hear of them, but clearly to see through them.

But even in the most excellent determination of goodness, what philosopher's counsel can so readily direct a prince, as the feigned Cyrus in Xenophon? or a virtuous man in all fortunes, as Aeneas in Virgil? or a whole commonwealth, as the way of Sir Thomas More's *Utopia*? I say the way, because where Sir Thomas More erred, it was the fault of the man, and not of the poet, for that way of patterning a commonwealth was most absolute, though he perchance hath not so absolutely performed it. For the question is, whether the feigned image of poesy or the regular instruction of philosophy hath the more force in teaching: wherein if the philosophers have more rightly showed themselves philosophers than the poets have attained to the high top of their profession, as in truth,

Mediocribus esse poetis
Non Di, non homines, non concessere columnae,[4]

it is, I say again, not the fault of the art, but that by few men that art can be accomplished.

Certainly, even our Saviour Christ could as well have given the moral commonplaces of uncharitableness and humbleness as the divine narration of Dives and Lazarus; or of disobedience and mercy, as that heavenly discourse of the lost child and the gracious father; but that his through-searching wisdom knew the estate of Dives burning in hell, and of Lazarus being in Abraham's bosom, would more constantly (as it were) inhabit both the memory and judgment. Truly, for myself, me seems I see before mine eyes the lost child's disdainful prodigality, turned to envy a swine's dinner: which by the learned divines are thought not historical acts, but instructing parables.

For conclusion, I say the philosopher teacheth, but he teacheth obscurely, so as the learned only can understand him; that is to say, he teacheth them that are already taught. But the poet is the food for the tenderest stomachs, the poet is indeed the right popular philosopher, whereof Aesop's tales give good proof; whose pretty allegories, stealing under the formal tales of beasts, make many, more beastly than beasts, begin to hear the sound of virtue from these dumb speakers.

But now may it be alleged that if this imagining of matters be so fit for the imagination, then must the historian needs surpass, who bringeth you images of true matters, such as indeed were done, and not such as fantastically or falsely may be suggested to have been done. Truly, Aristotle himself, in his discourse of poesy, plainly determineth this question, saying that poetry is *philosophoteron* and *spoudaioteron*, that is to say, it is more philosophical and more studiously serious than history. His reason is, because poesy dealeth with *katholou*, that is to say with the universal consideration, and the history with *kathekaston*, the particular: "now," saith he, "the universal weighs what is fit to be said or done, either in likelihood or necessity (which the poesy considereth in his imposed names), and the particular only marketh whether Alcibiades did, or suffered, this

---

[4] ["Not gods or men or booksellers permit poets to be mediocre." Horace, *Ars Poetica,* 372–373.]

or that." Thus far Aristotle: which reason of his (as all his) is most full of reason. For indeed, if the question were whether it were better to have a particular act truly or falsely set down, there is no doubt which is to be chosen, no more than whether you had rather have Vespasian's picture right as he was, or, at the painter's pleasure, nothing resembling. But if the question be for your own use and learning, whether it be better to have it set down as it should be, or as it was, then certainly is more doctrinable the feigned Cyrus of Xenophon than the true Cyrus in Justin, and the feigned Aeneas in Virgil than the right Aeneas in Dares Phrygius. As to a lady that desired to fashion her countenance to the best grace, a painter should more benefit her to portrait a most sweet face, writing Canidia upon it, than to paint Canidia as she was, who, Horace sweareth, was foul and ill-favored.

If the poet do his part aright, he will show you in Tantalus, Atreus, and such like, nothing that is not to be shunned; in Cyrus, Aeneas, Ulysses, each thing to be followed; where the historian, bound to tell things as things were, cannot be liberal (without he will be poetical) of a perfect pattern, but, as in Alexander, or Scipio himself, show doings, some to be liked, some to be misliked. And then how will you discern what to follow but by your own discretion, which you had without reading Quintus Curtius? And whereas a man may say, though in universal consideration of doctrine the poet prevaileth, yet that the history, in his saying such a thing was done, doth warrant a man more in that he shall follow, the answer is manifest: that if he stand upon that *was*—as if he should argue, because it rained yesterday, therefore it should rain today—then indeed it hath some advantage to a gross conceit; but if he know an example only informs a conjectured likelihood, and so go by reason, the poet doth so far exceed him as he is to frame his example to that which is most reasonable, be it in warlike, politic, or private matters; where the historian in his bare *was* hath many times that which we call fortune to overrule the best wisdom. Many times he must tell events whereof he can yield no cause; or, if he do, it must be poetical.

For that a feigned example hath as much force to teach as a true example (for as for to move, it is clear, since the feigned may be tuned to the highest key of passion), let us take one example wherein a poet and a historian do concur. Herodotus and Justin do both testify that Zopyrus, King Darius' faithful servant, seeing his master long resisted by the rebellious Babylonians, feigned himself in extreme disgrace of his king: for verifying of which, he caused his own nose and ears to be cut off: and so flying to the Babylonians, was received, and for his known valor so far credited, that he did find means to deliver them over to Darius. Much like matter doth Livy record of Tarquinius and his son. Xenophon excellently feigneth such another stratagem, performed by Abradates in Cyrus' behalf. Now would I fain know, if occasion be presented unto you to serve your prince by such an honest dissimulation, why do you not as well learn it of Xenophon's fiction as of the other's verity? And truly so much the better, as you shall save your nose by the bargain; for Abradates did not counterfeit so far. So then the best of the historian is subject to the poet; for whatsoever action, or faction, whatsoever counsel, policy, or war stratagem the historian is bound to recite, that may the poet (if he list) with his imitation make his own, beautifying it both for further teaching and more delighting, as it pleaseth him: having all, from Dante's heaven to his hell, under the authority of his pen. Which if I be asked what poets have done so, as I might well name some, yet say I, and say again, I speak of the art, and not of the artificer.

Now, to that which commonly is attributed to the praise of histories, in respect of the notable learning is gotten by marking the success, as though therein a man should see virtue exalted and vice punished—truly that commendation is peculiar to poetry, and far off from history. For indeed poetry ever setteth virtue so out in her best colors, making Fortune her well-waiting handmaid, that one must needs be enamored of her. Well may you see Ulysses in a storm, and in other hard plights; but they are but exercises of patience and magnanimity, to make them shine the more in the near-following prosperity. And of the contrary part, if evil men come to the stage, they ever go out (as the tragedy writer answered to one that misliked the show of such persons) so manacled as they little animate folks to follow them. But the historian, being captived to the truth of a foolish world, is many times a terror from well-doing, and an encouragement to unbridled wickedness.

For see we not valiant Miltiades rot in his fetters? the just Phocion and the accomplished Socrates put to death like traitors? the cruel Severus live prosperously? the excellent Severus miserably murdered? Sylla and Marius dying in their beds? Pompey and Cicero slain then when they would have thought exile a happiness? See we not virtuous Cato driven to kill himself, and rebel Caesar so advanced that his name yet, after sixteen hundred years, lasteth in the highest honor? And mark but even Caesar's own words of the forenamed Sylla (who in that only did honestly, to put down his dishonest tyranny), *literas nescivit*,[5] as if want of learning caused him to do well. He meant it not by poetry, which, not content with earthly plagues, deviseth new punishments in hell for tyrants; nor yet by philosophy, which teacheth *occidendos esse*;[6] but, no doubt, by skill in history, for that indeed can afford you Cypselus, Periander, Phalaris, Dionysius, and I know not how many more of the same kennel, that speed well enough in their abominable injustice or usurpation. I conclude, therefore, that he excelleth history, not only in furnishing the mind with knowledge, but in setting it forward to that which deserveth to be called and accounted good: which setting forward, and moving to well-doing, indeed setteth the laurel crown upon the poet as victorious, not only of the historian, but over the philosopher, howsoever in teaching it may be questionable.

For suppose it be granted (that which I suppose with great reason may be denied) that the philosopher, in respect of his methodical proceeding, doth teach more perfectly than the poet, yet do I think that no man is so much *philophilosophos* as to compare the philosopher, in moving, with the poet.

And that moving is of a higher degree than teaching, it may by this appear, that it is well nigh the cause and the effect of teaching. For who will be taught, if he be not moved with desire to be taught? and what so much good doth that teaching bring forth (I speak still of moral doctrine) as that it moveth one to do that which it doth teach? For, as Aristotle saith, it is not *gnosis* but *praxis*[7] must be the fruit. And how *praxis* cannot be, without being moved to practice, it is no hard matter to consider.

The philosopher showeth you the way, he informeth you of the particularities, as well of the tediousness of the way, as of the pleasant lodging you shall have when your journey is

[5] ["He was ignorant of letters." Suetonius, *Julius Caesar*, LXXVII.]
[6] ["They should be slain."]
[7] ["Not knowledge but action." *Ethics*, I, iii.]

ended, as of the many by-turnings that may divert you from
your way. But this is to no man but to him that will read him,
and read him with attentive, studious painfulness; which constant
desire whosoever hath in him, hath already passed half the
hardness of the way, and therefore is beholding to the philosopher
but for the other half. Nay truly, learned men have learnedly
thought that where once reason hath so much overmastered
passion as that the mind hath a free desire to do well, the inward
light each mind hath in itself is as good as a philosopher's book;
seeing in nature we know it is well to do well, and what is well
and what is evil, although not in the words of art which philosophers bestow upon us; for out of natural conceit the philosophers
drew it. But to be moved to do that which we know, or to be
moved with desire to know, *hoc opus, hic labor est.*[8]

Now therein of all sciences (I speak still of human, and
according to the human conceits) is our poet the monarch. For
he doth not only show the way, but giveth so sweet a prospect
into the way as will entice any man to enter into it. Nay, he doth,
as if your journey should lie through a fair vineyard, at the
first give you a cluster of grapes, that, full of that taste, you may
long to pass further. He beginneth not with obscure definitions,
which must blur the margin with interpretations, and load the
memory with doubtfulness; but he cometh to you with words
set in delightful proportion, either accompanied with, or prepared for, the well-enchanting skill of music; and with a tale
forsooth he cometh unto you, with a tale which holdeth children
from play, and old men from the chimney-corner. And, pretend-
ing no more, doth intend the winning of the mind from wickedness
to virtue: even as the child is often brought to take most wholesome things by hiding them in such other as have a pleasant
taste: which, if one should begin to tell them the nature of aloes
or rhubarb they should receive, would sooner take their physic
at their ears than at their mouth. So is it in men (most of which
are childish in the best things, till they be cradled in their
graves): glad they will be to hear the tales of Hercules, Achilles,
Cyrus, Aeneas; and, hearing them, must needs hear the right
description of wisdom, valor, and justice; which, if they had
been barely, that is to say philosophically, set out, they would
swear they be brought to school again.

That imitation, whereof poetry is, hath the most conveniency

[8] ["This is the work, this the labor." *Aeneid*, VI, 129.]

to nature of all other, insomuch that, as Aristotle saith, those things which in themselves are horrible, as cruel battles, unnatural monsters, are made in poetical imitation delightful. Truly, I have known men, that even with reading *Amadis de Gaule* (which God knoweth wanteth much of a perfect poesy) have found their hearts moved to the exercise of courtesy, liberality, and especially courage. Who readeth Aeneas carrying old Anchises on his back, that wisheth not it were his fortune to perform so excellent an act? Whom do not the words of Turnus move (the tale of Turnus having planted his image in the imagination)?

> *Fugientem haec terra videbit?*
> *Usque adeone mori miserum est?* [9]

Where the philosophers, as they scorn to delight, so must they be content little to move, saving wrangling whether virtue be the chief or the only good, whether the contemplative or the active life do excel: which Plato and Boethius well knew, and therefore made Mistress Philosophy very often borrow the masking raiment of Poesy. For even those hard-hearted evil men who think virtue a school name, and know no other good but *indulgere genio*,[10] and therefore despise the austere admonitions of the philosopher, and feel not the inward reason they stand upon, yet will be content to be delighted—which is all the goodfellow poet seemeth to promise—and so steal to see the form of goodness (which seen they cannot but love) ere themselves be aware, as if they took a medicine of cherries.

Infinite proofs of the strange effects of this poetical invention might be alleged; only two shall serve, which are so often remembered as I think all men know them. The one of Menenius Agrippa, who, when the whole people of Rome had resolutely divided themselves from the Senate, with apparent show of utter ruin, though he were (for that time) an excellent orator, came not among them upon trust either of figurative speeches or cunning insinuations, and much less with farfetched maxims of philosophy, which (especially if they were Platonic) they must have learned geometry before they could well have conceived; but forsooth he behaves himself like a homely and

---

[9] ["Shall this ground see (Turnus) fleeing? Is it so hard to die?" *Aeneid*, XII, 645–646.]
[10] ["To indulge one's nature."]

familiar poet. He telleth them a tale, that there was a time when all the parts of the body made a mutinous conspiracy against the belly, which they thought devoured the fruits of each other's labor: they concluded they would let so unprofitable a spender starve. In the end, to be short (for the tale is notorious, and as notorious that it was a tale), with punishing the belly they plagued themselves. This applied by him wrought such effect in the people, as I never read that ever words brought forth but then so sudden and so good an alteration; for upon reasonable conditions a perfect reconcilement ensued. The other is of Nathan the prophet, who, when the holy David had so far forsaken God as to confirm adultery with murder, when he was to do the tenderest office of a friend, in laying his own shame before his eyes, sent by God to call again so chosen a servant, how doth he it but by telling of a man whose beloved lamb was ungratefully taken from his bosom?—the application most divinely true, but the discourse itself feigned; which made David (I speak of the second and instrumental cause) as in a glass to see his own filthiness, as that heavenly psalm of mercy well testifieth.

By these, therefore, examples and reasons, I think it may be manifest that the poet, with that same hand of delight, doth draw the mind more effectually than any other art doth. And so a conclusion not unfitly ensueth: that, as virtue is the most excellent resting place for all worldly learning to make his end of, so poetry, being the most familiar to teach it, and most princely to move towards it, in the most excellent work is the most excellent workman.

But I am content not only to decipher him by his works (although works in commendation or dispraise must ever hold a high authority), but more narrowly will examine his parts: so that (as in a man) though all together may carry a presence full of majesty and beauty, perchance in some one defectious piece we may find a blemish. Now in his parts, kinds, or species (as you list to term them), it is to be noted that some poesies have coupled together two or three kinds, as tragical and comical, whereupon is risen the tragi-comical. Some, in the like manner, have mingled prose and verse, as Sannazzaro and Boethius. Some have mingled matters heroical and pastoral. But that cometh all to one in this question, for, if severed they be good, the conjunction cannot be hurtful. Therefore, perchance forgetting some, and leaving some as needless to be remembered, it shall not be amiss in a word to cite the special kinds, to see what faults may be found in the right use of them.

Is it then the pastoral poem which is misliked?(For perchance where the hedge is lowest they will soonest leap over.) Is the poor pipe disdained, which sometimes out of Meliboeus' mouth can show the misery of people under hard lords and ravening soldiers, and again, by Tityrus, what blessedness is derived to them that lie lowest from the goodness of them that sit highest? sometimes, under the pretty tales of wolves and sheep, can include the whole considerations of wrong doing and patience; sometimes show that contention for trifles can get but a trifling victory: where perchance a man may see that even Alexander and Darius, when they strave who should be cock of this world's dunghill, the benefit they got was that the after-livers may say:

> *Haec memini et victum frustra contendere Thirsin:*
> *Ex illo Coridon, Coridon est tempore nobis.*[11]

Or is it the lamenting elegiac, which in a kind heart would move rather pity than blame, who bewails with the great philosopher Heraclitus the weakness of mankind and the wretchedness of the world; who surely is to be praised, either for compassionate accompanying just causes of lamentation, or for rightly painting out how weak be the passions of woefulness? Is it the bitter but wholesome iambic, which rubs the galled mind, in making shame the trumpet of villainy with bold and open crying out against naughtiness? Or the satiric, who

> *Omne vafer vitium ridenti tangit amico;*[12]

who sportingly never leaveth until he make a man laugh at folly, and, at length ashamed to laugh at himself, which he cannot avoid, without avoiding the folly; who, while

> *circum praecordia ludit,*[13]

giveth us to feel how many headaches a passionate life bringeth us to; how, when all is done,

---

[11] ["These things I remember, how the vanquished Thyrsis struggled in vain. From that day on it has been Corydon, only Corydon, with us." Virgil, *Eclogues,* VII, 69–70.]

[12] ["Probes every fault while making his friend laugh." Persius, *Satires,* I, 116.]

[13] [He "plays about the strings of the heart." Persius, *Satires,* I, 117.]

Est Ulubris, animus si nos non deficit aequus? [14]

No, perchance it is the comic, whom naughty play-makers and stage-keepers have justly made odious. To the argument of abuse I will answer after. Only thus much now is to be said, that the comedy is an imitation of the common errors of our life, which he representeth in the most ridiculous and scornful sort that may be, so as it is impossible that any beholder can be content to be such a one.

Now, as in geometry the oblique must be known as well as the right, and in arithmetic the odd as well as the even, so in the actions of our life who seeth not the filthiness of evil wanteth a great foil to perceive the beauty of virtue. This doth the comedy handle so in our private and domestical matters, as with hearing it we get as it were an experience, what is to be looked for of a niggardly Demea, of a crafty Davus, of a flattering Gnatho, of a vainglorious Thraso; and not only to know what effects are to be expected, but to know who be such, by the signifying badge given them by the comedian. And little reason hath any man to say that men learn evil by seeing it so set out; since, as I said before, there is no man living but, by the force truth hath in nature, no sooner seeth these men play their parts, but wisheth them *in pristrinum:* [15] although perchance the sack of his own faults lie so behind his back that he seeth not himself dance the same measure; whereto yet nothing can more open his eyes than to find his own actions contemptibly set forth.

So that the right use of comedy will (I think) by nobody be blamed, and much less of the high and excellent tragedy, that openeth the greatest wounds, and showeth forth the ulcers that are covered with tissue; that maketh kings fear to be tyrants, and tyrants manifest their tyrannical humors; that, with stirring the effects of admiration and commiseration, teacheth the uncertainty of this world, and upon how weak foundations gilden roofs are builded; that maketh us know,

Qui sceptra saevus duro imperio regit,
Timet timentes, metus in auctorem redit. [16]

[14] ["What we seek can be found at Ulubrae (a squalid town; a dull place) if we keep a balanced mind." Horace, *Epistles,* I, xi, 30.]
[15] ["In a pounding mill" (where slaves were sent for punishment).]
[16] ["He who harshly wields the scepter with tyrannic sway (He who rules with an iron hand) fears those who fear him; the fear returns upon its author." Seneca, *Oedipus,* 705–706.]

But how much it can move, Plutarch yieldeth a notable testimony of the abominable tyrant Alexander Pheraeus, from whose eyes a tragedy, well made and represented, drew abundance of tears, who without all pity had murdered infinite numbers, and some of his own blood; so as he that was not ashamed to make matters for tragedies, yet could not resist the sweet violence of a tragedy. And if it wrought no further good in him, it was that he, in despite of himself, withdrew himself from hearkening to that which might mollify his hardened heart.

But it is not the tragedy they do mislike; for it were too absurd to cast out so excellent a representation of whatsoever is most worthy to be learned. Is it the lyric that most displeaseth, who with his tuned lyre and well-accorded voice, giveth praise, the reward of virtue, to virtuous acts? who gives moral precepts, and natural problems, who sometimes raiseth up his voice to the height of the heavens, in singing the lauds of the immortal God. Certainly, I must confess mine own barbarousness: I never heard the old song of Percy and Douglas that I found not my heart moved more than with a trumpet; and yet is it sung but by some blind crowder, with no rougher voice than rude style; which, being so evil appareled in the dust and cobwebs of that uncivil age, what would it work trimmed in the gorgeous eloquence of Pindar? In Hungary I have seen it the manner at all feasts, and other such meetings, to have songs of their ancestors' valor; which that right soldierlike nation think the chiefest kindlers of brave courage. The incomparable Lacedaemonians did not only carry that kind of music ever with them to the field, but even at home, as such songs were made, so were they all content to be singers of them, when the lusty men were to tell what they did, the old men what they had done, and the young men what they would do. And where a man may say that Pindar many times praiseth highly victories of small moment, matters rather of sport than virtue; as it may be answered, it was the fault of the poet, and not of the poetry, so indeed the chief fault was in the time and custom of the Greeks, who set those toys at so high a price that Philip of Macedon reckoned a horserace won at Olympus among his three fearful felicities. But as the unimitable Pindar often did, so is that kind most capable and most fit to awake the thoughts from the sleep of idleness, to embrace honorable enterprises.

There rests the heroical, whose very name (I think) should daunt all backbiters; for by what conceit can a tongue be directed to speak evil of that which draweth with it no less champions than Achilles, Cyrus, Aeneas, Turnus, Tydeus, and Rinaldo? who doth not only teach and move to a truth, but teacheth and moveth to the most high and excellent truth; who maketh magnanimity and justice shine throughout all misty fearfulness and foggy desires; who, if the saying of Plato and Tully be true, that who could see virtue would be wonderfully ravished with the love of her beauty—this man sets her out to make her more lovely in her holiday apparel, to the eye of any that will deign not to disdain until they understand. But if anything be already said in the defense of sweet poetry, all concurreth to the maintaining the heroical, which is not only a kind, but the best and most accomplished kind of poetry. For as the image of each action stirreth and instructeth the mind, so the lofty image of such worthies most inflameth the mind with desire to be worthy, and informs with counsel how to be worthy. Only let Aeneas be worn in the tablet of your memory; how he governeth himself in the ruin of his country; in the preserving his old father, and carrying away his religious ceremonies; in obeying the gods' commandment to leave Dido, though not only all passionate kindness, but even the human consideration of virtuous gratefulness, would have craved other of him; how in storms, how in sports, how in war, how in peace, how a fugitive, how victorious, how besieged, how besieging, how to strangers, how to allies, how to enemies, how to his own; lastly, how in his inward self, and how in his outward government; and I think, in a mind not prejudiced with a prejudicating humor, he will be found in excellency fruitful, yea, even as Horace saith,

melius Chrisippo et Crantore.[17]

But truly I imagine it falleth out with these poet-whippers as with some good women, who often are sick, but in faith they cannot tell where. So the name of poetry is odious to them, but neither his cause nor effects, neither the sum that contains him nor the particularities descending from him, give any fast handle to their carping dispraise.

[17] ["Better than (the philosophers) Chrysippus and Crantor." Horace, *Epistles,* I, ii, 4.]

Since, then, poetry is of all human learning the most ancient and of most fatherly antiquity, as from whence other learnings have taken their beginnings; since it is so universal that no learned nation doth despise it, nor no barbarous nation is without it; since both Roman and Greek gave divine names unto it, the one of "prophesying," the other of "making," and that indeed that name of "making" is fit for him, considering that whereas other arts retain themselves within their subject, and receive, as it were, their being from it, the poet only bringeth his own stuff, and doth not learn a conceit out of a matter, but maketh matter for a conceit; since neither his description nor his end containeth any evil, the thing described cannot be evil; since his effects be so good as to teach goodness and to delight the learners of it; since therein (namely in moral doctrine, the chief of all knowledges) he doth not only far pass the historian, but, for instructing, is well nigh comparable to the philosopher, and, for moving, leaves him behind him; since the Holy Scripture (wherein there is no uncleanness) hath whole parts in it poetical, and that even our Saviour Christ vouchsafed to use the flowers of it; since all his kinds are not only in their united forms but in their severed dissections fully commendable; I think (and think I think rightly) the laurel crown appointed for triumphing captains doth worthily (of all other learnings) honor the poet's triumph.

But because we have ears as well as tongues, and that the lightest reasons that may be will seem to weigh greatly, if nothing be put in the counterbalance, let us hear, and as well as we can, ponder, what objections may be made against this art, which may be worthy either of yielding or answering.

First, truly I note not only in these *mysomousoi,* poet-haters, but in all that kind of people who seek a praise by dispraising others, that they do prodigally spend a great many wandering words in quips and scoffs, carping and taunting at each thing which, by stirring the spleen, may stay the brain from a thorough beholding the worthiness of the subject. Those kind of objections, as they are full of very idle easiness, since there is nothing of so sacred a majesty but that an itching tongue may rub itself upon it, so deserve they no other answer, but, instead of laughing at the jest, to laugh at the jester. We know a playing wit can praise the discretion of an ass, the comfortableness of being in debt, and the jolly commodity of being sick of the plague. So of the contrary side, if we will turn Ovid's verse,

Ut lateat virtus proximitate mali,

"that good lie hid in nearness of the evil," Agrippa will be as merry in showing the vanity of science as Erasmus was in commending of folly. Neither shall any man or matter escape some touch of these smiling railers. But for Erasmus and Agrippa, they had another foundation than the superficial part would promise. Marry, these other pleasant faultfinders, who will correct the verb before they understand the noun, and confute others' knowledge before they confirm their own, I would have them only remember that scoffing cometh not of wisdom; so as the best title in true English they get with their merriments is to be called good fools, for so have our grave forefathers ever termed that humorous kind of jesters.

But that which giveth greatest scope to their scorning humors is rhyming and versing. It is already said (and, as I think, truly said) it is not rhyming and versing that maketh poesy. One may be a poet without versing, and a versifier without poetry. But yet presuppose it were inseparable (as indeed it seemeth Scaliger judgeth) truly it were an inseparable commendation. For if *oratio* next to *ratio*, speech next to reason, be the greatest gift bestowed upon mortality, that cannot be praiseless which doth most polish that blessing of speech; which considers each word, not only (as a man may say) by his forcible quality, but by his best-measured quantity, carrying even in themselves a harmony—without, perchance, number, measure, order, proportion be in our time grown odious. But lay aside the just praise it hath by being the only fit speech for music (music I say, the most divine striker of the senses), thus much is undoubtedly true, that if reading be foolish without remembering, memory being the only treasurer of knowledge, those words which are fittest for memory are likewise most convenient for knowledge.

Now, that verse far exceedeth prose in the knitting up of the memory, the reason is manifest: the words (besides their delight, which hath a great affinity to memory) being so set as one word cannot be lost but the whole work fails; which accuseth itself, calleth the remembrance back to itself, and so most strongly confirmeth it. Besides, one word so, as it were, begetting another, as, be it in rhyme or measured verse, by the former a man shall have a near guess to the follower. Lastly, even they that have taught the art of memory have showed nothing so apt for it as a certain room divided into many places well and thoroughly known. Now, that hath the verse in effect perfectly, every word having his natural seat, which seat must needs make the word remembered. But what needeth more in a thing so known to all men? Who is it that ever was a scholar that doth not carry away some verses of Virgil, Horace, or Cato, which in his youth he learned, and even to his old age serve him for hourly lessons? But the fitness it hath for memory is notably proved by all delivery of arts: wherein for the most part, from grammar to logic, mathematic, physic, and the rest, the rules chiefly necessary to be borne away are compiled in verses. So that verse being in itself sweet and orderly, and being best for memory, the only handle of knowledge, it must be in jest that any man can speak against it.

Now then go we to the most important imputations laid to the poor poets. For aught I can yet learn, they are these. First, that there being many other more fruitful knowledges, a man might better spend his time in them than in this. Secondly, that it is the mother of lies. Thirdly, that it is the nurse of abuse, infecting us with many pestilent desires, with a siren's sweetness drawing the mind to the serpent's tale of sinful fancy—and herein, especially, comedies give the largest field to ear (as Chaucer saith); how both in other nations and in ours, before poets did soften us, we were full of courage, given to martial exercises, the pillars of manlike liberty, and not lulled asleep in shady idleness with poets' pastimes. And lastly, and chiefly, they cry out with an open mouth, as if they outshot Robin Hood, that Plato banished them out of his commonwealth. Truly, this is much, if there be much truth in it.

First, to the first, that a man might better spend his time is a reason indeed; but it doth (as they say) but *petere principium:*[18] for if it be, as I affirm, that no learning is so good as that which teacheth and moveth to virtue, and that none can both teach and move thereto so much as poesy, then is the conclusion manifest that ink and paper cannot be to a more profitable purpose employed. And certainly, though a man should grant their first assumption, it should follow (me thinks) very unwillingly, that good is not good because better is better. But I still and utterly deny that there is sprung out of earth a more fruitful knowledge.

[18] ["Beg the question."]

To the second therefore, that they should be the principal liars, I answer paradoxically, but truly, I think truly, that of all writers under the sun the poet is the least liar, and, though he would, as a poet can scarcely be a liar. The astronomer, with his cousin the geometrician, can hardly escape when they take upon them to measure the height of the stars. How often, think you, do the physicians lie, when they aver things good for sicknesses, which afterwards send Charon a great number of souls drowned in a potion before they come to his ferry? And no less of the rest which take upon them to affirm. Now for the poet, he nothing affirms, and therefore never lieth. For, as I take it, to lie is to affirm that to be true which is false; so as the other artists, and especially the historian, affirming many things, can, in the cloudy knowledge of mankind, hardly escape from many lies. But the poet (as I said before) never affirmeth. The poet never maketh any circles about your imagination, to conjure you to believe for true what he writes. He citeth not authorities of other histories, but even for his entry calleth the sweet Muses to inspire into him a good invention; in truth, not laboring to tell you what is or is not, but what should or should not be. And therefore, though he recount things not true, yet because he telleth them not for true, he lieth not—without we will say that Nathan lied in his speech, before alleged, to David, which as a wicked man durst scarce say, so think I none so simple would say that Aesop lied in the tales of his beasts; for who thinks that Aesop wrote it for actually true were well worthy to have his name chronicled among the beasts he writeth of. What child is there that, coming to a play, and seeing *Thebes* written in great letters upon an old door, doth believe that it is Thebes? If then a man can arrive, at that child's age, to know that the poet's persons and doings are but pictures what should be, and not stories that have been, they will never give the lie to things not affirmatively but allegorically and figuratively written. And therefore, as in history looking for truth, they may go away full fraught with falsehood, so in poesy, looking for fiction, they shall use the narration but as an imaginative groundplot of a profitable invention.

But hereto is replied, that the poets give names to men they write of, which argueth a conceit of an actual truth, and so, not being true, proves a falsehood. And doth the lawyer lie then, when under the names of "John a Stile," and "John a Noakes," he puts his case? But that is easily answered. Their naming of men is but to make their picture the more lively, and not to build any history; painting men, they cannot leave men nameless. We see we cannot play at chess but that we must give names to our chessmen; and yet, me thinks, he were a very partial champion of truth that would say we lied for giving a piece of wood the reverend title of a bishop. The poet nameth Cyrus and Aeneas no other way than to show what men of their fames, fortunes, and estates should do.

Their third is, how much it abuseth men's wit, training it to wanton sinfulness and lustful love: for indeed that is the principal, if not the only abuse I can hear alleged. They say the comedies rather teach than reprehend amorous conceits. They say the lyric is larded with passionate sonnets, the elegiac weeps the want of his mistress, and that even to the heroical Cupid hath ambitiously climbed. Alas, Love, I would thou couldst as well defend thyself as thou canst offend others. I would those on whom thou dost attend could either put thee away, or yield good reason why they keep thee. But grant love of beauty to be a beastly fault (although it be very hard, since only man, and no beast, hath that gift to discern beauty); grant that lovely name of Love to deserve all hateful reproaches (although even some of my masters the philosophers spent a good deal of their lamp-oil in setting forth the excellency of it); grant, I say, whatsoever they will have granted, that not only love, but lust, but vanity, but (if they list) scurrility, possesseth many leaves of the poets' books; yet think I, when this is granted, they will find their sentence may with good manners put the last words foremost, and not say that poetry abuseth man's wit, but that man's wit abuseth poetry.

For I will not deny but that man's wit may make poesy, which should be *eikastike*, which some learned have defined, "figuring forth good things," to be *phantastike*, which doth contrariwise infect the fancy with unworthy objects; as the painter, that should give to the eye either some excellent perspective, or some fine picture, fit for building or fortification, or containing in it some notable example, as Abraham sacrificing his son Isaac, Judith killing Holofernes, David fighting with Goliath, may leave those, and please an ill-pleased eye with wanton shows of better-hidden matters. But what, shall the abuse of a thing make the right use odious? Nay truly, though I yield that poesy may not only be abused, but that being abused, by the reason of his sweet charming force, it can do more hurt than any other army of words, yet shall it be so far from concluding that the abuse should give reproach to the abused, that contrariwise it is a good reason, that whatsoever, being abused, doth most harm, being rightly used (and upon the right use each thing conceiveth his title), doth most good.

Do we not see the skill of physic (the best rampire to our often-assaulted bodies), being abused, teach poison, the most violent destroyer? Doth not knowledge of law, whose end is to even and right all things, being abused, grow the crooked fosterer of horrible injuries? Doth not (to go to the highest) God's word abused breed heresy, and his name abused become blasphemy? Truly a needle cannot do much hurt, and as truly (with leave of ladies be it spoken) it cannot do much good. With a sword thou mayst kill thy father, and with a sword thou mayst defend thy prince and country. So that, as in their calling poets the fathers of lies they say nothing, so in this their argument of abuse they prove the commendation.

They allege herewith, that before poets began to be in price, our nation hath set their hearts' delight upon action, and not upon imagination, rather doing things worthy to be written, than writing things fit to be done. What that beforetime was, I think scarcely Sphinx can tell, since no memory is so ancient that hath the precedence of poetry. And certain it is that, in our plainest homeliness, yet never was the Albion nation without poetry. Marry, this argument, though it be levelled against poetry, yet is it indeed a chainshot against all learning, or bookishness, as they commonly term it. Of such mind were certain Goths, of whom it is written that, having in the spoil of a famous city taken a fair library, one hangman (belike fit to execute the fruits of their wits) who had murdered a great number of bodies, would have set fire on it. "No," said another very gravely, "take heed what you do, for while they are busy about these toys, we shall with more leisure conquer their countries."

This indeed is the ordinary doctrine of ignorance, and many words sometimes I have heard spent in it; but because this reason is generally against all learning, as well as poetry, or rather, all learning but poetry; because it were too large a digression to handle, or at least too superfluous (since it is manifest that all government of action is to be gotten by knowledge, and

knowledge best by gathering many knowledges, which is reading), I only, with Horace, to him that is of that opinion,

Jubeo stultum esse libenter:[19]

for as for poetry itself, it is the freest from this objection. For
poetry is the companion of the camps.

I dare undertake, Orlando Furioso, or honest King Arthur, will
never displease a soldier: but the quiddity of *ens,* and *prima
materia,* will hardly agree with a corselet. And therefore, as I said
in the beginning, even Turks and Tartars are delighted with
poets. Homer, a Greek, flourished before Greece flourished. And
if to a slight conjecture a conjecture may be opposed, truly it
may seem, that as by him their learned men took almost their
first light of knowledge, so their active men received their first
motions of courage. Only Alexander's example may serve, who
by Plutarch is accounted of such virtue that Fortune was not his
guide but his footstool; whose acts speak for him, though Plutarch
did not; indeed the phoenix of warlike princes. This Alexander
left his schoolmaster, living Aristotle, behind him, but took dead
Homer with him. He put the philosopher Callisthenes to death
for his seeming philosophical, indeed mutinous, stubbornness, but
the chief thing he ever was heard to wish for was that Homer
had been alive. He well found he received more bravery of
mind by the pattern of Achilles than by hearing the definition
of fortitude. And therefore, if Cato misliked Fulvius for carrying
Ennius with him to the field, it may be answered, that if Cato
misliked it, the noble Fulvius liked it, or else he had not done it:
for it was not the excellent Cato Uticensis (whose authority I
would much more have reverenced) but it was the former, in
truth a bitter punisher of faults, but else a man that had never
well sacrificed to the Graces. He misliked and cried out upon
all Greek learning, and yet, being 80 years old, began to learn it,
belike fearing that Pluto understood not Latin. Indeed, the
Roman laws allowed no person to be carried to the wars but
he that was in the soldiers' roll, and therefore, though Cato misliked his unmustered person, he misliked not his work. And if
he had, Scipio Nasica, judged by common consent the best
Roman, loved him. Both the other Scipio brothers, who had by

[19] ["I bid him be as much a fool as he pleases." See Horace, *Satires,* I,
i, 63.]

their virtues no less surnames than of Asia and Afric, so loved him that they caused his body to be buried in their sepulchre. So as Cato's authority being but against his person, and that answered with so far greater than himself, is herein of no validity.

But now indeed my burden is great; now Plato's name is laid upon me, whom, I must confess, of all philosophers I have ever esteemed most worthy of reverence, and with great reason, since of all philosophers he is the most poetical. Yet if he will defile the fountain out of which his flowing streams have proceeded, let us boldly examine with what reasons he did it. First, truly a man might maliciously object that Plato, being a philosopher, was a natural enemy of poets. For indeed, after the philosophers had picked out of the sweet mysteries of poetry the right discerning true points of knowledge, they forthwith, putting it in method, and making a schoolart of that which the poets did only teach by a divine delightfulness, beginning to spurn at their guides, like ungrateful prentices, were not content to set up shops for themselves, but sought by all means to discredit their masters; which by the force of delight being barred them, the less they could overthrow them the more they hated them. For indeed, they found for Homer seven cities strove who should have him for their citizen; where many cities banished philosophers as not fit members to live among them. For only repeating certain of Euripides' verses, many Athenians had their lives saved of the Syracusans, when the Athenians themselves thought many philosophers unworthy to live. Certain poets, as Simonides and Pindar, had so prevailed with Hiero the First, that of a tyrant they made him a just king; where Plato could do so little with Dionysius, that he himself of a philosopher was made a slave. But who should do thus, I confess, should requite the objections made against poets with like cavillation against philosophers; as likewise one should do that should bid one read *Phaedrus* or *Symposium* in Plato, or the discourse of love in Plutarch, and see whether any poet do authorize abominable filthiness, as they do. Again, a man might ask out of what commonwealth Plato did banish them. In sooth, thence where he himself alloweth community of women. So as belike this banishment grew not for effeminate wantonness, since little should poetical sonnets be hurtful when a man might have what woman he listed. But I honor philosophical instructions, and bless the wits which bred them so as they be not abused, which is likewise stretched to poetry.

St. Paul himself (who yet, for the credit of poets allegeth twice two poets, and one of them by the name of a prophet) setteth a watchword upon philosophy,—indeed upon the abuse. So doth Plato upon the abuse, not upon poetry. Plato found fault that the poets of his time filled the world with wrong opinions of the gods, making light tales of that unspotted essence, and therefore would not have the youth depraved with such opinions. Herein may much be said; let this suffice: the poets did not induce such opinions, but did imitate those opinions already induced. For all the Greek stories can well testify that the very religion of that time stood upon many and many-fashioned gods, not taught so by the poets, but followed according to their nature of imitation. Who list may read in Plutarch the discourses of Isis and Osiris, of the cause why oracles ceased, of the divine providence, and see whether the theology of that nation stood not upon such dreams which the poets indeed superstitiously observed, and truly (since they had not the light of Christ) did much better in it than the philosophers, who, shaking off superstition, brought in atheism. Plato therefore (whose authority I had much rather justly construe than unjustly resist) meant not in general of poets, in those words of which Julius Scaliger saith, *Qua authoritate barbari quidam atque hispidi abuti velint ad poetas e republica exigendos;*[20] but only meant to drive out those wrong opinions of the Deity (whereof now, without further law, Christianity hath taken away all the hurtful belief), perchance (as he thought) nourished by the then esteemed poets. And a man need go no further than to Plato himself to know his meaning: who, in his dialogue called *Ion,* giveth high and rightly divine commendation to poetry. So as Plato, banishing the abuse, not the thing—not banishing it, but giving due honor unto it—shall be our patron and not our adversary. For indeed I had much rather (since truly I may do it) show their mistaking of Plato (under whose lion's skin they would make an ass-like braying against poesy) than go about to overthrow his authority, whom, the wiser a

[20] ["This authority certain barbarians and rude persons wish to use to expel poets from the state." *Poetices libri septem,* I, ii.]

man is, the more just cause he shall find to have in admiration; especially since he attributeth unto poesy more than myself do, namely, to be a very inspiring of a divine force, far above man's wit, as in the aforenamed dialogue is apparent.

Of the other side, who would show the honors have been by the best sort of judgments granted them, a whole sea of examples would present themselves: Alexanders, Caesars, Scipios, all favorers of poets; Laelius, called the Roman Socrates, himself a poet, so as part of *Heautontimoroumenos* in Terence was supposed to be made by him. And even the Greek Socrates, whom Apollo confirmed to be the only wise man, is said to have spent part of his old time in putting Aesop's fables into verses. And therefore, full evil should it become his scholar Plato to put such words in his master's mouth against poets. But what needs more? Aristotle writes the Art of Poesy: and why, if it should not be written? Plutarch teacheth the use to be gathered of them, and how, if they should not be read? And who reads Plutarch's either history or philosophy shall find he trimmeth both their garments with guards of poesy.

But I list not to defend poesy with the help of her underling historiography. Let it suffice that it is a fit soil for praise to dwell upon; and what dispraise may set upon it, is either easily overcome, or transformed into just commendation. So that, since the excellencies of it may be so easily and so justly confirmed, and the low-creeping objections so soon trodden down; it not being an art of lies, but of true doctrine; not of effeminateness, but of notable stirring of courage; not of abusing man's wit, but of strengthening man's wit; not banished, but honored by Plato; let us rather plant more laurels for to engarland our poets' heads (which honor of being laureate, as besides them only triumphant captains wear, is a sufficient authority to show the price they ought to be had in) than suffer the ill-favoring breath of such wrong-speakers once to blow upon the clear springs of poesy.

But since I have run so long a career in this matter, me thinks, before I give my pen a full stop, it shall be but a little more lost time to inquire why England (the mother of excellent minds) should be grown so hard a stepmother to poets, who certainly in wit ought to pass all others, since all only proceedeth from their wit, being indeed makers of themselves, not takers of others. How can I but exclaim,

Musa, mihi causas memora, quo numine laeso? [21]

Sweet poesy, that hath anciently had kings, emperors, senators, great captains, such as, besides a thousand others, David, Adrian, Sophocles, Germanicus, not only to favor poets, but to be poets; and of our nearer times can present for her patrons a Robert, King of Sicily, the great King Francis of France, King James of Scotland; such cardinals as Bembus and Bibbiena; such famous preachers and teachers as Beza and Melancthon; so learned philosophers as Fracastorius and Scaliger; so great orators as Pontanus and Muretus; so piercing wits as George Buchanan; so grave counselors as, besides many, but before all, that Hospital of France, than whom (I think) that realm never brought forth a more accomplished judgment, more firmly builded upon virtue —I say these, with numbers of others, not only to read others' poesies but to poetize for others' reading—that poesy, thus embraced in all other places, should only find in our time a hard welcome in England, I think the very earth lamenteth it, and therefore decketh our soil with fewer laurels than it was accustomed. For heretofore poets have in England also flourished, and, which is to be noted, even in those times when the trumpet of Mars did sound loudest. And now that an overfaint quietness should seem to strew the house for poets, they are almost in as good reputation as the mountebanks at Venice. Truly even that, as of the one side it giveth great praise to poesy, which like Venus (but to better purpose) hath rather be troubled in the net with Mars than enjoy the homely quiet of Vulcan; so serves it for a piece of a reason why they are less grateful to idle England, which now can scarce endure the pain of a pen. Upon this necessarily followeth, that base men with servile wits undertake it, who think it enough if they can be rewarded of the printer. And so as Epaminondas is said, with the honor of his virtue to have made an office, by his exercising it, which before was contemptible, to become highly respected, so these, no more but setting their names to it, by their own disgracefulness disgrace the most graceful poesy. For now, as if all the Muses were got with child, to bring forth bastard poets, without any commission they do post over the banks of Helicon, till they make the readers more weary than posthorses; while, in the mean time, they,

[21] ["O Muse, call to my mind the causes of these things: what divinity was injured?" *Aeneid*, I, 8.]

Queis meliore luto finxit praecordia Titan,[22]

are better content to suppress the outflowing of their wit than, by publishing them, to be accounted knights of the same order.

But I that, before ever I durst aspire unto the dignity, am admitted into the company of the paper-blurrers, do find the very true cause of our wanting estimation is want of desert, taking upon us to be poets in despite of Pallas. Now wherein we want desert were a thankworthy labor to express; but if I knew, I should have mended myself. But I, as I never desired the title, so have I neglected the means to come by it. Only, overmastered by some thoughts, I yielded an inky tribute unto them. Marry, they that delight in poesy itself should seek to know what they do and how they do; and, especially, look themselves in an unflattering glass of reason, if they be inclinable unto it. For poesy must not be drawn by the ears; it must be gently led, or rather it must lead; which was partly the cause that made the ancient-learned affirm it was a divine gift, and no human skill: since all other knowledges lie ready for any that hath strength of wit; a poet no industry can make, if his own genius be not carried unto it; and therefore is it an old proverb, *orator fit, poeta nascitur.*[23] Yet confess I always that as the fertilest ground must be manured, so must the highest flying wit have a Daedalus to guide him. That Daedalus, they say, both in this and in other, hath three wings to bear itself up into the air of due commendation: that is, art, imitation, and exercise. But these, neither artificial rules nor imitative patterns, we much cumber ourselves withal. Exercise indeed we do, but that very forebackwardly: for where we should exercise to know, we exercise as having known: and so is our brain delivered of much matter which never was begotten by knowledge. For, there being two principal parts— matter to be expressed by words, and words to express the matter—in neither we use art or imitation rightly.

·   ·   ·

Now for similitudes in certain printed discourses, I think all herbarists, all stories of beasts, fowls, and fishes are rifled up, that they may come in multitudes to wait upon any of our conceits; which certainly is as absurd a surfeit to the ears as is

---

[22] ["Whose hearts Titan made of finer clay." Juvenal, *Satires*, XIV, 34–35.]
[23] ["The orator is made, the poet is born."]

possible: for the force of a similitude not being to prove any thing to a contrary disputer but only to explain to a willing hearer, when that is done, the rest is a most tedious prattling, rather overswaying the memory from the purpose whereto they were applied than any whit informing the judgment, already either satisfied, or by similitudes not to be satisfied. For my part, I do not doubt, when Antonius and Crassus, the great fore-fathers of Cicero in eloquence, the one (as Cicero testifieth of them) pretended not to know art, the other not to set by it, be-cause with a plain sensibleness they might win credit of popular ears; which credit is the nearest step to persuasion; which per-suasion is the chief mark of oratory;—I do not doubt (I say) but that they used these tracks very sparingly; which, who doth generally use, any man may see doth dance to his own music, and so be noted by the audience more careful to speak curiously than to speak truly.

Undoubtedly (at least to my opinion undoubtedly) I have found in divers smally learned courtiers a more sound style than in some professors of learning; of which I can guess no other cause, but that the courtier, following that which by practice he findeth fittest to nature, therein (though he know it not) doth according to art, though not by art: where the other, using art to show art, and not to hide art (as in these cases he should do), flieth from nature, and indeed abuseth art.

But what? me thinks I deserve to be pounded for straying from poetry to oratory: but both have such an affinity in this wordish consideration that I think this digression will make my meaning receive the fuller understanding—which is not to take upon me to teach poets how they should do, but only, finding myself sick among the rest, to show some one or two spots of the common infection grown among the most part of writers; that, acknowledging ourselves somewhat awry, we may bend to the right use both of matter and manner: whereto our language giveth us great occasion, being indeed capable of any excellent exercising of it. I know some will say it is a mingled language. And why not so much the better, taking the best of both the other? Another will say it wanteth grammar. Nay truly, it hath that praise that it wanteth not grammar: for grammar it might have, but it needs it not; being so easy in itself, and so void of those cumbersome differences of cases, genders, moods, and tenses, which I think was a piece of the Tower of Babylon's curse, that a man should be put to school to learn his mother tongue. But for the uttering sweetly and properly the conceits of the mind, which is the end of speech, that hath it equally with any other tongue in the world; and is particularly happy in compositions of two or three words together, near the Greek, far beyond the Latin: which is one of the greatest beauties can be in a language.

Now of versifying there are two sorts, the one ancient, the other modern: the ancient marked the quantity of each syllable, and according to that framed his verse; the modern observing only number (with some regard of the accent), the chief life of it standeth in that like sounding of the words, which we call rhyme. Whether of these be the more excellent would bear many speeches. The ancient (no doubt) more fit for music, both words and tune observing quantity, and more fit lively to express divers passions, by the low and lofty sound of the well-weighed syllable. The latter likewise, with his rhyme, striketh a certain music to the ear: and, in fine, since it doth delight, though by another way, it obtains the same purpose: there being in either sweetness, and wanting in neither majesty. Truly the English, before any other vulgar language I know, is fit for both sorts: for, for the ancient, the Italian is so full of vowels that it must ever be cumbered with elisions; the Dutch so, of the other side, with consonants, that they cannot yield the sweet sliding fit for a verse; the French, in his whole language, hath not one word that hath his accent in the last syllable saving two, called *antepenultima;* and little more hath the Spanish and, therefore, very gracelessly may they use dactyls. The English is subject to none of these defects.

Now for the rhyme, though we do not observe quantity, yet we observe the accent very precisely: which other languages either cannot do, or will not do so absolutely. That *caesura,* or breathing place in the midst of the verse, neither Italian nor Spanish have, the French, and we, never almost fail of. Lastly, even the very rhyme itself the Italian cannot put in the last syllable, by the French named the "masculine rhyme," but still in the next to the last, which the French call the "female," or the next before that, which the Italians term *sdrucciola.* The example of the former is *buono: suono,* of the *sdrucciola, femina: semina.* The French, of the other side, hath both the male, as *bon: son,* and the female, as *plaise: taise,* but the *sdrucciola* he hath not: where the English hath all three, as *due: true, father: rather, motion: potion;* with much more which might be said, but that I find already the triflingness of this discourse is much too much enlarged.

So that since the ever-praiseworthy poesy is full of virtue-breeding delightfulness, and void of no gift that ought to be in the noble name of learning; since the blames laid against it are either false or feeble; since the cause why it is not esteemed in England is the fault of poet-apes, not poets; since, lastly, our tongue is most fit to honor poesy, and to be honored by poesy; I conjure you all that have had the evil luck to read this ink-wasting toy of mine, even in the name of the Nine Muses, no more to scorn the sacred mysteries of poesy, no more to laugh at the name of "poets," as though they were next inheritors to fools, no more to jest at the reverent title of a "rhymer"; but to believe, with Aristotle, that they were the ancient treasurers of the Grecians' divinity; to believe, with Bembus, that they were first bringers-in of all civility; to believe, with Scaliger, that no philosopher's precepts can sooner make you an honest man than the reading of Virgil; to believe, with Clauserus, the translator of Cornutus, that it pleased the heavenly Deity, by Hesiod and Homer, under the veil of fables, to give us all knowledge, logic, rhetoric, philosophy natural and moral, and *quid non?*; to believe, with me, that there are many mysteries contained in poetry which of purpose were written darkly, lest by profane wits it should be abused; to believe, with Landino, that they are so beloved of the gods that whatsoever they write proceeds of a divine fury; lastly, to believe themselves, when they tell you they will make you immortal by their verses.

Thus doing, your name shall flourish in the printers' shops; thus doing, you shall be of kin to many a poetical preface; thus doing, you shall be most fair, most rich, most wise, most all; you shall dwell upon superlatives. Thus doing, though you be *libertino patre natus,* you shall suddenly grow *Herculea proles,*[24]

> *Si quid mea carmina possunt.*[25]

Thus doing, your soul shall be placed with Dante's Beatrice or Virgil's Anchises. But if (fie of such a but) you be born so near

[24] ["Though you be the son of a freedman," you shall become "a descendant of Hercules."]

[25] ["If my songs are of any avail." *Aeneid,* IX, 446.]

the dull-making cataract of Nilus that you cannot hear the planet-like music of poetry, if you have so earth-creeping a mind that it cannot lift itself up to look to the sky of poetry, or rather, by a certain rustical disdain, will become such a mome as to be a Momus of poetry; then, though I will not wish unto you the ass's ears of Midas, nor to be driven by a poet's verses (as Bubonax was) to hang himself, nor to be rhymed to death, as is said to be done in Ireland; yet thus much curse I must send you, in the behalf of all poets, that while you live, you live in love, and never get favor for lacking skill of a sonnet, and when you die, your memory die from the earth for want of an epitaph.

QUESTIONS FOR STUDY
AND TOPICS FOR DISCUSSION
ON *An Apology for Poetry*

1. Sidney's essay is entitled an "apology," but that does not mean, as you might think from the way we use the word today, an "excuse," or "an expression of regret." For Sidney's readers the word meant "the pleading off from a charge or imputation, whether expressed, implied, or only conceived as possible; defense of a person, or vindication of an institution, etc., from accusation or aspersion." In short, the essay is a defense. A defense of what exactly? What are the charges? Who are the persons or parties who have brought the suit? What is the form of Sidney's plea? In several places in the essay Sidney seems to mock an action at law or a formal disputation on his subject. Why do you suppose he chose to present his argument in this manner?

The answers to these questions will be found in the performance of the whole work, but some facts about its occasion may help to start and focus your inquiry. *An Apology for Poetry* was first published in 1595, nine years after Sidney died of wounds received at the Battle of Zutphen. The date of its composition is uncertain; some scholars say it was written in 1580, but others argue for a date as late as 1585. Sidney states that he had been "provoked to say something" in defense of his vocation. The immediate provocation seems to have been the publication in 1579 of a polemic written by Stephen Gosson entitled *The School of Abuse*. This work was dedicated to Sidney, apparently without his foreknowledge and certainly without his blessing, and if we can take what Edmund Spenser said at face value, Gosson was "for his labor scorned" by his intended patron. Sidney's reaction is hardly to be wondered at since Gosson's purpose was to show that "Poets, Pipers, Players, Jesters, and such like Caterpillars" were preying on the Commonwealth and sapping its moral fiber. Gosson himself began as a dramatist, but smitten by the light, sincerely or opportunely, he proposed to play the censor. His work was dressed in the artificial elegance of the new literary style of Euphuism, and displays verve, bite, and wit, but his arguments were scarcely novel. Gosson was only repeating the major Puritan objections to poetry. What worried the poets was that the attacks had been lately mounting in number and vehemence. Plato's banishment of poetry began to look less like a fiction and more like something that might be enacted into law at any moment. The kind of imputations mirrored in *The School of Abuse* had become a cause for immediate concern to Sidney and his fellow poets.

2. Why does Sidney begin the essay with anecdotes about Pugliano? What purpose is served by the author's reminiscences? What is the *tone*? (*Tone* is a critical term designating the author's attitude toward what he is saying as conveyed by the way he says it. Tone is the manner in which what the author says is meant to be taken.) What characteristics of the author are revealed in his narrative? What sort of person does he seem to be? How do Pugliano's teachings and manner of discourse relate to the intention of the essay? (On this last question, consider the paragraph beginning "And that moving is . . ." on p. 36.)

3. According to K. O. Myrick (*Sir Philip Sidney as a Literary Craftsman*, 1935), Sidney's essay deliberately imitated the structure of a classical oration. The following is an outline of the structure: I. The *exordium* (introduction) comprises the first two paragraphs. II. The *narratio* (narration of the facts of the case) runs to the paragraph beginning "Now let us go . . ." on p. 26. III. The *propositio* (proposition) is the definition of poetry in the paragraph immediately following. IV. The *partitio* (partition of the points in controversy) runs to " . . . according to the dignity of the subject" (p. 28). V. The *confirmatio* (argument and proof) follows and runs until " . . . honor the poet's triumph" (p. 44). VI. The *reprehensio* (reprehension; refutation) picks up the confirmation and ends " . . . the clear springs of poesy" (p. 53). A *digressio* (digression), a portion of which is omitted here, contains Sidney's reflections on the state of contemporary English poetry; it begins "But since I have run so long a career . . . " (p. 53). VII. The *peroratio* (conclusion) begins "So that since the ever-praiseworthy poesy . . ." (p. 58).

Myrick asserts that Sidney's introduction is "in both substance and manner a classical exordium"; in manner because it creates a favorable mood for the reception of the argument of the oration; in substance because it expresses "the fundamental idea on which the argument is to be built." The opening of a classical oration is supposed to be "derived from the very essence of the cause." According to Myrick, the essence of Sidney's case is that poetry "giving both precept and example, is an eloquent speaking picture" and for that reason a more effective teacher than philosophy or history; therefore, the exordium of the essay exemplifies in the person of Pugliano the precepts of the author.

Myrick's analysis, in general as well as in this particular, raises a number of questions, which you might want to consider later. Does this kind of analysis suffice for a full understanding of the intention, form, and sense of the *Apology*? Assuming that Sidney's essay did imitate the form of the classical oration, what effects in the movement of the argument are achieved by this use of a conventional form? Does it always coincide with other modes of progression, or does it sometimes cross the others? And finally, why did Sidney choose to mimic the form of the classical oration? Was it just as a handy means of organizing his material—or did he have some expressive purpose besides?

4. Analyze the construction of the two sentences in the opening paragraph beginning "He said. . . . " How would you character-ize this style? Is it typical of the *Apology*? Sidney could write quite differently when he chose to do so. Here, for example, is one of his letters:

MR. MOLYNEUX:

Few words are best. My letters to my father have come to the eyes of some. Neither can I condemn any but you for it. If it be so you have played the very knave with me; and so I will make you know if I have good proof of it. But that for so much as is past. For that is to come, I assure you before God that if ever I know you do so much as read any letter I write to my father, without his commandment, or my consent, I will thrust my dagger into you. And trust to it, for I speak in earnest. In the mean time farewell. From Court this last of May 1578.

BY ME
PHILIP SIDNEY

Does Sidney use this manner in the essay? Why does he choose now one and then the other style?

5. What is the tone of "if I had not been a piece of a logician before I came to him, I think he would have persuaded me to have wished myself a horse" (p. 20)? Is there anything later in the essay which gives this statement a more serious aspect?

6. What is the manner and sense of the sentence "Wherein, if Pugliano's . . . the steps of his master" (p. 21)? Is this, as Myrick suggests, just an expression of the modesty expected of an advocate in a judicial oration in behalf of an accused client?

7. "And will they now play . . . kill their parents" (p. 21) is a parody of Gosson's style. How would you describe the style here? In answering this, consider the passage beginning "Now for similitudes . . . " on p. 55. Where else does Sidney mock that style? How does it differ from his own? Setting the parody aside, and taking the imagery at face value, what is Sidney saying? What is the tone? Compare the tone of the passage cited in Question 5.

8. What is the relation of the following passage to the intention of the *Apology*: "So as Amphion was said to move stones with his poetry to build Thebes, and Orpheus to be listened to by beasts—indeed stony and beastly people" (p. 21)?

One of the presiding patterns of imagery in the *Apology* is that of making, building, erecting. How does the passage cited relate to this pattern? The patterns of bestiality (or, more exactly, "animality") and civility (in the forms of taming and ordering) are less prominent, but they are obviously important. How are all of these patterns woven together, and what purpose do they serve?

9. Note the reference to Plato on p. 22. A major issue in the great debate of the Renaissance on the nature and purpose of poetry concerned the banishment of the poets by Plato from his ideal commonwealth. Sidney was himself a Platonist; his theory of poetry assimilates ideas from Aristotle and certain Italian Renaissance theorists, but it remains essentially Platonic. He and his like-minded contemporaries were torn between their reverence for the philosopher and their solicitude for their vocation, and they had to exercise great ingenuity in reconciling the two. Sidney's major argument on this score appears later in the essay. Why does he foreshadow that argument here? What contrasts are developed in this paragraph?

10. What is the literal sense of the word "passport" in "a great passport of poetry" (p. 22)? Is Sidney using the word *figuratively*? Is it a *trope*? (*Figurative language* is language which departs from what is taken to be the standard order, construction, and significance of words in order to achieve special meaning or effect. *Tropes* are a class of figures in which words are used with a decided change or extension in their literal and explicit meaning. *Simile* and *metaphor* are two of the most common tropes. Both of these compare or identify two things which are normally considered to be different. A simile compares them directly; e.g., "my love is *like* a red, red rose." A metaphor omits the specific word of comparison; e.g., "my love *is* a red, red rose.") How is the sense of "a great passport of poetry" related in structure to the preceding paragraphs, and in meaning to the argument that comes before and after?

11. How does Sidney develop his argument in the sections discussing the terms *areytos, vates,* and "maker"? Is there any progression in these terms? How does Sidney reconcile pagan ideas with his Christian convictions?

12. What does the passage "For what else is the awaking his musical instruments . . . scourged out of the church of God" (p. 24) reveal about the essay's intention? How does Sidney develop later as characteristic of the poet's handling of words what he says about the psalmist's handling of prophecy? What is the relation of this passage to the polemical occasion of the essay?

13. Analyze the intention, composition, and sense of the whole of the section "But now let us see . . . the name above all names of learning" (pp. 24–26). Consider the antitheses developed in the second and third paragraphs of this section. Consider the metaphors and meaning in "Only the poet . . . the poets only deliver a golden." What makes poetry superior to the other arts and sciences? What do you suppose Sidney meant by *nature*? Relate "our erected wit maketh us know what perfection is, and yet our infected will keepeth us from reaching unto it" (p. 26) to the matters discussed in Questions 8 and 12. How does this statement reflect on poetry, poet-haters, and lovers of poetry?

How does its meaning "change" by viewing it from each of these perspectives?

14. Why does Sidney say: "But these arguments will by few be understood, and by fewer granted" (p. 26)? In several places in the essay Sidney seems reluctant to sound the depths of his argument; he draws the curtain on a final mystery. "There are many mysteries contained in poetry," he says on p. 58, "which of purpose were written darkly, lest by profane wits it should be abused." He decides instead to "go to a more ordinary opening of him, that the truth may be more palpable" (p. 26). What does Sidney mean? What is the effect of the undercurrent of "mystery" on his argument? Why is Sidney sometimes open and sometimes enigmatical? Which is a pose, a mask for argument, and which is the true character of the person of the author?

Consider C. S. Lewis's commentary:

> In reality the "more ordinarie opening" is concessive and strategical. If the first account has seemed to some readers too ambitious and metaphysical, here for their comfort is something "which no man will denie." But when once we have been thus lured into agreement we shall find that it all comes to the same thing in the end and we are committed to Sidney's full doctrine.

15. Discuss the definition of poetry on p. 26 in connection with the form and purpose of the essay as a whole.

Poetry, Sidney says, is a speaking picture; it is a form of imitation, a counterfeit, and its end is to teach and delight. The word "counterfeit" is obviously meant to catch our attention. Sidney has already played with the notion of counterfeiting. We have seen that he delights in contraries, and his strategy on this point is apparent almost from the outset: although poetry "counterfeits," "feigns," and "lies" in its mode of representation, it alone, of all forms of knowledge, tells the truth. Why does Sidney use this strategy? Is he just trying to be witty and clever? Is he trying to confound his adversaries? How would the sense of the essay be changed if he had been more straightforward and less paradoxical in his argument?

How does Sidney's discussion on p. 27 of the painting of Lucretia (the wife of Tarquinius Collatinus, who killed herself after being violated by Sextus) relate to his definition of poetry?

An important pattern of imagery in the essay is that of perception, of seeing, and by this pattern Sidney intimates that there are two kinds of seeing: that which one sees with what might be called the "bodily" eye, and that which one sees with the "eyes of the mind." Trace this pattern and consider how it affects Sidney's arguments on the counterfeiting nature of poetry. Consider, also, how it relates to the other thematic contrasts of outward appearance and inner reality.

16. How is the paragraph beginning "These be subdivided . . . " (p. 27) linked with the next? How does Sidney employ the metaphor of "balance" elsewhere in the essay?

17. Analyze the intention and composition of the paragraph beginning "Now therefore it shall not be amiss . . . " (p. 28), especially the passage "the final end is to lead and draw us to as high a perfection as our degenerate souls, made worse by their clayey lodgings, can be capable of." Describe the tone of this and the passage "But all, one and other, having this scope [object]—to know, and by knowledge to lift up the mind from the dungeon of the body to the enjoying his own divine essence." How are the metaphors suggested by the verbs "to lead and draw" and "to lift" articulated elsewhere in the essay? What is the tone following the latter sentence?

18. How does Sidney's description of the "moral philosophers" on p. 29 relate to his discussion of *prosopopoeia* (a rhetorical figure: "personification") on p. 24?

19. Why does Sidney shift address on p. 30 and allow the historian to speak directly?

20. Following the boast of the historian that he teaches an active rather than a disputative virtue, Sidney disingenuously asks (p. 30): "Now whom shall we find (since the question standeth for the highest form in the school of learning) to be moderator?" Moderator is a technical term signifying the umpire or arbitrator in the university disputations that were a favorite exercise of Scholastic learning. What is the effect of Sidney's question? Describe his strategy in this section. How is Sidney's mockery of the language and procedures of formal disputation related to the sense of the whole essay?

21. Consider the style and sense of the passage in which Sidney explains why a poet gives a "perfect picture": "A perfect picture I say, for he yieldeth to the powers of the mind an image of that whereof the philosopher bestoweth but a wordish [i.e., "consisting of words" rather than "wordy"] description" (p. 31). Compare the meaning and effect derived from the logical argument on this point with the meaning the statement has taken on through the pattern of metaphor.

22. Why does Sidney contrast "outward things" and "inward conceits" (p. 31)? By reference to the *Oxford English Dictionary*, establish what "conceit" meant to his contemporaries. Compare Sidney's usage.

23. What is the tone and sense of "For conclusion, I say the philosopher teacheth . . . these dumb speakers" (p. 33)? What images and ideas does this passage pick up from earlier portions of the essay?

24. How does the sentence "But the historian, being captived to the truth of a foolish world . . . " (p. 35) condition the preceding argument on "feigned examples" and "true examples" (pp. 34–35)? What role does *passion* play in Sidney's argument?

25. Consider the section "And that moving is of a higher degree . . ." to ". . . they would swear they be brought to school again" (pp. 36–37) in the light of what you have discovered about the intention and the form of the essay.

26. Analyze the rhythm of the paragraph beginning "The philosopher showeth you the way . . . " (p. 36). Is any religious allusion suggested? What is the tone of the passage?

27. What idea of poetry is suggested by "even as the child is often brought to take most wholesome things by hiding them in such other as have a pleasant taste" (p. 37)? Is Sidney's notion similar to what his contemporary John Lyly said of instruction (in *Euphues*): "The admonition of a true friend should be like the practice of a wise physician, who wrapped his sharp pills in fine sugar"? In answering these questions, do not take the passage in isolation. Relate it to other passages of similar import, e.g., that on p. 22 on the "honest burgesses of Athens."

Relate it also to the pattern of ingestive imagery which informs the whole of the *Apology*. How does the tale of Menenius Agrippa (p. 38) bear on this point? Compare what Sidney says with Gosson's remark, "The deceitful physician giveth sweet syrups to make his poison go down the smoother."

28. What does Sidney mean by the phrase "masking raiment of Poesy" (p. 38)? Where else in the essay does he use the imagery of clothing and masking? To what purpose and with what effect?

29. On p. 46 Sidney finally takes up the "most important imputations laid to the poor poets" and addresses himself directly to Gosson's charges. Why has he waited so long? Would the sense of the essay be different if he had placed these charges earlier? Is the matter in this section the culmination of his case, what he has been leading up to all along, or is it ancillary to some other purpose? Is Sidney's "case" a negative or an affirmative one?

30. Consider the argument "of all writers under the sun the poet is the least liar" (p. 47) in connection with the preceding topic. How does Sidney's nimble fencing with contraries answer the charges of his adversaries, advance his own case, and delight the reader, all at the same time?

31. How does Sidney handle the ticklish problem of answering those critics who turn Plato against him and his vocation (pp. 51–53)? A number of scholars have argued that this is the weakest part of Sidney's refutation, as it surely is if regarded in isolation, but how is our judgment affected by viewing it in relation to the whole essay?

32. What is the relevance to the whole essay of the allusion to Daedalus (p. 55)? What metaphors and ideas are reflected?

33. Relate the famous passage on p. 56 in which Sidney contrasts the style of "divers smally learned courtiers" with that of "some professors of learning" to the style and the substance of the *Apology* itself.

34. Analyze the composition of the passage "I conjure you . . . immortal by their verses" (p. 58). Is this a change in tone? Is Sidney altering the tenor and temper of his plea? The

style? Point of view? If so, in what ways exactly? For what purpose? How does the passage affect your reflection on all that comes before?

Myrick says that this section imitates the *peroratio* of the classical oration in that it sums up the preceding argument and appeals to the feelings of judge and jury. According to Myrick, the appeal is "mock-heroic" in character, light in touch and tongue in cheek. To support his argument, he reads the clause "to believe, with Landino . . . " as "unmistakably a humorous exaggeration." Is this the way the statement is meant to be read? The whole section? Is Sidney's "peroration" just one more of the stratagems of rhetoric and disputation? Is it calculated and artful in quite the same way as the parts of the essay analyzed earlier? How does this section reflect the style discussed in Question 33?

Consider D. C. Allen's commentary:

> [Sidney] had the good sense to base his *Apologie for Poetrie* on supra-empirical arguments and to select his best weapons from the armory of the anti-poets. What he wrote was actually a lawyer's brief, and he opens his case by pleading that poetry requires no defense because it is all a matter of taste. It is something we like or dislike, and nothing can really be done about it. But having spoken as an advocate with full attention to the rites of forensic practice, he concludes, when he has reached the tail of his defense, as a theologian, inviting us to believe in revelation.

35. Is there yet another turn in the last paragraph? Is the end of the essay entirely flippant? How is the last paragraph linked to the one immediately preceding? What is the meaning of "if you have so earth-creeping a mind that it cannot lift itself up to look to the sky of poetry," and how is it meant to be taken?

36. Taking the turns of the last two paragraphs together, what image of mind and sensibility is figured forth? Which paragraph represents the true voice of the author? One or the other—or both? Is it possible to separate the serious from the sportive sides to his character? What is the relationship between the stylistic identity of the author and the sense of the whole essay?

THREE ESSAYS

BY *Sir Francis Bacon*

"Of Death"

Men fear Death, as children fear to go in the dark; and as
that natural fear in children is increased with tales, so is the
other. Certainly the contemplation of death, as the wages of
sin and passage to another world, is holy and religious, but the
fear of it, as a tribute due unto nature, is weak. Yet in religious
meditations there is sometimes mixture of vanity and of superstition. You shall read in some of the friars' books of mortification,
that a man should think with himself what the pain is if he
have but his finger's end pressed or tortured, and thereby imagine
what the pains of death are, when the whole body is corrupted
and dissolved; when many times death passeth with less pain
than the torture of a limb, for the most vital parts are not the
quickest of sense. And by him that spake only as a philosopher
and natural man, it was well said, *Pompa mortis magis terret,
quam mors ipsa.*[1] Groans and convulsions, and a discolored face,
and friends weeping, and blacks, and obsequies, and the like
show death terrible. It is worthy the observing that there is no
passion in the mind of man so weak, but it mates and masters
the fear of death; and therefore death is no such terrible enemy
when a man hath so many attendants about him that can win

[1] ["The circumstances attending death are more terrifying than death itself."]

the combat of him. Revenge triumphs over death; Love slights it; Honor aspireth to it; Grief flieth to it; Fear preoccupateth it; nay we read, after Otho the emperor had slain himself, Pity (which is the tenderest of affections) provoked many to die out of mere compassion to their sovereign, and as the truest sort of followers. Nay Seneca adds niceness and satiety: *Cogita quamdiu eadem feceris; mori velle, non tantum fortis, aut miser, sed etiam fastidiosus potest.*[2] A man would die, though he were neither valiant nor miserable, only upon a weariness to do the same thing so oft over and over. It is no less worthy to observe how little alteration in good spirits the approaches of death make, for they appear to be the same men till the last instant. Augustus Caesar died in a compliment: *Livia, conjugii nostri memor, vive et vale;*[3] Tiberius in dissimulation, as Tacitus saith of him: *Jam Tiberium vires et corpus, non dissimulatio, deserebant;*[4] Vespasian in a jest, sitting upon the stool: *Ut puto Deus fio;*[5] Galba with a sentence: *Feri, si ex re sit populi Romani,*[6] holding forth his neck; Septimius Severus in dispatch: *Adeste si quid mihi restat agendum.*[7] And the like. Certainly the Stoics bestowed too much cost upon death, and by their great preparations made it appear more fearful. Better saith he, *qui finem vitae extremum inter munera ponat naturae.*[8] It is as natural to die as to be born; and to a little infant, perhaps, the one is as painful as the other. He that dies in an earnest pursuit is like one that is wounded in hot blood, who, for the time, scarce feels the hurt; and therefore a mind fixed and bent upon somewhat that is good doth avert the dolors of death. But above all, believe it, the sweetest canticle is, *Nunc dimittis;*[9] when a man hath obtained worthy ends and expectations. Death hath this also, that it openeth the gate to good fame, and extinguisheth envy. *Extinctus amabitur idem.*[10]

[2] [Bacon's translation follows.]
[3] ["Mindful of our marriage, Livia, live and farewell."]
[4] ["His physical powers were deserting Tiberius, not his powers of dissimulation."]
[5] ["I think I am becoming a god."]
[6] ["Strike, if it be for the good of the Roman people."]
[7] ["Make haste, if anything remains for me to do."]
[8] ["Who considers the end of life one of the blessings of nature."]
[9] ["Now lettest thou thy servant depart."]
[10] ["The same man (that was envied while living) will be loved when dead."]

"Of Revenge"

Revenge is a kind of wild justice, which the more man's nature runs to, the more ought law to weed it out. For as for the first wrong, it doth but offend the law, but the revenge of that wrong putteth the law out of office. Certainly in taking revenge, a man is but even with his enemy, but in passing it over, he is superior, for it is a prince's part to pardon. And Solomon, I am sure, saith, "It is the glory of a man to pass by an offense." That which is past is gone and irrevocable, and wise men have enough to do with things present and to come; therefore they do but trifle with themselves that labor in past matters. There is no man doth a wrong for the wrong's sake, but thereby to purchase himself profit, or pleasure, or honor, or the like. Therefore why should I be angry with a man for loving himself better than me? And if any man should do wrong merely out of ill nature, why, yet it is but like the thorn or briar, which prick and scratch because they can do no other. The most tolerable sort of revenge is for those wrongs which there is no law to remedy, but then let a man take heed the revenge be such as there is no law to punish; else a man's enemy is still beforehand, and it is two for one. Some, when they take revenge, are desirous the party should know whence it cometh. This the more generous. For the delight seemeth to be not so much in doing the hurt as in making the party repent. But base and crafty cowards are like the arrow that flieth in the dark. Cosmus, duke of Florence, had a desperate saying against perfidious or neglecting friends, as if those wrongs were unpardonable: "You shall read," saith he, "that we are commanded to forgive our enemies; but you never read that we are commanded to forgive our friends." But yet the spirit of Job was in a better tune: "Shall we," saith he, "take good at God's hands, and not be content to take evil also?" And so of friends in a proportion. This is certain, that a man that studieth revenge keeps his own wounds green, which otherwise would heal and do well. Public revenges are for the most part fortunate, as that for the death of Caesar, for the death of Pertinax, for the death of Henry the Third of France, and many more. But in private revenges it is not so. Nay rather, vindictive persons live the life of witches, who, as they are mischievous, so end they infortunate.

"Of Studies"

1597 Version

Studies serve for pastimes, for ornaments and for abilities. Their chief use for pastime is in privateness and retiring; for ornament is in discourse, and for ability is in judgment. For expert men can execute, but learned men are fittest to judge or censure.

¶ To spend too much time in them is sloth, to use them too much for ornament is affectation: to make judgment wholly by their rules, is the humor of a scholar. ¶They perfect nature, and are perfected by experience. ¶ Crafty men contemn them, simple men admire them, wise men use them: For they teach not their own use, but that is a wisdom without them: and above them won by observation. ¶ Read not to contradict, nor to believe, but to weigh and consider. ¶ Some books are to be tasted, others to be swallowed, and some few to be chewed and digested: That is, some books are to be read only in parts; others to be read, but cursorily, and some few to be read wholly and with diligence and attention. ¶ Reading maketh a full man, conference a ready man, and writing an exact man. And therefore if a man write little, he had need have a great memory, if he confer little, he had need have a present wit, and if he read little, he had need have much cunning, to seem to know that he doth not. ¶ Histories make men wise, poets witty: the mathematics subtle, natural philosophy deep: moral grave, logic and rhetoric able to contend.

1612 Version

Studies serve for delight, for ornament, and for ability; their chief use for delight, is, in privateness, and retiring; for ornament, is in discourse, and for ability, is in judgment. For expert men can execute, but learned men are fittest to judge or censure. To spend too much time in them, is sloth; to use them too much for ornament, is affectation; to make judgment wholly by their rules, is the humor of a scholar. They perfect nature, and are perfected by experience. Crafty men contemn them, simple men admire them, and wise men use them. For they teach not their own use, but that is a wisdom without them, and above them, won by observation. Read not to contradict, nor to believe, but to weigh and consider. Some books are to be tasted, others to be swallowed, and some few to be chewed and digested. That is, some books are to be read only in parts; others to be read, but not curiously; and some few to be read wholly, and with diligence and attention. Reading maketh a full man, conference a ready man, and writing an exact man. And therefore if a man write little, he had need have a great memory; if he confer little, he had need have a present wit; and if he read little, he had need have much cunning, to seem to know that he doth not. Histories make men wise, poets witty, the mathematics subtle, natural philosophy deep, moral grave, logic and rhetoric able to contend. *Abeunt studia in mores.*[1] Nay, there is no stond or impediment in the wit, but may be wrought out by fit studies: like as diseases of the body may have appropriate exercises. Bowling is good for the stone and reins; shooting for the lungs and breast; gentle walking for the stomach; riding for the head: and the like. So if a man's wit be wandering, let him study the mathematics; if his wit be not apt to distinguish, or find difference, let him study the schoolmen; if it be not apt to beat over matters and to find out resemblances, let him study lawyers' cases. So every defect of the mind may have a special receipt.

1625 Version

Studies serve for delight, for ornament, and for ability. Their chief use for delight, is in privateness and retiring; for ornament, is in discourse; and for ability, is in the judgment and disposition of business. For expert men can execute, and perhaps judge of particulars, one by one; but the general counsels, and the plots, and marshalling of affairs, come best from those that are learned. To spend too much time in studies, is sloth; to use them too much for ornament, is affectation; to make judgment wholly by their rules is the humor of a scholar. They perfect nature, and are perfected by experience: for natural abilities, are like natural plants, that need pruning by study: and studies themselves, do give forth directions too much at large, except they be bounded in by experience. Crafty men contemn studies; simple men admire them; and wise men use them: for they teach not their own use; but that is a wisdom without them, and above them, won by observation. Read not to contradict, and confute; nor to believe and take for granted; nor to find talk and discourse; but to weigh

[1] ["Studies pass into manners."]

and consider. Some books are to be tasted, others to be swallowed, and some few to be chewed and digested: that is, some books are to be read only in parts; others to be read but not curiously; and some few to be read wholly, and with diligence and attention. Some books also may be read by deputy, and extracts made of them by others: but that would be, only in the less important arguments, and the meaner sort of books: else distilled books, are like common distilled waters, flashy things. Reading maketh a full man; conference a ready man; and writing an exact man. And therefore, if a man write little, he had need have a great memory; if he confer little, he had need have a present wit; and if he read little, he had need have much cunning, to seem to know that, he doth not. Histories make men wise; poets witty; the mathematics subtle; natural philosophy deep; moral grave; logic and rhetoric able to contend. *Abeunt studia in mores.* Nay there is no stond or impediment in the wit, but may be wrought out by fit studies: like as diseases of the body, may have appropriate exercises. Bowling is good for the stone and reins; shooting for the lungs and breast; gentle walking for the stomach; riding for the head; and the like. So if a man's wit be wandering, let him study the mathematics; for in demonstrations, if his wit be called away never so little, he must begin again. If his wit be not apt to distinguish or find differences, let him study the schoolmen; for they are *cymini sectores.*[2] If he be not apt to beat over matters, and to call up one thing to prove and illustrate another, let him study the lawyers' cases. So every defect of the mind may have a special receipt.

[2] ["Dividers of cuminseed," i.e., hairsplitters.]

QUESTIONS FOR STUDY
AND TOPICS FOR DISCUSSION
ON *Three Essays*

1. Bacon was the first English essayist. His first collection of *Essays* was published in 1597, seventeen years after the genre was given its name by the publication of Montaigne's *Essais*. The noun *essai* comes from *essaier,* the French verb meaning "to attempt," and by Montaigne's performance, the essay assumed the form of the writer's "attempt" to express himself in prose, on some restricted subject, in a tentative and unsystematic manner rather than with the formal elaboration of a philosophical or ethical treatise. Bacon borrowed Montaigne's title, and followed his example, but with certain significant differences in style and effect.

Both writers employ the form for personal expression; both make an "essay" into a topic, turning the thought over in the mind in active reflection as a "trial" or "experiment"; both make the mind and self of the author the focus of the work. Bacon, however, seems to be less intimate and casual. He is less revealing about his personal life; we learn next to nothing about Bacon's biography from his essays, while Montaigne's are packed with autobiographical details. Bacon seems colder and more distant in his tone; his reflections seem more formal and discursive.

Literary historians commonly separate the two writers into neat categories of contraries, asserting that Montaigne is intimate, informal, relaxed, and conversational in manner; Bacon, dogmatic, formal, intense, and expository. These differences may be magnified to a distorting degree, for both writers share a number of convictions common to men of the Renaissance, notably a consciousness of the gap between man's actual behavior and ideas of his nobility and dignity, and both writers employ disjunctive techniques of expression to convey the direct experience of thought. For all their similarities, however, Bacon is clearly more sententious in his speculations. His writing is closer to the kind of compression and verbal intricacy—the witty turns of speech, surprising juxtapositions, and lively leapings of thought—which are characteristic qualities of the poetry of his English contemporaries.

As you read through the essays included here, you might ask yourself: How does the form of the essay shape the content of its subject? How does the treatment of the subject differ from that of a formal argumentative or expository treatise? What is the reflective action of the essay? What are the premises in Bacon's arguments, what the conclusions, and by what procedures of reasoning does he move from premise to conclusion? The thinkers before Bacon who followed the Scholastic method had argued from established major premises taken from past authority and the revelations of religion. Bacon argued from general principles based on the observation of experience. How does Bacon appeal to experience in these essays? How does he make it the basis of judgment? Is the experience generalized or "personal"? What kind of person is revealed in the essays? If the style of an author is, as Gibbon said, the "image of his mind," what sort of mind and sensibility is mirrored in the form and language of Bacon's essays?

2. Like most of his contemporaries, Bacon kept a commonplace book—a journal—in which he collected his observations from experience, and, from his reading and reflections, certain striking anecdotes, apothegms, adages, and pithy sayings. In the three essays included here, which sentences have the look of journal entries? How is each sentence joined to the other? Does each sentence move from one to the next in an orderly and predictable fashion? Is the flow of the sentences smooth or choppy? How does the movement affect the sense?

3. How are the phrases and clauses within a sentence joined? Are the clauses connected by commas and semicolons loosely strung together? Is Bacon careless or indifferent in his syntax?

Bacon often uses a *paratactic* syntax. In *parataxis,* sentences, clauses, or phrases are placed together without connective words; in *hypotaxis,* on the other hand, these elements are joined by express subordinate relations. The classic instance of *parataxis* is Caesar's statement, "I came; I saw; I conquered." The effect of the construction is to suggest an ease and swiftness of conquest. All three events, each normally separate in character, are made to appear as one simultaneous action. The members of the series are close enough in length to make them seem of equal weight, but the last member of the series directs the sense of the whole, so that the conquest seems to have been accomplished in less time than the blinking of an eye. One can say more about the sentence—showing, for instance, that the laconic utterance has none of the hesitations and qualifications of a man of thought, and is thus appropriate to a man of action—but the point ought to be clear enough: the "style" of the sentence conveys not simply the "message" that Caesar was successful in a particular military engagement, but many other "meanings" besides. The order and choice of Caesar's words are more than an emphatic expression of the message; their performance, their total sense, adds scope and intricacy to the assertion.

Consider the sentence from the 1597 version of Bacon's "Of Studies": "Crafty men contemn them, simple men admire them, wise men use them" (p. 73). What is the relation of each clause to the others in the sentence? Do the clauses have equal value, or is one more important than others? Is there any progression in the units joined together? Try adding some subordinating conjunctions: e.g., "Although crafty men contemn them, and simple men admire them, wise men use them . . ."; or "Crafty men contemn them, and simple men admire them, yet wise men use them . . ." Does the addition of such words change the impression or sense of Bacon's statement? Are the syntactic relations of the items in the series clear enough without the addition of conjunctions? How is the total sense expressed by Bacon's construction altered by the use of hypotactic syntax?

4. What *antitheses* are developed in these essays, and how do they work to achieve the author's intentions? (Two or more adjacent phrases, clauses, or sentences having a similar syntactical structure form a *balance*; if these units express similar meanings they form a *parallelism*, if contrasting or opposite meanings they form an *antithesis*.) Bacon considers now one thing, now another; first one side, then the other. What is his own position? Is he simply putting down opinions impersonally and without evaluation? Bacon recommended that the writer always have commonplaces ready at hand "in which the question is argued

and handled on either side." Moreover, he advised that the case be "exaggerated both ways with the utmost force of the wit, and urged unfairly, as it were, and quite beyond the truth." In what ways are the questions in these essays "argued and handled on either side"? How are the questions wittily and unfairly "exaggerated both ways"? What are the effects of this handling of antitheses? Is the focus upon the conclusion reached, or upon the exploration of the question? How does this form affect the content of what is being said?

5. What kinds of figurative language does Bacon use in these essays? To what purpose, and with what effect? L. C. Knights has argued that "the great majority of Bacon's figures of speech are simple *illustrations* of the ideas that he wishes to convey"; and that the function of Bacon's images "is not to intensify the meaning, to make it deeper or richer, but simply to make more effective a meaning that was already formed before the application of the illustrative device." What does Knights mean exactly? Is he correct? What images, similes, and metaphors does Bacon employ? How do they work? Do they support a thought "already formed," or do they give the impression of a thought in the process of being formed? Do they enlarge the meaning, or do they simply emphasize the meaning?

The other class of figurative language besides *tropes* comprises *figures of thought. Figures of thought* also depart from standard usage of language in order to achieve artful effects. The distinction between the two classes is not sharp and firm—indeed, some critics call the devices of both classes *figures of speech*— but there is an important difference of focus in their verbal action. The departure from the standard in figures of thought is primarily in the arrangement or the rhetorical function of the words, without radical alteration of their literal meaning. *Antithesis* and *parataxis* are figures of thought.

Does Bacon depend more on tropes or on figures of thought in these essays? How do the syntactical devices affect the workings of the other kinds of figures—the similes and metaphors?

6. How does Bacon use quotations from classical literature and history? How does he differ in his use of such figures from Sidney? Why do you suppose he uses fewer classical allusions in the essays "Of Revenge" and "Of Studies" than in "Of Death"? What purpose do the allusions in "Of Death" serve? Are they all

delivered with the same tone? What is their connection with his own reflections? Do they give authority and reinforcement to his own reflections, or do they make the meaning deeper and richer?

7. Analyze the revisions of the essay "Of Studies." What does Bacon change exactly, and why? What effect does the expansion have upon the original sense of the essay? Is Bacon merely padding the content? Has he simply spruced up the expression of the first version, making it more decorous and correct? Has he altered the sense of the essay in any significant way? How do the revisions change the cadence and rhythm of the original piece? To what purpose?

Some general observations on Bacon's stylistic development may help in answering these questions. Bacon practiced a terse and curt manner of expression. He deliberately cultivated an "aphoristic" mode of discourse. This mode attempted to reproduce thought with the same form in which it originated and grew in the mind, unlike the "magistral" mode, which delivered knowledge in an orbicular fashion, with a rounded completeness. The 1597 *Essays* were little more than a collection of aphoristic "sentences" lifted from Bacon's commonplace books. The thoughts that made up each essay were given very little metaphoric or rhetorical elaboration.

The style of these essays was a conscious rejection of formal Elizabethan style, particularly the orotund manner of the so-called "Ciceronians"—writers who took as their model the stylistic devices and the grand manner of Cicero. This rejection Bacon shared with other contemporary writers, a loose assembly of "Anti-Ciceronians," who took their models of style from Seneca, Tacitus, or modern practitioners of the aphoristic mode.

Late in his career, however, Bacon felt that the reaction had gone too far, and he tried to dissociate himself from those who had cultivated an excessively "aculeate" and condensed manner of expression. Accordingly, in his later essays, especially in the collection of 1625, Bacon modified and enriched the spare manner of the 1597 *Essays*, recognizing apparently that a more magistral manner was better suited to his intentions. Anecdotes, tropes, and proverbs were added; the writing generally was made more concrete; transitions between thoughts were smoothed; and the organization of the whole was given more polish.

Even in his later prose, however, Bacon was predominantly aphoristic in his style, for he was constant to one purpose throughout his career: to "write what men do and not what they ought to do"—to write, that is, about the actualities of moral behavior, from experience and observation, rather than by prescription.

DEATH'S DUEL,

or, A Consolation to the Soul,
Against the Dying Life, and Living
Death of the Body

BY *John Donne*

TO THE READER

[*Preface to the first edition (1632) by*
Richard Redmer, the publisher]

This sermon was, by sacred authority, styled the author's own funeral sermon. Most fitly: whether we respect the time or the matter. It was preached not many days before his death, as if, having done this, there remained nothing for him to do but to die. And the matter is of death, the occasion and subject of all funeral sermons. It hath been observed of this reverend man that his faculty in preaching continually increased; and that, as he exceeded others at first, so at last he exceeded himself. This is his last sermon; I will not say it is therefore his best, because all his were excellent. Yet thus much: A dying man's words, if they concern ourselves, do usually make the deepest impression, as being spoken most feelingly and with least affectation. Now, whom doth it not concern to learn both the danger and benefit of death? Death is every man's enemy, and intends hurt to all, though to many he be occasion of greatest goods. This enemy we must all combat dying, whom he living did almost conquer, having discovered the utmost of his power, the utmost of his cruelty. May we make such use of this and other the like preparatives, that neither death, whensoever it shall come, may seem terrible, nor life tedious, how long soever it shall last.

*And unto God the Lord belong the issues
of death, i.e., from death.*

BUILDINGS STAND BY the benefit of their foundations that sustain
and support them, and of their buttresses that comprehend and
embrace them, and of their contignations that knit and unite
them: The foundations suffer them not to sink, the buttresses
suffer them not to swerve, and the contignation and knitting suffers them not to cleave. The body of our building is in the
former part of this verse. It is this: "He that is our God is the
God of salvation"; *ad salutes,*[1] of salvations in the plural, so it is
in the original; the God that gives us spiritual and temporal
salvation too.

But of this building, the foundation, the buttresses, the contignations are in this part of the verse, which constitutes our text,
and in the three divers acceptations of the words among our
expositors, "unto God the Lord belong the issues of death." For
first the foundation of this building (that our God is the God of
all salvations) is laid in this; that unto this "God the Lord belong the issues of death," that is, it is in his power to give us an
issue and deliverance, even then when we are brought to the
jaws and teeth of death, and to the lips of that whirlpool, the
grave. And so in this acceptation, this *exitus mortis,* this issue of
death, is *liberatio à morte,* a deliverance from death, and this is
the most obvious and most ordinary acceptation of these words,
and that upon which our translation lays hold, "the issues from
death."

And then secondly, the buttresses that comprehend and settle
this building, that he that is our God, is the God of all salvation,
are thus raised; "unto God the Lord belong the issues of death,"
that is, the disposition and manner of our death: what kind of
issue and transmigration we shall have out of this world, whether
prepared or sudden, whether violent or natural, whether in our
perfect senses or shaken and disordered by sickness; there is no
condemnation to be argued out of that, no judgment to be made
upon that, for howsoever they die, "precious in his sight is the
death of his saints,"[2] and with him are "the issues of death,"

[1] [Here and throughout the sermon Donne gives an English rendering immediately following the Latin allusion.]

[2] [Psalms 116 : 15.]

the ways of our departing out of this life are in his hands. And so in this sense of the words, this *exitus mortis,* the issue of death, is *liberatio in morte,* a deliverance in death. Not that God will deliver us from dying, but that he will have a care of us in the hour of death, of what kind soever our passage be. And this sense and acceptation of the words, the natural frame and contexture doth well and pregnantly administer unto us.

And then lastly, the contignation and knitting of this building, that he that is our God is the God of all salvations, consists in this; "unto this God the Lord belong the issues of death," that is, that this God the Lord having united and knit both natures in one, and being God, having also come into this world, in our flesh, he could have no other means to save us, he could have no other issue out of this world, nor return to his former glory, but by death. And so in this sense, this *exitus mortis,* this issue of death, is *liberatio per mortem,* a deliverance by death, by the death of this God, our Lord Christ Jesus. And this is St. Augustine's acceptation of the words, and those many and great persons that have adhered to him.

In all these three lines then, we shall look upon these words: first, as the God of power, the Almighty Father rescues his servants from the jaws of death; and then, as the God of mercy, the glorious Son rescued us, by taking upon himself this issue of death; and then between these two, as the God of comfort, the Holy Ghost rescues us from all discomfort by his blessed impressions beforehand, that what manner of death soever be ordained for us, yet this *exitus mortis* shall be *introitus in vitam,* our issue in death shall be an entrance into everlasting life. And these three considerations, our deliverance *à morte, in morte, per mortem,* from death, in death, and by death, will abundantly do all the offices of the foundations, of the buttresses, of the contignation of this our building: that "He that is our God is the God of all salvation," because "unto this God the Lord belong the issues of death."

First, then, we consider this *exitus mortis* to be *liberatio à morte,* that with God the Lord are the issues of death, and therefore in all our deaths, and deadly calamities of this life, we may justly hope of a good issue from him; and all our periods and transitions in this life are so many passages from death to death. Our very birth and entrance into this life is *exitus à morte,* an issue from death, for in our mother's womb we are dead so, as that we do not know we live, not so much as we do in our sleep; neither is there any grave so close, or so putrid a prison, as the womb would be unto us if we stayed in it beyond our time, or died there before our time. In the grave the worms do not kill us, we breed and feed, and then kill those worms which we ourselves produced. In the womb the dead child kills the mother that conceived it, and is a murderer, nay a parricide, even after it is dead. And if we be not dead so in the womb, so as that being dead, we kill her that gave us our first life, our life of vegetation, yet we are dead so, as David's idols are dead. In the womb we have "eyes and see not, ears and hear not." [3] There in the womb we are fitted for works of darkness, all the while deprived of light. And there in the womb we are taught cruelty, by being fed with blood, and may be damned, though we be never born.

Of our very making in the womb, David says, "I am wonderfully and fearfully made," and, "Such knowledge is too excellent for me," for even that is the Lord's doing, and "it is wonderful in our eyes." [4] *Ipse fecit nos*, "it is he that hath made us, and not we ourselves," [5] no, nor our parents neither. "Thy hands have made me and fashioned me round about," saith Job, and (as the original word is) "thou hast taken pains about me," and "yet," says he, "thou dost destroy me." [6] Though I be the masterpiece of the greatest Master (man is so), yet if thou do no more for me, if thou leave me where thou madest me, destruction will follow. The womb which should be the house of life becomes death itself if God leave us there. That which God threatens so often, the shutting of the womb, is not so heavy nor so discomfortable a curse in the first as in the latter shutting, nor in the shutting of barrenness as in the shutting of weakness, when children are come to the birth and "there is not strength to bring forth." [7]

It is the exaltation of misery to fall from a near hope of happiness. And in that vehement imprecation the prophet expresses the highest of God's anger, "Give them O Lord, what wilt thou give them? give them a miscarrying womb." [8] Therefore as soon as we are men (that is, inanimated, quickened in the womb), though we cannot ourselves, our parents have reason to say in our behalf, "Wretched man that he is, who shall deliver him from

[3] Psalms 115 : 5, 6.   [4] Psalms 139 : 14, 6; 118 : 23.   [5] Psalms 100 : 3.
[6] Job 10 : 8.   [7] Isaiah 37 : 3.   [8] Hosea 9 : 14.

this body of death?" [9] for even the womb is a body of death if there be no deliverer. It must be he that said to Jeremiah, "Before I formed thee I knew thee, and before thou camest out of the womb I sanctified thee." [10]

We are not sure that there was no kind of ship nor boat to fish in, nor to pass by, till God prescribed Noah that absolute form of the Ark. That word which the Holy Ghost by Moses useth for the Ark, is common to all kinds of boats, *Thebah,* and is the same word that Moses useth for the boat that he was exposed in, that his mother laid him in an ark of bulrushes. But we are sure that Eve had no midwife when she was delivered of Cain; therefore she might well say, *possedi virum à Domino,* "I have gotten a man from the Lord," [11] wholly, entirely from the Lord; it is the Lord that enabled me to conceive, the Lord that infused a quickening soul into that conception, the Lord that brought into the world that which himself had quickened. Without all this might Eve say, My body had been but the house of death, and *Domini Domini sunt exitus mortis,* to God the Lord belong the issues of death.

But then this *exitus à morte* is but *introitus in mortem,* this issue, this deliverance from that death, the death of the womb, is an entrance, a delivering over to another death, the manifold deaths of this world. We have a winding sheet in our mother's womb, which grows with us from our conception, and we come into the world wound up in that winding sheet, for we come to seek a grave. And as prisoners discharged of actions may lie for fees, so when the womb hath discharged us, yet we are bound to it by cords of flesh, by such a string as that we cannot go thence, nor stay there. We celebrate our own funerals with cries, even at our birth; as though our threescore and ten years life were spent in our mother's labor, and our circle made up in the first point thereof. We beg one baptism with another, a sacrament of tears; and we come into a world that lasts many ages, but we last not.

In domo Patris, says our blessed Saviour, speaking of heaven, *multae mansiones,* "there are many mansions," [12] divers and durable, so that if a man cannot possess a martyr's house (he hath shed no blood for Christ), yet he may have a confessor's, he

---

[9] Romans 7 : 24.   [10] Jeremiah 1 : 5.   [11] Genesis 4 : 1.
[12] John 14 : 2.

hath been ready to glorify God in the shedding of his blood. And if a woman cannot possess a virgin's house (she hath embraced the holy state of marriage), yet she may have a matron's house, she hath brought forth and brought up children in the fear of God. *In domo patris,* in my father's house, in heaven there are many mansions; but here upon earth, "the son of man hath not where to lay his head," says he himself.[13] *Nonne terram dedit filiis hominum?* How then hath God given this earth to the sons of men?[14] he hath given them earth for their materials to be made of earth, and he hath given them earth for their grave and sepulchre, to return and resolve to earth, but not for their possession: "Here we have no continuing city,"[15] nay no cottage that continues, nay no persons, no bodies that continue.

Whatsoever moved St. Jerome to call the journeys of the Israelites in the wilderness, mansions, the word (the word is *Nasang*) signifies but a journey, but a peregrination. Even the Israel of God hath no mansions, but journeys, pilgrimages in this life. By that measure did Jacob measure his life to Pharaoh, "the days of the years of my pilgrimage."[16] And though the Apostle would not say *morimur,* that whilst we are in the body we are dead, yet he says, *peregrinamur,* whilst we are in the body we are but in a pilgrimage, and "we are absent from the Lord."[17] He might have said dead, for this whole world is but an universal churchyard, but our common grave; and the life and motion that the greatest persons have in it is but as the shaking of buried bodies in their graves by an earthquake.

That which we call life is but *hebdomada mortium,* a week of deaths, seven days, seven periods of our life spent in dying, a dying seven times over; and there is an end. Our birth dies in infancy, and our infancy dies in youth, and youth and the rest die in age, and age also dies, and determines all. Nor do all these, youth out of infancy, or age out of youth arise so, as a phoenix out of the ashes of another phoenix formerly dead, but as a wasp or a serpent out of a carrion, or as a snake out of dung. Our youth is worse than our infancy, and our age worse than our youth. Our youth is hungry and thirsty after those sins which our infancy knew not; and our age is sorry and angry that it cannot pursue those sins which our youth did. And besides, all

[13] Matthew 8 : 20.   [14] [See Psalms 115 : 16.]   [15] Hebrews 13 : 14.
[16] Genesis 47 : 9.   [17] II Corinthians 5 : 6.

the way, so many deaths, that is, so many deadly calamities accompany every condition, and every period of this life, as that death itself would be an ease to them that suffer them.

Upon this sense doth Job wish that God had not given him an issue from the first death, from the womb: "Wherefore has thou brought me forth out of the womb? O that I had given up the ghost, and no eye had seen me; I should have been, as though I had not been." [18] And not only the impatient Israelites in their murmuring ("Would to God we had died by the hand of the Lord in the land of Egypt" [19]), but Elijah himself, when he fled from Jezebel and went for his life, as that text says, under the juniper tree, requested that he might die, and said, "It is enough, now O Lord, take away my life." [20] So Jonah justifies his impatience, nay his anger towards God himself. "Now O Lord take, I beseech thee, my life from me, for it is better for me to die than to live." And when God asked him, "Doest thou well to be angry for this?" and after (about the gourd), "Doest thou well to be angry for that?" he replies, "I do well to be angry, even unto death." [21] How much worse a death than death is this life, which so good men would so often change for death!

But if my case be as St. Paul's case, *quotidiè morior,* that "I die daily," [22] that something heavier than death fall upon me every day; if my case be David's case, *tota die mortificamur,* "all the day long we are killed," [23] that not only every day, but every hour of the day something heavier than death falls upon me, though that be true of me, *Conceptus in peccatis,* "I was shapen in iniquity, and in sin did my mother conceive me" [24] (there I died one death), though that be true of me (*Natus filius irae*) I was born not only the child of sin, but the child of wrath, of the wrath of God for sin, which is a heavier death; yet *Domini Domini sunt exitus mortis,* with God the Lord are the issues of death, and after a Job, and a Joseph, and a Jeremiah, and a Daniel, I cannot doubt of a deliverance. And if no other deliverance conduce more to his glory and my good, yet he hath the "keys of death," [25] and he can let me out at that door, that is, deliver me from the manifold deaths of this world, the *omni die* and the *tota die,* the every day's death and every hour's death, by

[18] Job 10 : 18–19.　　[19] Exodus 16 : 3.　　[20] I Kings 19 : 4.
[21] Jonah 4 : 3, 4, 9.　　[22] I Corinthians 15 : 31.　　[23] Psalms 44 : 22.
[24] Psalms 51 : 5.　　[25] Revelation 1 : 18.

that one death, the final dissolution of body and soul, the end of all.

But then is that the end of all? Is that dissolution of body and soul the last death that the body shall suffer? (For of spiritual death we speak not now.) It is not. Though this be *exitus à morte*, it is *introitus in mortem*: though it be an issue from the manifold deaths of this world, yet it is an entrance into the death of corruption and putrefaction and vermiculation and incineration, and dispersion in and from the grave, in which every dead man dies over again.

It was a prerogative peculiar to Christ not to die this death, not to see corruption. What gave him this privilege? Not Joseph's great proportion of gums and spices, that might have preserved his body from corruption and incineration longer than he needed it, longer than three days, but it would not have done it forever. What preserved him then? Did his exemption and freedom from original sin preserve him from this corruption and incineration? 'Tis true that original sin hath induced this corruption and incineration upon us. If we had not sinned in Adam, "mortality had not put on immortality" (as the Apostle speaks), nor "corruption had not put on incorruption," [26] but we had had our transmigration from this to the other world, without any mortality, any corruption at all.

But yet since Christ took sin upon him, so far as made him mortal, he had it so far too, as might have made him see this corruption and incineration, though he had no original sin in himself. What preserved him then? Did the hypostatical union of both natures, God and man, preserve him from this corruption and incineration? 'Tis true that this was a most powerful embalming, to be embalmed with the divine nature itself, to be embalmed with eternity, was able to preserve him from corruption and incineration forever. And he was embalmed so, embalmed with the divine nature itself, even in his body as well as in his soul; for the Godhead, the divine nature, did not depart, but remained still united to his dead body in the grave.

But yet for all this powerful embalming, this hypostatical union of both natures, we see Christ did die; and for all this union which made him God and man, he became no man (for

[26] I Corinthians 15 : 53.

the union of the body and soul makes the man, and he whose soul and body are separated by death, as long as that state lasts, is properly no man). And therefore as in him the dissolution of body and soul was no dissolution of the hypostatical union, so is there nothing that constrains us to say, that though the flesh of Christ had seen corruption and incineration in the grave, this had been any dissolution of the hypostatical union, for the divine nature, the Godhead, might have remained with all the elements and principles of Christ's body, as well as it did with the two constitutive parts of his person, his body and his soul.

This incorruption then was not in Joseph's gums and spices, nor was it in Christ's innocency and exemption from original sin, nor was it (that is, it is not necessary to say it was) in the hypostatical union. But this incorruptibleness of his flesh is most conveniently placed in that, *Non dabis*, "thou wilt not suffer thy holy one to see corruption." [27] We look no further for causes or reasons in the mysteries of religion, but to the will and pleasure of God: Christ himself limited his inquisition in that *ita est*, "even so Father, for so it seemed good in thy sight." [28] Christ's body did not see corruption, therefore, because God had decreed it should not.

The humble soul (and only the humble soul is the religious soul) rests himself upon God's purposes and his decrees; but then, it is upon those purposes and decrees of God which he hath declared and manifested, not such as are conceived and imagined in ourselves, though upon some probability, some verisimilitude. So, in our present case, Peter proceeded in his sermon at Jerusalem, and so Paul in his at Antioch. They preached Christ to have been risen without seeing corruption, not only because God had decreed it, but because he had manifested that decree in his prophet. Therefore doth St. Paul cite by special number the second Psalm for that decree; and therefore both St. Peter and St. Paul cite for it that place in the sixteenth Psalm, for when God declares his decree and purpose in the express words of his prophet, or when he declares it in the real execution of the decree, then he makes it ours, then he manifests it to us. And therefore as the mysteries of our religion are not the objects of our reason, but by faith we rest on God's decree and purpose (It is so, O God, because it is thy will it should be so), so God's decrees are ever to be considered in the manifestation thereof.

[27] Psalms 16 : 10.   [28] Matthew 11 : 26.

All manifestation is either in the word of God, or in the execution of the decree; and when these two concur and meet, it is the strongest demonstration that can be. When therefore I find those marks of adoption and spiritual filiation which are delivered in the word of God to be upon me, when I find that real execution of his good purpose upon me, as that actually I do live under the obedience, and under the conditions which are evidences of adoption and spiritual filiation; then, and so long as I see these marks and live so, I may safely comfort myself in a holy certitude and a modest infallibility of my adoption. Christ determines himself in that, the purpose of God; because the purpose of God was manifest to him. St. Peter and St. Paul determine themselves in those two ways of knowing the purpose of God, the word of God before, the execution of the decree in the fullness of time. It was prophesied before, say they, and it is performed now: Christ is risen without seeing corruption.

Now this which is so singularly peculiar to him, that his flesh should not see corruption, at his second coming, his coming to judgment, shall extend to all that are then alive, their flesh shall not see corruption, because (as the Apostle says, and says as a secret, as a mystery, "Behold I show you a mystery") "we shall not all sleep" (that is, not continue in the state of the dead in the grave), "but we shall all be changed." [29] In an instant we shall have a dissolution, and in the same instant a reintegration, a recompacting of body and soul, and that shall be truly a death and truly a resurrection, but no sleeping, no corruption. But for us that die now and sleep in the state of the dead, we must all pass this posthumous death, this death after death, nay this death after burial, this dissolution after dissolution, this death of corruption and putrefaction, of vermiculation and incineration, of dissolution and dispersion in and from the grave. When those bodies that have been the children of royal parents, and the parents of royal children, must say with Job, "Corruption thou art my father," and to the worm, "Thou art my mother and my sister." [30]

Miserable riddle, when the same worm must be my mother and my sister and myself. Miserable incest, when I must be married to my mother and my sister, and be both father and mother to my own mother and sister, beget and bear that worm

[29] Corinthians 15 : 51.   [30] Job 17 : 14.

which is all that miserable penury; when my mouth shall be filled with dust, and the worm shall feed, and feed sweetly upon me, when the ambitious man shall have no satisfaction if the poorest alive tread upon him, nor the poorest receive any contentment in being made equal to princes, for they shall be equal but in dust. "One dieth at his full strength, being wholly at ease and in quiet"; "and another dies in the bitterness of his soul, and never eats with pleasure"; but "they lie down alike in the dust, and the worm covers them." [31] The worm covers them in Job and in Isaiah, it covers them and is spread under them; "the worm is spread under thee, and the worm covers thee." [32] There's the mats and the carpets that lie under, and there's the state and the canopy that hangs over the greatest of the sons of men. Even those bodies that were the temples of the Holy Ghost come to this dilapidation, to ruin, to rubbish, to dust; even the Israel of the Lord, and Jacob himself, hath no other specification, no other denomination, but that *vermis Jacob*, "thou worm of Jacob." [33]

Truly the consideration of this posthumous death, this death after burial, that after God (with whom are the issues of death) hath delivered me from the death of the womb by bringing me into the world, and from the manifold deaths of the world by laying me in the grave, I must die again in an incineration of this flesh and in a dispersion of that dust. That that monarch who spread over many nations alive must in his dust lie in a corner of that sheet of lead, and there but so long as that lead will last; and that private and retired man that thought himself his own forever, and never came forth, must in his dust of the grave be published, and (such are the revolutions of the graves) be mingled in his dust with the dust of every highway, and of every dunghill, and swallowed in every puddle and pond: this is the most inglorious and contemptible vilification, the most deadly and peremptory nullification of man, that we can consider.

God seems to have carried the declaration of his power to a great height when he sets the prophet Ezekiel in the valley of dry bones and says, "Son of man, can these bones live?" [34] as though it had been impossible, and yet they did; the Lord laid sinews upon them, and flesh, and breathed into them, and they did live. But in that case there were bones to be seen, something visible, of which it might be said, Can this thing live? But in

[31] Job 21 : 23, 25, 26.   [32] Isaiah 14 : 11.   [33] Isaiah 41 : 14.
[34] [Ezekiel 37 : 3.]

this death of incineration and dispersion of dust, we see nothing that we call that man's. If we say, Can this dust live? perchance it cannot, it may be the mere dust of the earth, which never did live, nor never shall. It may be the dust of that man's worm, which did live, but shall no more. It may be the dust of another man, that concerns not him of whom it was asked. This death of incineration and dispersion is, to natural reason, the most ir- recoverable death of all, and yet *Domini Domini sunt exitus mortis,* unto God the Lord belong the issues of death, and by recompacting this dust into the same body, and reanimating the same body with the same soul, he shall in a blessed and glorious resurrection give me such an issue from this death as shall never pass into any other death, but establish me into a life that shall last as long as the Lord of life himself.

And so have you that that belongs to the first acceptation of these words ("unto God the Lord belong the issues of death"), that though from the womb to the grave and in the grave itself we pass from death to death, yet, as Daniel speaks, "The Lord our God is able to deliver us, and he will deliver us."

And so we pass unto our second accommodation of these words ("unto God the Lord belong the issues of death"), that it belongs to God, and not to man, to pass a judgment upon us at our death, or to conclude a dereliction on God's part upon the manner thereof.

Those indications which the physicians receive, and those presagitions which they give for death or recovery in the patient, they receive and they give out of the grounds and the rules of their art. But we have no such rule or art to give a presagition of spiritual death and damnation upon any such indication as we see in any dying man; we see often enough to be sorry, but not to despair; we may be deceived both ways. We use to com- fort ourself in the death of a friend, if it be testified that he went away like a lamb, that is, without any reluctation. But, God knows that he may be accompanied with a dangerous damp and stupefaction, and insensibility of his present state. Our blessed Saviour suffered colluctations with death, and a sadness even in his soul to death, and an agony even to a bloody sweat in his body, and expostulations with God, and exclamations upon the cross.

He was a devout man who said upon his deathbed or death- turf (for he was an hermit) *septuaginta annos Domino servivisti, et mori times?* "Hast thou served a good master threescore and ten years, and now art thou loath to go into his presence?" Yet Hilarion was loath. Barlaam was a devout man (an hermit too) that said that day he died, *Cogita te hodie coepisse servire Domino, et hodie finiturum,* "Consider this to be the first day's service that ever thou didst thy Master, to glorify him in a Christianly and a constant death, and if thy first day be thy last day too, how soon dost thou come to receive thy wages?" Yet Barlaam could have been content to have stayed longer for it.

Make no ill conclusions upon any man's loathness to die, for the mercies of God work momentarily in minutes, and many times insensibly to bystanders or any other than the party departing. And then, upon violent deaths inflicted, as upon malefactors, Christ himself hath forbidden us by his own death to make any ill conclusion; for his own death had those impressions in it; he was reputed, he was executed as a malefactor, and no doubt many of them who concurred to his death did believe him to be so. Of sudden death there are scarce examples to be found in the Scriptures upon good men, for death in battle cannot be called sudden death; but God governs not by examples, but by rules, and therefore make no ill conclusion upon sudden death nor upon distempers neither, though perchance accompanied with some words of diffidence and distrust in the mercies of God.

The tree lies as it falls,[35] 'tis true, but yet it is not the last stroke that fells the tree, nor the last word nor gasp that qualifies the soul. Still pray we for a peaceable life against violent death, and for time of repentance against sudden death, and for sober and modest assurance against distempered and diffident death, but never make ill conclusions upon persons overtaken with such deaths; *Domini Domini sunt exitus mortis,* to God the Lord belong the issues of death. And he received Samson, who went out of this world in such a manner (consider it actively, consider it passively in his own death, and in those whom he slew with himself) as was subject to interpretation hard enough. Yet the Holy Ghost hath moved St. Paul to celebrate Samson in his great catalogue, and so doth all the Church.

Our critical day is not the very day of our death, but the whole course of our life. I thank him that prays for me when my bell tolls, but I thank him much more that catechizes me, or preaches

[35] [See Ecclesiastes 11 : 3.]

to me, or instructs me how to live. *Fac hoc et vives*, there's my security, the mouth of the Lord hath said it, "do this and thou shalt live." [36] But though I do it, yet I shall die too, die a bodily, a natural death. But God never mentions, never seems to consider that death, the bodily, the natural death. God doth not say, Live well and thou shalt die well, that is, an easy, a quiet death; but, Live well here, and thou shalt live well forever. As the first part of a sentence pieces well with the last, and never respects, never hearkens after the parenthesis that comes between, so doth a good life here flow into an eternal life, without any consideration what manner of death we die. But whether the gate of my prison be opened with an oiled key (by a gentle and preparing sickness), or the gate be hewn down by a violent death, or the gate be burnt down by a raging and frantic fever, a gate into heaven I shall have, for from the Lord is the cause of my life, and with God the Lord are the issues of death. And further we carry not this second acceptation of the words, as this issue of death is *liberatio in morte*, God's care that the soul be safe, what agonies soever the body suffers in the hour of death; but pass to our third part and last part: as this issue of death is *liberatio per mortem*, a deliverance by the death of another, by the death of Christ.

Sufferentiam Job audiistis, et vidistis finem Domini, says St. James 5:11: "You have heard of the patience of Job," says he. All this while you have done that, for in every man, calamitous, miserable man, a Job speaks. Now "see the end of the Lord," sayeth that Apostle, which is not that end that the Lord proposed to himself (salvation to us), nor the end which he proposes to us (conformity to him), but "see the end of the Lord," says he, the end that the Lord himself came to, death, and a painful and a shameful death.

But why did he die? and why die so? *Quia Domini Domini sunt exitus mortis* (as St. Augustine, interpreting this text, answers that question),[37] because to this God our Lord belonged the issues of death. *Quid apertius diceretur?* says he there, what can be more obvious, more manifest than this sense of these words? In the former part of this verse, it is said, "He that is our God is the God of salvation," *Deus salvos faciendi*, so he reads it, the God that must save us. Who can that be, says he, but Jesus? for

---

[36] [Luke 10 : 28.]　　　[37] *De Civitate Dei*, XVII, c. 18.

therefore that name was given him, because he was to save us.
And to this Jesus, says he, this Saviour, belong the issues of
death. *Nec oportuit eum de hac vita alios exitus habere quam
mortis*; being come into this life in our mortal nature, he could
not go out of it any other way than by death. *Ideo dictum*, says
he, therefore it is said, "To God the Lord belong the issues of
death"; *ut ostenderetur moriendo nos salvos facturum*, to show
that his way to save us was to die. And from this text doth St.
Isidore prove that Christ was truly man (which as many sects
of heretics denied as that he was truly God), because to him,
though he were *Dominus Dominus* (as the text doubles it), God
the Lord, yet to him, to God the Lord belonged the issues of
death. *Oportuit eum pati*, more cannot be said than Christ himself says of himself, "these things Christ ought to suffer"; he
had no other way but by death.

So then this part of our sermon must needs be a passion
sermon. Since all his life was a continual passion, all our Lent
may well be a continual Good Friday. Christ's painful life took
off none of the pains of his death; he felt not the less then for
having felt so much before. Nor will anything that shall be
said before lessen, but rather enlarge your devotion to that
which shall be said of his passion at the time of due solemnization
thereof. Christ bled not a drop the less at the last for having bled
at his circumcision before, nor will you shed a tear the less then,
if you shed some now. And therefore be now content to consider
with me how to this God the Lord belonged the issues of death.

That God, this Lord, the Lord of life could die, is a strange
contemplation. That the Red Sea could be dry, that the sun could
stand still, that an oven could be seven times heat and not burn,
that lions could be hungry and not bite, is strange, miraculously
strange;[38] but supermiraculous that God could die. But that God
would die is an exaltation of that. But even of that also it is a
superexaltation that God should die, must die, and *non exitus*
(said Saint Augustine), "God the Lord had no issue but by
death," and *oportuit pati* (says Christ himself), "all this Christ
ought to suffer," was bound to suffer. *Deus ultionum Deus*, says
David, "God is the God of revenges," he would not pass over
the sin of man unrevenged, unpunished.[39] But then *Deus ultionum
liberè egit* (says that place), the God of revenges works freely,

[38] [See Exodus 14 : 21; Joshua 10 : 12; Daniel 3 : 19; Daniel 6 : 22.]
[39] Psalms 94 : 1.

he punishes, he spares whom he will. And would he not spare himself? He would not. *Dilectio fortis ut mors,* "love is as strong as death," [40] stronger; it drew in death that naturally is not welcome. *Si possible,* says Christ, "if it be possible, let this cup pass," [41] when his love expressed in a former decree with his Father had made it impossible. "Many waters quench not love"; [42] Christ tried many. He was baptized out of his love, and his love determined not there. He wept over Jerusalem out of his love, and his love determined not there. He mingled blood with water in his agony, and that determined not his love. He wept pure blood, all his blood at all his eyes, at all his pores, in his flagellation and thorns (to the Lord our God belonged the issues of death), and these expressed, but these did not quench his love.

He would not spare, nay he could not spare himself. There was nothing more free, more voluntary, more spontaneous than the death of Christ. 'Tis true, *liberè egit,* he died voluntarily, but yet when we consider the contract that had passed between his Father and him, there was an *oportuit,* a kind of necessity upon him. All this Christ ought to suffer. And when shall we date this obligation, this *oportuit,* this necessity? When shall we say that began? Certainly this decree by which Christ was to suffer all this was an eternal decree, and was there anything before that, that was eternal? Infinite love, eternal love; be pleased to follow this home, and to consider it seriously, that what liberty soever we can conceive in Christ to die or not to die, this necessity of dying, this decree is as eternal as that liberty; and yet how small a matter made he of this necessity and this dying? His Father calls it but a bruise, and but a bruising of his heel ("the serpent shall bruise his heel" [43]), and yet that was that the serpent should practice and compass his death. Himself calls it but a baptism, as though he were to be the better for it. "I have a baptism to be baptized with," [44] and he was in pain till it was accomplished, and yet this baptism was his death. The Holy Ghost calls it joy ("for the joy which was set before him he endured the cross" [45]) which was not a joy of his reward after his passion, but a joy that filled him even in the midst of his torments, and arose from them. When Christ calls his passion *calicem,* a cup, and no worse ("Can ye drink of my cup?" [46]),

[40] Song of Solomon 8 : 6.   [41] [Matthew 26 : 39.]   [42] Song of Solomon 8 : 7.
[43] Genesis 3 : 15.   [44] Luke 12 : 50.   [45] Hebrews 12 : 2.
[46] Matthew 20 : 22.

he speaks not odiously, not with detestation of it. Indeed it was a cup, *salus mundo,* a health to all the world. And *quid retribuam,* says David, "what shall I render to the Lord?" Answer you with David, *accipiam calicem,* "I will take the cup of salvation." [47] Take it, that cup of salvation, his passion, if not into your present imitation, yet into your present contemplation. And behold how that Lord that was God yet could die, would die, must die, for your salvation.

That Moses and Elijah talked with Christ in the transfiguration, both St. Matthew and St. Mark tell us, but what they talked of, only St. Luke. *Dicebant excessum eius,* says he, "they talked of his decease, of his death which was to be accomplished at Jerusalem." [48] The word is of his *Exodus,* the very word of our text, *exitus,* his issue by death. Moses, who in his Exodus had prefigured this issue of our Lord, and in passing Israel out of Egypt through the Red Sea had foretold in that actual prophecy, Christ's passing of mankind through the sea of his blood; and Elijah, whose Exodus and issue of this world was a figure of Christ's ascension, had no doubt a great satisfaction in talking with our blessed Lord *de excessu eius,* of the full consummation of all this in his death, which was to be accomplished at Jerusalem.

Our meditation of his death should be more visceral and affect us more because it is of a thing already done. The ancient Romans had a certain tenderness and detestation of the name of death; they could not name death, no, not in their wills. There they could not say *Si mori contigerit,* but *si quid humanitus contingat,* not "if or when I die," but "when the course of nature is accomplished upon me." To us that speak daily of the death of Christ (he was crucified, dead, and buried), can the memory or the mention of our own death be irksome or bitter? There are in these latter times amongst us those that name death freely enough, and the death of God, but in blasphemous oaths and execrations. Miserable men, who shall therefore be said never to have named Jesus, because they have named him too often; and therefore hear Jesus say, *Nescivi vos,* "I never knew you," [49] because they made themselves too familiar with him.

Moses and Elijah talked with Christ of his death only in a holy and joyful sense of the benefit which they and all the

---

[47] Psalms 116 : 12–13.   [48] Luke 9 : 31.   [49] Matthew 7 : 23.

world were to receive by that. Discourses of religion should not be out of curiosity, but to edification. And then they talked with Christ of his death at that time, when he was in the greatest height of glory that ever he admitted in this world, that is, his transfiguration. And we are afraid to speak to the great men of this world of their death, but nourish in them a vain imagination of immortality and immutability. But *bonum est nobis esse hic* (as St. Peter said there), "it is good to dwell here," in this consideration of his death, and therefore transfer we our tabernacle (our devotions) through some of those steps which God the Lord made to his issue of death that day.

Take in the whole day from the hour that Christ received the passover upon Thursday unto the hour in which he died the next day. Make this present day that day in your devotion, and consider what he did, and remember what you have done. Before he instituted and celebrated the sacrament (which was after the eating of the passover), he proceeded to that act of humility, to wash his disciples' feet, even Peter's, who for a while resisted him. In thy preparation to the holy and blessed sacrament, hast thou with a sincere humility sought a reconciliation with all the world, even with those that have been averse from it and refused that reconciliation from thee? If so (and not else) thou hast spent that first part of his last day in a conformity with him.

After the sacrament he spent the time till night in prayer, in preaching, in psalms. Hast thou considered that a worthy receiving of the sacrament consists in a continuation of holiness after, as well as in a preparation before? If so, thou hast therein also conformed thyself to him; so Christ spent his time till night. At night he went into the garden to pray, and he prayed prolixius; he spent much time in prayer. How much? Because it is literally expressed that he prayed there three several times, and that returning to his Disciples after his first prayer, and finding them asleep, said, "Could ye not watch with me one hour?" [50] it is collected that he spent three hours in prayer. I dare scarce ask thee whither thou wentest, or how thou disposedst of thyself, when it grew dark and after last night. If that time were spent in a holy recommendation of thyself to God, and a submission of thy will to his, it was spent in a conformity to him. In that time and in those prayers was his agony and bloody sweat. I will

[50] Matthew 26 : 40.

hope that thou didst pray; but not every ordinary and customary prayer, but prayer actually accompanied with shedding of tears, and dispositively in a readiness to shed blood for his glory in necessary cases, puts thee into a conformity with him.

About midnight he was taken and bound with a kiss. Art thou not too conformable to him in that? Is not that too literally, too exactly thy case—at midnight to have been taken and bound with a kiss? From thence he was carried back to Jerusalem, first to Annas, then to Caiaphas, and (as late as it was) then he was examined and buffeted, and delivered over to the custody of those officers, from whom he received all those irrisions and violences, the covering of his face, the spitting upon his face, the blasphemies of words, and the smartness of blows which that Gospel mentions. In which compass fell that *gallicinium,* that crowing of the cock, which called up Peter to his repentance. How thou passedst all that time last night, thou knowest. If thou didst anything then that needed Peter's tears, and hast not shed them, let me be thy cock; do it now. Now thy Master (in the unworthiest of his servants) looks back upon thee; do it now.

Betimes, in the morning, so soon as it was day, the Jews held a counsel in the high priest's hall, and agreed upon their evidence against him, and then carried him to Pilate, who was to be his judge. Didst thou accuse thyself when thou wakedst this morning, and wast thou content to admit even false accusations, (that is) rather to suspect actions to have been sin, which were not, than to smother and justify such as were truly sins? Then thou spentst that hour in conformity to him. Pilate found no evidence against him, and therefore to ease himself and to pass a compliment upon Herod, Tetrarch of Galilee, who was at that time at Jerusalem (because Christ being a Galilean was of Herod's jurisdiction), Pilate sent him to Herod, and rather as a madman than a malefactor, Herod remanded him (with scorns) to Pilate to proceed against him; and this was about eight of the clock.

Hast thou been content to come to this inquisition, this examination, this agitation, this cribration, this pursuit of thy conscience, to sift it, to follow it from the sins of thy youth to thy present sins, from the sins of thy bed to the sins of thy board, and from the substance to the circumstance of thy sins? That's time spent like thy Saviour's. Pilate would have saved Christ by using the privilege of the day in his behalf, because that day one prisoner was to be delivered, but they chose Barabbas. He would have saved him from death by satisfying their fury, with inflicting other torments upon him, scourging and crowning with thorns, and loading him with many scornful and ignominious contumelies. But this redeemed him not; they pressed a crucifying.

Hast thou gone about to redeem thy sin by fasting, by alms, by disciplines and mortifications, in way of satisfaction to the justice of God? That will not serve, that's not the right way; we press an utter crucifying of that sin that governs thee: and that conforms thee to Christ. Towards noon Pilate gave judgment, and they made such haste to execution as that by noon he was upon the cross. There now hangs that sacred body upon the cross, rebaptized in his own tears and sweat, and embalmed in his own blood alive. There are those bowels of compassion, which are so conspicuous, so manifested, as that you may see them through his wounds. There those glorious eyes grew faint in their light: so as the sun, ashamed to survive them, departed with his light too. And then that Son of God, who was never from us, and yet had now come a new way unto us in assuming our nature, delivers that soul (which was never out of his Father's hands) by a new way, a voluntary emission of it into his Father's hands.

For though to this God our Lord belonged these issues of death, so that considered in his own contract, he must necessarily die, yet at no breach or battery, which they had made upon his sacred body, issued his soul, but *emisit*, he gave up the ghost, and as God breathed a soul into the first Adam, so this second Adam breathed his soul into God, into the hands of God. There we leave you in that blessed dependency, to hang upon him that hangs upon the cross, there bathe in his tears, there suck at his wounds, and lie down in peace in his grave, till he vouchsafe you a resurrection, and an ascension into that kingdom, which he hath purchased for you with the inestimable price of his incorruptible blood. Amen.

QUESTIONS FOR STUDY
AND TOPICS FOR DISCUSSION
on *Death's Duel*

1. John Donne is famous today as one of the great English poets, but in his own time he was better known and more highly esteemed as a preacher. He was, in fact, the most popular and eloquent preacher in London. When he preached at St. Paul's Cathedral, where he was Dean for the ten years before his death, he spoke to a packed congregation who listened, as Izaak Walton testifies, with rapt wonder and excited sympathy. He preached before more learned and sophisticated auditories as well, before the King's court and before the lawyers at Lincoln's Inn, but all the congregations were responsive to eloquence in preaching. They wanted instruction, assuredly, but they delighted in verbal virtuosity, and they appreciated an artful performance.

Death's Duel was preached before the King at Whitehall at the beginning of Lent in 1631. Donne had contracted an illness the year before, and during the winter it became so severe that he was rumored to have died. His friends tried to keep him from delivering the Lenten sermon because they feared the effort would kill him, but he went ahead anyway. His appearance of a man near death and the aptness of the topic of the sermon made a macabre drama of the event. His audience watched a man preaching his own funeral sermon. Five weeks later, after the strange preparations for burial recounted by Walton, Donne died.

The occasion of the sermon is a meditation on Lent; its purpose is to prepare the congregation for Lent, Good Friday, and Easter. Lent is a season of mortification, but that mortification is a preparation for meditation on the passion of Christ in Holy Week, and his agony on the cross of Good Friday. The form of the sermon is an exposition of the text from Donne's favorite portion of the Bible.

How does the doctrinal and liturgical significance of the Lenten season in the Anglican church year govern the selection of the text, the treatment of its matter, and the content and form of the whole sermon? How is this entwined with Donne's personal condition? Does the sermon concern his own deliverance? What is the connection between his own deliverance and the final section in which he meditates on the death of Christ? Is the sermon a study of the good death or a reflection on the good life in awareness of death? Is Donne, as some critics have claimed, in love with death? Why is the sermon entitled "Death's Duel"? What is the significance of the subtitle? What is the intention of the sermon?

2. *Death's Duel* begins with a painstaking elaboration of the metaphor of building. How does Donne extend the literal sense of the word to several "levels" of meaning? According to I. A. Richards, a metaphor has two items or subjects: the principal subject, to which the metaphoric word is applied, and the secondary subject, or the literal meaning of the metaphoric word itself. Richards devised the term *tenor* for the principal subject, and *vehicle* for the secondary subject. In the expression "My love is a red, red rose," the word "love" would be designated the tenor, and the word "rose" the vehicle. What is the tenor of Donne's metaphor of building and what the vehicle at each of the several levels of his extension of the figure? How far into the sermon does he carry the metaphor? Does he drop it? To what other figures does it yield place or give rise? Why does he use the metaphor?

3. Donne divides "the issues of death" in his text into three considerations: deliverance from death, deliverance in death, and deliverance by death. What further considerations do these subsume? What is Donne's authority for his "acceptations" of the word "issue"? What conjunctions does he establish between the three accommodations of the text, the three parts of a building, and the three persons of God? Are these combinations too intricate to be intelligible to an auditor? How does Donne keep them lucid?

This part of the sermon is largely a disquisition upon certain words and interpretations of the text. In color and feeling it seems to differ markedly from the more emotive portions that follow. To the modern reader it is likely to appear finicking and labored. However, Donne is only following the customary procedure of an expositor of a scriptural text. Moreover, he is fashioning the first part of the three-part structure which is characteristic of his sermons. (The first part is typically an analysis of the natural divisions of the text; the second, the disposition and amplification of these divisions with illustrations, chiefly Biblical, and arguments; and the third, the drawing together of the several lines of proof into a general or specific application.) Would an auditor or reader familiar with the conventions of scriptural exegesis and with Donne's practice find this portion of the sermon tedious? How do these procedures order the discourse and aid in its comprehension?

How does Donne link the first and second parts of his text, Psalms 68 : 20? What key words and phrases does he repeat and vary? What is the rhetorical effect when Donne finally brings the two parts of the text together on p. 84? Does it look contrived? Does it seem any less so if you read the section aloud? How important is oral delivery to the form and sense of *Death's Duel*?

4. Donne opens the first accommodation of the text by considering the deliverance, the issue, of life from the "death" of the womb (pp. 84–85). He treats the topic in lurid terms. If the congregation has been nodding, he makes it sit bolt upright with this terrifying excursion. What is Donne trying to get his auditors to feel and understand? Is the picture of the putrid prison of the womb meant to be taken literally? Is it just a gruesome depiction of the condition of original sin? Is Donne trying to make mortality seem repulsive and hopeless? Or is he setting the stage for the later deliverance, in order to make that more affecting and desirable?

How do the conceits of this section differ from the preceding disquisition on the text? What drives the torrent of words? How does Donne keep them within banks and under control? How does the statement "our very birth and entrance into this life is *exitus à morte,* an issue from death" (p. 84) govern what follows?

5. What is the tone and rhetoric of the two paragraphs beginning "It is the exaltation of misery . . . " (pp. 85–86), and how do they compare with the two paragraphs preceding? Are they an interlude? Is Donne giving his auditors a chance to catch their breath before he pours on more of the same? Or

is he drawing out the implications of a key idea? What is the relationship between the apothegm which heads the paragraph and the string of thoughts which follows?

6. Beginning at "But then this *exitus à morte* . . . " (p. 86), Donne describes the manifold deaths of the world into which one is "delivered" from the death of the womb. The passage "We have a winding sheet . . . an ease to them that suffer them" (pp. 86–88) is one of the most famous portions of the sermon. What is its function in the developing argument and rhetoric of the whole? Analyze its composition, especially its imagery, its syntax, and its cadence. How does Donne handle conjunctions and prepositions? What kind and degree of subordinate clauses does he employ? What kind and degree of balanced structures? Are the parallelisms and antitheses symmetrical or asymmetrical? Consider the rhythm of "That which we call life . . . and there is an end" (p. 87). What is the subject, verb, and complement? Where does the main accent fall? Do the repetitions slow or quicken the pace? Why does Donne shape the sentence this way?

What purpose is served by the allegory of the house of God and the journey of man (pp. 86–87)? Is the prominent imagery throughout this portion relevant to the allegorical structure? Are there any other passages in the sermon whose imagery is significantly applicable to the allegory?

7. Donne begins the concluding section of the first accommodation with the abrupt turn "But then is that the end of all?" (p. 89). Is this a rhetorical question? Does it signal a turning point in the sermon's tone and tenor? He follows shortly after with a piling up of epithets describing the nature of death. Is he only repeating what he has said before, hammering them home for emphasis, or is he preparing the way for: "It was a prerogative peculiar to Christ not to die this death, not to see corruption" (p. 89)? Why does "not" seem to require a special stress? Much of this portion of the sermon is devoted to the incorruptibility of Christ's body. What purpose does the discussion of incorruptibility serve? Does it contradict Donne's later insistence on the human nature of Christ?

8. In the remaining part of the first accommodation Donne often uses the first-person singular. Is Donne expressing his

own desire for liberation from death? Is this an intrusion of
Donne's "personality"? If not, what then? Why does Donne use
the personal mode of address?

9. The second accommodation of the text, which runs from
"And so we pass unto our second accommodation . . . " to
" . . . by the death of Christ" (pp. 93–95), is much shorter
than the first. Why? What has Donne achieved in the first that
makes it unnecessary for him to dwell upon in the second?

He begins the argument by suggesting that a man may find
more security in the prognosis of a doctor of medicine than in
the speculation of a doctor of the spirit. How does this comparison
between man's physical sickness and his spiritual infection serve
the intention of the section?

Donne concludes the second accommodation with a discussion
of sudden death. What is the relevance of this discussion to the
section as a whole? Consider especially: "The tree lies as it
falls . . . that qualifies the soul" (p. 94). Why do you suppose
Donne is reminded of the death of Samson here? Why does
Donne emphasize the distinction between living well and dying
well? How does the image of the oiled key (p. 95) pick up an
earlier reference? What other images are gathered together in
the conclusion? How are prisons, gates, liberations, and deliver-
ances combined?

10. Why does Donne feel it important in the third accommodation to insist that Christ was truly man (p. 96)? Why doesn't
Donne follow the first paragraph of the section with a description
of Christ's "painful and shameful" death (p. 95)? Why does he
ask instead: "But why did he die? and why die so?" Why does
Donne say, "this part of our sermon must needs be a passion
sermon" (p. 96)?

Analyze the composition of "That God, this Lord . . . but
these did not quench his love" (pp. 96–97). How is Donne
trying to impress upon his auditors the surpassing wonder of
Christ's suffering and death? Donne says elsewhere that to him
the passion of Christ was a subject for adoring love and ecstasy,
not for an exercise of rhetorical skill: "The passion of Christ
Jesus is rather an amazement, an astonishment, an ecstasy, a
consternation, than an instruction." Does the passage from
Death's Duel embody this tone? Is it without "rhetoric"? In

what ways is the passage typical or atypical of other portions of the sermon?

How does Donne use the allusion and notion of exodus to conclude his exposition of *exitus mortis*? What patterns of imagery and thought from the whole are drawn together in this reference?

11. In the last section of the sermon (beginning "Take in the whole day . . . " on p. 99) Donne shifts his address and brings the lessons of his text and meditations directly to his audience. The passage is carefully composed. As Donne promises, he carries the congregation step by step through the last day of Christ, from the hour of the Passover Feast to the hour of his death. Interlaced in this narrative is an exhortation to consider whether the auditors have imitated the perfect pattern set by Christ. What does Donne ask them to consider? How are the literal events of Christ's last day invested with allegorical, moral, and mystical or spiritual significance? What is the relation of Donne's interpretation of the text to the narrative, discursive, and symbolic composite of this section of the sermon? What is the tone?

At the end, beginning " . . . by noon he was upon the cross" (p. 101), Donne draws a ghastly picture of the crucifixion. This has been hard for many readers to stomach; it seems grotesque. What is Donne's purpose? Was T. S. Eliot justified in charging that Donne "is a little of the religious spellbinder, the Reverend Billy Sunday of his time, the flesh-creeper, the sorcerer of emotional orgy"? Is Donne trying to terrify his auditors? Is he trying to make their flesh creep?

from THE LIFE OF DR. JOHN DONNE

BY *Izaak Walton*

I RETURN FROM my account of the vision to tell the reader that both before Mr. Donne's going into France, at his being there, and after his return, many of the nobility and others that were powerful at court were watchful and solicitous to the king for some secular employment for him. The king had formerly both known and put a value upon his company, and had also given him some hopes of a state-employment; being always much pleased when Mr. Donne attended him, especially at his meals, where there were usually many deep discourses of general learning and very often friendly disputes or debates of religion betwixt His Majesty and those divines whose places required their attendance on him at those times: particularly the Dean of the Chapel, who then was Bishop Montague (the publisher of the learned and eloquent works of His Majesty) and the most Reverend Doctor Andrewes the late learned Bishop of Winchester, who then was the king's almoner.

About this time there grew many disputes that concerned the Oath of Supremacy and Allegiance, in which the king had appeared, and engaged himself by his public writings now extant: and His Majesty discoursing with Mr. Donne concerning many of the reasons which are usually urged against the taking of those oaths, apprehended such a validity and clearness in his stating the questions, and his answers to them, that His Majesty commanded him to bestow some time in drawing the arguments into a method, and then to write his answers to them; and, having done that, not to send, but be his own messenger and bring them to him. To this he presently and diligently applied himself, and within six weeks brought them to him under his own hand-writing, as they be now printed; the book bearing the name of *Pseudo-Martyr*, printed *anno* 1610.

When the king had read and considered that book, he persuaded Mr. Donne to enter into the ministry; to which, at that time, he was, and appeared, very unwilling, apprehending it (such was his mistaking modesty) to be too weighty for his abilities: and though His Majesty had promised him a favor, and many persons of worth mediated with His Majesty for some secular employment for him (to which his education had apted him), and particularly the Earl of Somerset when in his greatest height of favor; who being then at Theobald's with the king, where one of the clerks of the council died that night, the Earl posted a messenger for Mr. Donne to come to him immediately, and at Mr. Donne's coming, said, "Mr. Donne, to testify the reality of my affection, and my purpose to prefer you, stay in this garden till I go up to the king, and bring you word that you are clerk of the council: doubt not my doing this, for I know the king loves you, and know the king will not deny me." But the king gave a positive denial to all requests, and, having a discerning spirit, replied, "I know Mr. Donne is a learned man, has the abilities of a learned divine, and will prove a powerful preacher; and my desire is to prefer him that way, and in that way I will deny you nothing for him." After that time, as he professeth, "the king descended to a persuasion, almost to a solicitation, of him to enter into sacred orders": which, though he then denied not, yet he deferred it for almost three years. All which time he applied himself to an incessant study of textual divinity, and to the attainment of a great perfection in the learned languages, Greek and Hebrew.

In the first and most blessed times of Christianity, when the clergy were looked upon with reverence, and deserved it, when they overcame their opposers by high examples of virtue, by a blessed patience and long suffering, those only were then judged worthy the ministry whose quiet and meek spirits did make them look upon that sacred calling with an humble adoration and fear to undertake it; which indeed requires such great degrees of

humility, and labor, and care, that none but such were then
thought worthy of that celestial dignity. And such only were then
sought out and solicited to undertake it. This I have mentioned
because forwardness and inconsideration could not in Mr. Donne,
as in many others, be an argument of insufficiency or unfitness;
for he had considered long, and had many strifes within himself
concerning the strictness of life and competency of learning required in such as enter into sacred orders; and doubtless, considering his own demerits, did humbly ask God with St. Paul,
"Lord, who is sufficient for these things?" and with meek Moses,
"Lord, who am I?" [1] And sure, if he had consulted with flesh
and blood, he had not for these reasons put his hand to that
holy plow. But God, who is able to prevail, wrestled with him,
as the angel did with Jacob, and marked him; marked him for his
own; marked him with a blessing, a blessing of obedience to the
motions of his blessed spirit. And then, as he had formerly asked
God with Moses, "Who am I?" so now, being inspired with an
apprehension of God's particular mercy to him, in the king's
and other solicitations of him, he came to ask King David's
thankful question; "Lord, who am I, that thou art so mindful of
me?" [2] So mindful of me as to lead me for more than forty years
through this wilderness of the many temptations and various
turnings of a dangerous life; so merciful to me as to move the
learnedest of kings to descend to move me to serve at the altar;
so merciful to me as at last to move my heart to embrace this
holy motion! Thy motions I will and do embrace: and I now
say with the blessed Virgin, "Be it with thy servant as seemeth
best in thy sight":[3] and so, blessed Jesus, I do take the cup of
salvation and will call upon thy name and will preach thy gospel.

Such strifes as these St. Augustine had, when St. Ambrose
endeavored his conversion to Christianity; with which he con-
fesseth he acquainted his friend Alipius. Our learned author
(a man fit to write after no mean copy) did the like. And declaring his intentions to his dear friend Dr. King, then Bishop
of London, a man famous in his generation and no stranger to
Mr. Donne's abilities (for he had been chaplain to the Lord
Chancellor at the time of Mr. Donne's being his lordship's sec-
retary), that reverend man did receive the news with much

[1] [II Corinthians 2 : 16 and Exodus 3 : 11.]
[2] [See Psalms 8 : 4.]
[3] [Cf. Luke 1 : 38.]

gladness; and, after some expressions of joy, and a persuasion to be constant in his pious purpose, he proceeded with all convenient speed to ordain him first deacon, and then priest not long after.

Now the English Church had gained a second St. Augustine, for I think none was so like him before his conversion, none so like St. Ambrose after it: and if his youth had the infirmities of the one, his age had the excellencies of the other; the learning and holiness of both.

And now all his studies, which had been occasionally diffused, were all concentered in divinity. Now he had a new calling, new thoughts, and a new employment for his wit and eloquence. Now all his earthly affections were changed into divine love; and all the faculties of his own soul were engaged in the conversion of others: in preaching the glad tidings of remission to repenting sinners and peace to each troubled soul. To these he applied himself with all care and diligence: and now such a change was wrought in him that he could say with David, "O how amiable are thy tabernacles. O Lord God of Hosts!" [4] Now he declared openly, "That when he required a temporal, God gave him a spiritual blessing." And that "he was now gladder to be a doorkeeper in the House of God, than he could be to enjoy the noblest of all temporal employments."

Presently after he entered into his holy profession, the king sent for him, and made him his Chaplain in Ordinary, and promised to take a particular care for his preferment.

And though his long familiarity with scholars and persons of greatest quality was such as might have given some men boldness enough to have preached to any eminent auditory; yet his modesty in this employment was such that he could not be persuaded to it, but went, usually accompanied with some one friend, to preach privately in some village not far from London; his first sermon being preached at Paddington. This he did till His Majesty sent and appointed him a day to preach to him at Whitehall, and, though much were expected from him, both by His Majesty and others, yet he was so happy (which few are) as to satisfy and exceed their expectations: preaching the Word so, as showed his own heart was possessed with those very thoughts and joys that he labored to distill into others: a preacher in earnest; weeping sometimes for his auditory, sometimes with

[4] [Psalms 84 : 1.]

them; always preaching to himself, like an angel from a cloud, but in none; carrying some, as St. Paul was, to heaven in holy raptures, and enticing others by a sacred art and courtship to amend their lives; here picturing a vice so as to make it ugly to those that practiced it; and a virtue so as to make it be beloved, even by those that loved it not; and all this with a most particular grace and an unexpressible addition of comeliness.

·   ·   ·

Before that month ended, he was appointed to preach upon his old constant day, the first Friday in Lent; he had notice of it, and had in his sickness so prepared for that employment, that as he had long thirsted for it, so he resolved his weakness should not hinder his journey; he came therefore to London some few days before his appointed day of preaching. At his coming thither, many of his friends (who with sorrow saw his sickness had left him but so much flesh as did only cover his bones) doubted his strength to perform that task, and did therefore dissuade him from undertaking it, assuring him, however, it was like to shorten his life; but he passionately denied their requests, saying, "he would not doubt that that God, who in so many weaknesses had assisted him with an unexpected strength, would now withdraw it in his last employment;" professing an holy ambition to perform that sacred work. And when, to the amazement of some beholders, he appeared in the pulpit, many of them thought he presented himself not to preach mortification by a living voice, but mortality by a decayed body and a dying face. And doubtless many did secretly ask that question in Ezekiel, "Do these bones live?" Or can that soul organize that tongue to speak so long time as the sand in that glass will move towards its center and measure out an hour of this dying man's unspent life? Doubtless it cannot. And yet, after some faint pauses in his zealous prayer, his strong desires enabled his weak body to discharge his memory of his preconceived meditations, which were of dying, the text being, "To God the Lord belong the issues from death." Many that then saw his tears, and heard his faint and hollow voice, professing they thought the text prophetically chosen, and that Dr. Donne had preached his own funeral sermon.

Being full of joy that God had enabled him to perform this desired duty, he hastened to his house; out of which he never moved till, like St. Stephen, "he was carried by devout men to his grave." [5]

. . .

It is observed that a desire of glory or commendation is rooted in the very nature of man; and that those of the severest and most mortified lives, though they may become so humble as to banish self-flattery, and such weeds as naturally grow there; yet they have not been able to kill this desire of glory, but that like our radical heat, it will both live and die with us; and many think it should do so; and we want not sacred examples to justify the desire of having our memory to outlive our lives; which I mention, because Dr. Donne, by the persuasion of Dr. Fox, easily yielded at this very time to have a monument made for him; but Dr. Fox undertook not to persuade him how, or what monument it should be; that was left to Dr. Donne himself.

A monument being resolved upon, Dr. Donne sent for a carver to make for him in wood the figure of an urn, giving him directions for the compass and height of it; and to bring with it a board, of the just height of his body. These being got, then without delay a choice painter was got to be in readiness to draw his picture, which was taken as followeth. Several charcoal fires being first made in his large study, he brought with him into that place his winding-sheet in his hand, and having put off all his clothes, had this sheet put on him, and so tied with knots at his head and feet, and his hands so placed as dead bodies are usually fitted to be shrouded and put into their coffin or grave. Upon this urn he thus stood with his eyes shut and with so much of the sheet turned aside as might show his lean, pale, and deathlike face, which was purposely turned towards the east, from whence he expected the second coming of his and our Saviour Jesus. In this posture he was drawn at his just height; and when the picture was fully finished, he caused it to be set by his bedside, where it continued and became his hourly object till his death, and was then given to his dearest friend and executor Dr. Henry King, then chief residentiary of St. Paul's, who caused him to be thus carved in one entire piece of white marble, as it now stands in that church; and by Dr. Donne's own appointment, these words were to be affixed to it as his epitaph:

[5] [Cf. Acts 8 : 2.]

JOHANNES DONNE
Sac. Theol. Profess.

Post varia studia quibus ab annis tenerrimis
fideliter, nec infeliciter incubuit,
instinctu et impulsu Sp. Sancti, monitu
et hortatu

REGIS JACOBI, *ordines sacros*
amplexus, anno sui Jesu, 1614, et suae aetatis 42,
decanatu hujus ecclesiae indutus 27
Novembris, 1621,

exutus morte ultimo die Martii, 1631,
hic licet in occiduo cinere aspicit eum
cujus nomen est Oriens.[6]

And now, having brought him through the many labyrinths and perplexities of a various life, even to the gates of death and the grave, my desire is, he may rest till I have told my reader that I have seen many pictures of him in several habits and at several ages and in several postures; and I now mention this, because I have seen one picture of him, drawn by a curious hand, at his age of eighteen, with his sword, and what other adornments might then suit with the present fashions of youth and the giddy gaieties of that age; and his motto then was,

How much shall I be changed,
Before I am changed.

And if that young and his now dying picture were at this time set together, every beholder might say, "Lord! how much is Dr. Donne already changed, before he is changed!" And the view of them might give my reader occasion to ask himself with some

[6] ["John Donne, Professor of Sacred Theology. After various studies, which he plied from his tenderest youth faithfully and not unsuccessfully, moved by the instinct and impulse of the Holy Spirit and the admonition and encouragement of King James, he took holy orders in the year of our Lord 1614 at the age of 42. On the 27th of November, 1621, he was made deacon of this church; and he died on the last day of March, 1631. Here in the decline and decay of ashes, may he look upon him whose name is a Rising Sun."]

amazement, "Lord! how much may I also, that am now in health, be changed before I am changed; before this vile, this changeable body shall put off mortality!" and therefore to prepare for it. But this is not writ so much for my reader's memento as to tell him that Dr. Donne would often in his private discourses, and often publicly in his sermons, mention the many changes both of his body and mind; especially of his mind from a vertiginous giddiness; and would as often say, "his great and most blessed change was from a temporal to a spiritual employment"; in which he was so happy that he accounted the former part of his life to be lost; and the beginning of it to be from his first entering into sacred orders and serving his most merciful God at his altar.

Upon Monday, after the drawing this picture, he took his last leave of his beloved study; and, being sensible of his hourly decay, retired himself to his bedchamber; and that week sent at several times for many of his most considerable friends, with whom he took a solemn and deliberate farewell, commending to their considerations some sentences useful for the regulation of their lives; and then dismissed them, as good Jacob did his sons, with a spiritual benediction. The Sunday following, he appointed his servants, that if there were any business yet undone that concerned him or themselves, it should be prepared against Saturday next; for after that day he would not mix his thoughts with anything that concerned this world; nor ever did; but, as Job, so he "waited for the appointed day of his dissolution."

And now he was so happy as to have nothing to do but to die, to do which he stood in need of no longer time; for he had studied it long and to so happy a perfection that in a former sickness he called God to witness, "he was that minute ready to deliver his soul into his hands, if that minute God would determine his dissolution." In that sickness he begged of God the constancy to be preserved in that estate forever; and his patient expectation to have his immortal soul disrobed from her garment of mortality makes me confident that he now had a modest assurance that his prayers were then heard and his petition granted. He lay fifteen days earnestly expecting his hourly change; and in the last hour of his last day, as his body melted away and vapored into spirit, his soul having, I verily believe, some revelation of the beatifical vision, he said, "I were miserable if I might not die"; and after those words, closed many periods of his faint breath by saying often, "Thy kingdom come, thy will be done." His speech, which had long been his ready and faithful servant, left him not till the last minute of his life, and then forsook him, not to serve another master (for who speaks like him) but died before him; for that it was then become useless to him that now conversed with God on earth as angels are said to do in heaven, only by thoughts and looks. Being speechless, and seeing heaven by that illumination by which he saw it, he did, as St. Stephen, "look steadfastly into it, till he saw the Son of Man standing at the right hand of God his Father";[7] and being satisfied with this blessed sight, as his soul ascended and his last breath departed from him, he closed his own eyes; and then disposed his hands and body into such a posture as required not the least alteration by those that came to shroud him.

Thus variable, thus virtuous was the life; thus excellent, thus exemplary was the death of this memorable man.

He was buried in that place of St. Paul's Church which he had appointed for that use some years before his death; and by which he passed daily to pay his public devotions to Almighty God (who was then served twice a day by a public form of prayer and praises in that place): but he was not buried privately, though he desired it; for, besides an unnumbered number of others, many persons of nobility, and of eminency for learning, who did love and honor him in his life, did show it at his death by a voluntary and sad attendance of his body to the grave, where nothing was so remarkable as a public sorrow.

To which place of his burial some mournful friends repaired, and, as Alexander the Great did to the grave of the famous Achilles, so they strewed his with an abundance of curious and costly flowers; which course, they (who were never yet known) continued morning and evening for many days, not ceasing, till the stones that were taken up in that church to give his body admission into the cold earth (now his bed of rest) were again by the mason's art so leveled and firmed as they had been formerly, and his place of burial undistinguishable to common view.

The next day after his burial, some unknown friend, some one of the many lovers and admirers of his virtue and learning, wrote this epitaph with a coal on the wall over his grave:

[7] [Cf. Acts 7 : 55.]

Reader! I am to let thee know,
Donne's body only lies below;
For, could the grave his soul comprise,
Earth would be richer than the skies.

Nor was this all the honor done to his reverend ashes; for, as there be some persons that will not receive a reward for that for which God accounts himself a debtor, persons that dare trust God with their charity and without a witness; so there was by some grateful unknown friend that thought Dr. Donne's memory ought to be perpetuated, an hundred marks sent to his two faithful friends and executors, towards the making of his monument. It was not for many years known by whom; but after the death of Dr. Fox, it was known that it was he that sent it; and he lived to see as lively a representation of his dead friend as marble can express: a statue indeed so like Dr. Donne that (as his friend Sir Henry Wotton hath expressed himself) "it seems to breathe faintly, and posterity shall look upon it as a kind of artificial miracle."

He was of stature moderately tall; of a straight and equally proportioned body, to which all his words and actions gave an unexpressible addition of comeliness.

The melancholy and pleasant humor were in him so contempered that each gave advantage to the other, and made his company one of the delights of mankind.

His fancy was unimitably high, equaled only by his great wit; both being made useful by a commanding judgment.

His aspect was cheerful, and such as gave a silent testimony of a clear knowing soul, and of a conscience at peace with itself.

His melting eye showed that he had a soft heart, full of noble compassion; of too brave a soul to offer injuries and too much a Christian not to pardon them in others.

He did much contemplate (especially after he entered into his sacred calling) the mercies of Almighty God, the immortality of the soul, and the joys of heaven: and would often say in a kind of sacred ecstasy—"Blessed be God that he is God, only and divinely like himself."

He was by nature highly passionate, but more apt to reluct at the excesses of it. A great lover of the offices of humanity, and of so merciful a spirit that he never beheld the miseries of mankind without pity and relief.

He was earnest and unwearied in the search of knowledge, with which his vigorous soul is now satisfied, and employed in a continual praise of that God that first breathed it into his active body: that body, which once was a temple of the Holy Ghost and is now become a small quantity of Christian dust:

But I shall see it reanimated.

QUESTIONS FOR STUDY
AND TOPICS FOR DISCUSSION
ON *The Life of Dr. John Donne*

1. Walton's *Life* of Donne originated as a preface to the 1640 edition of Donne's *LXXX Sermons*. This was the first of several biographies of contemporary English writers and prelates. A devout Anglican himself, Walton turned to biography when the Civil Wars were threatening, and all of his writing in biography was done during the time the High Church was under attack from the Puritans or struggling to re-establish itself after the Restoration. He conceived his subjects as examples of Anglican piety, even as saints and martyrs. His portraits reflect his High Church principles, his political persuasion, and his moral outlook; Walton might well have said of the biographies what he acknowledged in *The Compleat Angler*: "the whole discourse is a kind of picture of my own disposition."

Walton's portrait of Donne has been criticized for mistakes and distortions of fact, and, on more serious grounds, for whitewashing or slighting the characteristics of "Jack" Donne, the rakish and earthly figure that emerges from such poems as *Songs and Sonnets*. But Walton was not interested in making an "objective" and complete record of the life of his subject. His purpose was to compose an appreciation and a commemoration of the author of *LXXX Sermons*: Dr. John Donne, Late Dean of St. Paul's Church; Donne the preacher and the Anglican divine.

In the first extract (pp. 108–112) Walton describes Donne's "conversion"—which was actually a decision reversing his earlier refusal to take Anglican orders. What qualities does Walton portray? How do his religious principles shape the content? How does he draw the picture? Does the writing convey Donne's "wrestling" with the decision to enter sacred orders? Does Walton's language reproduce the tortured introversions of *Death's*

Duel? Analyze the composition of the paragraph beginning "Now the English Church had gained . . ." (p. 111). Note especially the balance of its construction. Is it ornate and affected? In this and the passage that follows how does the adverb "now" work? What impression does it create?

2. Walton disclaimed artifice. In the introduction to the *Life* of Donne he resolved that "the world should see the best plain picture of the author's life that my artless pencil, guided by the hand of truth, could present to it." But his art is, of course, plainly visible, and it is studied and subtle. Walton's prose is remarkable chiefly for its limpidity and pace. The texture is relatively spare (though tending towards rhetorical balance, coupled adjectives, and alliteration) and the syntax is unencumbered. Each word strikes with clean precision and moves effortlessly and with a continuous rhythm.

Donne writes a very different kind of prose. He shapes his words so as to arouse a strong visceral response in the reader. The dense and violent metaphors, the nervous rhythms, and the startling leaps from one thought to another convey a direct equivalent of action. Physical states are rendered intensely and with sharp particularity. Language has the quality of animated gesture.

Donne's prose forces active participation by the reader. Walton, on the other hand, is interested in creating a *distance* between the action and the reader's response. There is no design to enlist and arouse the reader's physical states of feeling. Each kind of writing is artful, and each fits the respective intentions of the authors.

Continue the kind of analysis suggested here by a fuller and more specific consideration of the styles of *Death's Duel* and Walton's *Life*. What are the differences in texture, syntax, and rhythm? What makes each style of expression fitting for the intentions of the two works? What effects are created by each style?

3. In the second extract (pp. 112–113) Walton describes Donne's delivery of *Death's Duel*. Walton may have been present at the event, but that is not certain. Does he write like an eyewitness? Is his narrative a "realistic" factual account? How does he pick up and exploit the reference to Ezekiel in the sermon? How does Walton's use of the Biblical illustration differ from

Donne's? What is the construction of the sentence "And when, to the amazement . . ." (p. 112)? What use does Walton make of the Epistle to the Reader from *Death's Duel* (p. 82) in his narrative? How does he use the same "source" in the next extract?

4. In the third extract (pp. 113–118) Walton describes Donne's last days and gives a summary of his character. Donne's posing in a winding sheet, and his contemplation of the finished picture, seems to be a bizarre episode. Most modern readers are likely to view this as a clear indication of Donne's morbid fascination with death. Does Walton regard it so? What does Walton choose to emphasize in his account? What is the tone? Is it too pietistic to be convincing? Are Donne's last days rendered in a fashion too much like an object of art—too marmoreal? Walton's enumeration of Donne's features and qualities is reminiscent of the convention of the "character." This literary form, which flourished in the seventeenth century, is a brief descriptive sketch of a personage who typifies some definite quality. Walton was fond of the form and he used it extensively in his biographies. What is the purpose and effect of the form in *The Life of Donne*? Is Donne treated as an individual or as a type? Is there any progression in the things enumerated? Walton brings Donne down to "a small quantity of Christian dust" and then promises his reanimation (p. 118). How does the language enact the thought? What echoes of *Death's Duel* sound in the closing paragraphs?

AREOPAGITICA

A Speech for the Liberty of Unlicensed Printing, To the Parliament of England

BY *John Milton*

This is true liberty, when free-born men,
Having to advise the public, may speak free,
Which he who can, and will, deserves high praise;
Who neither can, nor will, may hold his peace:
What can be juster in a state than this?

EURIPIDES, The Suppliants

THEY WHO TO STATES and governors of the Commonwealth direct their speech, High Court of Parliament, or, wanting such access in a private condition, write that which they foresee may advance the public good; I suppose them, as at the beginning of no mean endeavor, not a little altered and moved inwardly in their minds: some with doubt of what will be the success, others with fear of what will be the censure; some with hope, others with confidence of what they have to speak. And me perhaps each of these dispositions, as the subject was whereon I entered, may have at other times variously affected; and likely might in these foremost expressions now also disclose which of them swayed most, but that the very attempt of this address thus made, and the thought of whom it hath recourse to, hath got the power within me to a passion, far more welcome than incidental to a preface.

Which though I stay not to confess ere any ask, I shall be

blameless, if it be no other than the joy and gratulation which it brings to all who wish and promote their country's liberty; whereof this whole discourse proposed will be a certain testimony, if not a trophy. For this is not the liberty which we can hope, that no grievance ever should arise in the Commonwealth —that let no man in this world expect; but when complaints are freely heard, deeply considered, and speedily reformed, then is the utmost bound of civil liberty attained that wise men look for. To which if I now manifest, by the very sound of this which I shall utter, that we are already in good part arrived, and yet from such a steep disadvantage of tyranny and superstition grounded into our principles as was beyond the manhood of a Roman recovery, it will be attributed first, as is most due, to the strong assistance of God our deliverer, next to your faithful guidance and undaunted wisdom, Lords and Commons of England. Neither is it in God's esteem the diminution of his glory, when honorable things are spoken of good men and worthy magistrates; which if I now first should begin to do, after so fair a progress of your laudable deeds, and such a long obligement upon the whole realm to your indefatigable virtues, I might be justly reckoned among the tardiest and the unwillingest of them that praise ye.

Nevertheless there being three principal things, without which all praising is but courtship and flattery: first, when that only is praised which is solidly worth praise; next, when greatest likelihoods are brought that such things are truly and really in those persons to whom they are ascribed; the other, when he who praises, by showing that such his actual persuasion is of whom he writes, can demonstrate that he flatters not; the former two of these I have heretofore endeavored, rescuing the employment from him who went about to impair your merits with a trivial and malignant encomium; the latter, as belonging chiefly to mine own acquittal, that whom I so extolled I did not flatter, hath been reserved opportunely to this occasion.

For he who freely magnifies what hath been nobly done, and fears not to declare as freely what might be done better, gives ye the best covenant of his fidelity; and that his loyalest affection and his hope waits on your proceedings. His highest praising is not flattery, and his plainest advice is a kind of praising; for though I should affirm and hold by argument that it would fare better with truth, with learning, and the Commonwealth, if one of your published Orders, which I should name, were called in; yet at the same time it could not but much redound to the luster of your mild and equal government, whenas private persons are hereby animated to think ye better pleased with public advice than other statists have been delighted heretofore with public flattery. And men will then see what difference there is between the magnanimity of a triennial Parliament and that jealous haughtiness of prelates and cabin counselors that usurped of late, whenas they shall observe ye in the midst of your victories and successes more gently brooking written exceptions against a voted Order than other courts, which had produced nothing worth memory but the weak ostentation of wealth, would have endured the least signified dislike at any sudden proclamation.

If I should thus far presume upon the meek demeanor of your civil and gentle greatness, Lords and Commons, as what your published Order hath directly said, that to gainsay, I might defend myself with ease, if any should accuse me of being new or insolent, did they but know how much better I find ye esteem it to imitate the old and elegant humanity of Greece than the barbaric pride of a Hunnish and Norwegian stateliness. And out of those ages, to whose polite wisdom and letters we owe that we are not yet Goths and Jutlanders, I could name him who from his private house wrote that discourse to the parliament of Athens that persuades them to change the form of democracy which was then established. Such honor was done in those days to men who professed the study of wisdom and eloquence, not only in their own country but in other lands, that cities and signiories heard them gladly, and with great respect, if they had aught in public to admonish the state. Thus did Dion Prusaeus, a stranger and a private orator, counsel the Rhodians against a former edict; and I abound with other like examples, which to set here would be superfluous.

But if from the industry of a life wholly dedicated to studious labors, and those natural endowments haply not the worse for two and fifty degrees of northern latitude, so much must be derogated as to count me not equal to any of those who had this privilege, I would obtain to be thought not so inferior as yourselves are superior to the most of them who received their counsel: and how far you excel them, be assured, Lords and Commons, there can no greater testimony appear than when your prudent spirit acknowledges and obeys the voice of reason, from what quarter soever it be heard speaking; and renders ye as willing to repeal any Act of your own setting forth, as any set forth by your predecessors.

If ye be thus resolved, as it were injury to think ye were not, I know not what should withhold me from presenting ye with a fit instance wherein to show both that love of truth which ye eminently profess, and that uprightness of your judgment which is not wont to be partial to yourselves; by judging over again that Order which ye have ordained *to regulate printing: that no book, pamphlet, or paper shall be henceforth printed, unless the same be first approved and licensed by such,* or at least one of such, as shall be thereto appointed. For that part which preserves justly every man's copy to himself, or provides for the poor, I touch not, only wish they be not made pretenses to abuse and persecute honest and painful men, who offend not in either of these particulars. But that other clause of Licensing Books, which we thought had died with his brother *quadragesimal* and *matrimonial* when the prelates expired, I shall now attend with such a homily as shall lay before ye, first, the inventors of it to be those whom ye will be loath to own; next, what is to be thought in general of reading, whatever sort the books be; and that this Order avails nothing to the suppressing of scandalous, seditious, and libelous books, which were mainly intended to be suppressed. Last, that it will be primely to the discouragement of all learning, and the stop of truth, not only by disexercising and blunting our abilities in what we know already, but by hindering and cropping the discovery that might be yet further made both in religious and civil wisdom.

I deny not but that it is of greatest concernment in the Church and Commonwealth to have a vigilant eye how books demean themselves as well as men; and thereafter to confine, imprison, and do sharpest justice on them as malefactors. For books are not absolutely dead things, but do contain a potency of life in them to be as active as that soul was whose progeny they are; nay, they do preserve as in a vial the purest efficacy and extraction of that living intellect that bred them. I know they are as lively, and as vigorously productive, as those fabulous dragon's teeth; and being sown up and down, may chance to spring up armed men. And yet, on the other hand, unless wariness be used, as good almost kill a man as kill a good book: who kills a man kills a reasonable creature, God's image; but he who destroys a good book, kills reason itself, kills the image of God, as it were, in the eye. Many a man lives a burden to the earth; but a good book is the precious life-blood of a master spirit, embalmed and treasured up on purpose to a life beyond life. 'Tis true, no age can restore a life, whereof perhaps there is no great loss; and revolutions of ages do not oft recover the loss of a rejected truth, for the want of which whole nations fare the worse. We should be wary therefore what persecution we raise against the living labors of public men, how we spill that seasoned life of man preserved and stored up in books; since we see a kind of homicide may be thus committed, sometimes a martyrdom, and if it extend to the whole impression, a kind of massacre, whereof the execution ends not in the slaying of an elemental life, but strikes at that ethereal and fifth essence, the breath of reason itself, slays an immortality rather than a life. But lest I should be condemned of introducing license, while I oppose licensing, I refuse not the pains to be so much historical as will serve to show what hath been done by ancient and famous commonwealths against this disorder, till the very time that this project of licensing crept out of the Inquisition, was catched up by our prelates, and hath caught some of our presbyters.

In Athens, where books and wits were ever busier than in any other part of Greece, I find but only two sorts of writings which the magistrate cared to take notice of; those either blasphemous and atheistical, or libelous. Thus the books of Protagoras were by the judges of Areopagus commanded to be burnt, and himself banished the territory for a discourse begun with his confessing not to know "whether there were gods, or whether not." And against defaming, it was decreed that none should be traduced by name, as was the manner of Vetus Comoedia, whereby we may guess how they censured libeling: and this course was quick enough, as Cicero writes, to quell both the desperate wits of other atheists and the open way of defaming, as the event showed. Of other sects and opinions, though tending to voluptuousness, and the denying of divine providence, they took no heed. Therefore we do not read that either Epicurus, or that libertine school of Cyrene, or what the Cynic impudence uttered, was ever questioned by the laws. Neither is it recorded that the writings of those old comedians were suppressed, though the acting of them were forbid; and that Plato commended the reading of Aristophanes, the loosest of them all, to his royal scholar

Dionysius, is commonly known, and may be excused, if holy Chrysostom, as is reported, nightly studied so much the same author and had the art to cleanse a scurrilous vehemence into the style of a rousing sermon.

That other leading city of Greece, Lacedaemon, considering that Lycurgus their lawgiver was so addicted to elegant learning as to have been the first that brought out of Ionia the scattered works of Homer, and sent the poet Thales from Crete to prepare and mollify the Spartan surliness with his smooth songs and odes, the better to plant among them law and civility, it is to be wondered how museless and unbookish they were, minding nought but the feats of war. There needed no licensing of books among them, for they disliked all but their own laconic apothegms, and took a slight occasion to chase Archilochus out of their city, perhaps for composing in a higher strain than their own soldierly ballads and roundels could reach to; or if it were for his broad verses, they were not therein so cautious, but they were as dissolute in their promiscuous conversing; whence Euripides affirms, in *Andromache,* that their women were all unchaste. Thus much may give us light after what sort of books were prohibited among the Greeks.

The Romans also, for many ages trained up only to a military roughness, resembling most the Lacedaemonian guise, knew of learning little but what their Twelve Tables and the Pontific College with their augurs and flamens taught them in religion and law, so unacquainted with other learning that when Carneades and Critolaus, with the Stoic Diogenes coming ambassadors to Rome, took thereby occasion to give the city a taste of their philosophy, they were suspected for seducers by no less a man than Cato the Censor, who moved it in the Senate to dismiss them speedily, and to banish all such Attic babblers out of Italy. But Scipio and others of the noblest senators withstood him and his old Sabine austerity; honored and admired the men; and the Censor himself at last, in his old age, fell to the study of what whereof before he was so scrupulous. And yet at the same time, Naevius and Plautus, the first Latin comedians, had filled the city with all the borrowed scenes of Menander and Philemon. Then began to be considered there also what was to be done to libelous books and authors; for Naevius was quickly cast into prison for his unbridled pen, and released by the tribunes upon his recantation: we read also that libels were burnt, and the makers punished by Augustus. The like severity, no doubt, was used if aught were impiously written against their esteemed gods. Except in these two points, how the world went in books, the magistrate kept no reckoning. And therefore Lucretius without impeachment versifies his Epicurism to Memmius, and had the honor to be set forth the second time by Cicero, so great a father of the commonwealth; although himself disputes against that opinion in his own writings. Nor was the satirical sharpness or naked plainness of Lucilius, or Catullus, or Flaccus, by any order prohibited. And for matters of state, the story of Titus Livius, though it extolled that part which Pompey held, was not therefore suppressed by Octavius Caesar of the other faction. But that Naso was by him banished in his old age, for the wanton poems of his youth, was but a mere covert of state over some secret cause: and besides, the books were neither banished nor called in. From hence we shall meet with little else but tyranny in the Roman empire, that we may not marvel if not so often bad as good books were silenced. I shall therefore deem to have been large enough in producing what among the ancients was punishable to write, save only which, all other arguments were free to treat on.

By this time the emperors were become Christians, whose discipline in this point I do not find to have been more severe than what was formerly in practice. The books of those whom they took to be grand heretics were examined, refuted, and condemned in the general councils; and not till then were prohibited, or burnt, by authority of the emperor. As for the writings of heathen authors, unless they were plain invectives against Christianity, as those of Porphyrius and Proclus, they met with no interdict that can be cited, till about the year 400, in a Carthaginian Council, wherein bishops themselves were forbid to read the books of Gentiles, but heresies they might read: while others long before them, on the contrary, scrupled more the books of heretics than of Gentiles. And that the primitive councils and bishops were wont only to declare what books were not commendable, passing no further, but leaving it to each one's conscience to read or to lay by, till after the year 800, is observed already by Padre Paolo, the great unmasker of the Trentine Council. After which time the popes of Rome, engrossing what they pleased of political rule into their own hands, extended their dominion over men's eyes, as they had before over their judgments, burning and prohibiting to be read what they fancied not; yet sparing in their censures, and the books not many which they so dealt with: till Martin V by his bull not only prohibited, but was the first that excommunicated the reading of heretical books; for about that time Wyclif and Huss growing terrible, were they who first drove the Papal Court to a stricter policy of prohibiting. Which course Leo X and his successors followed, until the Council of Trent and the Spanish Inquisition, engendering together, brought forth or perfected those catalogues and expurging Indexes that rake through the entrails of many an old good author with a violation worse than any could be offered to his tomb.

Nor did they stay in matters heretical, but any subject that was not to their palate, they either condemned in a prohibition, or had it straight into the new purgatory of an Index. To fill up the measure of encroachment, their last invention was to ordain that no book, pamphlet, or paper should be printed (as if St. Peter had bequeathed them the keys of the press also out of Paradise) unless it were approved and licensed under the hands of two or three glutton friars. For example:

> Let the Chancellor Cini be pleased to see if in this present work be contained aught that may withstand the printing.
> VINCENT RABATTA, Vicar of Florence.

> I have seen this present work, and find nothing athwart the Catholic faith and good manners: in witness whereof I have given, etc.
>
> NICOLÒ CINI, Chancellor of Florence.

> Attending the precedent relation, it is allowed that this present work of Davanzati may be printed,
> VINCENT RABATTA, etc.

> It may be printed, July 15.
> FRIAR SIMON MOMPEI D'AMELIA, Chancellor of the holy office in Florence.

Sure they have a conceit, if he of the bottomless pit had not long since broke prison, that this quadruple exorcism would bar him down. I fear their next design will be to get into their custody the licensing of that which they say Claudius intended, but went not through with. Vouchsafe to see another of their forms, the Roman stamp:

Imprimatur, If it seem good to the reverend Master of the holy Palace,

BELCASTRO, Viceregent

Imprimatur,

FRIAR NICOLÒ RODOLPHI, Master of the holy Palace.

Sometimes five Imprimaturs are seen together dialogue-wise in the piazza of one title page, complimenting and ducking each to other with their shaven reverences, whether the author, who stands by in perplexity at the foot of his epistle, shall to the press or to the sponge. These are the pretty responsories, these are the dear antiphonies that so bewitched of late our prelates and their chaplains with the goodly echo they made; and besotted us to the gay imitation of a lordly Imprimatur, one from Lambeth House, another from the west end of Paul's, so apishly Roman- izing that the word of command still was set down in Latin; as if the learned grammatical pen that wrote it would cast no ink without Latin; or perhaps, as they thought, because no vulgar tongue was worthy to express the pure conceit of an Imprimatur; but rather, as I hope, for that our English, the language of men ever famous and foremost in the achievements of liberty, will not easily find servile letters enow to spell such a dictatory presump- tion English.

And thus ye have the inventors and the original of book- licensing ripped up and drawn as lineally as any pedigree. We have it not, that can be heard of, from any ancient state, or polity, or church, nor by any statute left us by our ancestors elder or later; nor from the modern custom of any reformed city or church abroad; but from the most antichristian council and the most tyrannous inquisition that ever inquired. Till then books were ever as freely admitted into the world as any other birth; the issue of the brain was no more stifled than the issue of the womb: no envious Juno sat cross-legged over the nativity of any man's intellectual offspring; but if it proved a monster, who denies but that it was justly burnt, or sunk into the sea? But that a book, in worse condition than a peccant soul, should be to stand before a jury ere it be born to the world, and undergo yet in darkness the judgment of Radamanth and his colleagues, ere it can pass the ferry backward into light, was never heard before, till that mysterious iniquity, provoked and troubled at the first entrance of Reformation, sought out new limbos and

new hells wherein they might include our books also within the
number of their damned. And this was the rare morsel so of-
ficiously snatched up, and so ill-favoredly imitated by our in-
quisiturient bishops and the attendant minorities their chaplains.
That ye like not now these most certain authors of this licensing
order, and that all sinister intention was far distant from your
thoughts, when ye were importuned the passing it, all men who
know the integrity of your actions, and how ye honor truth, will
clear ye readily.

But some will say, what though the inventors were bad, the
thing for all that may be good. It may be so; yet if that thing
be no such deep invention, but obvious and easy for any man
to light on, and yet best and wisest commonwealths through all
ages and occasions have forborne to use it, and falsest seducers
and oppressors of men were the first who took it up, and to no
other purpose but to obstruct and hinder the first approach of
Reformation; I am of those who believe it will be a harder al-
chemy than Lullius ever knew, to sublimate any good use out
of such an invention. Yet this only is what I request to gain
from this reason, that it may be held a dangerous and suspicious
fruit, as certainly it deserves, for the tree that bore it, until I
can dissect one by one the properties it has. But I have first to
finish, as was propounded, what is to be thought in general of
reading books, whatever sort they be, and whether be more the
benefit or the harm that thence proceeds.

Not to insist upon the examples of Moses, Daniel, and Paul,
who were skillful in all the learning of the Egyptians, Chaldeans,
and Greeks, which could not probably be without reading their
books of all sorts, in Paul especially, who thought it no defilement
to insert into Holy Scripture the sentences of three Greek poets,
and one of them a tragedian; the question was notwithstanding
sometimes controverted among the primitive doctors, but with
great odds on that side which affirmed it both lawful and profitable, as was then evidently perceived when Julian the Apostate,
and subtlest enemy to our faith, made a decree forbidding Christians the study of heathen learning: for, said he, they wound us
with our own weapons, and with our own arts and sciences they
overcome us. And indeed the Christians were put so to their
shifts by this crafty means, and so much in danger to decline
into all ignorance, that the two Apollinarii were fain, as a man
may say, to coin all the seven liberal sciences out of the Bible,

reducing it into divers forms of orations, poems, dialogues, even
to the calculating of a new Christian grammar. But, saith the
historian Socrates, the providence of God provided better than
the industry of Apollinarius and his son, by taking away that
illiterate law with the life of him who devised it. So great an
injury they then held it to be deprived of Hellenic learning; and
thought it a persecution more undermining, and secretly decay-
ing the church, than the open cruelty of Decius or Diocletian.

And perhaps it was the same politic drift that the devil
whipped St. Jerome in a Lenten dream for reading Cicero; or else
it was a phantasm bred by the fever which had then seized him.
For had an angel been his discipliner, unless it were for dwelling too much upon Ciceronianisms, and had chastised the reading, not the vanity, it had been plainly partial; first to correct
him for grave Cicero, and not for scurril Plautus, whom he confesses to have been reading not long before; next to correct him
only, and let so many more ancient fathers wax old in those
pleasant and florid studies without the lash of such a tutoring
apparition; insomuch that Basil teaches how some good use may
be made of *Margites,* a sportful poem, not now extant, writ by
Homer; and why not then of *Morgante,* an Italian romance much
to the same purpose?

But if it be agreed we shall be tried by visions, there is a
vision recorded by Eusebius, far ancienter than this tale of Jerome
to the nun Eustochium, and besides, has nothing of a fever in
it. Dionysius Alexandrinus was, about the year 240, a person of
great name in the church for piety and learning, who had wont
to avail himself much against heretics by being conversant in
their books; until a certain presbyter laid it scrupulously to his
conscience, how he durst venture himself among those defiling
volumes. The worthy man, loath to give offense, fell into a new
debate with himself what was to be thought; when suddenly
a vision sent from God (it is his own epistle that so avers it)
confirmed him in these words: "Read any books whatever come
to thy hands, for thou art sufficient both to judge aright and to
examine each matter." To this revelation he assented the sooner,
as he confesses, because it was answerable to that of the Apostle
to the Thessalonians: "Prove all things, hold fast that which is
good."

And he might have added another remarkable saying of the
same author: "To the pure all things are pure"; not only meats

and drinks, but all kind of knowledge, whether of good or evil; the knowledge cannot defile, nor consequently the books, if the will and conscience be not defiled. For books are as meats and viands are, some of good, some of evil substance; and yet God in that unapocryphal vision said without exception, "Rise, Peter, kill and eat," leaving the choice to each man's discretion. Wholesome meats to a vitiated stomach differ little or nothing from unwholesome; and best books to a naughty mind are not unappliable to occasions of evil. Bad meats will scarce breed good nourishment in the healthiest concoction; but herein the difference is of bad books, that they to a discreet and judicious reader serve in many respects to discover, to confute, to forewarn, and to illustrate. Whereof what better witness can ye expect I should produce than one of your own now sitting in Parliament, the chief of learned men reputed in this land, Mr. Selden, whose volume of natural and national laws proves, not only by great authorities brought together, but by exquisite reasons and theorems almost mathematically demonstrative, that all opinions, yea errors, known, read, and collated, are of main service and assistance toward the speedy attainment of what is truest.

I conceive, therefore, that when God did enlarge the universal diet of man's body, saving ever the rules of temperance, he then also, as before, left arbitrary the dieting and repasting of our minds; as wherein every mature man might have to exercise his own leading capacity. How great a virtue is temperance, how much of moment through the whole life of man! Yet God commits the managing so great a trust, without particular law or prescription, wholly to the demeanor of every grown man. And therefore when he himself tabled the Jews from heaven, that omer, which was every man's daily portion of manna, is computed to have been more than might have well sufficed the heartiest feeder thrice as many meals. For those actions which enter into a man, rather than issue out of him, and therefore defile not, God uses not to captivate under a perpetual childhood of prescription, but trusts him with the gift of reason to be his own chooser; there were but little work left for preaching, if law and compulsion should grow so fast upon those things which heretofore were governed only by exhortation. Solomon informs us that much reading is a weariness to the flesh; but neither he nor other inspired author tells us that such or such reading is unlawful: yet certainly had God thought good to limit us herein,

it had been much more expedient to have told us what was unlawful than what was wearisome.

As for the burning of those Ephesian books by St. Paul's converts; 'tis replied the books were magic, the Syriac so renders
them. It was a private act, a voluntary act, and leaves us to a
voluntary imitation: the men in remorse burnt those books which
were their own; the magistrate by this example is not appointed:
these men practiced the books, another might perhaps have read
them in some sort usefully.

Good and evil we know in the field of this world grow up
together almost inseparably; and the knowledge of good is so
involved and interwoven with the knowledge of evil, and in so
many cunning resemblances hardly to be discerned, that those
confused seeds which were imposed on Psyche as an incessant
labor to cull out and sort asunder were not more intermixed. It
was from out the rind of one apple tasted that the knowledge
of good and evil, as two twins cleaving together, leapt forth into
the world. And perhaps this is that doom which Adam fell into
of knowing good and evil, that is to say, of knowing good by
evil.

As therefore the state of man now is, what wisdom can there
be to choose, what continence to forbear without the knowledge
of evil? He that can apprehend and consider vice with all her
baits and seeming pleasures, and yet abstain, and yet distinguish,
and yet prefer that which is truly better, he is the true wayfaring
Christian. I cannot praise a fugitive and cloistered virtue, un-
exercised and unbreathed, that never sallies out and sees her adversary, but slinks out of the race, where that immortal garland
is to be run for, not without dust and heat. Assuredly we bring
not innocence into the world, we bring impurity much rather:
that which purifies us is trial, and trial is by what is contrary.
That virtue therefore which is but a youngling in the contemplation of evil, and knows not the utmost that vice promises to
her followers, and rejects it, is but a blank virtue, not a pure;
her whiteness is but an excremental whiteness; which was the
reason why our sage and serious poet Spenser, whom I dare be
known to think a better teacher than Scotus or Aquinas, describing true temperance under the person of Guyon, brings him
in with his palmer through the Cave of Mammon, and the Bower
of Earthly Bliss, that he might see and know, and yet abstain.

Since therefore the knowledge and survey of vice is in this

world so necessary to the constituting of human virtue, and the scanning of error to the confirmation of truth, how can we more safely, and with less danger, scout into the regions of sin and falsity than by reading all manner of tractates and hearing all manner of reason? And this is the benefit which may be had of books promiscuously read.

But of the harm that may result hence, three kinds are usually reckoned. First is feared the infection that may spread; but then all human learning and controversy in religious points must remove out of the world, yea the Bible itself; for that ofttimes relates blasphemy not nicely, it describes the carnal sense of wicked men not unelegantly, it brings in holiest men passionately murmuring against providence through all the arguments of Epicurus: in other great disputes it answers dubiously and darkly to the common reader: and ask a Talmudist what ails the modesty of his marginal Keri, that Moses and all the prophets cannot persuade him to pronounce the textual Chetiv. For these causes we all know the Bible itself put by the papist into the first rank of prohibited books. The ancientest fathers must be next removed, as Clement of Alexandria, and that Eusebian book of evangelic preparation, transmitting our ears through a hoard of heathenish obscenities to receive the Gospel. Who finds not that Irenaeus, Epiphanius, Jerome, and others discover more heresies than they well confute, and that oft for heresy which is the truer opinion?

Nor boots it to say for these, and all the heathen writers of greatest infection, if it must be thought so, with whom is bound up the life of human learning, that they writ in an unknown tongue, so long as we are sure those languages are known as well to the worst of men, who are both most able and most diligent to instill the poison they suck, first into the courts of princes, acquainting them with the choicest delights and criticisms of sin. As perhaps did that Petronius whom Nero called his Arbiter, the master of his revels; and that notorious ribald of Arezzo, dreaded and yet dear to the Italian courtiers. I name not him for posterity's sake, whom Harry VIII named in merriment his vicar of hell. By which compendious way all the contagion that foreign books can infuse will find a passage to the people far easier and shorter than an Indian voyage, though it could be sailed either by the north of Cathay eastward, or of Canada westward, while our Spanish licensing gags the English press never so severely.

But on the other side, that infection which is from books of controversy in religion is more doubtful and dangerous to the learned than to the ignorant; and yet those books must be permitted untouched by the licenser. It will be hard to instance where any ignorant man hath been ever seduced by papistical book in English, unless it were commended and expounded to him by some of that clergy: and indeed all such tractates, whether false or true, are as the prophecy of Isaiah was to the eunuch, not to be "understood without a guide." But of our priests and doctors how many have been corrupted by studying the comments of Jesuits and Sorbonists, and how fast they could transfuse that corruption into the people, our experience is both late and sad. It is not forgot, since the acute and distinct Arminius was perverted merely by the perusing of a nameless discourse written at Delft, which at first he took in hand to confute.

Seeing therefore that those books, and those in great abundance, which are likeliest to taint both life and doctrine, cannot be suppressed without the fall of learning and of all ability in disputation, and that these books of either sort are most and soonest catching to the learned, from whom to the common people whatever is heretical or dissolute may quickly be conveyed, and that evil manners are as perfectly learnt without books a thousand other ways which cannot be stopped, and evil doctrine not with books can propagate, except a teacher guide, which he might also do without writing, and so beyond prohibiting, I am not able to unfold how this cautelous enterprise of licensing can be exempted from the number of vain and impossible attempts. And he who were pleasantly disposed could not well avoid to liken it to the exploit of that gallant man who thought to pound up the crows by shutting his park gate.

Besides another inconvenience, if learned men be the first receivers out of books and dispreaders both of vice and error, how shall the licensers themselves be confided in, unless we can confer upon them, or they assume to themselves above all others in the land, the grace of infallibility and uncorruptedness? And again, if it be true that a wise man like a good refiner can gather gold out of the drossiest volume, and that a fool will be a fool with the best book, yea or without book, there is no reason that we should deprive a wise man of any advantage to his wisdom, while we seek to restrain from a fool that which being restrained will be no hindrance to his folly. For if there should be so much exactness always used to keep that from him which is unfit for his reading, we should in the judgment of Aristotle not only, but of Solomon, and of our Saviour, not vouchsafe him good precepts, and by consequence not willingly admit him to good books; as being certain that a wise man will make better use of an idle pamphlet than a fool will do of sacred Scripture.

'Tis next alleged we must not expose ourselves to temptations without necessity, and next to that, not employ our time in vain things. To both these objections one answer will serve, out of the grounds already laid, that to all men such books are not temptations, nor vanities, but useful drugs and materials wherewith to temper and compose effective and strong medicines, which man's life cannot want. The rest, as children and childish men, who have not the art to qualify and prepare these working minerals, well may be exhorted to forbear, but hindered forcibly they cannot be by all the licensing that sainted Inquisition could ever yet contrive; which is what I promised to deliver next: that this order of licensing conduces nothing to the end for which it was framed; and hath almost prevented me by being clear already while thus much hath been explaining. See the ingenuity of Truth, who, when she gets a free and willing hand, opens herself faster than the pace of method and discourse can overtake her.

It was the task which I began with, to show that no nation, or well instituted state, if they valued books at all, did ever use this way of licensing; and it might be answered that this is a piece of prudence lately discovered. To which I return, that as it was a thing slight and obvious to think on, so if it had been difficult to find out, there wanted not among them long since who suggested such a course; which they not following, leave us a pattern of their judgment that it was not the not knowing, but the not approving, which was the cause of their not using it.

Plato, a man of high authority indeed, but least of all for his commonwealth, in the book of his laws, which no city ever yet received, fed his fancy by making many edicts to his airy burgomasters, which they who otherwise admire him wish had been rather buried and excused in the genial cups of an Academic night sitting. By which laws he seems to tolerate no kind of learning but by unalterable decree, consisting most of practical traditions, to the attainment whereof a library of smaller bulk than his own dialogues would be abundant. And there also enacts that no poet should so much as read to any private man what he had written, until the judges and lawkeepers had seen it and allowed it; but that Plato meant this law peculiarly to that commonwealth which he had imagined, and to no other, is evident. Why was he not else a lawgiver to himself, but a transgressor, and to be expelled by his own magistrates, both for the wanton epigrams and dialogues which he made, and his perpetual reading of Sophron Mimus and Aristophanes, books of grossest infamy; and also for commending the latter of them, though he were the malicious libeler of his chief friends, to be read by the tyrant Dionysius, who had little need of such trash to spend his time on? But that he knew this licensing of poems had reference and dependence to many other provisos there set down in his fancied republic, which in this world could have no place: and so neither he himself, nor any magistrate, or city ever imitated that course, which, taken apart from those other collateral injunctions, must needs be vain and fruitless.

For if they fell upon one kind of strictness, unless their care were equal to regulate all other things of like aptness to corrupt the mind, that single endeavor they knew would be but a fond labor; to shut and fortify one gate against corruption, and be necessitated to leave others round about wide open. If we think to regulate printing, thereby to rectify manners, we must regulate all recreations and pastimes, all that is delightful to man. No music must be heard, no song be set or sung, but what is grave and Doric. There must be licensing dancers, that no gesture, motion, or deportment be taught our youth but what by their allowance shall be thought honest; for such Plato was provided of. It will ask more than the work of twenty licensers to examine all the lutes, the violins, and the guitars in every house; they must not be suffered to prattle as they do, but must be licensed what they may say. And who shall silence all the airs and madrigals that whisper softness in chambers? The windows also, and the balconies, must be thought on; there are shrewd books, with dangerous frontispieces, set to sale: who shall prohibit them, shall twenty licensers? The villages also must have their visitors to inquire what lectures the bagpipe and the rebec reads, even to the balladry and the gamut of every municipal fiddler, for these are the countryman's *Arcadias,* and his Monte Mayors.

Next, what more national corruption, for which England hears ill abroad, than household gluttony? Who shall be the rectors of our daily rioting? And what shall be done to inhibit the multitudes that frequent those houses where drunkenness is sold and

harbored? Our garments also should be referred to the licensing
of some more sober workmasters to see them cut into a less
wanton garb. Who shall regulate all the mixed conversation of
our youth, male and female together, as is the fashion of this
country? Who shall still appoint what shall be discoursed, what
presumed, and no further? Lastly, who shall forbid and separate
all idle resort, all evil company? These things will be, and must
be; but how they shall be least hurtful, how least enticing,
herein consists the grave and governing wisdom of a state.

To sequester out of the world into Atlantic and Utopian poli-
ties, which never can be drawn into use, will not mend our
condition; but to ordain wisely as in this world of evil, in the
midst whereof God hath placed us unavoidably. Nor is it Plato's
licensing of books will do this, which necessarily pulls along with
it so many other kinds of licensing as will make us all both
ridiculous and weary, and yet frustrate; but those unwritten, or
at least unconstraining, laws of virtuous education, religious and
civil nurture, which Plato there mentions as the bonds and liga-
ments of the commonwealth, the pillars and the sustainers of
every written statute; these they be which will bear chief sway
in such matters as these, when all licensing will be easily eluded.
Impunity and remissness, for certain, are the bane of a commonwealth; but here the great art lies, to discern in what the law
is to bid restraint and punishment, and in what things persuasion only is to work. If every action which is good or evil in
man at ripe years were to be under pittance and prescription
and compulsion, what were virtue but a name, what praise could
be then due to well-doing, what gramercy to be sober, just, or
continent?

Many there be that complain of divine providence for suffering
Adam to transgress; foolish tongues! When God gave him reason,
he gave him freedom to choose, for reason is but choosing; he
had been else a mere artificial Adam, such an Adam as he is in
the motions. We ourselves esteem not of that obedience, or love,
or gift, which is of force: God therefore left him free, set before
him a provoking object ever almost in his eyes; herein consisted
his merit, herein the right of his reward, the praise of his ab-
stinence. Wherefore did he create passions within us, pleasures
round about us, but that these rightly tempered are the very
ingredients of virtue? They are not skillful considerers of human
things who imagine to remove sin by removing the matter of

sin; for, besides that it is a huge heap increasing under the very act of diminishing, though some part of it may for a time be withdrawn from some persons, it cannot from all, in such a universal thing as books are; and when this is done, yet the sin remains entire. Though ye take from a covetous man all his treasure, he has yet one jewel left, ye cannot bereave him of his covetousness. Banish all objects of lust, shut up all youth into the severest discipline that can be exercised in any hermitage, ye cannot make them chaste, that came not thither so: such great care and wisdom is required to the right managing of this point.

Suppose we could expel sin by this means; look how much we thus expel of sin, so much we expel of virtue: for the matter of them both is the same; remove that, and ye remove them both alike. This justifies the high providence of God, who, though he command us temperance, justice, continence, yet pours out before us even to a profuseness all desirable things, and gives us minds that can wander beyond all limit and satiety. Why should we then affect a rigor contrary to the manner of God and of nature, by abridging or scanting those means, which books freely permitted are, both to the trial of virtue and the exercise of truth? It would be better done to learn that the law must needs be frivolous which goes to restrain things uncertainly and yet equally working to good and to evil. And were I the chooser, a dram of well-doing should be preferred before many times as much the forcible hindrance of evil-doing. For God sure esteems the growth and completing of one virtuous person more than the restraint of ten vicious.

And albeit whatever thing we hear or see, sitting, walking, travelling, or conversing, may be fitly called our book, and is of the same effect that writings are, yet grant the thing to be prohibited were only books, it appears that this Order hitherto is far insufficient to the end which it intends. Do we not see, not once or oftener but weekly, that continued court-libel against the Parliament and City, printed, as the wet sheets can witness, and dispersed among us, for all that licensing can do? Yet this is the prime service, a man would think, wherein this Order should give proof of itself. If it were executed, you'll say. But certain, if execution be remiss or blindfold now, and in this particular, what will it be hereafter and in other books?

If then the Order shall not be vain and frustrate, behold a new labor, Lords and Commons: ye must repeal and proscribe all scandalous and unlicensed books already printed and divulged; after ye have drawn them up into a list, that all may know which are condemned, and which not; and ordain that no foreign books be delivered out of custody till they have been read over. This office will require the whole time of not a few overseers, and those no vulgar men. There be also books which are partly useful and excellent, partly culpable and pernicious; this work will ask as many more officials, to make expurgations and expunctions, that the commonwealth of learning be not damnified. In fine, when the multitude of books increase upon their hands, ye must be fain to catalogue all those printers who are found frequently offending, and forbid the importation of their whole suspected typography. In a word, that this your Order may be exact and not deficient, ye must reform it perfectly according to the model of Trent and Seville, which I know ye abhor to do.

Yet though ye should condescend to this, which God forbid, the Order still would be but fruitless and defective to that end whereto ye meant it. If to prevent sects and schisms, who is so unread or so uncatechized in story that hath not heard of many sects refusing books as a hindrance, and preserving their doctrine unmixed for many ages, only by unwritten traditions? The Christian faith, for that was once a schism, is not unknown to have spread all over Asia, ere any Gospel or Epistle was seen in writing. If the amendment of manners be aimed at, look into Italy and Spain, whether those places be one scruple the better, the honester, the wiser, the chaster, since all the inquisitional rigor that hath been executed upon books.

Another reason, whereby to make it plain that this Order will miss the end it seeks, consider by the quality which ought to be in every licenser. It cannot be denied but that he who is made judge to sit upon the birth or death of books, whether they may be wafted into this world or not, had need to be a man above the common measure, both studious, learned, and judicious; there may be else no mean mistakes in the censure of what is passable or not; which is also no mean injury. If he be of such worth as behooves him, there cannot be a more tedious and unpleasing journey-work, a greater loss of time levied upon his head, than to be made the perpetual reader of unchosen books and pamphlets, ofttimes huge volumes. There is no book that is acceptable unless at certain seasons; but to be enjoined the reading of that at all times, and in a hand scarce legible, whereof three pages would not down at any time in the fairest print, is an imposition which I cannot believe how he that values time and his own studies, or is but of a sensible nostril, should be able to endure.

In this one thing I crave leave of the present licensers to be pardoned for so thinking: who doubtless took this office up, looking on it through their obedience to the Parliament, whose command perhaps made all things seem easy and unlaborious to them; but that this short trial hath wearied them out already, their own expressions and excuses to them who make so many journeys to solicit their license are testimony enough. Seeing therefore those who now possess the employment by all evident signs wish themselves well rid of it, and that no man of worth, none that is not a plain unthrift of his own hours, is ever likely to succeed them, except he mean to put himself to the salary of a press corrector, we may easily foresee what kind of licensers we are to expect hereafter, either ignorant, imperious, and remiss, or basely pecuniary. This is what I had to show, wherein this Order cannot conduce to that end whereof it bears the intention.

I lastly proceed from the no good it can do, to the manifest hurt it causes, in being first the greatest discouragement and affront that can be offered to learning and to learned men.

•   •   •

Truth indeed came once into the world with her divine Master, and was a perfect shape most glorious to look on: but when he ascended, and his Apostles after him were laid asleep, then straight arose a wicked race of deceivers, who, as that story goes of the Egyptian Typhon with his conspirators, how they dealt with the good Osiris, took the virgin Truth, hewed her lovely form into a thousand pieces, and scattered them to the four winds. From that time ever since, the sad friends of Truth, such as durst appear, imitating the careful search that Isis made for the mangled body of Osiris, went up and down gathering up limb by limb still as they could find them. We have not yet found them all, Lords and Commons, nor ever shall do, till her Master's second coming; he shall bring together every joint and member, and shall mold them into an immortal feature of loveliness and perfection. Suffer not these licensing prohibitions to stand at every place of opportunity forbidding and disturbing them that continue seeking, that continue to do our obsequies to the torn body of our martyred saint.

We boast our light; but if we look not wisely on the sun itself, it smites us into darkness. Who can discern those planets that are oft combust, and those stars of brightest magnitude that rise and set with the sun, until the opposite motion of their orbs bring them to such a place in the firmament, where they may be seen evening or morning? The light which we have gained was given us, not to be ever staring on, but by it to discover onward things more remote from our knowledge. It is not the unfrocking of a priest, the unmitering of a bishop, and the removing him from off the Presbyterian shoulders, that will make us a happy nation; no, if other things as great in the Church, and in the rule of life both economical and political, be not looked into and reformed, we have looked so long upon the blaze that Zwingli and Calvin hath beaconed up to us that we are stark blind.

There be who perpetually complain of schisms and sects, and make it such a calamity that any man dissents from their maxims. 'Tis their own pride and ignorance which causes the disturbing, who neither will hear with meekness, nor can convince, yet all must be suppressed which is not found in their *syntagma*. They are the troublers, they are the dividers of unity, who neglect and permit not others to unite those dissevered pieces which are yet wanting to the body of Truth. To be still searching what we know not by what we know, still closing up truth to truth as we find it (for all her body is homogeneal and proportional), this is the golden rule in theology as well as in arithmetic, and makes up the best harmony in a church; not the forced and outward union of cold and neutral and inwardly divided minds.

Lords and Commons of England, consider what nation it is whereof ye are, and whereof ye are the governors: a nation not slow and dull, but of a quick, ingenious, and piercing spirit, acute to invent, subtle and sinewy to discourse, not beneath the reach of any point the highest that human capacity can soar to. Therefore the studies of learning in her deepest sciences have been so ancient and so eminent among us that writers of good antiquity and ablest judgment have been persuaded that even the school of Pythagoras and the Persian wisdom took beginning from the old philosophy of this island. And that wise and civil Roman, Julius Agricola, who governed once here for Caesar, preferred the natural wits of Britain before the labored studies of the French. Nor is it for nothing that the grave and frugal Transylvanian

sends out yearly from as far as the mountainous borders of
Russia, and beyond the Hercynian wilderness, not their youth,
but their staid men, to learn our language and our theologic
arts.

Yet that which is above all this, the favor and the love of
heaven, we have great argument to think in a peculiar manner
propitious and propending towards us. Why else was this nation
chosen before any other, that out of her, as out of Sion, should
be proclaimed and sounded forth the first tidings and trumpet
of Reformation to all Europe? And had it not been the obstinate
perverseness of our prelates against the divine and admirable
spirit of Wyclif, to suppress him as a schismatic and innovator,
perhaps neither the Bohemian Huss and Jerome, no, nor the
name of Luther or of Calvin, had been ever known: the glory
of reforming all our neighbors had been completely ours. But
now, as our obdurate clergy have with violence demeaned the
matter, we are become hitherto the latest and the backwardest
scholars, of whom God offered to have made us the teachers.

Now once again by all concurrence of signs, and by the
general instinct of holy and devout men, as they daily and
solemnly express their thoughts, God is decreeing to begin some
new and great period in his Church, even to the reforming of
Reformation itself: what does he then but reveal himself to his
servants, and as his manner is, first to his Englishmen? I say, as
his manner is, first to us, though we mark not the method of his
counsels, and are unworthy. Behold now this vast city: a city
of refuge, the mansion house of liberty, encompassed and surrounded with his protection; the shop of war hath not there
more anvils and hammers waking, to fashion out the plates and
instruments of armed Justice in defense of beleaguered Truth,
than there be pens and heads there, sitting by their studious
lamps, musing, searching, revolving new notions and ideas
wherewith to present, as with their homage and their fealty
the approaching Reformation: others as fast reading, trying all
things, assenting to the force of reason and convincement.

What could a man require more from a nation so pliant and
so prone to seek after knowledge? What wants there to such
a towardly and pregnant soil, but wise and faithful laborers,
to make a knowing people, a nation of prophets, of sages, and
of worthies? We reckon more than five months yet to harvest;
there need not be five weeks, had we but eyes to lift up; the

fields are white already. Where there is much desire to learn, there of necessity will be much arguing, much writing, many opinions; for opinion in good men is but knowledge in the making. Under these fantastic terrors of sect and schism, we wrong the earnest and zealous thirst after knowledge and understanding which God hath stirred up in this city. What some lament of, we rather should rejoice at, should rather praise this pious forwardness among men, to reassume the ill-deputed care of their religion into their own hands again. A little generous prudence, a little forbearance of one another, and some grain of charity might win all these diligences to join and unite in one general and brotherly search after truth; could we but forego this prelatical tradition of crowding free consciences and Christian liberties into canons and precepts of men. I doubt not, if some great and worthy stranger should come among us, wise to discern the mold and temper of a people, and how to govern it, observing the high hopes and aims, the diligent alacrity of our extended thoughts and reasonings in the pursuance of truth and freedom, but that he would cry out as Pyrrhus did, admiring the Roman docility and courage, "If such were my Epirots, I would not despair the greatest design that could be attempted to make a church or kingdom happy."

Yet these are the men cried out against for schismatics and sectaries; as if, while the temple of the Lord was building, some cutting, some squaring the marble, others hewing the cedars, there should be a sort of irrational men who could not consider there must be many schisms and many dissections made in the quarry and in the timber, ere the house of God can be built. And when every stone is laid artfully together, it cannot be united into a continuity, it can but be contiguous in this world; neither can every piece of the building be of one form; nay rather the perfection consists in this, that out of many moderate varieties and brotherly dissimilitudes that are not vastly disproportional, arises the goodly and the graceful symmetry that commends the whole pile and structure.

Let us therefore be more considerate builders, more wise in spiritual architecture, when great reformation is expected. For now the time seems come, wherein Moses the great prophet may sit in heaven rejoicing to see that memorable and glorious wish of his fulfilled, when not only our seventy elders, but all the Lord's people, are become prophets. No marvel then though some men, and some good men too perhaps, but young in goodness, as Joshua then was, envy them. They fret, and out of their own weakness are in agony, lest these divisions and subdivisions will undo us. The adversary again applauds, and waits the hour. When they have branched themselves out, saith he, small enough into parties and partitions, then will be our time. Fool! he sees not the firm root, out of which we all grow, though into branches; nor will beware until he see our small divided maniples cutting through at every angle of his ill-united and unwieldly brigade. And that we are to hope better of all these supposed sects and schisms, and that we shall not need that solicitude, honest perhaps, though over-timorous, of them that vex in this behalf, but shall laugh in the end at those malicious applauders of our differences, I have these reasons to persuade me.

First, when a city shall be as it were besieged and blocked about, her navigable river infested, inroads and incursions round, defiance and battle oft rumored to be marching up even to her walls and suburb trenches; that then the people, or the greater part, more than at other times, wholly taken up with the study of highest and most important matters to be reformed, should be disputing, reasoning, reading, inventing, discoursing, even to a rarity and admiration, things not before discoursed or written of, argues first a singular goodwill, contentedness, and confidence in your prudent foresight and safe government, Lords and Commons; and from thence derives itself to a gallant bravery and well-grounded contempt of their enemies, as if there were no small number of as great spirits among us, as his was who, when Rome was nigh besieged by Hannibal, being in the city, bought that piece of ground at no cheap rate whereon Hannibal himself encamped his own regiment.

Next, it is a lively and cheerful presage of our happy success and victory. For as in a body, when the blood is fresh, the spirits pure and vigorous, not only to vital but to rational faculties, and those in the acutest and the pertest operations of wit and sub-tlety, it argues in what good plight and constitution the body is; so when the cheerfulness of the people is so sprightly up, as that it has not only wherewith to guard well its own freedom and safety, but to spare, and to bestow upon the solidest and sublimest points of controversy and new invention, it betokens us not degenerated, nor drooping to a fatal decay, but casting off the old and wrinkled skin of corruption to outlive these pangs and wax young again, entering the glorious ways of truth and prosperous virtue, destined to become great and honorable in these latter ages.

Methinks I see in my mind a noble and puissant nation rousing herself like a strong man after sleep, and shaking her invincible locks: methinks I see her as an eagle mewing her mighty youth, and kindling her undazzled eyes at the full midday beam; purging and unscaling her long-abused sight at the fountain itself of heavenly radiance; while the whole noise of timorous and flocking birds, with those also that love the twilight, flutter about, amazed at what she means, and in their envious gabble would prognosticate a year of sects and schisms.

What should ye do then, should ye suppress all this flowery crop of knowledge and new light sprung up and yet springing daily in this city? Should ye set an oligarchy of twenty engrossers over it, to bring a famine upon our minds again, when we shall know nothing but what is measured to us by their bushel? Believe it, Lords and Commons, they who counsel ye to such a suppressing do as good as bid ye suppress yourselves; and I will soon show how. If it be desired to know the immediate cause of all this free writing and free speaking, there cannot be assigned a truer than your own mild and free and humane government; it is the liberty, Lords and Commons, which your own valorous and happy counsels have purchased us, liberty which is the nurse of all great wits: this is that which hath rarefied and enlightened our spirits like the influence of heaven: this is that which hath enfranchised, enlarged, and lifted up our apprehensions degrees above themselves. Ye cannot make us now less capable, less knowing, less eagerly pursuing of the truth, unless ye first make yourselves, that made us so, less the lovers, less the founders of our true liberty. We can grow ignorant again, brutish, formal, and slavish, as ye found us; but you then must first become that which ye cannot be, oppressive, arbitrary, and tyrannous, as they were from whom ye have freed us. That our hearts are now more capacious, our thoughts more erected to the search and expectation of greatest and exactest things, is the issue of your own virtue propagated in us; ye cannot suppress that unless ye reinforce an abrogated and merciless law, that fathers may dispatch at will their own children. And who shall then stick closest to ye and excite others? not he who takes up arms for coat and conduct, and his four nobles of Danegelt. Although I dispraise not the defense of just immunities, yet love my peace better, if that were all. Give me the liberty to know, to utter, and to argue freely according to conscience, above all liberties.

What would be best advised then, if it be found so hurtful and so unequal to suppress opinions for the newness or the unsuitableness to a customary acceptance, will not be my task to say. I only shall repeat what I have learnt from one of your own honorable number, a right noble and pious lord, who, had he not sacrificed his life and fortunes to the Church and Commonwealth, we had not now missed and bewailed a worthy and undoubted patron of this argument. Ye know him, I am sure; yet I for honor's sake, and may it be eternal to him, shall name him, the Lord Brook. He, writing of episcopacy, and by the way treating of sects and schisms, left ye his vote, or rather now the last words of his dying charge, which I know will ever be of dear and honored regard with ye, so full of meekness and breathing charity that next to His last testament, who bequeathed love and peace to His disciples, I cannot call to mind where I have read or heard words more mild and peaceful. He there exhorts us to hear with patience and humility those, however they be miscalled, that desire to live purely, in such a use of God's ordinances as the best guidance of their conscience gives them, and to tolerate them, though in some disconformity to ourselves. The book itself will tell us more at large, being published to the world, and dedicated to the Parliament by him who, both for his life and for his death, deserves that what advice he left be not laid by without perusal.

And now the time in special is, by privilege, to write and speak what may help to the further discussing of matters in agitation. The temple of Janus, with his two controversial faces, might now not unsignificantly be set open. And though all the winds of doctrine were let loose to play upon the earth, so Truth be in the field, we do injuriously by licensing and prohibiting to misdoubt her strength. Let her and Falsehood grapple; who ever knew Truth put to the worse, in a free and open encounter? Her confuting is the best and surest suppressing. He who hears what praying there is for light and clearer knowledge to be sent down among us, would think of other matters to be constituted beyond the discipline of Geneva, framed and fabricked already to our hands.

Yet when the new light which we beg for shines in upon us, there be who envy and oppose, if it come not first in at their casements. What a collusion is this, whenas we are exhorted by the wise man to use diligence, "to seek for wisdom as for hidden treasures" early and late, that another order shall enjoin us to know nothing but by statute. When a man hath been laboring the hardest labor in the deep mines of knowledge, hath furnished out his findings in all their equipage, drawn forth his reasons as it were a battle ranged, scattered and defeated all objections in his way, calls out his adversary into the plain, offers him the advantage of wind and sun, if he please, only that he may try the matter by dint of argument; for his opponents then to skulk, to lay ambushments, to keep a narrow bridge of licensing where the challenger should pass, though it be valor enough in soldiership, is but weakness and cowardice in the wars of Truth. For who knows not that Truth is strong, next to the Almighty. She needs no policies, nor stratagems, nor licensings to make her victorious; those are the shifts and the defenses that error uses against her power. Give her but room, and do not bind her when she sleeps, for then she speaks not true, as the old Proteus did, who spake oracles only when he was caught and bound, but then rather she turns herself into all shapes except her own, and perhaps tunes her voice according to the time, as Micaiah did before Ahab, until she be adjured into her own likeness.

Yet is it not impossible that she may have more shapes than one. What else is all that rank of things indifferent, wherein Truth may be on this side or on the other, without being unlike herself? What but a vain shadow else is the abolition of "those ordinances, that handwriting nailed to the cross"; what great purchase is this Christian liberty which Paul so often boasts of? His doctrine is, that he who eats or eats not, regards a day or regards it not, may do either to the Lord. How many other things might be tolerated in peace, and left to conscience, had we but charity, and were it not the chief stronghold of our hypocrisy to be ever judging one another. I fear yet this iron yoke of outward conformity hath left a slavish print upon our necks; the ghost of a linen decency yet haunts us. We stumble and are impatient at the least dividing of one visible congregation from another, though it be not in fundamentals; and through our forwardness to suppress, and our backwardness to recover any enthralled piece of truth out of the gripe of custom, we care not to keep truth separated from truth, which is the fiercest rent and disunion of all. We do not see that while we still affect by all means a rigid external formality, we may as soon fall again into a gross conforming stupidity, a stark and dead congealment of "wood and hay and stubble" forced and frozen together, which is more to the sudden degenerating of a church than many subdichotomies of petty schisms.

Not that I can think well of every light separation, or that all in a church is to be expected "gold and silver and precious stones:" it is not possible for man to sever the wheat from the tares, the good fish from the other fry; that must be the angels' ministry at the end of mortal things. Yet if all cannot be of one mind—as who looks they should be?—this doubtless is more wholesome, more prudent, and more Christian, that many be tolerated rather than all compelled. I mean not tolerated popery, and open superstition, which, as it extirpates all religions and civil supremacies, so itself should be extirpate, provided first that all charitable and compassionate means be used to win and regain the weak and the misled: that also which is impious or evil absolutely, either against faith or manners, no law can possibly permit, that intends not to unlaw itself: but those neighboring differences, or rather indifferences, are what I speak of, whether in some point of doctrine or of discipline, which though they may be many, yet need not interrupt "the unity of Spirit," if we could but find among us "the bond of peace."

In the meanwhile, if any one would write, and bring his helpful hand to the slow-moving Reformation which we labor under, if Truth have spoken to him before others, or but seemed at least to speak, who hath so bejesuited us that we should trouble that man with asking license to do so worthy a deed? and not consider this, that if it come to prohibiting, there is not aught more likely to be prohibited than Truth itself; whose first appearance to our eyes bleared and dimmed with prejudice and custom, is more unsightly and unplausible than many errors, even as the person is of many a great man slight and contemptible to see to. And what do they tell us vainly of new opinions, when this very opinion of theirs, that none must be heard but whom they like, is the worst and newest opinion of all others; and is the chief cause why sects and schisms do so much abound, and true knowledge is kept at distance from us; besides yet a greater danger which is in it. For when God shakes a kingdom with strong and healthful commotions to a general reforming, 'tis not untrue that many sectaries and false teachers are then busiest in seducing; but yet more true it is that God then raises to his own work men of rare abilities, and more than common industry, not only to look back and revise what hath been taught heretofore, but to gain further and to go on some new enlightened steps in the discovery of truth.

For such is the order of God's enlightening his Church, to dispense and deal out by degrees his beam, so as our earthly eyes may best sustain it. Neither is God appointed and confined, where and out of what place these his chosen shall be first heard to speak; for he sees not as man sees, chooses not as man chooses, lest we should devote ourselves again to set places and assemblies and outward callings of men; planting our faith one while in the old Convocation house, and another while in the Chapel at Westminster; when all the faith and religion that shall be there canonized, is not sufficient without plain convincement and the charity of patient instruction, to supple the least bruise of conscience, to edify the meanest Christian who desires to walk in the Spirit and not in the letter of human trust, for all the number of voices that can be there made; no, though Harry VII himself there, with all his liege tombs about him, should lend them voices from the dead to swell their number.

And if the men be erroneous who appear to be the leading schismatics, what withholds us but our sloth, our self-will, and distrust in the right cause, that we do not give them gentle meeting and gentle dismissions, that we debate not and examine the matter thoroughly with liberal and frequent audience; if not for their sakes, yet for our own? seeing no man who hath tasted learning but will confess the many ways of profiting by those who, not contented with stale receipts, are able to manage and set forth new positions to the world. And were they but as the dust and cinders of our feet, so long as in that notion they may yet serve to polish and brighten the armory of Truth, even for that respect they were not utterly to be cast away. But if they be of those whom God hath fitted for the special use of these times with eminent and ample gifts, and those perhaps neither among the priests nor among the pharisees, and we in the haste of a precipitant zeal shall make no distinction, but resolve to stop their mouths, because we fear they come with new and dangerous opinions, as we commonly forejudge them ere we understand them, no less than woe to us while, thinking thus to defend the Gospel, we are found the persecutors.

There have been not a few since the beginning of this Parliament, both of the Presbytery and others, who by their unlicensed books to the contempt of an Imprimatur first broke that triple ice clung about our hearts, and taught the people to see day: I hope that none of those were the persuaders to renew upon us this bondage which they themselves have wrought so much good by contemning. But if neither the check that Moses gave to young Joshua, nor the countermand which our Saviour gave to young John, who was so ready to prohibit those whom he thought unlicensed, be not enough to admonish our elders how unacceptable to God their testy mood of prohibiting is; if neither their own remembrance what evil hath abounded in the Church by this let of licensing, and what good they themselves have begun by transgressing it, be not enough, but that they will persuade and execute the most Dominican part of the Inquisition over us, and are already with one foot in the stirrup so active at suppressing, it would be no unequal distribution in the first place to suppress the suppressors themselves: whom the change of their condition hath puffed up, more than their late experience of harder times hath made wise.

And as for regulating the press, let no man think to have the honor of advising ye better than yourselves have done in that Order published next before this, "that no book be printed, unless the printer's and the author's name, or at least the printer's, be registered." Those which otherwise come forth, if they be found mischievous and libelous, the fire and the executioner will be the timeliest and the most effectual remedy that man's prevention can use. For this authentic Spanish policy of licensing books, if I have said aught, will prove the most unlicensed book itself within a short while; and was the immediate image of a Star Chamber decree to that purpose made in those very times when that Court did the rest of those her pious works, for which she is now fallen from the stars with Lucifer. Whereby ye may guess what kind of state prudence, what love of the people, what care of religion or good manners there was at the contriving, although with singular hypocrisy it pretended to bind books to their good behavior. And how it got the upper hand of your precedent Order so well constituted before, if we may believe those men whose profession gives them cause to inquire most, it may be doubted there was in it the fraud of some old patentees and monopolizers in the trade of bookselling; who, under pretense of the poor in their Company not to be defrauded, and the just retaining of each man his several copy, which God forbid should be gainsaid, brought divers glosing colors to the House, which were indeed but colors, and serving to no end except it be to exercise a superiority over their neighbors; men who do not therefore labor in an honest profession to which learning is indebted, that they should be made other men's vassals. Another end is thought was aimed at by some of them in procuring by petition this Order, that, having power in their hands, malignant books might the easier scape abroad, as the event shows.

But of these sophisms and elenchs of merchandise I skill not. This I know, that errors in a good government and in a bad are equally almost incident; for what magistrate may not be misinformed, and much the sooner, if liberty of printing be reduced into the power of a few? But to redress willingly and speedily what hath been erred, and in highest authority to esteem a plain advertisement more than others have done a sumptuous bribe, is a virtue (honored Lords and Commons) answerable to your highest actions, and whereof none can participate but greatest and wisest men.

QUESTIONS FOR STUDY
AND TOPICS FOR DISCUSSION
ON *Areopagitica*

1. The *Areopagitica* was published in 1644 as Milton's plea "for the liberty of unlicensed printing." It originated as a polemical tract for the times, and while the range and depth of its treatment of the subject makes it an epic of prose argument which is "relatively inexhaustible to meditation," any attempt at a full understanding of its whole performance in words must begin with the occasion for its composition.

On June 14, 1643, the English Parliament passed an ordinance for the control of printing. The Licensing Order enjoined, among other things, the printing or sale of any book or pamphlet without the approval and license of an official appointed by either the Lords or Commons. Licensing was nothing new in English history. Control of the press had been zealously exercised by all the Tudors and both the early Stuarts. Charles' Star Chamber Decree of 1637 was only the most elaborate and complete instrument for the suppression of undesired publication. With the abolition of the Star Chamber by the Long Parliament in 1641, the press was left virtually without legal regulation. A rash of pamphlets against the government followed the lifting of the restrictions, and the new governors of England, anxious to check the "great abuses and the frequent disorders in printing," commenced to devise their own licensing system. The Licensing Order of 1643 was one of several steps in the formulation by the Long Parliament of a body of laws and policies for the regulation of all forms of printing. These acts were difficult to enforce, as Milton had foreseen. The *Areopagitica* was itself unlicensed, and indeed, it was the third pamphlet he had published since the passage of the Order. The attacks by Milton and others had little effect on the Long Parliament's policy; the Order of 1643 was supplanted but not softened by later acts.

It should be clear at the outset that Milton is not arguing in the *Areopagitica* for the abolition of all forms of control. He does not plead, as a nineteenth- or twentieth-century libertarian would, for complete freedom of speech. His immediate object is to persuade Parliament to rescind the Licensing Order. He believed that the ordinance endangered some basic principles of the Puritan Revolution, and he presses that issue in his argument, but he may have been provoked by other motives as well. Milton had been annoyed by the suspicious attitudes of the official censor when he applied for a license to publish his controversial tract on divorce. He may have been nettled at having to submit his work to judgment by inferior and uncomprehending minds. Something of this attitude is revealed in his remarks in his *Second Defense* (1654):

> I wrote, after the model of a regular speech, *Areopagitica,* on the liberty of printing, that the determination of true and false, of what ought to be published and what suppressed, might not be in the hands of the few who may be charged with the inspection of books, men commonly without learning and of vulgar judgment, and by whose license and pleasure, no one is suffered to publish any thing which may be above vulgar apprehension.

But whatever all the reasons for undertaking the work may have been, Milton engages the topic of licensing in the *Areopagitica* as a matter of broad and urgent principle touching not only his person but the whole of the commonwealth.

What restraints upon the freedom of the press does Milton acknowledge? What forms of control does he admit? How are books that offend to be punished? What are Milton's assumptions about liberty and how do they differ from your own? What does Milton think of licensers? What qualifications does he require of them? Why are they unlikely to be fit to judge books? By what means does Milton make licensing appear to be un-English in tradition and substance? According to Milton's history, who instituted licensing, and for what reasons? How sound is his history? What does he omit or tone down? What does Milton say or imply are the ways in which the Licensing Order threatens the ideals of the Puritan reformers? What senses of the word "license" does Milton play upon in his argument? Consider this paraphrase of his case: Unlicensed printing makes possible the purging of licentious behavior; licensed printing encourages it to flourish. Are these propositions apt for understanding Milton's purpose? How do they inform and order the essay?

2. The title means "things to be said before the Areopagus." The work is written as if it were an oration before the Areopagus, or Great Council, of ancient Athens. Isocrates, a famous teacher of rhetoric, wrote in 355 B.C. an oration called the *Areopagiticus;* as with all of his speeches, this was meant to be read rather than delivered aloud. Like Isocrates, Milton presents himself as a citizen pleading for a change in public policy, and he addresses his arguments in the form of a "speech" to be read, not spoken. Milton's title implies a comparison between the Areopagus and the English Parliament, but if that is his intent, the parallel is curious, for in the fourth century the Areopagus had declined in status and power, being then principally a court for the trial of homicide.

Whatever the motive for the comparison, the image of a speech addressed to some great court or forum is essential to the form of the work. The *Areopagitica* is conceived dramatically; it is a *play* of ideas. Milton intends a stage for his great argument and a theater of contending temperaments, interests, and opinions. He is addressing a specific audience, the High Court of Parliament, at a critical juncture in English history, and he speaks as an advocate for the cause of the revolution and the destiny of the nation. If we take the dramatic situation of the piece as a governing fiction rather than a mere learned allusion, the work pulses with all the excitement and feeling that attends a forensic contest on a question of great moment.

The speaker, Milton himself, is no ordinary citizen. He has friends and enemies among the assembly. He is familiar to the judges he must persuade. He is no anonymous scrivener who must bow and scrape before their eminences, for he has been close to the springs of power. As a pamphleteer, he has served cause and party zealously—and he has exhibited a formidable way with words. He has proved to be scurrilous in debate. He is capable of savage invective, and he knows all the tricks of persuasion by which to carry a case. Moreover, certain members of the assembly are wary of his opinions. He has been loyal, but he has shown an independent and stubborn streak; he may end in disaffection or even apostasy. A man like this is capable of anything. They will watch his conduct closely. They are on guard.

On his side, Milton knows that he has his work cut out. He must prove that the men to whom he pleads his case are in danger of reverting to a Romish theory and practice. Harder yet, he must get them to acknowledge error by repealing their policy. He knows, then, that his audience will be a hard one. He cannot count on any sentimentalists among them. They are tough-minded realists, hardened by terrible battles of arms and words, and fortified by a sense of righteousness in their cause and actions. They are not likely to be won over by the artful graces of a Sidney, or the wit and wiles of a Bacon, or the lofty conceits of a Donne; they want plain speaking. And yet Milton must be subtle. He cannot risk offending by playing on them the tricks he has used against their common enemies.

What picture of himself does Milton draw in the *Areopagitica*? What references does he make to his past performances as a polemicist? What is the image of Parliament? Where does Milton address Parliament and where some larger audience? What is the effect of the sense of audience on the form and content of the work? By what means does Milton achieve, in the words of Douglas Bush, the "effect of a living voice"? With what dispositions does Milton come before Parliament? What connections does he establish between his private condition and the public good? What is the relevance of the epigraph? Why does he say that he will deliver a "homily"? What range of dispositions does he employ in his argument? How does this variety affect the intention and sense of the whole? Put yourself in the "theater" as one of several characters suggested by the dramatic situation— i.e., a person familiar with Milton's reputation and friendly, a person suspicious of his motives and manner, a person indifferent to licensing but very jealous of Parliament's dignity, etc. How would you receive and judge his case in each of these roles?

3. Like *An Apology for Poetry*, the *Areopagitica* observes the formal divisions of a classical oration. The following outline observes the analysis made by Ernest Sirluck in his recent edition of the *Areopagitica* (*Complete Prose Works of John Milton*, Vol. II, Yale University Press, 1959). The exordium comprises the first six paragraphs. The proposition runs from "If ye be thus resolved . . ." to ". . . slays an immortality rather than a life"

(pp. 125–126), and includes a fourfold partition. The confirmation takes up the four issues of the proposition: 1) begins "But lest I should be condemned . . ." (p. 126); 2), "But I have first to finish . . . " (p. 131); 3), "which is what I promised to deliver next . . . " (p. 137); 4), "I lastly proceed . . ." (p. 142). The peroration follows, commencing "What would be best advised then . . ." (p. 148), and runs to the end of the speech. The narration comprises several particular narratives rather than a single comprehensive one; e.g., "In Athens, where books . . . clear ye readily" (pp. 126–131). The reprehension is similarly scattered throughout; e.g., p. 131, pp. 135–137, pp. 137–139, etc. There are two formal digressions: the first of these is to be found in the portion omitted here; the second is "Lords and Commons of England . . . above all liberties" (pp. 143–148).

While this kind of descriptive analysis is helpful for comprehending one structure in the *Areopagitica,* and while it establishes a pattern of expectations Milton could assume would be effective with his audience, it hardly suffices for a full understanding of his intention and strategy. Although Milton himself acknowledged his debt to the "model of a regular speech," he was enough of a master in language and argument to play with the convention rather than to imitate it slavishly. Consider, as instance, his treatment of the exordium. The purpose of the exordium is to secure a favorable atmosphere for the speech's reception, and one of the tricks by which this is achieved is to flatter the judges. But what is Milton's tone toward his judges? What conditions does he lay down "without which all praising is but courtship and flattery" (p. 123)? How does he cross what the judges expect according to the convention of the exordium? Doesn't he come rather close to being "new and insolent"? Why does he take the risk? What is his purpose?

Furthermore, what other modes of progression does he use besides the conventional mode inherent in the structure of the classical oration? Obviously, he uses a discursive mode. His arguments in the confirmation observe a logical sequence. These can be named by their familiar labels: The first is historical; the second is an argument from principle (though, as Sirluck shows, it seems on first glance to be an argument from authority); the third is a practical argument; and the fourth is an argument from consequences. What pattern of expectations does each of these arouse and fulfill?

Does Milton also use a qualitative mode of progression? Does his case move from one part to another by means of associated states of feeling? Do his images and figures form their own pattern of expectations?

Once these several structures have been located and described, the question becomes: In what ways do the modes of progression move together, confirm or reinforce one another, diverge or conflict? What is the effect of the interaction upon the workings of each separate mode? How do they affect the sense of the piece?

4. Analyze the sense and composition of the eighth paragraph (beginning "I deny not . . ." on p. 125). Milton obviously considers the passage important, for he interrupts the continuity of the case. Instead of moving directly to the arguments he has just listed, he pauses, first to concede that books must be guarded as closely as if they were men since they too are alive and potent, and then to affirm that caution must be exercised in persecuting books since the suppression may slay the quintessence of life, the breath of reason itself. Taken at face value, this seems to be a preposterous claim. Milton must know that it is hardly likely to convince or sway his tough-minded audience. What is he up to? What is the connection between this passage and the logical arguments he has proposed? Has he wandered from the point?

John Middleton Murry has said of the *Areopagitica*: "whenever I read it, the last thing I find myself thinking about, whether during the process or at the end, is the liberty of unlicensed printing. It might much rather be a poem on the immortality of the soul." At first glance, the *Areopagitica* may appear to be more affecting as a panegyric on human reason and the inquiring mind than as a brief against the licensing system. But what is the connection between the eighth paragraph and the later passages on the nature of human reason, such as those on p. 134 and p. 139? What do these reveal about the relationship between the immortality of the soul and the liberty of unlicensed printing? What religious doctrine underlies the two topics? How would Milton's appeal to this doctrine discomfit Parliament and turn the case to his advantage? Assume that the gravamen of his case is the charge that the framers of the Licensing Order have imperiled the real end of civil and religious government, which is to save man from his original state of impurity. How does this affect the tone and tenor of his argument in the eighth paragraph and the rest of the work? How does it affect Milton's relation to his audience? What, then, is the intention of the eighth paragraph? The intention of the whole work?

5. Consider the grammar and syntax of the opening sentence. What is its subject, verb, and complement? How is each member connected to the other? In shifting from "They" to "I," the sentence breaks consistent grammatical sequence. When such an inconsistency is deliberate it is called an *anacoluthon*. Why does Milton employ the device? Two explanations are possible: 1) since English grammar was relatively unformed in the seventeenth century, he followed the rules of classical syntax (*anacoluthon* being common in classical Greek prose); 2) he broke the regular syntax in order to get the effect of an actual spoken utterance. Without taking issue with these "motives," consider the effects of the construction on the sense of the passage. How does the sentence move? Where does the emphasis of its meaning fall? What impression does it make upon the reader?

Extend this kind of analysis to other sentences in the work. Milton's style is usually described as being "dense" and "crabbed," but these words are actually metaphors signifying a certain kind of syntax and a certain kind of figurative texture. A prose with many subordinate clauses, parenthetic qualifications, and suspended predications seems "crabbed," while a prose of simpler structure seems "crisp" or "flowing" or "prancing." What is the characteristic form of Milton's sentence structure? What is the typical order of subject, verb, and complement? What is the type and position of modifying elements? How are these joined together? What effects are created by the constructions? Why did Milton use the particular forms he did? What alternatives were possible? What variations from his "typical" sentence structure are used in the work? Why the variation?

Milton is commonly said to have favored the long *periodic sentence* characteristic of Latin prose. A *periodic sentence* is a complex sentence in which the main clause comes at the end. A *loose sentence* is one in which the main clause comes first, followed by dependent clauses and other modifying elements. The general effect of postponing or suspending the main clause in a periodic sentence is to cause the reader to consider first the various details upon which the main thought is based. Suspension is

easier in Latin than in English because, being more highly in-
flected, its noun and verb endings keep the structural relationships in a sentence clear and unimpeded. What devices in English compensate for the properties of Latin sentence structure?
Does the periodic sentence go against the grain of English? How
effective are Milton's "Latinate" sentences? Are all his sentences
periodic, or does he mix in some loose ones? Are all his sentences
long? Is Milton's syntax always intelligible? What accounts for
any lapse? Is Milton capable of writing plain and straightforward
prose? Where does he do so in the *Areopagitica*?

6. What are the presiding patterns of imagery in the *Areopagitica*? The idea of the state of man's impurity, in original sin,
is basic to the argument of both Milton's and Sidney's essays.
What are the differences in imagery between the two? If Sidney
treats the escape from infection in terms of flying above the
condition, how does Milton deal with the same doctrine?

In the passage where Milton says he prefers the true "wayfaring" Christian (p. 134), the printed text has "wayfaring," although several of Milton's presentation copies have the "y"
crossed out and an "r" written above. Sirluck argues on textual
and other extrinsic evidence that "warfaring" is what Milton
meant. Which of these seems more in keeping with the imagery
of the whole work?

Consider the composition and effect of the imagery of the passage beginning "Till then books were ever as freely admitted . . ." (p. 130). (The story of Juno is found in Ovid's *Meta-
morphoses*, IX, 281–323. Rhadamanthus was one of the judges of
Hades.) What is the relation of this imagery to Milton's larger
intention? What patterns of the whole are reflected here? Why
does Milton conclude the first argument of the confirmation with
this passage? What connections link it with the metaphors and
sense of the eighth paragraph?

Analyze the construction and purpose of the myth of Osiris
in the passage beginning "Truth indeed came once into the
world . . ." (p. 142). The source is Plutarch's *Moralia* (Loeb
Library, V, 9). What is the relation of the figures in this passage
to the design of the whole work? How does Milton's treatment of
this myth differ from Sidney's handling of the myth of Daedalus?

Does Milton draw all his images and figures from literary
sources? What other sources does he exploit? How much of his

imagery comes from the activities and scenery of everyday life? Does Milton rely more on allusions (classical, historical, Biblical) than on images and metaphors from ordinary experience?

7. What kinds of diction does Milton use, and to what effect? It is usually said that he combines colloquial and learned, homely and ornate words. The modern reader will find it hard to judge which are colloquial and which learned, but Milton is not so far from modern usage as one might think, and a careful reading will reveal the range of his diction, if not all of its subtleties. Consider, for example, the diction in the passage deriding Imprimaturs on p. 130, and consider as a contrast the language of the passage beginning "For if they fell upon one kind of strictness . . ." on p. 138, or that beginning "Behold now this vast city . . ." on p. 144, or that beginning "When a man hath been laboring . . ." on p. 149. Why does Milton move from one kind of diction to the other? What purpose governs his choice of language at any particular point?

8. How does Milton close the *Areopagitica*? Does he save any forceful thought or expression for the end, or does he soften his tone and lower his pitch? Is there any irony at the close? Compare the ending of Sidney's *Apology*.

A MODEST PROPOSAL

For Preventing the Children of Poor People in Ireland from Being a Burden to Their Parents or Country, and for Making Them Beneficial to the Public

BY *Jonathan Swift*

IT IS A MELANCHOLY object to those who walk through this great town or travel in the country, when they see the streets, the roads, and cabin doors crowded with beggars of the female sex, followed by three, four, or six children, all in rags and importuning every passenger for an alms. These mothers, instead of being able to work for their honest livelihood, are forced to employ all their time in strolling to beg sustenance for their helpless infants, who, as they grow up, either turn thieves for want of work, or leave their dear native country to fight for the Pretender in Spain, or sell themselves to the Barbadoes.

I think it is agreed by all parties that this prodigious number of children in the arms, or on the backs, or at the heels of their mothers, and frequently of their fathers, is in the present deplorable state of the kingdom a very great additional grievance; and therefore whoever could find out a fair, cheap, and easy method of making these children sound and useful members of the commonwealth would deserve so well of the public as to have his statue set up for a preserver of the nation.

But my intention is very far from being confined to provide only for the children of professed beggars; it is of a much greater extent, and shall take in the whole number of infants at a certain age who are born of parents in effect as little able to support them as those who demand our charity in the streets.

As to my own part, having turned my thoughts for many years upon this important subject, and maturely weighed the several schemes of other projectors, I have always found them grossly mistaken in their computation. It is true a child just dropped from its dam may be supported by her milk for a solar year with little other nourishment, at most not above the value of two shillings, which the mother may certainly get, or the value in scraps, by her lawful occupation of begging; and it is exactly at one year old that I propose to provide for them in such a manner as instead of being a charge upon their parents or the parish, or wanting food and raiment for the rest of their lives, they shall, on the contrary, contribute to the feeding and partly to the clothing of many thousands.

There is likewise another great advantage in my scheme, that it will prevent those voluntary abortions, and that horrid practice of women murdering their bastard children, alas! too frequent among us, sacrificing the poor innocent babes, I doubt, more to avoid the expense than the shame, which would move tears and pity in the most savage and inhuman breast.

The number of souls in this kingdom being usually reckoned one million and a half, of these I calculate there may be about two hundred thousand couples whose wives are breeders; from which number I subtract thirty thousand couples who are able to maintain their own children, although I apprehend there cannot be so many, under the present distress of the kingdom; but this being granted, there will remain an hundred and seventy thousand breeders. I again subtract fifty thousand for those women who miscarry, or whose children die by accident or disease within the year. There only remain an hundred and twenty thousand children of poor parents annually born. The question therefore is, how this number shall be reared and provided for, which, as I have already said, under the present situation of affairs is utterly impossible by all the methods hitherto proposed. For we can neither employ them in handicraft or agriculture; we neither build houses (I mean in the country) nor cultivate land: they can very seldom pick up a livelihood by stealing till they arrive at six years old, except where they are of towardly parts; although I confess they learn the rudiments much earlier, during which time they can, however, be properly looked upon only as probationers, as I have been informed by a principal gentleman in the county of Cavan, who protested to me that he never knew above one or two instances under the age of six, even in a part of the kingdom so renowned for the quickest proficiency in that art.

I am assured by our merchants that a boy or girl before twelve years old is no salable commodity; and even when they come to this age they will not yield above three pounds or three pounds and half-a-crown at most on the Exchange; which cannot turn to account either to the parents or the kingdom, the charge of nutriment and rags having been at least four times that value.

I shall now therefore humbly propose my own thoughts, which I hope will not be liable to the least objection.

I have been assured by a very knowing American of my acquaintance in London that a young healthy child well nursed is at a year old a most delicious, nourishing, and wholesome food, whether stewed, roasted, baked, or boiled; and I make no doubt that it will equally serve in a fricassee or a ragout.

I do therefore humbly offer it to public consideration that of the hundred and twenty thousand children already computed, twenty thousand may be reserved for breed, whereof only one-fourth part to be males, which is more than we allow to sheep, black cattle or swine; and my reason is that these children are seldom the fruits of marriage, a circumstance not much regarded by our savages; therefore one male will be sufficient to serve four females. That the remaining hundred thousand may at a year old be offered in sale to the persons of quality and fortune through the kingdom, always advising the mother to let them suck plentifully in the last month, so as to render them plump and fat for a good table. A child will make two dishes at an entertainment for friends; and when the family dines alone, the fore or hind quarter will make a reasonable dish, and seasoned with a little pepper or salt will be very good boiled on the fourth day, especially in winter.

I have reckoned upon a medium that a child just born will weigh twelve pounds, and in a solar year if tolerably nursed increaseth to twenty-eight pounds.

I grant this food will be somewhat dear, and therefore very proper for landlords, who, as they have already devoured most of the parents, seem to have the best title to the children.

Infants' flesh will be in season throughout the year, but more plentiful in March, and a little before and after; for we are told by a grave author, an eminent French physician, that fish being a prolific diet, there are more children born in Roman Catholic countries about nine months after Lent than at any other season; therefore reckoning a year after Lent, the markets will be more glutted than usual, because the number of popish infants is at least three to one in this kingdom; and therefore it will have one other collateral advantage, by lessening the number of Papists among us.

I have already computed the charge of nursing a beggar's child (in which list I reckon all cottagers, laborers, and four-fifths of the farmers) to be about two shillings per annum, rags included; and I believe no gentleman would repine to give ten shillings for the carcass of a good fat child, which, as I have said, will make four dishes of excellent nutritive meat, when he hath only some particular friend or his own family to dine with him. Thus the squire will learn to be a good landlord, and grow popular among his tenants; the mother will have eight shillings net profit, and be fit for work till she produces another child.

Those who are more thrifty (as I must confess the times require) may flay the carcass; the skin of which artificially dressed will make admirable gloves for ladies, and summer boots for fine gentlemen.

As to our city of Dublin, shambles may be appointed for this purpose in the most convenient parts of it, and butchers we may be assured will not be wanting; although I rather recommend buying the children alive, and dressing them hot from the knife, as we do roasting pigs.

A very worthy person, a true lover of his country, and whose virtues I highly esteem, was lately pleased, in discoursing on this matter, to offer a refinement upon my scheme. He said that many gentlemen of this kingdom, having of late destroyed their deer, he conceived that the want of venison might be well supplied by the bodies of young lads and maidens, not exceeding fourteen years of age nor under twelve, so great a number of both sexes in every country being now ready to starve for want of work and service: and these to be disposed of by their parents, if alive, or otherwise by their nearest relations. But with due deference to so excellent a friend and so deserving a patriot, I cannot be altogether in his sentiments. For as to the males, my American acquaintance assured me from frequent experience that their flesh was generally tough and lean, like that of our schoolboys, by continual exercise, and their taste disagreeable; and to fatten them would not answer the charge. Then as to the females, it would, I think, with humble submission, be a loss to the public, because they soon would become breeders themselves: and besides, it is not improbable that some scrupulous people might be apt to censure such a practice (although indeed very unjustly) as a little bordering upon cruelty; which, I confess, hath always been with me the strongest objection against any project, how well soever intended.

But in order to justify my friend, he confessed that this expedient was put into his head by the famous Psalmanazar, a native of the island Formosa, who came from thence to London above twenty years ago, and in conversation told my friend that in his country when any young person happened to be put to death, the executioner sold the carcass to persons of quality as a prime dainty, and that in his time the body of a plump girl of fifteen, who was crucified for an attempt to poison the emperor, was sold to his Imperial Majesty's prime minister of state, and other great mandarins of the court, in joints from the gibbet, at four hundred crowns. Neither indeed can I deny that if the same use were made of several plump young girls in this town, who, without one single groat to their fortunes, cannot stir abroad without a chair, and appear at the playhouse and assemblies in foreign fineries, which they never will pay for, the kingdom would not be the worse.

Some persons of a desponding spirit are in great concern about that vast number of poor people, who are aged, diseased, or maimed, and I have been desired to employ my thoughts what course may be taken to ease the nation of so grievous an encumbrance. But I am not in the least pain upon that matter, because it is very well known that they are every day dying and rotting, by cold and famine, and filth and vermin, as fast as can be reasonably expected. And as to the younger laborers, they are now in almost as hopeful a condition. They cannot get work, and consequently pine away for want of nourishment, to a degree that if at any time they are accidentally hired to common labor, they have not strength to perform it; and thus the country and themselves are happily delivered from the evils to come.

I have too long digressed, and therefore shall return to my subject. I think the advantages by the proposal which I have made are obvious and many, as well as of the highest importance.

For first, as I have already observed, it would greatly lessen the number of Papists, with whom we are yearly overrun, being the principal breeders of the nation as well as our most dangerous enemies; and who stay at home on purpose with a design to deliver the kingdom to the Pretender, hoping to take their advantage by the absence of so many good Protestants, who have chosen rather to leave their country than stay at home and pay tithes against their conscience to an Episcopal curate.

Secondly, the poorer tenants will have something valuable of their own, which by law may be made liable to distress, and help to pay their landlord's rent; their corn and cattle being already seized, and money a thing unknown.

Thirdly, whereas the maintenance of an hundred thousand children, from two years old and upwards, cannot be computed at less than ten shillings apiece per annum, the nation's stock will be thereby increased fifty thousand pounds per annum, besides the profit of a new dish introduced to the tables of all gentlemen of fortune in the kingdom who have any refinement in taste. And the money will circulate among ourselves, the goods being entirely of our own growth and manufacture.

Fourthly, the constant breeders, besides the gain of eight shillings sterling per annum by the sale of their children, will be rid of the charge of maintaining them after the first year.

Fifthly, this food would likewise bring great custom to taverns, where the vintners will certainly be so prudent as to procure the best receipts for dressing it to perfection, and consequently have their houses frequented by all the fine gentlemen, who justly value themselves upon their knowledge in good eating; and a skillful cook, who understands how to oblige his guests, will contrive to make it as expensive as they please.

Sixthly, this would be a great inducement to marriage, which all wise nations have either encouraged by rewards or enforced by laws and penalties. It would increase the care and tenderness of mothers toward their children, when they were sure of a settlement for life to the poor babes, provided in some sort by the public, to their annual profit instead of expense. We should see an honest emulation among the married women, which of them could bring the fattest child to the market. Men would become as fond of their wives during the time of their pregnancy as they are now of their mares in foal, their cows in calf, or sows when they are ready to farrow; nor offer to beat or kick them (as is too frequent a practice) for fear of miscarriage.

Many other advantages might be enumerated. For instance, the addition of some thousand carcasses in our exportation of barreled beef, the propagation of swine's flesh, and improvement in the art of making good bacon, so much wanted among us by the great destruction of pigs, too frequent at our tables, and are no way comparable in taste or magnificence to a well-grown, fat yearling child, which roasted whole will make a considerable figure at a lord mayor's feast, or any other public entertainment. But this and many others I omit, being studious of brevity.

Supposing that one thousand families in this city would be constant customers for infants' flesh, besides others who might have it at merry meetings, particularly weddings and christenings, I compute that Dublin would take off annually about twenty thousand carcasses, and the rest of the kingdom (where probably they will be sold somewhat cheaper) the remaining eighty thousand.

I can think of no one objection that will possibly be raised against this proposal, unless it should be urged that the number of people will be thereby much lessened in the kingdom. This I freely own, and it was indeed one principal design in offering it to the world. I desire the reader will observe that I calculate my remedy for this one individual kingdom of Ireland, and for no other that ever was, is, or, I think, ever can be upon earth. Therefore let no man talk to me of other expedients: of taxing our absentees at five shillings a pound; of using neither clothes nor household furniture except what is of our own growth and manufacture; of utterly rejecting the materials and instruments that promote foreign luxury; of curing the expensiveness of pride, vanity, idleness, and gaming in our women; of introducing a vein of parsimony, prudence, and temperance; of learning to love our country, in the want of which we differ even from Laplanders and the inhabitants of Topinamboo; of quitting our animosities and factions, nor act any longer like the Jews, who were murdering one another at the very moment their city was taken; of being a little cautious not to sell our country and consciences for nothing; of teaching landlords to have at least one degree of mercy toward their tenants; lastly, of putting a spirit of honesty, industry, and skill into our shopkeepers, who, if a resolution could now be taken to buy only our native goods, would immediately unite to cheat and exact upon us in the price, the measure, and the goodness, nor could ever yet be brought to make one fair proposal of just dealing, though often and earnestly invited to it.

Therefore I repeat, let no man talk to me of these and the like expedients, till he has at least some glimpse of hope that there will be ever some hearty and sincere attempt to put them in practice.

But as to myself, having been wearied out for many years with offering vain, idle, visionary thoughts, and at length utterly despairing of success, I fortunately fell upon this proposal, which, as it is wholly new, so it has something solid and real, of no expense and little trouble, full in our own power, and whereby we can incur no danger in disobliging England. For this kind of commodity will not bear exportation, the flesh being of too tender a consistence to admit a long continuance in salt, although perhaps I could name a country which would be glad to eat up our whole nation without it.

After all, I am not so violently bent upon my own opinion as to reject any offer proposed by wise men, which shall be found equally innocent, cheap, easy, and effectual. But before something of that kind shall be advanced in contradiction to my scheme, and offering a better, I desire the author or authors will be pleased maturely to consider two points. First, as things now stand, how they will be able to find food and raiment for an hundred thousand useless mouths and backs. And secondly, there being a round million of creatures in human figure throughout this kingdom, whose whole subsistence put into a common stock would leave them in debt two millions of pounds sterling, adding those who are beggars by profession to the bulk of farmers, cottagers, and laborers, with their wives and children, who are beggars in effect; I desire those politicians who dislike my overture, and may perhaps be so bold as to attempt an answer, that they will first ask the parents of these mortals whether they would not at this day think it a great happiness to have been sold for food at a year old in the manner I prescribe, and thereby have avoided such a perpetual scene of misfortunes as they have since gone through by the oppression of landlords, the impossibility of paying rent without money or trade, the want of common sustenance, with neither house nor clothes to cover them from the inclemencies of the weather, and the most inevitable prospect of entailing the like or greater miseries upon their breed for ever.

I profess, in the sincerity of my heart, that I have not the least personal interest in endeavoring to promote this necessary work, having no other motive than the public good of my country, by advancing our trade, providing for infants, relieving the poor, and giving some pleasure to the rich. I have no children by which I can propose to get a single penny; the youngest being nine years old, and my wife past child-bearing.

QUESTIONS FOR STUDY
AND TOPICS FOR DISCUSSION
ON *A Modest Proposal*

1. *A Modest Proposal* is a masterpiece of irony. It says one thing and means another; not many people are likely to take at face value a proposal for cannibalism, the use of the children of the poor for food, as a final solution of the Irish problem. There are, however, several kinds and modes of irony. One kind, commonly called *verbal irony*, establishes a contrast between what is stated and what is more or less wryly suggested. This is the equivalent of what happens in speech when one says something like "He is a generous fellow" but makes it clear by intonation, facial expression, and gesture that quite the opposite is meant. Another kind, usually called *dramatic irony*, establishes a discrepancy between what the character who is the subject of the irony believes and what the audience knows to be the case. The character acts in ignorance of his condition; he is naïve or self-deceived; he puts an interpretation on his words and actions which the audience alters or reverses. Is the irony of *A Modest Proposal* primarily verbal or dramatic?

In thinking about this question, consider the *voice* and *perspective* of the author and speaker. When an author looks at a character or a subject obliquely rather than directly, it is said that he adopts a *persona*, a mask, a voice other than his own. A *persona* can be used in verbal as well as dramatic irony, the difference being that in the former the speaker is masking his intentions from the audience specified or assumed in the work, while in the latter the speaker is cast in a role that is deliberately mocked and unmasked before the audience.

Where is Swift himself located in *A Modest Proposal*? Is he identical with the speaker? Does Swift speak in the person of the speaker, or does he stand apart and mock the character of the speaker? If it is the first of these, the speaker is himself playing a role and wearing a mask. He is assuming the guise and manner of those who make proposals like his own and who would be receptive to solutions like his own. He is masking his true purpose by verbal irony. If it is the second, Swift is ridiculing the speaker as well as the dispositions and actions mirrored in the proposal. Swift is unmasking the pretensions of the speaker by dramatic irony.

What kind of person is the speaker? He presents himself as a public-spirited, benevolent humanitarian genuinely concerned about the miserable state of his country, Ireland; he is decent, rational, and sensitive. He seems to be an economic planner and a political arithmetician—somewhat of a technocrat. He says that he has maturely weighed the schemes of "other projectors" (p. 164). Now, a projector signified to Swift's contemporaries a person who proposed foolish or impractical projects. Many of these projects were proposed in pamphlets very similar in form to that of *A Modest Proposal*. Is Swift's pamphlet, then, a *parody* of these proposals? Is the speaker, too, a parody of the typical projector? Is he stupid and ingenuous, however well-intentioned? Is he sublimely unaware of the horrid nature of his plan? Or is the speaker deliberately playing the role of a typical projector and mocking the tone and tenor of a typical projector's scheme?

What difference does it make whether the speaker is identical with or separate from the author? Is the content and effect of the piece the same in either case? What bearing does the question of verbal or dramatic irony have on the consistency of the composition? Is there any place where Swift breaks in with his own voice? Is this an intrusion? Is it explained better by verbal or dramatic irony? Which form of irony better accommodates the tone of the piece? Which form more completely encompasses Swift's intention? Why does he use irony at all? What can he say ironically that he cannot say any other way? Why is Swift's indirect method of castigating the exploitations of the English governors and their Irish accomplices more effective than any straightforward catalogue of abuses?

2. The title is an obvious understatement; the word "modest" makes it an instance of the rhetorical figure called *meiosis,* which means presenting something as less than it really is (and hence the contrary of *hyperbole*). Where else is the device used? To what purpose and with what effect?

Is the word "poor" in the full title used in the sense of "indigent"; "emaciated"; or "unfortunate, hapless, pitiful"? Which of these senses is more common? How is the word "burden" used? Is the speaker deliberately trying to restrict the meanings of "poor" and "burden" to non-affective senses? Does it seem unnatural to do so?

3. The mention in the second paragraph of "the present deplorable state of the kingdom" may be a reference to the preceding three years of bad harvests in Ireland. There are similar phrases elsewhere, e.g., "the present distress of the kingdom" (p. 164); "the present situation of affairs" (p. 164). Is the speaker referring specifically to economic conditions, or is he obscuring the larger misery of the Irish problem by resorting to *euphemism* and *periphrasis*?

4. In the fourth paragraph the speaker, having established the desirability of finding a "fair, cheap, and easy method" for making beggar-children and all the infants of the poor "sound and useful members of the commonwealth," criticizes the computations of other projectors. This is the first of many references to the language of computation. Swift's purpose is to satirize the statistical approach to the problems of poverty and misery common in the writings of the political economists of the period. How does Swift's mockery of the language of computation serve his intention? Why is this language unnatural? With what manner does the speaker deliver his remarks? His own scheme has not been proposed yet. Why does he begin with a negative rather than affirmative argument?

The paragraph also suggests two other clusters of language prominent in the work: 1) the language of trade and commerce; 2) the language of animal husbandry and animality generally. How are these used? Is the implied metaphor in the sentence "It is true a child just dropped from its dam . . ." (p. 164) characteristic of Swift's figurative construction in *A Modest Proposal*? Does the speaker call human beings "beasts" by simile or metaphor? Does he say that the Irish are treated "like" things of commerce? What is literal and what is figurative in his argument for the proposal? Is *A Modest Proposal* allegorical?

Dr. Johnson said of Swift: "The rogue never hazards a metaphor." Herbert Read (*English Prose Style*, 1942) acknowledges this may be an exaggeration, but, he claims, "it is true that we may read Swift for many pages without encountering imagery of any kind, except such as was at that time embodied in common speech." Perhaps, however, it is precisely Swift's play upon metaphors in common speech that is one of the main sources of his irony. Irony exploits incongruity to produce the shock of the unexpected. Swift works his surprises by altering or reversing the usual acceptation of a word or concept. But he does this not so much by figurative expansion—by new and surprising combinations—as by a literal reduction of common metaphoric usage. Generally speaking, Swift's favorite rhetorical tactic is to push a proposition to an absurdly logical conclusion. In *A Modest Proposal* he treats the figurative expression "The Irish are being devoured" in real and concrete terms; he treats the premise of his argument literally. He forces a radical scrutiny of *dead metaphors* (i.e., figurative expressions which are so common that they are no longer recognized as such, e.g., "the leg of a table," "poor creatures"), clichés, stock responses, and other figurative properties of everyday speech.

Where does the speaker seem to urge a literal and concrete meaning when we expect a figurative sense? Is he meant to be taken as a literalist, or is that a mask? How can we, as readers, tell when he is being serious and when mocking? What are the effects of Swift's technique of literal reduction? How does he give a double meaning to such words as "grievance," "encumbrance," "commonwealth," "nutriment"?

5. In the fifth paragraph the speaker argues that his scheme will prevent "that horrid practice of women murdering their bastard children" (p. 164). Here and elsewhere in the work he seems to display shock at the immoral behavior of the Irish poor, yet he proposes an expedient equally horrid and murderous. Is the speaker mocking the conventional moral responses of the typical projector, or is Swift exhibiting in the character of the speaker the split moral sensibilities of the projectors?

6. How does the speaker broach his proposal (p. 165)? Why has he waited this long before presenting it? Is it only chance that he had been assured of the excellence of children as food by an American acquaintance in London? What aspects of the Irish problem does the speaker choose to emphasize? What aspects does he ignore? What makes his argument seem so plausible? Its logic? Its air of compassion and good intentions? Its reasonable and thoughtful tone? How does the speaker try to make the proposal inviting and attractive? To what does he appeal?

7. What is the tone and effect of the paragraph beginning "I grant this food will be somewhat dear . . ." (p. 165)? In other tracts Swift bitterly attacked the large landowners as being chiefly responsible for Ireland's miserable condition. How are the words "dear," "proper," and "title" meant to be taken? Is the speaker blandly unaware of what he is saying, or is he deliberately playing on the conception of "devouring" which frames the piece? Does Swift make it seem as if this is an unconscious exposure on the part of the speaker, or is he speaking in the person of the speaker?

8. The speaker continues his argument by claiming that in addition to providing "excellent nutritive meat" the carcass of a good fat child will make admirable gloves for ladies and summer boots for gentlemen (p. 166). This picks up the mention in the fourth paragraph, carried throughout the pamphlet, of the "food and raiment" that can be provided by the children of the poor. What irony on self-help is expressed in this grotesque development? "Food and raiment" is an echo of a famous Biblical phrase. Can you supply the context? What ironic dimension is added by the Biblical allusion? How does Swift vary the phrase in the course of the pamphlet?

9. With an almost insane insouciance the speaker recommends buying the children alive "and dressing them hot from the knife, as we do roasting pigs" (p. 166). Here and throughout he "pleads" for the application to human beings of the same kind of efficiency and solicitude that are accorded to the breeding and slaughtering of animals. By what means has Swift identified the condition of the poor people of Ireland as worse than that of livestock?

10. Having reached this extremity of gruesomeness, the speaker digresses into a refinement on his scheme which was advanced by a friend who had obtained the "expedient" from one Psalmanazar, a contemporary impostor. Why does the speaker take the trouble to discuss the refinement? Why does he think this "expedient" is likely to be received as bordering upon cruelty and

his own proposal not? What is the target of the irony in the sentence beginning "Neither indeed can I deny . . ." (p. 167)?

11. Analyze the tone and language of the paragraph beginning "Some persons of a desponding spirit . . ." (p. 167). How do the following words and phrases function: "desponding"; "ease . . . of so grievous an encumbrance"; "I am not in the least pain"; "rotting"; "in almost as hopeful a condition"; "happily delivered from the evils to come"?

12. After the digression the speaker enumerates the advantages of his proposal (pp. 168–169). Each of these is itself a sardonic reversal. He says, for example, that once the poorer tenants have something valuable of their own, it will by law "be made liable to distress"—i.e., subject to seizure for payment of debts—and help to pay their landlord's rent. As another advantage, the policy would be a great inducement to marriage; it would increase the care and tenderness of mothers toward their children, and men would become as fond of their wives, during their pregnancy, as they are now of their breed animals. Cannibalism, that is to say, would engender humane sentiments and behavior. The children would be looked after as tenderly as any commodity which advances prosperity. The parents would become tradesmen, mercantilists, owners of "property." They could then indulge in the same moral luxuries as the wealthy. Analyze the content of all of the advantages listed by the speaker and show how they achieve their ironic effect. Consider especially the way in which Swift *inverts* moral properties, benefits, and values.

13. The speaker concedes his proposal will shrink the population of Ireland (p. 169), but he freely admits that object as part of his intent. As Louis Landa has shown, the *persona's* argument here is a gibe at the widely held economic assumption that "people are the riches of a nation." What relevance does Swift's irony on this point have to the design and sense of the whole? Why does he have the speaker say that the remedy is calculated "for this one individual kingdom of Ireland, and for no other that ever was, is, or, I think, ever can be upon earth" (p. 169)?

14. Why does the speaker take the trouble to list the "other expedients" he seems so firmly to reject? What does "expedient"

mean? How would you go about finding the particular sense Swift gives to the word? Most of the expedients are policies that Swift himself had proposed in various tracts before *A Modest Proposal*. Is Swift presenting the speaker as a representative of those who have failed to accept his own modest proposals?

15. What is the tone, voice, and perspective of the paragraph beginning "But as to myself . . ." (p. 170)? Does the speaker seem to be, at this point, the obtuse and bland "projector" who is the object of Swift's dramatic irony—or is he rather an agent of verbal irony? The country "which would be glad to eat up our whole nation" is England. The idea of this passage coincides with Swift's own view that England was the chief cause of Ireland's difficulties by virtue of the restrictions it had imposed on the dependency's commerce. Is Swift speaking in his own voice here? Does he intrude his own bitterness? If it is an intrusion, does it threaten the consistency of the *dramatic* irony?

16. The speaker closes with a sincere disclaimer of any personal motive. After the bitter outburst of the preceding paragraphs, he recovers his aplomb. He steps back into character and resumes either the dry mockery of his verbal irony or the obtuseness of a well-meaning projector. In what sense are the words of his summary of the arguments of the proposal double-edged? He says, for example, that he wishes to "relieve" the poor, which means, of course, easing their burdens—but this worthy object is to be achieved by "removing" their children. How are the other words given an ironic double reference? How is the last sentence meant to be taken? Is it funny? What final irony is lodged in the report that the speaker's wife is no longer burdened by "child-bearing"?

❦

"THE RETREAT AND DEATH OF JULIAN"

FROM *The Decline and Fall of the Roman Empire*

BY *Edward Gibbon*

JULIAN WAS AN OBJECT of terror and hatred to the Persians; and the painters of that nation represented the invader of their country under the emblem of a furious lion, who vomited from his mouth a consuming fire. To his friends and soldiers the philosophic hero appeared in a more amiable light; and his virtues were never more conspicuously displayed than in the last and most active period of his life. He practiced, without effort, and almost without merit, the habitual qualities of temperance and sobriety. According to the dictates of that artificial wisdom which assumes an absolute dominion over the mind and body, he sternly refused himself the indulgence of the most natural appetites. In the warm climate of Assyria, which solicited a luxurious people to the gratification of every sensual desire, a youthful conqueror preserved his chastity pure and inviolate: nor was Julian ever tempted, even by a motive of curiosity, to visit his female captives of exquisite beauty, who, instead of resisting his power, would have disputed with each other the honor of his embraces. With the same firmness that he resisted the allurements of love, he sustained the hardships of war. When the Romans marched through the flat and flooded country, their sovereign, on foot, at the head of his legions, shared their fatigues and animated their diligence. In every useful labor the hand of Julian was prompt and strenuous; and the Imperial purple was wet and dirty, as the coarse garment of the meanest soldier. The two sieges allowed him some remarkable opportunities of signalizing his personal valor, which, in the improved state of the military art, can seldom be exerted by a prudent general. The emperor stood before the citadel of Perisabor, insensible of his extreme danger, and encouraged his troops to burst open the gates of iron, till he was almost overwhelmed under a cloud of missile weapons and huge stones that were directed against his person. As he examined the exterior fortifications of Maogamalcha, two Persians, devoting themselves for their country, suddenly rushed upon him with drawn scimitars: the emperor dexterously received their blows on his uplifted shield; and, with a steady and well-aimed thrust, laid one of his adversaries dead at his feet. The esteem of a prince who possesses the virtues which he approves is the noblest recompense of a deserving subject; and the authority which Julian derived from his personal merit enabled him to revive and enforce the rigor of ancient discipline. He punished with death, or ignominy, the misbehavior of three troops of horse, who, in a skirmish with the Surenas, had lost their honor and one of their standards: and he distinguished with *obsidional* crowns the valor of the foremost soldiers who had ascended into the city of Maogamalcha. After the siege of Perisabor the firmness of the emperor was exercised by the insolent avarice of the army, who loudly complained that their services were rewarded by a trifling donative of one hundred pieces of silver. His just indignation was expressed in the grave and manly language of a Roman. "Riches are the object of your desires; those riches are in the hands of the Persians: and the spoils of this fruitful country are proposed as the prize of your valor and discipline. Believe me," added Julian, "the Roman republic, which formerly possessed such immense treasures, is now reduced to want and wretchedness; since our princes have been persuaded, by weak and interested ministers, to purchase with gold the tranquillity of the barbarians. The revenue is exhausted; the cities are ruined; the provinces are dispeopled. For myself, the only inheritance that I have received from my royal ancestors is a soul incapable of fear; and as long as I am convinced that every real advantage is seated in the mind, I shall not blush to acknowledge an honorable poverty, which in the days of ancient virtue was considered as the glory of Fabricius. That glory, and that virtue, may be your own, if you will listen to the voice of Heaven and of your leader. But if you will rashly persist, if you are determined to renew the shameful and mischievous examples of old seditions, proceed. As it becomes an emperor who has filled the first rank among men, I am prepared to die standing, and to despise a precarious life which every hour may depend on an accidental fever. If I have been found unworthy of the command, there are now among you (I speak it with pride and pleasure), there are many chiefs whose merit and experience are equal to the conduct of the most important war. Such has been the temper of my reign, that I can retire, without regret and without apprehension, to the obscurity of a private station." The modest resolution of Julian was answered by the unanimous applause and cheerful obedience of the Romans, who declared their confidence of victory while they fought under the banners of their heroic prince. Their courage was kindled by his frequent and familiar asseverations (for such wishes were the oaths of Julian), "So may I reduce the Persians under the yoke!" "Thus may I restore the strength and splendor of the republic!" The love of fame was the ardent passion of his soul: but it was not before he trampled on the ruins of Maogamalcha that he allowed himself to say, "We have now provided some materials for the sophist of Antioch."

The successful valor of Julian had triumphed over all the obstacles that opposed his march to the gates of Ctesiphon. But the reduction, or even the siege, of the capital of Persia was still at a distance: nor can the military conduct of the emperor be clearly apprehended without a knowledge of the country which was the theater of his bold and skillful operations. Twenty miles to the south of Bagdad, and on the eastern bank of the Tigris, the curiosity of travelers has observed some ruins of the palaces of Ctesiphon, which in the time of Julian was a great and populous city. The name and glory of the adjacent Seleucia were for ever extinguished; and the only remaining quarter of that Greek colony had resumed, with the Assyrian language and manners, the primitive appelation of Coche. Coche was situate on the western side of the Tigris; but it was naturally considered as a suburb of Ctesiphon, with which we may suppose it to have been connected by a permanent bridge of boats. The united parts contributed to form the common epithet of Al Modain, THE CITIES, which the Orientals have bestowed on the winter residence of the Sassanides; and the whole circumference of the Persian capital was strongly fortified by the waters of the river, by lofty walls, and by impracticable morasses. Near the ruins of Seleucia the camp of Julian was fixed, and secured by a ditch and rampart against the sallies of the numerous and enterprising garrison of Coche. In this fruitful and pleasant country the Romans were plentifully supplied with water and forage: and several forts, which might have embarrassed the motions of the army, submitted, after some resistance, to the efforts of their valor. The fleet passed from the Euphrates into an artificial deviation of that river, which pours a copious and navigable stream into the Tigris at a small distance *below* the great city. If they had followed this royal canal, which bore the name of Nahar-Malcha, the intermediate situation of Coche would have separated the fleet and army of Julian; and the rash attempt of steering against the current of the Tigris, and forcing their way through the midst of a hostile capital, must have been attended with the total destruction of the Roman navy. The prudence of the emperor foresaw the danger, and provided the remedy. As he had minutely studied the operations of Trajan in the same country, he soon recollected that his warlike predecessor had dug a new and navigable canal, which, leaving Coche on the right hand, conveyed the waters of the Nahar-Malcha into the river Tigris at some distance *above* the cities. From the information of the peasants Julian ascertained the vestiges of this ancient work, which were almost obliterated by design or accident. By the indefatigable labor of the soldiers a broad and deep channel was speedily prepared for the reception of the Euphrates. A strong dyke was constructed to interrupt the ordinary current of the Nahar-Malcha: a flood of waters rushed impetuously into their new bed; and the Roman fleet, steering their triumphant course into the Tigris, derided the vain and ineffectual barriers which the Persians of Ctesiphon had erected to oppose their passage.

As it became necessary to transport the Roman army over the Tigris, another labor presented itself, of less toil, but of more danger, than the preceding expedition. The stream was broad and rapid, the ascent steep and difficult; and the entrenchments which had been formed on the ridge of the opposite bank were lined with a numerous army of heavy cuirassiers, dexterous archers, and huge elephants; who (according to the extravagant hyperbole of Libanius) could trample with the same ease a field of corn or a legion of Romans. In the presence of such an enemy the construction of a bridge was impracticable; and the intrepid prince, who instantly seized the only possible expedient, concealed his design, till the moment of execution, from the knowledge of the barbarians, of his own troops, and even of his generals themselves. Under the specious pretense of examining the state of the magazines, fourscore vessels were gradually unladen; and a select detachment, apparently destined for some secret expedition, was ordered to stand to their arms on the first signal. Julian disguised the silent anxiety of his own mind with smiles of confidence and joy; and amused the hostile nations with the spectacle of military games, which he insultingly celebrated under the walls of Coche. The day was consecrated to pleasure; but, as soon as the hour of supper was past, the emperor summoned the generals to his tent, and acquainted them that he had fixed that night for the passage of the Tigris. They stood in silent and respectful astonishment; but when the venerable Sallust assumed the privilege of his age and experience, the rest of the chiefs supported with freedom the weight of his prudent remonstrances. Julian contented himself with observing that conquest and safety depended on the attempt; that, instead of diminishing, the number of their enemies would be increased by successive reinforcements; and that a longer delay would neither contract the breadth of the stream nor level the height of the bank. The signal was instantly given, and obeyed: the most impatient of the legionaries leaped into five vessels that lay nearest to the bank; and, as they plied their oars with intrepid diligence, they were lost after a few moments in the darkness of the night. A flame arose on the opposite side; and Julian, who too clearly understood that his foremost vessels in attempting to land had been fired by the enemy, dexterously converted their extreme danger into a presage of victory. "Our fellow-soldiers," he eagerly exclaimed, "are already masters of the bank: see—they make the appointed signal; let us hasten to emulate and assist their courage." The united and rapid motion of a great fleet broke the violence of the current, and they reached the eastern shore of the Tigris with sufficient speed to extinguish the flames and rescue their adventurous companions. The difficulties of a steep and lofty ascent were increased by the weight of armor and the darkness of the night. A shower of stones, darts, and fire was incessantly discharged on the heads of the assailants; who, after an arduous struggle, climbed the bank and stood victorious upon the rampart. As soon as they possessed a more equal field, Julian, who with his light infantry had led the attack, darted through the ranks a skillful and experienced eye: his bravest soldiers, according to the precepts of Homer, were distributed in the front and rear; and all the trumpets of the Imperial army sounded to battle. The Romans, after sending up a military shout, advanced in measured steps to the animating notes of martial music; launched their formidable javelins, and rushed forwards with drawn swords to deprive the barbarians, by a closer onset, of the advantage of their missile weapons. The whole engagement lasted above twelve hours; till the gradual retreat of the Persians was changed into a disorderly flight, of which the shameful example was given by the principal leaders and the Surenas himself. They were pursued to the gates of Ctesiphon; and the conquerors might have entered the dismayed city, if their general, Victor, who was dangerously wounded with an arrow, had not conjured them to desist from a rash attempt, which must be fatal if it were not successful. On *their* side the Romans acknowledged the loss of only seventy-five men; while they affirmed that the barbarians had left on the field of battle two thousand five hundred, or even six thousand, of their bravest soldiers. The spoil was such as might be expected from the riches and luxury of an Oriental camp; large quantities of silver and gold, splendid arms and trappings, and beds and tables of massive silver. The victorious emperor distributed, as the rewards of valor, some honorable gifts, civic, and mural, and naval crowns; which he, and perhaps he alone, esteemed more precious than the wealth of Asia. A solemn sacrifice was offered to the god of war, but the appearances of the victims threatened the most inauspicious events; and Julian soon discovered, by less ambiguous signs, that he had now reached the term of his prosperity.

On the second day after the battle the domestic guards, the Jovians and Herculians, and the remaining troops, which composed near two-thirds of the whole army, were securely wafted over the Tigris. While the Persians beheld from the walls of Ctesiphon the desolation of the adjacent country, Julian cast many an anxious look towards the North, in full expectation that, as he himself had victoriously penetrated to the capital of Sapor, the march and junction of his lieutenants, Sebastian and Procopius, would be executed with the same courage and diligence. His expectations were disappointed by the treachery of the Armenian king, who permitted, and most probably directed, the desertion of his auxiliary troops from the camp of the Romans; and by the dissensions of the two generals, who were incapable of forming or executing any plan for the public service. When the emperor had relinquished the hope of this important reinforcement, he condescended to hold a council of war, and approved, after a full debate, the sentiment of those generals who dissuaded the siege of Ctesiphon, as a fruitless and pernicious undertaking. It is not easy for us to conceive by what arts of fortification a city thrice besieged and taken by the predecessors of Julian could be rendered impregnable against an army of sixty thousand Romans, commanded by a brave and experienced general, and abundantly supplied with ships, provisions, battering engines, and military stores. But we may rest assured, from the love of glory, and contempt of danger, which formed the character of Julian, that he was not discouraged by any trivial or imaginary obstacles. At the very time when he declined the siege of Ctesiphon, he rejected, with obstinacy and disdain, the most flattering offers of a negotiation of peace. Sapor, who had been so long accustomed to the tardy ostentation of Constantius, was surprised by the intrepid diligence of his successor. As far as the confines of India and Scythia, the satraps of the distant provinces were ordered to assemble their troops, and to march, without delay, to the assistance of their monarch. But their preparations were dilatory, their motions slow; and before Sapor could lead an army into the field, he received the melancholy intelligence of the devastation of Assyria, the ruin of his palaces, and the slaughter of his bravest troops, who defended the passage of the Tigris. The pride of royalty was humbled in the dust; he took his repasts on the ground; and the disorder of his hair expressed the grief and anxiety of his mind. Perhaps he would not have refused to purchase, with one half of his kingdom, the safety of the remainder; and he would have gladly subscribed himself, in a treaty of peace, the faithful and dependent ally of the Roman conqueror. Under the pretense of private business, a minister of rank and confidence was secretly dispatched to embrace the knees of Hormisdas, and to request, in the language of a suppliant, that he might be introduced into the presence of the emperor. The Sassanian prince, whether he listened to the voice of pride or humanity, whether he consulted the sentiments of his birth or the duties of his situation, was equally inclined to promote a salutary measure which would terminate the calamities of Persia, and secure the triumph of Rome. He was astonished by the inflexible firmness of a hero who remembered, most unfortunately for himself and for his country, that Alexander had uniformly rejected the propositions of Darius. But as Julian was sensible that the hope of a safe and honorable peace might cool the ardor of his troops, he earnestly requested that Hormisdas would privately dismiss the minister of Sapor, and conceal this dangerous temptation from the knowledge of the camp.

The honor, as well as interest, of Julian, forbade him to consume his time under the impregnable walls of Ctesiphon; and as often as he defied the barbarians, who defended the city, to meet him on the open plain, they prudently replied that, if he desired to exercise his valor, he might seek the army of the Great King. He felt the insult, and he accepted the advice. Instead of confining his servile march to the banks of the Euphrates and Tigris, he resolved to imitate the adventurous spirit of Alexander, and boldly to advance into the inland provinces, till he forced his rival to contend with him, perhaps in the plains of Arbela, for the empire of Asia. The magnanimity of Julian was applauded and betrayed by the arts of a noble Persian, who, in the cause of his country, had generously submitted to act a part full of danger, of falsehood, and of shame. With a train of faithful followers he deserted to the Imperial camp; exposed, in a specious tale, the injuries which he had sustained; exaggerated the cruelty of Sapor, the discontent of the people, and the weakness of the monarchy; and confidently offered himself as the hostage and guide of the Roman march. The most rational grounds of suspicion were urged, without effect, by the wisdom and experience of Hormisdas; and the credulous Julian, receiving the traitor into his bosom, was persuaded to issue an hasty order, which, in the opinion of mankind, appeared to arraign his prudence and to endanger his safety. He destroyed in a single hour the whole navy, which had been transported above five hundred miles, at so great an expense of toil, of treasure, and of blood. Twelve, or, at the most, twenty-two, small vessels were saved, to accompany, on carriages, the march of the army, and to form occasional bridges for the passage of the rivers. A supply of twenty days' provisions was reserved for the use of the soldiers; and the rest of the magazines, with a fleet of eleven hundred vessels, which rode at anchor in the Tigris, were abandoned to the flames by the absolute command of the emperor. The Christian bishops, Gregory and Augustin, insult the madness of the apostate, who executed, with his own hands, the sentence of divine justice. Their authority, of less weight, perhaps, in a military question, is confirmed by the cool judgment of an experienced soldier, who was himself spectator of the conflagration, and who could not disapprove the reluctant murmurs of the troops. Yet there are not wanting some specious, and perhaps solid, reasons, which might justify the resolution of Julian. The navigation of the Euphrates never ascended above Babylon, nor that of the Tigris above Opis. The distance of the last-mentioned city from the Roman camp was not very considerable; and Julian must soon have renounced the vain and impracticable attempt of forcing upwards a great fleet against the stream of a rapid river, which in several places was embarrassed by natural or artificial cataracts. The power of sails and oars was insufficient, it became necessary to tow the ships against the current of the river; the strength of twenty thousand soldiers was exhausted in this tedious and servile labor; and if the Romans continued to march along the banks of the Tigris, they could only expect to return home without achieving any enterprise worthy of the genius or fortune of their leader. If, on the contrary, it was advisable to advance into the inland country, the destruction of the fleet and magazines was the only measure which could save that valuable prize from the hands of the numerous and active troops which might suddenly be poured from the gates of Ctesiphon. Had the arms of Julian been victorious, we should now admire the conduct as well as the courage of a hero who, by depriving his soldiers of the hopes of a retreat, left them only the alternative of death or conquest.

The cumbersome train of artillery and waggons, which retards the operations of a modern army, was in a great measure unknown in the camps of the Romans. Yet, in every age, the subsistence of sixty thousand men must have been one of the most important cares of a prudent general; and that subsistence could only be drawn from his own or from the enemy's country. Had it been possible for Julian to maintain a bridge of communication on the Tigris, and to preserve the conquered places of Assyria, a desolated province could not afford any large or regular supplies in a season of the year when the lands were covered by the inundation of the Euphrates, and the unwholesome air was darkened with swarms of innumerable insects. The appearance of the hostile country was far more inviting. The extensive region that lies between the river Tigris and the mountains of Media was filled with villages and towns; and the fertile soil, for the most part, was in a very improved state of cultivation. Julian might expect that a conqueror who possessed the two forcible instruments of persuasion, steel and gold, would easily procure a plentiful subsistence from the fears or avarice of the natives. But on the approach of the Romans this rich and smiling prospect was instantly blasted. Wherever they moved, the inhabitants deserted the open villages and took shelter in the fortified towns; the cattle was driven away; the grass and ripe corn were consumed with fire; and, as soon as the flames had subsided which interrupted the march of Julian, he beheld the melancholy face of a smoking and naked desert. This desperate but effectual method of defense can only be executed by the enthusiasm of a people who prefer their independence to their property; or by the rigor of an arbitrary government, which consults the public safety without submitting to their inclinations the liberty of choice. On the present occasion the zeal and obedience of the Persians seconded the commands of Sapor; and the emperor was soon reduced to the scanty stock of provisions which continually wasted in his hands. Before they were entirely consumed he might still have reached the wealthy and unwarlike cities of Ecbatana or Susa by the effort of a rapid and well-directed march; but he was deprived of this last resource by his ignorance of the roads and by the perfidy of his guides. The Romans wandered several days in the country to the eastward of Bagdad; the Persian deserter, who had artfully led them into the snare, escaped from their resentment; and his followers, as soon as they were put to the torture, confessed the secret of the conspiracy. The visionary conquests of Hyrcania and India, which had so long amused, now tormented, the mind of Julian. Conscious that his own imprudence was the cause of the public distress, he anxiously balanced the hopes of safety or success without obtaining a satisfactory answer either from gods or men. At length, as the only practicable measure, he embraced the resolution of directing his steps towards the banks of the Tigris, with the design of saving the army by a hasty march to the confines of Corduene, a fertile and friendly province, which acknowledged the sovereignty of Rome. The desponding troops obeyed the signal of the retreat, only seventy days after they had passed the Chaboras with the sanguine expectation of subverting the throne of Persia.

As long as the Romans seemed to advance into the country, their march was observed and insulted from a distance by several bodies of Persian cavalry; who, showing themselves, sometimes in loose, and sometimes in closer order, faintly skirmished with the advanced guards. These detachments were, however, supported by a much greater force; and the heads of the columns were no sooner pointed towards the Tigris than a cloud of dust arose on the plain. The Romans, who now aspired only to the permission of a safe and speedy retreat, endeavored to persuade themselves that this formidable appearance was occasioned by a troop of wild asses, or perhaps by the approach of some friendly Arabs. They halted, pitched their tents, fortified their camp, passed the whole night in continual alarms; and discovered at the dawn of day that they were surrounded by an army of Persians. This army, which might be considered only as the van of the barbarians, was soon followed by the main body of cuirassiers, archers, and elephants, commanded by Meranes, a general of rank and reputation. He was accompanied by two of the king's sons and many of the principal satraps; and fame and expectation exaggerated the strength of the remaining powers, which slowly advanced under the conduct of Sapor himself. As the Romans continued their march, their long array, which was forced to bend or divide, according to the varieties of the ground, afforded frequent and favorable opportunities to their vigilant enemies. The Persians repeatedly charged with fury; they were repeatedly repulsed with firmness; and the action at Maronga, which almost deserved the name of a battle, was marked by a considerable loss of satraps and elephants, perhaps of equal value in the eyes of their monarch. These splendid advantages were not obtained without an adequate slaughter on the side of the Romans: several officers of distinction were either killed or wounded; and the emperor himself, who, on all occasions of danger, inspired and guided the valor of his troops, was obliged to expose his person and exert his abilities. The weight of offensive and defensive arms, which still constituted the strength and safety of the Romans, disabled them from making any long or effectual pursuit; and as the horsemen of the East were trained to dart their javelins and shoot their arrows at full speed, and in every possible direction, the cavalry of Persia was never more formidable than in the moment of a rapid and disorderly flight. But the most certain and irreparable loss of the Romans was that of time. The hardy veterans, accustomed to the cold climate of Gaul and Germany, fainted under the sultry heat of an Assyrian summer; their vigor was exhausted by the incessant repetition of march and combat; and the progress of the army was suspended by the precautions of a slow and dangerous retreat in the presence of an active enemy. Every day, every hour, as the supply diminished, the value and price of subsistence increased in the Roman camp. Julian, who always contented himself with such food as a hungry soldier would have disdained, distributed, for the use of the troops, the provisions of the Imperial household, and whatever could be spared from the sumpter-horses of the tribunes and generals. But this feeble relief served only to aggravate the sense of the public distress; and the Romans began to entertain the most gloomy apprehensions that, before they could reach the frontiers of the empire, they should all perish, either by famine or by the sword of the barbarians.

While Julian struggled with the almost insuperable difficulties of his situation, the silent hours of the night were still devoted to study and contemplation. Whenever he closed his eyes in short and interrupted slumbers, his mind was agitated with painful anxiety: nor can it be thought surprising that the Genius of the empire should once more appear before him, covering with a funeral veil his head and his horn of abundance, and slowly retiring from the Imperial tent. The monarch started from his couch, and, stepping forth to refresh his wearied spirits with the coolness of the midnight air, he beheld a fiery meteor, which shot athwart the sky, and suddenly vanished. Julian was convinced that he had seen the menacing countenance of the god of war; the council which he summoned, of Tuscan Haruspices, unanimously pronounced that he should abstain from action; but, on this occasion, necessity and reason were more prevalent than superstition; and the trumpets sounded at the break of day. The army marched through a hilly country; and the hills had been secretly occupied by the Persians. Julian led the van with the skill and attention of a consummate general; he was alarmed by the intelligence that his rear was suddenly attacked. The heat of the weather had tempted him to lay aside his cuirass; but he snatched a shield from one of his attendants, and hastened, with a sufficient reinforcement, to the relief of the rear guard. A similar danger recalled the intrepid prince to the defense of the front; and, as he galloped between the columns, the center of the left was attacked, and almost overpowered, by a furious charge of the Persian cavalry and elephants. This huge body was soon defeated by the well-timed evolution of the light infantry, who aimed their weapons, with dexterity and effect, against the backs of the horsemen, and the legs of the elephants. The barbarians fled: and Julian, who was foremost in every danger, animated the pursuit with his voice and gestures. His trembling guards, scattered and oppressed by the disorderly throng of friends and enemies, reminded their fearless sovereign that he was without armor; and conjured him to decline the fall of the impending ruin. As they exclaimed, a cloud of darts and arrows was discharged from the flying squadrons; and a javelin, after razing the skin of his arm, transpierced the ribs, and fixed in the inferior part of the liver. Julian attempted to draw the deadly weapon from his side; but his fingers were cut by the sharpness of the steel, and he fell senseless from his horse. His guards flew to his relief; and the wounded emperor was gently raised from the ground, and conveyed out of the tumult of the battle into an adjacent tent. The report of the melancholy event passed from rank to rank; but the grief of the Romans inspired them with invincible valor, and the desire of revenge. The bloody and obstinate conflict was maintained by the two armies till they were separated by the total darkness of the night. The Persians derived some honor from the advantage which they obtained against the left wing, where Anatolius, master of the offices, was slain, and the praefect Sallust very narrowly escaped. But the event of the day was adverse to the barbarians. They abandoned the field; their two generals, Meranes and Nohordates, fifty nobles or satraps, and a multitude of their bravest soldiers [were slain]: and the success of the Romans, if Julian had survived, might have been improved into a decisive and useful victory.

The first words that Julian uttered, after his recovery from the fainting fit into which he had been thrown by loss of blood, were expressive of his martial spirit. He called for his horse and arms, and was impatient to rush into the battle. His remaining strength was exhausted by the painful effort; and the surgeons, who examined his wound, discovered the symptoms of approaching death. He employed the awful moments with the firm temper of a hero and a sage; the philosophers who had accompanied him in this fatal expedition compared the tent of Julian with the prison of Socrates; and the spectators, whom duty, or friendship, or curiosity, had assembled round his couch, listened with respectful grief to the funeral oration of their dying emperor. "Friends and fellow-soldiers, the seasonable period of my departure is now arrived, and I discharge, with the cheerfulness of a ready debtor, the demands of nature. I have learned from philosophy how much the soul is more excellent than the body; and that the separation of the nobler substance should be the subject of joy, rather than of affliction. I have learned from religion that an early death has often been the reward of piety; and I accept, as a favor of the gods, the mortal stroke that secures me from the danger of disgracing a character which has hitherto been supported by virtue and fortitude. I die without remorse, as I have lived without guilt. I am pleased to reflect on the innocence of my private life; and I can affirm with confidence that the supreme authority, that emanation of the Divine Power, has been preserved in my hands pure and immaculate. Detesting the corrupt and destructive maxims of despotism, I have considered the happiness of the people as the end of government. Submitting my actions to the laws of prudence, of justice, and of moderation, I have trusted the event to the care of Providence. Peace was the object of my counsels, as long as peace was consistent with the public welfare; but when the imperious voice of my country summoned me to arms, I exposed my person to the dangers of war, with the clear foreknowledge (which I had acquired from the art of divination) that I was destined to fall by the sword. I now offer my tribute of gratitude to the Eternal Being, who has not suffered me to perish by the cruelty of a tyrant, by the secret dagger of conspiracy, or by the slow tortures of lingering disease. He has given me, in the midst of an honorable career, a splendid and glorious departure from this world; and I hold it equally absurd, equally base, to solicit, or to decline, the stroke of fate.— Thus much I have attempted to say; but my strength fails me, and I feel the approach of death.—I shall cautiously refrain from any word that may tend to influence your suffrages in the election of an emperor. My choice might be imprudent or injudicious; and if it should not be ratified by the consent of the army, it might be fatal to the person whom I should recommend. I shall only, as a good citizen, express my hopes that the Romans may be blessed with the government of a virtuous sovereign." After this discourse, which Julian pronounced in a firm and gentle tone of voice, he distributed, by a military testament, the remains of his private fortune; and making some inquiry why Anatolius was not present, he understood, from the answer of Sallust, that Anatolius was killed; and bewailed, with amiable inconsistency, the loss of his friend. At the same time he reproved the immoderate grief of the spectators; and conjured them not to disgrace, by unmanly tears, the fate of a prince who in a few moments would be united with heaven and with the stars. The spectators were silent; and Julian entered into a metaphysical argument with the philosophers Priscus and Maximus on the nature of the soul. The efforts which he made, of mind as well as body, most probably hastened his death. His wound began to bleed with fresh violence: his respiration was embarrassed by the swelling of the veins: he called for a draught of cold water, and, as soon as he had drunk it, expired without pain, about the hour of midnight. Such was the end of that extraordinary man, in the thirty-second year of his age, after a reign of one year and about eight months from the death of Constantius. In his last moments he displayed, perhaps with some ostentation, the love of virtue and of fame, which had been the ruling passions of his life.

●   ●   ●

After Jovian had performed those engagements which the voice of his people might have tempted him to violate, he hastened away from the scene of his disgrace, and proceeded with his whole court to enjoy the luxury of Antioch. Without consulting the dictates of religious zeal, he was prompted, by humanity and gratitude, to bestow the last honors on the remains of his deceased sovereign; and Procopius, who sincerely bewailed the loss of his kinsman, was removed from the command of the army, under the decent pretense of conducting the funeral. The corpse of Julian was transported from Nisibis to Tarsus in a slow march of fifteen days, and, as it passed through the cities of the East, was saluted by the hostile factions with mournful lamentations and clamorous insults. The Pagans already placed their beloved hero in the rank of those gods whose worship he had restored, while the invectives of the Christians pursued the soul of the apostate to hell, and his body to the grave. One party lamented the approaching ruin of their altars, the other celebrated the marvellous deliverance of the church. The Christians applauded, in lofty and ambiguous strains, the stroke of divine vengeance which had been so long suspended over the guilty head of Julian. They acknowledged that the death of the tyrant, at the instant he expired beyond the Tigris, was *revealed* to the saints of Egypt, Syria, and Cappadocia; and instead of suffering him to fall by the Persian darts, their indiscretion ascribed the heroic deed to the obscure hand of some mortal or immortal champion of the faith. Such imprudent declarations were eagerly adopted by the malice or credulity of their adversaries, who darkly insinuated or confidently asserted that the governors of the church had instigated and directed the fanaticism of a domestic assassin. Above sixteen years after the death of Julian, the charge was solemnly and vehemently urged in a public oration addressed by Libanius to the emperor Theodosius. His suspicions are unsupported by fact or argument, and we can only esteem the generous zeal of the sophist of Antioch for the cold and neglected ashes of his friend.

It was an ancient custom in the funerals, as well as in the triumphs of the Romans, that the voice of praise should be corrected by that of satire and ridicule, and that, in the midst of the splendid pageants which displayed the glory of the living or of the dead, their imperfections should not be concealed from the eyes of the world. This custom was practiced in the funeral of Julian. The comedians, who resented his contempt and aversion for the theatre, exhibited, with the applause of a Christian audience, the lively and exaggerated representation of the faults and follies of the deceased emperor. His various character and singular manners afforded an ample scope for pleasantry and ridicule. In the exercise of his uncommon talents he often descended below the majesty of his rank. Alexander was transformed into Diogenes—the philosopher was degraded into a priest. The purity of his virtue was sullied by excessive vanity; his superstition disturbed the peace and endangered the safety of a mighty empire; and his irregular sallies were the less entitled to indulgence, as they appeared to be the laborious efforts of art, or even of affectation. The remains of Julian were interred at Tarsus in Cilicia; but his stately tomb, which arose in that city on the banks of the cold and limpid Cydnus, was displeasing to the faithful friends who loved and revered the memory of that extraordinary man. The philosopher expressed a very reasonable wish that the disciple of Plato might have reposed amidst the groves of the Academy, while the soldier exclaimed, in bolder accents, that the ashes of Julian should have been mingled with those of Caesar, in the field of Mars, and among the ancient monuments of Roman virtue. The history of princes does not very frequently renew the example of a similar competition.

QUESTIONS FOR STUDY
AND TOPICS FOR DISCUSSION
ON *"The Retreat and Death of Julian"*

1. This account of the last campaign and death of Julian the Apostate is taken from Chapter XXIV of Gibbon's history. The figure of Julian occupies a pivotal position in *The Decline and Fall of the Roman Empire*. Gibbon originally intended to carry his history only as far as the decline of the Roman Empire in the West, and he planned the reign of Julian as the climax of the work. The Emperor's rule lasted only one year and seven months (from December A.D. 361 to June 363), and it ended disastrously, yet Gibbon gave Julian three of his best chapters. The events were hardly significant enough to justify such prominence. Julian's importance is determined more by his role in Gibbon's vast tragic drama than by his actual historical position.

Julian was a vigorous reformer and a stern enemy of the Christian Church. His ambition was to reverse the decline of Roman imperial power and "to restore the strength and splendor of the republic." To this end he embarked on a career of military conquest in imitation of Caesar and Alexander. In 363 he invaded Persia. His campaign was successful at first and he reached Ctesiphon in triumph, but when he spurned a flattering offer of peace by the Persians, his fortunes took a calamitous turn. He overreached himself, his supplies dwindled, the Persian resistance hardened, and he was forced to withdraw. He was slain during the retreat. For Gibbon, the death of Julian put an end to any hope of saving the Empire from its final fall.

Gibbon saw Julian as an "extraordinary man," and he found much to admire in his character, but he cast a coolly appraising eye on his subject. How does Gibbon conceive his portrait? In what ways does he emulate the funeral custom of the Romans and correct "the voice of praise" (p. 194)? What qualities does he depict? What flaws? What relationship between thought and

action underlies Gibbon's treatment? Is Julian represented as a
person divided between the two? What assumptions of his own
does Gibbon reveal in this motif? How does he play on Julian's
"ostentation"? Where is Julian shown to be unpretentious and
where ostentatious? How does Gibbon play on his subject's
"merit"? What does he think of Julian's "philosophy"? How does
he treat Julian's skills as a soldier? Does he see him as only a
mockery of the great Roman generals? What kinds of irony are
evident in Gibbon's portrait? Does he use "satire and ridicule"—
or "pleasantry"? How hard is he upon Julian's "imperfections"?

2. Analyze the form of the first paragraph. Gibbon is a virtuoso
of the paragraph. He is able to encompass a huge quantity of
material with masterful control of detail and movement. He
worked hard to achieve this perfection; as he said: "It has always
been my practice to cast a long paragraph in a single mold, to
try it by my ear, to deposit it in my memory, but to suspend the
action of the pen till I had given the last polish to my work."
How does Gibbon shape the first paragraph? What is the connection between the first and last sentences? What material do
they frame? What unit of the narrative is set off by the paragraph? What is its single mold? What is there about its grammar,
punctuation, and syntax that suggests it may have been tried
by ear? Are there any instances where Gibbon violates "correct"
syntax in order to emphasize the flow and balance of his ca-
dences? Does the whole have the quality of spoken discourse?
If so, how does Gibbon's "speech" compare with that of Milton or
Donne? Is Gibbon's too mannered, too polished?

3. Looking now at the smaller elements of composition, the
most conspicuous feature of Gibbon's prose is its rhetorical balance. Does he favor antithesis or parallelism? How does the
balance of Gibbon's sentences compare with that of Milton or
Walton? Which is more symmetrical? Which has greater variety?
Which seems more stylized? Notice the frequent doubling of
adjectives in Gibbon's writing. Is this merely a device for in-
tensification, or is it a means of achieving clarity and exactness?
Gibbon often joins adjectives by the coordinating particle "or"
to signify alternatives. Are they genuine alternatives? Why does
Gibbon use this device rather than any other? Is the effect simply
one of specious sonority? Is Gibbon's habit of coupling modifiers
in parallelism or contrast a device of precision or of distention?

Does it impede the movement of the sentence? To what elements of the thought of the sentence does it direct the mind of the reader?

4. Like Milton, Gibbon is partial to the long periodic sentence. The main thought comes last with many qualifications intervening among the subject, verb, and complement. According to Harold Bond (*The Literary Art of Edward Gibbon,* 1960), the usual form of Gibbon's sentence is a period made of three or more members. Gibbon likes to consider several parts of an assertion or situation simultaneously and not complete his thought until these parts have been brought into a clear relationship to each other. How many of the sentences in the first paragraph exemplify Gibbon's characteristic sentence formation? Compare the sentences in the other paragraphs of the selection. Gibbon uses many devices to vary the pattern of his periods and avoid monotony—e.g., inversion, surprise endings, alterations in tone, variations in length of parts and of the whole, variations in the kinds of relationships examined. Pick out instances of each of these departures from the "norm" of Gibbon's periodic sentence, and consider their effect on the style and sense of the passage. How do Gibbon's periods differ from Milton's?

5. Consider Gibbon's rendition of Julian's speech to the army after the siege of Perisabor (p. 180). In what ways does it convey "the grave and manly language of a Roman"? How does the diction of this speech compare with the diction in the rest of the paragraph? Are there significant differences in sentence structure? What qualities of Julian's character are exhibited by the speech? How does Julian handle his troops?

6. Analyze the composition of the third paragraph (beginning "As it became necessary . . ." on p. 182). How does Gibbon render the military engagement recounted on p. 183? Does he dwell on the tactics, terrain, order of battle, etc. with the kind of detail dear to military historians? Does he try to enact in his writing the violence and the movement of the battle, or does he depict the action in static terms, catching its essential contours with the arrested motion of a painting or a frieze? What does Gibbon choose to emphasize in his narrative? How does the success of Julian's tactics and the ease of his victory here contrast with his later reverses? Is there more to the detail of "darkness" than meets the eye? Why does Gibbon end the paragraph with the remark that Julian "had now reached the term of his prosperity" (p. 184)? What does this tell the reader about the intention of the paragraph?

7. What surprises and ironies does Gibbon represent in the next paragraph (beginning "On the second day . . ." at p. 184)? Explain the ironic effects of the sentence "Sapor, who had been . . ." (p. 185). How would you describe the construction of the sentence "The pride of royalty . . ."? Analyze the composition of the sentence "The Sassanian prince . . ." Gibbon inserts several qualifications between the subject and verb in the form of a neatly balanced consideration of alternative motives for the prince's action. In what other ways could this sentence have been written, and how would each of these forms of expression alter its sense or effect? Why did Gibbon choose this form?

8. The ruse of the Persian secret agent described on p. 186 would seem to offer rich dramatic possibilities. An imaginative writer ought to be able to make more of this episode. Why doesn't Gibbon exploit the opportunity? Does he underplay the treason? What is uppermost in his mind at this juncture? What is he trying to show? Why does Gibbon bother to explain and defend Julian's actions here? Is he exonerating his "hero"?

9. Analyze the sense and composition of the paragraph beginning "The cumbersome train . . ." (p. 187). What is the rhythmic effect of "blasted" in the sentence "But on the approach of the Romans this rich and smiling prospect was instantly blasted" (p. 188)? Why does Gibbon set this off as a separate sentence? What is its connection to the one before and the one after? How would you characterize the writing in the account of the scorched-earth policy? What makes "the emperor was soon reduced to the scanty stock of provisions which continually wasted in his hands" so effective? How is the sense of time running out and fortunes dwindling rendered in Gibbon's narrative?

10. Is there a figurative tracery in the narrative of the paragraph beginning "As long as the Romans . . ." (p. 189)? Does the account of the losses suffered by the retreating Romans in their skirmishes with the Persians suggest an attrition of strength and resolve—a wasting away of energy, the wearing down of a cumbersome body? What part do Gibbon's verbs play in creating

this impression? What is the relation of this pattern to the design of the whole?

11. Consider the voice and perspective of the author in the sentence "But this feeble relief . . . ," which closes the seventh paragraph (p. 190). The Roman soldiers may well have felt what Gibbon relates, but as readers we are less concerned with how they actually felt and more with the lessons to be drawn from the action. The aim of his history is moral and philosophic instruction. Our responses are directed to judgment and evaluation rather than to the vicarious experience of the events recounted. The vise tightens on Julian's army and the plight becomes more desperate, but we are meant to be detached, our minds engaged by the example Gibbon is making of the decline of the Emperor's fortunes and the collapse of his ambitions. Gibbon sometimes looks at a situation from the point of view of the participants, but he does not dwell there. He carries the reader some distance above and away from the events to gaze upon the actors on his stage. Gibbon is a magisterial writer. He does not mask his presence, and he does not conceal the artifice of his art. He is openly deliberate. He is as much an artist in history as a novelist is in fiction. He makes his history in a manner very like a dramatist.

Are Sidney's objections to the historian pertinent to Gibbon's kind of history? How does Gibbon's practice differ from that of twentieth-century historians? How would you answer the charges made by Herbert Read (*English Prose Style,* 1942) with Gibbon in mind?

> . . . most historians have considered it necessary to eke out the scantiness of their facts with personal affectations; the narrative is subordinated to theoretical disquisitions and hypothetical motivations. The historian makes no attempt to see the events in their concreteness, but reacts to what he considers the historical significance of these events. We are given, not a narrative of facts, but a contemporaneous philosophy of history—an amalgam of politics, psychology, metaphysics and prejudice.

What makes Gibbon's account of the apprehensions of Julian's soldiers affecting and convincing—even if it were conceded to be an imaginative invention? Why has Gibbon's work endured? Only

because of its "style"? Has his history been discredited or super-
seded? Why should we read *The Decline and Fall of the Roman
Empire*? How should we read it? As a chronicle, or as something
else?

12. In the paragraph beginning "While Julian struggled . . ."
(p. 190) Gibbon leaves the broad field of the campaign and
focuses upon Julian's last hours. Gibbon makes it clear that he
regards Julian's visions as "superstition." How does he convey this
attitude in the form of his expression? What does Gibbon think
of Julian's "anxieties"? What split in his character is depicted?
Is there a suggestion that the division has played a significant
part in his demise—that, dramatically speaking, Julian's character
is his fate? Julian is made to seem frantic and foolhardy in his
last fight (p. 191). Why? Is Gibbon recounting something besides Julian's courage? Why doesn't Gibbon break off the paragraph at "and conveyed out of the tumult of the battle into an
adjacent tent"?

13. How are the first two sentences of the paragraph beginning "The first words . . ." (p. 191) meant to be taken? What
does Gibbon think of Julian's dying talk? Does he agree with
the hired philosophers who compared Julian's tent with the prison
of Socrates? Analyze the intent, form, and sense of Julian's funeral
oration. How does the writing compare with Gibbon's own characteristic expression? In a footnote Gibbon remarked: "The
character and situation of Julian might countenance the suspicion
that he had previously composed the elaborate oration." What
does this reveal about his own attitude toward the speech?
How does Gibbon render the expressions of grief at Julian's
dying, particularly the Emperor's bewailing the loss of Anatolius?
Why does Gibbon say "amiable" inconsistency? What is the tone
of "The efforts which he made, of mind as well as body, most
probably hastened his death" (p. 193)? Why does Gibbon bother
with the details in the sentence "His wound began to bleed . . ."?
Why doesn't Gibbon write something like the following: "His
wound began to bleed with fresh violence, and about the hour of
midnight, he died"? What is the tone of the last sentence in the
paragraph?

"WHERE I LIVED, AND WHAT I LIVED FOR"

FROM *Walden*

BY *Henry David Thoreau*

AT A CERTAIN SEASON of our life we are accustomed to consider every spot as the possible site of a house. I have thus surveyed the country on every side within a dozen miles of where I live. In imagination I have bought all the farms in succession, for all were to be bought, and I knew their price. I walked over each farmer's premises, tasted his wild apples, discoursed on husbandry with him, took his farm at his price, at any price, mortgaging it to him in my mind; even put a higher price on it,—took everything but a deed of it,—took his word for his deed, for I dearly love to talk,—cultivated it, and him too to some extent, I trust, and withdrew when I had enjoyed it long enough, leaving him to carry it on. This experience entitled me to be regarded as a sort of real-estate broker by my friends. Wherever I sat, there I might live, and the landscape radiated from me accordingly. What is a house but a *sedes*, a seat?—better if a country seat. I discovered many a site for a house not likely to be soon improved, which some might have thought too far from the village, but to my eyes the village was too far from it. Well, there I might live, I said; and there I did live, for an hour, a summer and a winter life; saw how I could let the years run off, buffet the winter through, and see the spring come in. The future inhabitants of this region, wherever they may place their houses, may be sure that they have been anticipated. An afternoon sufficed to lay out the land into orchard, woodlot, and pasture, and to decide what fine oaks or pines should be left to stand before the door, and whence each blasted tree could be seen to the best advantage; and then I let it lie, fallow perchance, for a man is rich in proportion to the number of things which he can afford to let alone.

My imagination carried me so far that I even had the refusal of several farms,—the refusal was all I wanted,—but I never got my fingers burned by actual possession. The nearest that I came to actual possession was when I bought the Hollowell place, and had begun to sort my seeds, and collected materials with which to make a wheelbarrow to carry it on or off with; but before the owner gave me a deed of it, his wife—every man has such a wife —changed her mind and wished to keep it, and he offered me ten dollars to release him. Now, to speak the truth, I had but ten cents in the world, and it surpassed my arithmetic to tell, if I was the man who had ten cents, or who had a farm, or ten dollars, or all together. However, I let him keep the ten dollars and the farm too, for I had carried it far enough; or rather, to be generous, I sold him the farm for just what I gave for it, and, as he was not a rich man, made him a present of ten dollars, and still had my ten cents, and seeds, and materials for a wheelbarrow left. I found thus that I had been a rich man without any damage to my poverty. But I retained the landscape, and I have since annually carried off what it yielded without a wheelbarrow. With respect to landscapes,—

> I am monarch of all I *survey*,
> My right there is none to dispute.

I have frequently seen a poet withdraw, having enjoyed the most valuable part of a farm, while the crusty farmer supposed that he had got a few wild apples only. Why, the owner does not know it for many years when a poet has put his farm in rhyme, the most admirable kind of invisible fence, has fairly impounded it, milked it, skimmed it, and got all the cream, and left the farmer only the skimmed milk.

The real attractions of the Hollowell farm, to me, were: its complete retirement, being about two miles from the village, half a mile from the nearest neighbor, and separated from the highway by a broad field; its bounding on the river, which the owner

said protected it by its fogs from frosts in the spring, though
that was nothing to me; the gray color and ruinous state of the
house and barn, and the dilapidated fences, which put such an
interval between me and the last occupant; the hollow and
lichen-covered apple trees, gnawed by rabbits, showing what
kind of neighbors I should have; but above all, the recollection
I had of it from my earliest voyages up the river, when the house
was concealed behind a dense grove of red maples, through
which I heard the house-dog bark. I was in haste to buy it, before the proprietor finished getting out some rocks, cutting down
the hollow apple trees, and grubbing up some young birches
which had sprung up in the pasture, or, in short, had made any
more of his improvements. To enjoy these advantages I was
ready to carry it on; like Atlas, to take the world on my shoulders,
—I never heard what compensation he received for that,—and
do all those things which had no other motive or excuse but that
I might pay for it and be unmolested in my possession of it; for
I knew all the while that it would yield the most abundant crop
of the kind I wanted if I could only afford to let it alone. But it
turned out as I have said.

All that I could say, then, with respect to farming on a large
scale, (I have always cultivated a garden,) was, that I had had
my seeds ready. Many think that seeds improve with age. I have
no doubt that time discriminates between the good and the bad;
and when at last I shall plant, I shall be less likely to be disappointed. But I would say to my fellows, once for all, As long as
possible live free and uncommitted. It makes but little difference
whether you are committed to a farm or the county jail.

Old Cato, whose "De Re Rustica" is my "Cultivator," says, and
the only translation I have seen makes sheer nonsense of the passage, "When you think of getting a farm turn it thus in your
mind, not to buy greedily; nor spare your pains to look at it, and
do not think it enough to go round it once. The oftener you go
there the more it will please you, if it is good." I think I shall not
buy greedily, but go round and round it as long as I live, and be
buried in it first, that it may please me the more at last.

The present was my next experiment of this kind, which I
purpose to describe more at length, for convenience, putting the
experience of two years into one. As I have said, I do not propose

to write an ode to dejection, but to brag as lustily as chanticleer in the morning, standing on his roost, if only to wake my neighbors up.

When first I took up my abode in the woods, that is, began to spend my nights as well as days there, which, by accident, was on Independence day, or the fourth of July, 1845, my house was not finished for winter, but was merely a defense against the rain, without plastering or chimney, the walls being of rough weather-stained boards, with wide chinks, which made it cool at night. The upright white hewn studs and freshly planed door and window casings gave it a clean and airy look, especially in the morning, when its timbers were saturated with dew, so that I fancied that by noon some sweet gum would exude from them. To my imagination it retained throughout the day more or less of this auroral character, reminding me of a certain house on a mountain which I had visited a year before. This was an airy and unplastered cabin, fit to entertain a travelling god, and where a goddess might trail her garments. The winds which passed over my dwelling were such as sweep over the ridges of mountains, bearing the broken strains, or celestial parts only, of terrestrial music. The morning wind forever blows, the poem of creation is uninterrupted; but few are the ears that hear it. Olympus is but the outside of the earth everywhere.

The only house I had been the owner of before, if I except a boat, was a tent, which I used occasionally when making excursions in the summer, and this is still rolled up in my garret; but the boat, after passing from hand to hand, has gone down the stream of time. With this more substantial shelter about me, I had made some progress toward settling in the world. This frame, so slightly clad, was a sort of crystallization around me, and reacted on the builder. It was suggestive somewhat as a picture in outlines. I did not need to go out doors to take the air, for the atmosphere within had lost none of its freshness. It was not so much within doors as behind a door where I sat, even in the rainiest weather. The Harivansa says, "An abode without birds is like a meat without seasoning." Such was not my abode, for I found myself suddenly neighbor to the birds; not by having imprisoned one, but having caged myself near them. I was not only nearer to some of those which commonly frequent the garden and the orchard, but to those wilder and more thrilling songsters of the forest which never, or rarely, serenade a villager, —the wood-thrush, the veery, the scarlet tanager, the field-sparrow, the whippoorwill, and many others.

I was seated by the shore of a small pond, about a mile and a half south of the village of Concord and somewhat higher than it, in the midst of an extensive wood between that town and Lincoln, and about two miles south of that our only field known to fame, Concord Battle Ground; but I was so low in the woods that the opposite shore, half a mile off, like the rest, covered with wood, was my most distant horizon. For the first week, whenever I looked out on the pond it impressed me like a tarn high up on the side of a mountain, its bottom far above the surface of other lakes, and, as the sun arose, I saw it throwing off its nightly clothing of mist, and here and there, by degrees, its soft ripples or its smooth reflecting surface was revealed, while the mists, like ghosts, were stealthily withdrawing in every direction into the woods, as at the breaking up of some nocturnal conventicle. The very dew seemed to hang upon the trees later into the day than usual, as on the sides of mountains.

This small lake was of most value as a neighbor in the intervals of a gentle rain storm in August, when, both air and water being perfectly still, but the sky overcast, mid-afternoon had all the serenity of evening, and the wood-thrush sang around, and was heard from shore to shore. A lake like this is never smoother than at such a time; and the clear portion of the air above it being shallow and darkened by clouds, the water, full of light and reflections, becomes a lower heaven itself so much the more important. From a hill top near by, where the wood had been recently cut off, there was a pleasing vista southward across the pond, through a wide indentation in the hills which form the shore there, where their opposite sides sloping toward each other suggested a stream flowing out in that direction through a wooded valley, but stream there was none. That way I looked between and over the near green hills to some distant and higher ones in the horizon, tinged with blue. Indeed, by standing on tiptoe I could catch a glimpse of some of the peaks of the still bluer and more distant mountain ranges in the north-west, those true-blue coins from heaven's own mint, and also of some portion of the village. But in other directions, even from this point, I could not see over or beyond the woods which surrounded me. It is well to have some water in your neighborhood, to give buoyancy to and float the earth. One value even of the smallest well is, that when you look into it you see that earth is not continent but insular. This is as important as that it keeps butter cool. When I looked across the pond from this peak toward the Sudbury meadows, which in time of flood I distinguished elevated perhaps by a mirage in their seething valley, like a coin in a basin, all the earth beyond the pond appeared like a thin crust insulated and floated even by this small sheet of intervening water, and I was reminded that this on which I dwelt was but *dry land.*

Though the view from my door was still more contracted, I did not feel crowded or confined in the least. There was pasture enough for my imagination. The low shrub-oak plateau to which the opposite shore arose, stretched away toward the prairies of the West and the steppes of Tartary, affording ample room for all the roving families of men. "There are none happy in the world but beings who enjoy freely a vast horizon,"—said Damodara, when his herds required new and larger pastures.

Both place and time were changed, and I dwelt nearer to those parts of the universe and to those eras in history which had most attracted me. Where I lived was as far off as many a region viewed nightly by astronomers. We are wont to imagine rare and delectable places in some remote and more celestial corner of the system, behind the constellation of Cassiopeia's Chair, far from noise and disturbance. I discovered that my house actually had its site in such a withdrawn, but forever new and unprofaned, part of the universe. If it were worth the while to settle in those parts near to the Pleiades or the Hyades, to Aldebaran or Altair, then I was really there, or at an equal remoteness from the life which I had left behind, dwindled and twinkling with as fine a ray to my nearest neighbor, and to be seen only in moonless nights by him. Such was that part of creation where I had squatted;—

> There was a shepherd that did live,
>   And held his thoughts as high
> As were the mounts whereon his flocks
>   Did hourly feed him by.

What should we think of the shepherd's life if his flocks always wandered to higher pastures than his thoughts?

Every morning was a cheerful invitation to make my life of equal simplicity, and I may say innocence, with Nature herself.

I have been as sincere a worshipper of Aurora as the Greeks. I got up early and bathed in the pond; that was a religious exercise, and one of the best things which I did. They say that characters were engraven on the bathing tub of king Tching-thang to this effect: "Renew thyself completely each day; do it again, and again, and forever again." I can understand that. Morning brings back the heroic ages. I was as much affected by the faint hum of a mosquito making its invisible and unimaginable tour through my apartment at earliest dawn, when I was sitting with door and windows open, as I could be by any trumpet that ever sang of fame. It was Homer's requiem; itself an Iliad and Odyssey in the air, singing its own wrath and wanderings. There was something cosmical about it; a standing advertisement, till forbidden, of the everlasting vigor and fertility of the world. The morning, which is the most memorable season of the day, is the awakening hour. Then there is least somnolence in us; and for an hour, at least, some part of us awakes which slumbers all the rest of the day and night. Little is to be expected of that day, if it can be called a day, to which we are not awakened by our Genius, but by the mechanical nudgings of some servitor, are not awakened by our own newly-acquired force and aspirations from within, accompanied by the undulations of celestial music, instead of factory bells, and a fragrance filling the air—to a higher life than we fell asleep from; and thus the darkness bear its fruit, and prove itself to be good, no less than the light. That man who does not believe that each day contains an earlier, more sacred, and auroral hour than he has yet profaned, has despaired of life, and is pursuing a descending and darkening way. After a partial cessation of his sensuous life, the soul of man, or its organs rather, are reinvigorated each day, and his Genius tries again what noble life it can make. All memorable events, I should say, transpire in morning time and in a morning atmosphere. The Vedas say, "All intelligences awake with the morning." Poetry and art, and the fairest and most memorable of the actions of men, date from such an hour. All poets and heroes, like Memnon, are the children of Aurora, and emit their music at sunrise. To him whose elastic and vigorous thought keeps pace with the sun, the day is a perpetual morning. It matters not what the clocks say or the attitudes and labors of men. Morning is when I am awake and there is a dawn in me. Moral reform is the effort to throw off sleep. Why is it that men give so poor an account of their day if they have not been slumbering? They are not such poor calculators. If they had not been overcome with drowsiness they would have performed something. The millions are awake enough for physical labor; but only one in a million is awake enough for effective intellectual exertion, only one in a hundred millions to a poetic or divine life. To be awake is to be alive. I have never yet met a man who was quite awake. How could I have looked him in the face?

We must learn to reawaken and keep ourselves awake, not by mechanical aids, but by an infinite expectation of the dawn, which does not forsake us in our soundest sleep. I know of no more encouraging fact than the unquestionable ability of man to elevate his life by a conscious endeavor. It is something to be able to paint a particular picture, or to carve a statue, and so to make a few objects beautiful; but it is far more glorious to carve and paint the very atmosphere and medium through which we look, which morally we can do. To affect the quality of the day, that is the highest of arts. Every man is tasked to make his life, even in its details, worthy of the contemplation of his most elevated and critical hour. If we refused, or rather used up, such paltry information as we get, the oracles would distinctly inform us how this might be done.

I went to the woods because I wished to live deliberately, to front only the essential facts of life, and see if I could not learn what it had to teach, and not, when I came to die, discover that I had not lived. I did not wish to live what was not life, living is so dear; nor did I wish to practice resignation, unless it was quite necessary. I wanted to live deep and suck out all the marrow of life, to live so sturdily and Spartan-like as to put to rout all that was not life, to cut a broad swath and shave close, to drive life into a corner, and reduce it to its lowest terms, and, if it proved to be mean, why then to get the whole and genuine meanness of it, and publish its meanness to the world; or if it were sublime, to know it by experience, and be able to give a true account of it in my next excursion. For most men, it appears to me, are in a strange uncertainty about it, whether it is of the devil or of God, and have *somewhat hastily* concluded that it is the chief end of man here to "glorify God and enjoy him forever."

Still we live meanly, like ants; though the fable tells us that we were long ago changed into men; like pygmies we fight with cranes; it is error upon error, and clout upon clout, and our best

virtue has for its occasion a superfluous and evitable wretchedness. Our life is frittered away by detail. An honest man has
hardly need to count more than his ten fingers, or in extreme
cases he may add his ten toes, and lump the rest. Simplicity,
simplicity, simplicity! I say, let your affairs be as two or three,
and not a hundred or a thousand; instead of a million count half
a dozen, and keep your accounts on your thumb nail. In the
midst of this chopping sea of civilized life, such are the clouds
and storms and quicksands and thousand-and-one items to be allowed for, that a man has to live, if he would not founder and go
to the bottom and not make his port at all, by dead reckoning,
and he must be a great calculator indeed who succeeds. Simplify,
simplify. Instead of three meals a day, if it be necessary eat but
one; instead of a hundred dishes, five; and reduce other things
in proportion. Our life is like a German Confederacy, made up
of petty states, with its boundary forever fluctuating, so that even
a German cannot tell you how it is bounded at any moment. The
nation itself, with all its so-called internal improvements, which,
by the way, are all external and superficial, is just such an un-
wieldy and overgrown establishment, cluttered with furniture
and tripped up by its own traps, ruined by luxury and heedless
expense, by want of calculation and a worthy aim, as the million
households in the land; and the only cure for it as for them is in
a rigid economy, a stern and more than Spartan simplicity of
life and elevation of purpose. It lives too fast. Men think that it
is essential that the *Nation* have commerce, and export ice, and
talk through a telegraph, and ride thirty miles an hour, without a
doubt, whether *they* do or not; but whether we should live like
baboons or like men, is a little uncertain. If we do not get out
sleepers, and forge rails, and devote days and nights to the work,
but go to tinkering upon our *lives* to improve *them,* who will
build railroads? And if railroads are not built, how shall we get
to heaven in season? But if we stay at home and mind our business, who will want railroads? We do not ride on the railroad; it
rides upon us. Did you ever think what those sleepers are that
underlie the railroad? Each one is a man, an Irishman, or a
Yankee man. The rails are laid on them, and they are covered
with sand, and the cars run smoothly over them. They are sound
sleepers, I assure you. And every few years a new lot is laid down
and run over; so that, if some have the pleasure of riding on a
rail, others have the misfortune to be ridden upon. And when

they run over a man that is walking in his sleep, a supernumerary sleeper in the wrong position, and wake him up, they suddenly stop the cars, and make a hue and cry about it, as if this were an exception. I am glad to know that it takes a gang of men for every five miles to keep the sleepers down and level in their beds as it is, for this is a sign that they may sometime get up again.

Why should we live with such hurry and waste of life? We are determined to be starved before we are hungry. Men say that a stitch in time saves nine, and so they take a thousand stitches to-day to save nine to-morrow. As for *work*, we haven't any of any consequence. We have the Saint Vitus' dance, and cannot possibly keep our heads still. If I should only give a few pulls at the parish bell-rope, as for a fire, that is, without setting the bell, there is hardly a man on his farm in the outskirts of Concord, notwithstanding that press of engagements which was his excuse so many times this morning, nor a boy, nor a woman, I might almost say, but would forsake all and follow that sound, not mainly to save property from the flames, but, if we will confess the truth, much more to see it burn, since burn it must, and we, be it known, did not set it on fire,—or to see it put out, and have a hand in it, if that is done as handsomely; yes, even if it were the parish church itself. Hardly a man takes a half hour's nap after dinner, but when he wakes he holds up his head and asks, "What's the news?" as if the rest of mankind had stood his sentinels. Some give directions to be waked every half hour, doubtless for no other purpose; and then, to pay for it, they tell what they have dreamed. After a night's sleep the news is as indispensable as the breakfast. "Pray tell me anything new that has happened to a man anywhere on this globe,"—and he reads it over his coffee and rolls, that a man has had his eyes gouged out this morning on the Wachito River; never dreaming the while that he lives in the dark unfathomed mammoth cave of this world, and has but the rudiment of an eye himself.

For my part, I could easily do without the post-office. I think that there are very few important communications made through it. To speak critically, I never received more than one or two letters in my life—I wrote this some years ago—that were worth the postage. The penny-post is, commonly, an institution through which you seriously offer a man that penny for his thoughts which is so often safely offered in jest. And I am sure that I never read any memorable news in a newspaper. If we read of one man robbed, or murdered, or killed by accident, or one house burned, or one vessel wrecked, or one steamboat blown up, or one cow run over on the Western Railroad, or one mad dog killed, or one lot of grasshoppers in the winter,—we never need read of another. One is enough. If you are acquainted with the principle, what do you care for a myriad instances and applications? To a philosopher all *news,* as it is called, is gossip, and they who edit and read it are old women over their tea. Yet not a few are greedy after this gossip. There was such a rush, as I hear, the other day at one of the offices to learn the foreign news by the last arrival, that several large squares of plate glass belonging to the establishment were broken by the pressure,—news which I seriously think a ready wit might write a twelvemonth or twelve years beforehand with sufficient accuracy. As for Spain, for instance, if you know how to throw in Don Carlos and the Infanta, and Don Pedro and Seville and Granada, from time to time in the right proportions,—they may have changed the names a little since I saw the papers,—and serve up a bull-fight when other entertainments fail, it will be true to the letter, and give us as good an idea of the exact state or ruin of things in Spain as the most succinct and lucid reports under this head in the newspapers: and as for England, almost the last significant scrap of news from that quarter was the revolution of 1649; and if you have learned the history of her crops for an average year, you never need attend to that thing again, unless your speculations are of a merely pecuniary character. If one may judge who rarely looks into the newspapers, nothing new does ever happen in foreign parts, a French revolution not excepted.

What news! how much more important to know what that is which was never old! "Kieou-he-yu (great dignitary of the state of Wei) sent a man to Khoung-tseu to know his news. Khoung-tseu caused the messenger to be seated near him, and questioned him in these terms: What is your master doing? The messenger answered with respect: My master desires to diminish the number of his faults, but he cannot come to the end of them. The messenger being gone, the philosopher remarked: What a worthy messenger! What a worthy messenger!" The preacher, instead of vexing the ears of drowsy farmers on their day of rest at the end of the week,—for Sunday is the fit conclusion of an ill-spent week, and not the fresh and brave beginning of a new one,—with this one other draggle-tail of a sermon, should shout with thundering voice,—"Pause! Avast! Why so seeming fast, but deadly slow?"

Shams and delusions are esteemed for soundest truths, while reality is fabulous. If men would steadily observe realities only, and not allow themselves to be deluded, life, to compare it with such things as we know, would be like a fairy tale and the Arabian Nights' Entertainments. If we respected only what is inevitable and has a right to be, music and poetry would resound along the streets. When we are unhurried and wise, we perceive that only great and worthy things have any permanent and absolute existence,—that petty fears and petty pleasures are but the shadow of the reality. This is always exhilarating and sublime. By closing the eyes and slumbering, and consenting to be deceived by shows, men establish and confirm their daily life of routine and habit everywhere, which still is built on purely illusory foundations. Children, who play life, discern its true law and relations more clearly than men, who fail to live it worthily, but who think that they are wiser by experience, that is, by failure. I have read in a Hindoo book, that "there was a king's son, who, being expelled in infancy from his native city, was brought up by a forester, and, growing up to maturity in that state, imagined himself to belong to the barbarous race with which he lived. One of his father's ministers having discovered him, revealed to him what he was, and the misconception of his character was removed, and he knew himself to be a prince. So soul," continues the Hindoo philosopher, "from the circumstances in which it is placed, mistakes its own character, until the truth is revealed to it by some holy teacher, and then it knows itself to be *Brahme*." I perceive that we inhabitants of New England live this mean life that we do because our vision does not penetrate the surface of things. We think that that *is* which *appears* to be. If a man should walk through this town and see only the reality, where, think you, would the "Mill-dam" go to? If he should give us an account of the realities he beheld there, we should not recognize the place in his description. Look at a meeting-house, or a courthouse, or a jail, or a shop, or a dwelling-house, and say what that thing really is before a true gaze, and they would all go to pieces in your account of them. Men esteem truth remote, in the outskirts of the system, behind the farthest star, before Adam and after the last man. In eternity there is indeed something true and sublime. But all these times and places and occasions are now and here. God himself culminates in the present moment, and will never be more divine in the lapse of all the ages. And we are enabled to apprehend at all what is sublime and noble only by the perpetual instilling and drenching of the reality that surrounds us. The universe constantly and obediently answers to our conceptions; whether we travel fast or slow, the track is laid for us. Let us spend our lives in conceiving then. The poet or the artist never yet had so fair and noble a design but some of his posterity at least could accomplish it.

Let us spend one day as deliberately as Nature, and not be thrown off the track by every nutshell and mosquito's wing that falls on the rails. Let us rise early and fast, or break fast, gently and without perturbation; let company come and let company go, let the bells ring and the children cry,—determined to make a day of it. Why should we knock under and go with the stream? Let us not be upset and overwhelmed in that terrible rapid and whirlpool called a dinner, situated in the meridian shallows. Weather this danger and you are safe, for the rest of the way is down hill. With unrelaxed nerves, with morning vigor, sail by it, looking another way, tied to the mast like Ulysses. If the engine whistles, let it whistle till it is hoarse for its pains. If the bell rings, why should we run? We will consider what kind of music they are like. Let us settle ourselves, and work and wedge our feet downward through the mud and slush of opinion, and prejudice, and tradition, and delusion, and appearance, that alluvion which covers the globe, through Paris and London, through New York and Boston and Concord, through church and state, through poetry and philosophy and religion, till we come to a hard bottom and rocks in place, which we can call *reality*, and say, This is, and no mistake; and then begin, having a *point d'appui*, below freshet and frost and fire, a place where you might found a wall or a state, or set a lamp-post safely, or perhaps a gauge, not a Nilometer, but a Realometer, that future ages might know how deep a freshet of shams and appearances had gathered from time to time. If you stand right fronting and face to face to a fact, you will see the sun glimmer on both its surfaces, as if it were a cimeter, and feel its sweet edge dividing you through the heart and marrow, and so you will happily conclude your mortal career. Be it life or death, we crave only reality. If we are really dying, let us hear the rattle in our throats and feel cold in the extremities; if we are alive, let us go about our business.

Time is but the stream I go a-fishing in. I drink at it; but while I drink I see the sandy bottom and detect how shallow it is. Its thin current slides away, but eternity remains. I would drink deeper; fish in the sky, whose bottom is pebbly with stars. I cannot count one. I know not the first letter of the alphabet. I have always been regretting that I was not as wise as the day I was born. The intellect is a cleaver; it discerns and rifts its way into the secret of things. I do not wish to be any more busy with my hands than is necessary. My head is hands and feet. I feel all my best faculties concentrated in it. My instinct tells me that my head is an organ for burrowing, as some creatures use their snout and fore-paws, and with it I would mine and burrow my way through these hills. I think that the richest vein is somewhere hereabouts; so by the divining rod and thin rising vapors I judge; and here I will begin to mine.

QUESTIONS FOR STUDY
AND TOPICS FOR DISCUSSION
on *"Where I Lived, and What I Lived For"*

1. The first six paragraphs of this selection, Chapter II of *Walden* (1854), comprise a complete unit. Paragraphs 1, 2, 3, and 5 were first published as "A Poet Buying a Farm," in a magazine in 1852. Why does Thoreau add paragraphs 4 and 6? Are the joints between the paragraphs neat and tight? Why does Thoreau set this off as a separate section? What is its connection with what follows? Thoreau is whimsically recounting his "buying" of farms, real and fancied, before taking up residence at Walden. He contrasts the poet's imaginative possession and use of property with that of more practical owners and real-estate brokers. How does this section prepare for the later discussion, in the two paragraphs before the last (pp. 213–214), of the differences between appearance and reality? Why is the poet's fiction a vision of reality, and the "realist's" vision only a perception of deceiving appearances?

2. *Walden* is a work of high seriousness, but it is lightened by wit. Thoreau is passionate in his convictions and fiercely honest—he had, as Emerson says, such a dangerous frankness that he was called "the terrible Thoreau"—but his writing is gay and artful, almost frolicsome. He loves to play with words. Many of his favorite tricks are exhibited in the first section of this chapter. He fools with the word "survey," punning on his own profession as a surveyor. He toys with the root-meaning of "seat" (and ties this to the fact that he is living on Emerson's acres at Walden Pond as a "squatter"). He drily mocks the "improvements" of the proprietor of the Hollowell place. He satirizes the "crusty farmer" and all his breed of possessors. He exploits the ambiguities of "commitment," playing the legal and financial senses of the word against his own concern. Most of all, he delights in paradox: e.g., "a man is rich in proportion to the number of things which he can afford to let alone." Threading the whole is a play on the language and notion of "buying," and a cluster of affiliations: possession, entailments, yields, value.

What is the intention and effect of these several devices? Why does Thoreau employ them? Why, for example, does he choose to play upon "commitment"? How does the multiplicity of meanings expand the scope of the statement? How does the ambiguity reflect the sense of the whole chapter? Does the verbal play disturb the consistency of the later portions that treat the notion of commitment? How does this play on words, and all the other tricks here and in the rest of the chapter, express Thoreau's serious purpose? In what ways are the paradoxes of this section picked up and elaborated in other terms later in the piece? What metaphoric patterns order the paradoxes, and how are these developed? Are the paradoxes forced and artificial?

3. What does the seventh paragraph (p. 204) tell us about the intention and the form of the chapter (and the whole of *Walden*)? Thoreau lived at Walden from July 4, 1845 to September 6, 1847. Why did he condense the experience of two years into one? Is it just an accident that he took occupancy on Independence day? Thoreau placed the statement "I do not propose . . ." as the epigraph to the book. What is its significance for this chapter? Why does he say "brag"? How does he play upon the language and idea of "waking up" throughout the chapter? To whom does he address his piece? Literally his neighbors? What is his disposition and manner?

4. Analyze the sense and composition of Thoreau's description of his house in the two paragraphs beginning "When I first took up my abode . . ." on p. 205. The character of this house is as surely figurative as Donne's metaphor (pp. 83 ff.), but the description seems to be so factual, so much that of an actual building, that it is impossible to separate the literal from the figurative. Almost every literal detail, every fact, in Thoreau's work turns figurative upon close inspection. Why are we prepared to receive the material of these paragraphs as "symbolic"? What is being symbolized exactly? What part does the form and content of the first section play in directing us to the symbolic quality here? Why does Thoreau remark the "auroral character" of his abode? Why does he take satisfaction in its being open and unfinished?

Why does he choose to remember another house on a mountain which he had visited a year before? Is there any ulterior significance to the description of the mountain winds which passed over his dwelling? Is the writing of the passage "my house was not finished . . . would exude from them" appreciably different in construction and effect from that of "This was an airy . . . of the earth everywhere"? Is the latter more conventionally "poetic"? Why does Thoreau emphasize the music heard by the imaginative faculties? Does this remind you of anything in Sidney's *An Apology for Poetry*?

5. Why does Thoreau make so much of the position and the optical effects of his perception of the pond (pp. 206–207)? Why does he dwell upon his view? Is he simply describing where he lived before taking up what he lived for, or are the two inseparable parts of a certain mode of apprehending nature and reality? What is the significance of the contrast between water and land? What other symbolic contrasts are expressed?

6. Why does Thoreau play on remoteness and nearness in the paragraph beginning "Both place and time . . ." (p. 207)? In what sense has he "settled into the world" (p. 205) and yet soared beyond the environs of Concord? Is he escaping something?

7. Analyze the sense and composition of the paragraph beginning "Every morning was a cheerful invitation . . ." (p. 207). Why does he say his morning bath was "a religious exercise"? How important is the theme of *renewal* to the entire chapter? What kind of renewal is Thoreau after? After the long paean to morning at the beginning, why does he turn around and say: "It matters not what the clocks say or the attitudes and labors of men. Morning is when I am awake and there is a dawn in me"? Is "being awake" literal or figurative? Which is "morning"; "dawn"; "bathing"? Toward the end of the paragraph, Thoreau's sentences assume a crisp and terse quality. What makes the last three sentences of the paragraph (p. 209) so effective? Is it just that the sentences are shorter and more pointed? How would you compare the sentences earlier in the paragraph, e.g., the three sentences beginning "Little is to be expected . . ."? Why does Thoreau choose one style for the former and another for the latter?

8. In the paragraph beginning "I went to the woods because . . ." (p. 209) Thoreau declares the purpose of his excursion to Walden. Why has he delayed the declaration? Why does he place it here? How does it issue from the paragraphs immediately preceding? What is the sense of "front"? How does he play on "live" and "die"? How does this word play compare with that of the first section? The tone? What is the sense of "dear"? Of "mean"? Is his reduction ascetic? Is he trying to annihilate sense experience? Why does Thoreau use so many negatives here? What is their rhetorical effect?

Analyze the composition of the sentence "I wanted to live deep . . ." (p. 209). Thoreau objected to De Quincey's style as too diffuse and flowing in detail, not sufficiently "concentrated and nutty." The sentence "I wanted to live deep . . ." approaches the ideal of style implicit in this criticism, for it is packed with meaning, taut in construction, yet supple in motion. Are there any sentences in the chapter which lapse into De Quincey's "faults"?

The last sentence alludes to the Shorter Catechism in the *New England Primer*. Is Thoreau being ironical? Why? Why does he italicize *somewhat hastily*?

9. Why does Thoreau allude to the fable of Aeacus and to the cranes and pygmies of the *Iliad*, III, at the beginning of the next paragraph (p. 209)? Is he showing off his learning? How often does he employ allusions to classical and Oriental literature? What is the effect of following allusions with the colloquial idiom of "Our life is frittered away by detail"? Does the alteration from learned writing to everyday idiom jar?

Why does Thoreau repeat "simplicity" three times? What does he mean exactly? In what ways has superfluity, one of the contraries to simplicity, been articulated earlier in the chapter? What words suggesting the notion of encumbrance have been used before? Is there any connection between "simplicity" and "commitment"?

In the passage beginning with the sentence "I say, let your affairs be . . ." (p. 210) Thoreau addresses the reader directly, in an imperative mode and in a tone of exhortation. He has done this before far back in the first section ("But I would say to my fellows . . . ," p. 204), and much of the material intervening has a quality of thinly-disguised moral argument, but from here on he is openly moralistic, almost sermonizing. He lashes out at the follies of his neighbors with biting sarcasm. He continues his play on the word "waking," but the tone is altogether different. What has triggered this change? Why does he alter his tone? How far into the chapter does Thoreau carry his rage? Where does it peak and modulate into something else? How does the change of disposition affect the style of expression?

Many of the analogies in this paragraph are similes. How often does he use this particular figurative device elsewhere in the piece? What is the difference between the figure in "Our life is like a German Confederacy . . ." and that in "In the midst of this chopping sea of civilized life . . ."? Is "keep your accounts on your thumb nail" figurative? What kind of figures are prominent in the paragraph immediately preceding? Which of these are more effective? Why?

Analyze the composition of the sentences beginning "Men think that it is essential . . ." Why does he use a triplet of questions? Are they rhetorical questions? With what tone are they delivered? How are they linked to one another? What does the sentence "We do not ride on the railroad; it rides upon us" do for the cadence of the passage? What is the rhythmical effect of "The rails are laid on them . . ."? A terse and ironic sentence follows, and then two long ones, each commencing with the conjunction "and," concluding with a sarcastic affirmation. What are the rhythmical effects of this construction? What is Thoreau saying in this passage? That the price of progress is the death of those who build railroads; that improvements cost lives? Does he mean this literally? What does this passage have to do with the main thought of the paragraph? With the opening sentence? How do the stops and starts, the turns and surprises of rhythm serve the intention and sense of the passage?

10. What is the relation of the paragraph beginning "Shams and delusions . . ." (p. 213) to what has come before? Is it the next necessary logical step from the paragraph immediately preceding? It opens with an aphoristic statement. As with many of the first and last sentences of Thoreau's paragraphs, the statement has the polished concision of an epigram. It has the air of a journal entry. Like Bacon, Thoreau was a conscientious journal keeper. A substantial portion of his finished writing was

rehearsed in his journals. *Walden* itself included not only a direct account of his experience in the woods during his two years of residence, but a distillation from his journals going back to 1838. Does this paragraph show traces of having been lifted from one of Thoreau's journals? Is it detachable from the whole piece? Can it be placed anywhere else?

What does Thoreau mean by "fabulous"? How does the idea of the sublimity of reality contrast with that of the meanness of the slumber and shows of the daily life of routine and habit? How does the thought "I perceive that . . . which *appears* to be" (p. 213) govern the entire section? Has Thoreau made his meaning of "reality" tangible? He returns to the notion that men search for remote truth instead of finding it "now and here." Is he simply repeating himself, or has he carried the reader through the encrustations of habit and the encumbrances of appearances *by the very form of the work*? Is Thoreau's fable of reality, the publication he promised, an enactment of his experience and an example to the reader? Has Thoreau awakened in the reader by the art of his words the truth he discovered at Walden? Is *Walden* shaped as an excursion into thought—the verbal equivalent of Thoreau's own fronting of life and his awakening into reality?

11. How do the exhortations of the next paragraph (p. 214) differ from those referred to in Question 9? What is Thoreau's tone? How does he pick up figures and ideas which have come before? Almost every significant word sounds an echo or catches an overtone from some earlier passage: deliberately; rails; break fast; bell; stream; music; etc. What is the effect of these repetitions? Does Thoreau define reality? How does he treat the idea of reality? What is the form of the last sentence? What makes the sentence so impressive?

12. Analyze the sense and composition of the last paragraph. How is each sentence joined to the other? How does one thought follow another? Are the sentences and thoughts strung together like separate beads, or are they animated and dynamic in their motion? Is the style typical of the rest of the selection? Why does Thoreau close with this style of writing? What is he saying exactly? What is the sense of the metaphor of the stream and the

metaphor of burrowing? Is the paragraph a point of departure for what is to follow in the rest of the book, or is it the culmination of the thought of this chapter? Is Thoreau marking a stage in his progress?

"A CRISIS IN MY MENTAL HISTORY"
FROM *Autobiography*

BY *John Stuart Mill*

FOR SOME YEARS AFTER this time I wrote very little, and nothing regularly, for publication: and great were the advantages which I derived from the intermission. It was of no common importance to me, at this period, to be able to digest and mature my thoughts for my own mind only, without any immediate call for giving them out in print. Had I gone on writing, it would have been much disturbed the important transformation in my opinions and character, which took place during those years. The origin of this transformation, or at least the process by which I was prepared for it, can only be explained by turning some distance back.

From the winter of 1821, when I first read Bentham, and especially from the commencement of the Westminster Review, I had what might truly be called an object in life; to be a reformer of the world. My conception of my own happiness was entirely identified with this object. The personal sympathies I wished for were those of fellow laborers in this enterprise. I endeavored to pick up as many flowers as I could by the way; but as a serious and permanent personal satisfaction to rest upon, my whole reliance was placed on this; and I was accustomed to felicitate myself on the certainty of a happy life which I enjoyed, through placing my happiness in something durable and distant, in which some progress might be always making, while it could never be exhausted by complete attainment. This did very well for several years, during which the general improvement going on in the world and the idea of myself as engaged with others in struggling to promote it, seemed enough to fill up an interesting and animated existence. But the time came when I awakened from this as from a dream. It was in the autumn of 1826. I was in a dull state of nerves, such as everybody is occasionally liable to; unsusceptible to enjoyment or pleasurable excitement; one of those moods when what is pleasure at other times, becomes insipid or indifferent; the state, I should think, in which converts to Methodism usually are, when smitten by their first "conviction of sin." In this frame of mind it occurred to me to put the question directly to myself: "Suppose that all your objects in life were realized; that all the changes in institutions and opinions which you are looking forward to, could be completely effected at this very instant: would this be a great joy and happiness to you?" And an irrepressible self-consciousness distinctly answered, "No!" At this my heart sank within me: the whole foundation on which my life was constructed fell down. All my happiness was to have been found in the continual pursuit of this end. The end had ceased to charm, and how could there ever again be any interest in the means? I seemed to have nothing left to live for.

At first I hoped that the cloud would pass away of itself; but it did not. A night's sleep, the sovereign remedy for the smaller vexations of life, had no effect on it. I awoke to a renewed consciousness of the woeful fact. I carried it with me into all companies, into all occupations. Hardly anything had power to cause me even a few minutes' oblivion of it. For some months the cloud seemed to grow thicker and thicker. The lines in Coleridge's "Dejection"—I was not then acquainted with them—exactly describe my case:

> A grief without a pang, void, dark and drear,
> A drowsy, stifled, unimpassioned grief,
> Which finds no natural outlet or relief
> In word, or sigh, or tear.

In vain I sought relief from my favorite books; those memorials of past nobleness and greatness from which I had always hitherto drawn strength and animation. I read them now without feeling, or with the accustomed feeling *minus* all its charm; and I became persuaded, that my love of mankind, and of excellence for its own sake, had worn itself out. I sought no comfort by speaking to others of what I felt. If I had loved any one sufficiently to make confiding my griefs a necessity, I should not have been in the condition I was. I felt, too, that mine was not an interesting, or in any way respectable distress. There was nothing in it to attract sympathy. Advice, if I had known where to seek it, would have been most precious. The words of Macbeth to the physician often occurred to my thoughts. But there was no one on whom I could build the faintest hope of such assistance. My father, to whom it would have been natural to me to have recourse in any practical difficulties, was the last person to whom, in such a case as this, I looked for help. Everything convinced me that he had no knowledge of any such mental state as I was suffering from, and that even if he could be made to understand it, he was not the physician who could heal it. My education, which was wholly his work, had been conducted without any regard to the possibility of its ending in this result; and I saw no use in giving him the pain of thinking that his plans had failed, when the failure was probably irremediable, and, at all events, beyond the power of *his* remedies. Of other friends, I had at that time none to whom I had any hope of making my condition intelligible. It was however abundantly intelligible to myself; and the more I dwelt upon it, the more hopeless it appeared.

My course of study had led me to believe, that all mental and moral feelings and qualities, whether of a good or of a bad kind, were the results of association; that we love one thing, and hate another, take pleasure in one sort of action or contemplation, and pain in another sort, through the clinging of pleasurable or painful ideas to those things, from the effect of education or of experience. As a corollary from this, I had always heard it maintained by my father, and was myself convinced, that the object of education should be to form the strongest possible associations of the salutary class; associations of pleasure with all things beneficial to the great whole, and of pain with all things hurtful to it. This doctrine appeared inexpugnable; but it now seemed to me, on retrospect, that my teachers had occupied themselves but superficially with the means of forming and keeping up these salutary associations. They seemed to have trusted altogether to the old familiar instruments, praise and blame, reward and punishment. Now, I did not doubt that by these means, begun early, and applied unremittingly, intense associations of pain and pleasure, especially of pain, might be created, and might produce desires and aversions capable of lasting undiminished to the end of life. But there must always be something artificial and casual in associations thus produced. The pains and pleasures thus forcibly associated with things, are not connected with them by any natural tie; and it is therefore, I thought, essential to the durability of these associations, that they should have become so intense and inveterate as to be practically indissoluble, before the habitual exercise of the power of analysis had commenced. For I now saw, or thought I saw, what I had always before received with incredulity—that the habit of analysis has a tendency to wear away the feelings: as indeed it has, when no other mental habit is cultivated, and the analyzing spirit remains without its natural complements and correctives. The very excellence of analysis (I argued) is that it tends to weaken and undermine whatever is the result of prejudice; that it enables us mentally to separate ideas which have only casually clung together: and no associations whatever could ultimately resist this dissolving force, were it not that we owe to analysis our clearest knowledge of the permanent sequences in nature; the real connections between Things, not dependent on our will and feelings; natural laws, by virtue of which, in many cases, one thing is inseparable from another in fact; which laws, in proportion as they are clearly perceived and imaginatively realized, cause our ideas of things which are always joined together in Nature, to cohere more and more closely in our thoughts. Analytic habits may thus even strengthen the associations between causes and effects, means and ends, but tend altogether to weaken those which are, to speak familiarly, a *mere* matter of feeling. They are therefore (I thought) favorable to prudence and clear-sightedness, but a perpetual worm at the root both of the passions and of the virtues; and, above all, fearfully undermine all desires, and all pleasures, which are the effects of association, that is, according to the theory I held, all except the purely physical and organic; of the entire insufficiency of which to make life desirable, no one had a stronger conviction than I had. These were the laws of human nature, by which, as it seemed to me, I had been brought to my present state. All those to whom I looked up, were of opinion that the pleasure of sympathy with human beings, and the feelings which made the good of others, and especially of mankind on a large scale, the object of existence, were the greatest and surest sources of happiness. Of the truth of this I was convinced, but to know that a feeling would make me happy if I had it, did not give me the feeling. My education, I thought, had failed to create these feelings in sufficient strength to resist the dissolving influence of analysis, while the whole course of my intellectual cultivation had made precocious and premature analysis the inveterate habit of my mind. I was thus, as I said to myself, left stranded at the commencement of my voyage, with a well-equipped ship and a rudder, but no sail; without any real desire for the ends which I had been so carefully fitted out to work for: no delight in virtue, or the general good, but also just as little in anything else. The fountains of vanity and ambition seemed to have dried up within me, as completely as those of benevolence. I had had (as I reflected) some gratification of vanity at too early an age: I had obtained some distinction, and felt myself of some importance, before the desire of distinction and of importance had grown into a passion: and little as it was which I had attained, yet having been attained too early, like all pleasures enjoyed too soon, it had made me *blasé* and indifferent to the pursuit. Thus neither selfish nor unselfish pleasures were pleasures to me. And there seemed no power in nature sufficient to begin the formation of my character anew, and create in a mind now irretrievably analytic, fresh associations of pleasure with any of the objects of human desire.

These were the thoughts which mingled with the dry heavy dejection of the melancholy winter of 1826–7. During this time I was not incapable of my usual occupations. I went on with them mechanically, by the mere force of habit. I had been so drilled in a certain sort of mental exercise, that I could still carry it on when all the spirit had gone out of it. I even composed and spoke several speeches at the debating society, how, or with what degree of success, I know not. Of four years continual speaking at that society, this is the only year of which I remember next to nothing. Two lines of Coleridge, in whom alone of all writers I have found a true description of what I felt, were often in my thoughts, not at this time (for I had never read them), but in a later period of the same mental malady:

> Work without hope draws nectar in a sieve,
> And hope without an object cannot live.

In all probability my case was by no means so peculiar as I fancied it, and I doubt not that many others have passed through a similar state; but the idiosyncrasies of my education had given to the general phenomenon a special character, which made it seem the natural effect of causes that it was hardly possible for time to remove. I frequently asked myself, if I could, or if I was bound to go on living, when life must be passed in this manner. I generally answered to myself, that I did not think I could possibly bear it beyond a year. When, however, not more than half that duration of time had elapsed, a small ray of light broke in upon my gloom. I was reading, accidentally, Marmontel's "Memoires," and came to the passage which relates his father's death, the distressed position of the family, and the sudden inspiration by which he, then a mere boy, felt and made them feel that he would be everything to them—would supply the place of all that they had lost. A vivid conception of that scene and its feelings came over me, and I was moved to tears. From this moment my burden grew lighter. The oppression of the thought that all feeling was dead within me, was gone. I was no longer hopeless: I was not a stock or a stone. I had still, it seemed, some of the material out of which all worth of character, and all capacity for happiness, are made. Relieved from my ever present sense of irremediable wretchedness, I gradually found that the ordinary incidents of life could again give me some pleasure; that I could again find enjoyment, not intense, but sufficient for cheerfulness, in sunshine and sky, in books, in conversation, in public affairs; and that there was, once more, excitement, though of a moderate kind, in exerting myself for my opinions, and for the public good. Thus the cloud gradually drew off, and I again enjoyed life: and though I had several relapses, some of which lasted many months, I never again was as miserable as I had been.

QUESTIONS FOR STUDY
AND TOPICS FOR DISCUSSION
ON *"A Crisis in My Mental History"*

1. This selection is taken from Chapter V of Mill's *Autobiography*. The autobiography was written over a long stretch of time, partly before 1861, partly after 1871, and it was not published until 1873, shortly after Mill's death. The events described in this section occurred when he was twenty years old. What was the precise nature of Mill's crisis, and what were its causes? Was it a fit of depression? Was it the fatigue and exhaustion of a bout of overwork? Or was it something like what we call today a nervous breakdown? With what manner does Mill render the experience? Why this rather than any other manner?

Mill's biographers and modern critics have puzzled over these questions and have found the answers hard to pin down. They have been struck more by the elusiveness and circumspection of Mill's account than by its apparent candor, and they have concluded either that he failed to probe deeply enough, concealing the whole truth in the calm and reasoned surfaces of his prose, or that he lacked the diagnostic and psychological concepts by which he could define his condition in exact terms.

Most modern interpretations of Mill's mental crisis locate its origins and significance in the circumstances of his upbringing by his father and in the psychological conflicts induced by his attempt to assert his independence of his father's influence. Mill had been educated by his father under an astonishing regimen. From the age of three he was taught, first, Greek, Latin, and history, and later, mathematics, logic, philosophy, and political economy. All of his early training was dominated by eighteenth-century psychology and philosophy. His father effectively attempted to turn his son into an eighteenth-century *philosophe* as well as a prodigy of Utilitarianism. When Mill was fifteen he read the works of Jeremy Bentham and became, like his father, an enthusiastic advocate of the Utilitarian philosophy. Before he was twenty Mill became an active propagandist for various Reform causes; founded the Utilitarian Society, a study and discussion group; helped found the London Debating Society; contributed to the Utilitarian periodical, *The Westminster Review;* and edited Bentham's *Rationale of Judicial Evidence.* But even while he was performing these precocious intellectual feats, he began to feel some dissatisfaction with the mental outlook of the Utilitarians and with the course of study so sternly administered by his father. His discontent grew and the conflict in his loyalties deepened until finally, shortly after he was twenty, they erupted into the mental crisis which upset his plans, challenged his beliefs, and threatened, as he says, his very life.

Mill's crisis has been accounted for in a number of ways by modern critics: physically, as the fatigue following the prolonged and over-intense intellectual activity of his childhood education; spiritually, as the affliction of the condition of spiritual dryness and depression known in the Middle Ages as *accidia;* philosophically, as a reaction against the eighteenth-century rationalism he had been saturated with since boyhood; and psychologically, as the acting-out of an unconscious wish to escape the tyrannical domination of his father. Many critics favor the psychological explanation. The strongest advocate of this view, A. W. Levi, has said that the real cause of Mill's crisis was "his repressed death wishes against his father, the vague and unarticulated guilt which he had in consequence, and the latent, though still present, dread that never now should he be free of his father's domination."

All of these explanations have sought to probe beneath the surface of Mill's account into something which was deliberately or unconsciously hidden from sight. Whatever justification there may be for this kind of depth analysis, it obscures the part the narrative plays in the work—its expressive motive. Whether Mill realized the full implications of the event of his mental crisis, he knew what he was about in the *Autobiography;* he had a design in mind and he shaped the experience to express that design. Mill intended a history of his intellectual development and the progress of his opinions. In this respect his work is one of several great nineteenth-century apologies for an author's life.

Mill's biographers will justifiably be interested in the psychological motives behind the narrative, but the general reader of the *Autobiography*—the reader interested in its performance as a work of artful prose—will be more curious about its expressive motives. He will ask: What emotions are articulated, and what significance do these emotions have for the sense of the work? How does Mill shape the experience? To what purpose, and with what effect?

2. Mill begins by noting that for some years after 1828, when he ceased to write for *The Westminster Review*, the intermission from public debate and argument had a beneficial effect on his development. In what way does this change of direction from public controversy to private reflection govern the account which follows?

3. What is the basis of Mill's objection to the Benthamite philosophy and the course of study administered by his father? How does Mill unfold his objections? Why doesn't he begin by stating directly the objections taken up in the paragraph beginning "My course of study . . ." (p. 225)?

4. Analyze the composition of the passage "I endeavored to pick up . . . I seemed to have nothing left to live for" in the second paragraph. What is the order of subject, verb, and complement, and the pattern of subordination and modification of the sentences at the beginning of the passage? Of the sentences at the end of the passage? Why does he say "But the time came when I awakened from this as from a dream"? What is the effect of the last sentence in the paragraph? Note the last sentence in each of the following paragraphs of the selection. How does Mill shape the drift of his paragraphs? With what kind of resolution does he end? How does he begin each paragraph? At what stage of his thought does he pick up a paragraph?

5. Is the writing in the third and fourth paragraphs any different in manner and quality from that of the preceding paragraph? How? Why? How is the sentence "If I had loved any one sufficiently . . ." (p. 225) meant to be taken? What makes this statement so surprising? What degree of self-awareness does it show? How does Mill deliver the next five sentences? Does he show any self-pity? What makes what he is saying moving and affecting? What is the tone of Mill's explanation of why he did not turn to his father in his distress? Is there any criticism in his remark that his father "had no knowledge of any such mental state as I was suffering from"? Does he feel any bitterness or any blame, hidden or open? Why doesn't he bother to berate his father?

6. In the next paragraph Mill makes a long analysis of the defects of his early course of study. He criticizes the assumptions and consequences of the Utilitarian philosophy and psychology of his father, and he makes it seem, by the parenthetical insertions "I argued," "I thought," "I reflected," as if these objections were in his mind at the time. Most critics seem to be agreed that these thoughts were not so completely formed as Mill suggests, and that rather they were more in accord with his opinions at the time of the writing of the *Autobiography,* many years after the events being chronicled. What is Mill up to here? Why does he give this paragraph so much emphasis? Is the philosophical air of this discussion a reversion to the earlier abstract language appropriate to a treatise and an abandonment of the more concrete language of reminiscence and personal experience? What is the relation between his own life and the philosophical position he is expounding? Is he trying to make his life exemplary of a certain philosophical view? In what ways does this paragraph describe the pattern of change and transformation of Mill's beliefs, and how does this coincide with the patterns of transformation elsewhere in the piece?

7. In the last paragraph he returns to the dry heavy dejection of the melancholy winter of 1826–7 and says that he carried on his usual occupations "mechanically, by the mere force of habit." What makes the sentence "I had been so drilled . . ." so effective? He brings the account of his crisis to the point of revealing that he could not have lived much longer in this mechanical fashion, and then rather suddenly, with the subdued matter-of-factness that has characterized the whole of the narrative, he sets down the incident that proved to be the turning-point in his crisis—the reading of a passage from Jean François Marmontel's *Mémoires d'un père.* That a man of Mill's sophistication could be so sentimental (and that he could fail to detect an underlying irony in Marmontel's account) has puzzled many modern critics. It is here, some have said, that Mill reveals his guilts and his unconscious death-wish for his father. What is

Mill saying exactly? What is the relation of this episode to all that has gone before? Analyze the style of the writing which follows "A vivid conception of that scene . . ." (p. 228).

One way of explaining the significance of the episode is to say that Mill's tears showed him that he had not, after all, lost his capacity for *imaginative sympathy*. This was his notion that one is able to enter into and participate in another person's inner thoughts and feelings only by sympathetic awareness. Once Mill felt that he had recovered this power to feel a mental event, he turned the corner of his crisis. In the years immediately following 1826 he undertook to reconcile the split between poetry and philosophy which had been opened by the Utilitarians. He asserted sensibility to be equal in importance to intellect, the feelings to reason, imaginative sympathy to rational argument. Hence, the incident of his tears at reading Marmontel may be seen as emblematic of a certain transformation of his character and opinions. The question, then, is: Which is more pertinent to the intention of the selection and the *Autobiography* as a whole— this kind of explanation, or the "Freudian" explanation of the kind given by A. W. Levi?

8. This selection invites comparison with F. Scott Fitzgerald's essay, "The Crack-Up" (pp. 246–251), since both works are accounts of a personal emotional crisis. After you have read that essay, think of both works together and try to analyze the differences in intention, style, and sense of their treatment of the subject.

WHY THE NOVEL MATTERS

BY *D. H. Lawrence*

WE HAVE CURIOUS IDEAS of ourselves. We think of ourselves as a body with a spirit in it, or a body with a soul in it, or a body with a mind in it. *Mens sana in corpore sano.* The years drink up the wine, and at last throw the bottle away, the body, of course, being the bottle.

It is a funny sort of superstition. Why should I look at my hand, as it so cleverly writes these words, and decide that it is a mere nothing compared to the mind that directs it? Is there really any huge difference between my hand and my brain? Or my mind? My hand is alive, it flickers with a life of its own. It meets all the strange universe in touch, and learns a vast number of things, and knows a vast number of things. My hand, as it writes these words, slips gaily along, jumps like a grasshopper to dot an *i*, feels the table rather cold, gets a little bored if I write too long, has its own rudiments of thought, and is just as much *me* as is my brain, my mind, or my soul. Why should I imagine that there is a *me* which is more *me* than my hand is? Since my hand is absolutely alive, me alive.

Whereas, of course, as far as I am concerned, my pen isn't alive at all. My pen *isn't me* alive. Me alive ends at my finger-tips.

Whatever is me alive is me. Every tiny bit of my hands is alive,

From *Phoenix: The Posthumous Papers of D. H. Lawrence*, edited by Edward D. McDonald (New York: The Viking Press, 1936), pp. 533–538. Copyright 1936 by Frieda Lawrence, 1964 by The Estate of the late Frieda Lawrence Ravagli. Reprinted by permission of The Viking Press, Inc.

every little freckle and hair and fold of skin. And whatever is me alive is me. Only my finger-nails, those ten little weapons between me and an inanimate universe, they cross the mysterious Rubicon between me alive and things like my pen, which are not alive, in my own sense.

So, seeing my hand is all alive, and me alive, wherein is it just a bottle, or a jug, or a tin can, or a vessel of clay, or any of the rest of that nonsense? True, if I cut it it will bleed, like a can of cherries. But then the skin that is cut, and the veins that bleed, and the bones that should never be seen, they are all just as alive as the blood that flows. So the tin can business, or vessel of clay, is just bunk.

And that's what you learn, when you're a novelist. And that's what you are very liable *not* to know, if you're a parson, or a philosopher, or a scientist, or a stupid person. If you're a parson, you talk about souls in heaven. If you're a novelist, you know that paradise is in the palm of your hand, and on the end of your nose, because both are alive; and alive, and man alive, which is more than you can say, for certain, of paradise. Paradise is after life, and I for one am not keen on anything that is *after* life. If you are a philosopher, you talk about infinity, and the pure spirit which knows all things. But if you pick up a novel, you realize immediately that infinity is just a handle to this self-same jug of a body of mine; while as for knowing, if I find my finger in the fire, I know that fire burns, with a knowledge so emphatic and vital, it leaves Nirvana merely a conjecture. Oh, yes, my body, me alive, *knows*, and knows intensely. And as for the sum of all knowledge, it can't be anything more than an accumulation of all the things I know in the body, and you, dear reader, know in the body.

These damned philosophers, they talk as if they suddenly went off in steam, and were then much more important than they are when they're in their shirts. It is nonsense. Every man, philosopher included, ends in his own finger-tips. That's the end of his man alive. As for the words and thoughts and sighs and aspirations that fly from him, they are so many tremulations in the ether, and not alive at all. But if the tremulations reach another man alive, he may receive them into his life, and his life may take on a new color, like a chameleon creeping from a brown rock on to a green leaf. All very well and good. It still doesn't alter the fact that the so-called spirit, the message or teaching of the philosopher or the saint, isn't alive at all, but just a tremulation upon the ether, like a radio message. All this spirit stuff is just tremulations upon the ether. If you, as man alive, quiver from the tremulation of the ether into new life, that is because you are man alive, and you take sustenance and stimulation into your alive man in a myriad ways. But to say that the message, or the spirit which is communicated to you, is more important than your living body, is nonsense. You might as well say that the potato at dinner was more important.

Nothing is important but life. And for myself, I can absolutely see life nowhere but in the living. Life with a capital L is only man alive. Even a cabbage in the rain is cabbage alive. All things that are alive are amazing. And all things that are dead are subsidiary to the living. Better a live dog than a dead lion. But better a live lion than a live dog. *C'est la vie!*

It seems impossible to get a saint, or a philosopher, or a scientist, to stick to this simple truth. They are all, in a sense, renegades. The saint wishes to offer himself up as spiritual food for the multitude. Even Francis of Assisi turns himself into a sort of angel-cake, of which anyone may take a slice. But an angel-cake is rather less than man alive. And poor St. Francis might well apologize to his body, when he is dying: "Oh, pardon me, my body, the wrong I did you through the years!" It was no wafer, for others to eat.

The philosopher, on the other hand, because he can think, decides that nothing but thoughts matter. It is as if a rabbit, because he can make little pills, should decide that nothing but little pills matter. As for the scientist, he has absolutely no use for me so long as I am man alive. To the scientist, I am dead. He puts under the microscope a bit of dead me, and calls it me. He takes me to pieces, and says first one piece, and then another piece, is me. My heart, my liver, my stomach have all been scientifically me, according to the scientist; and nowadays I am either a brain, or nerves, or glands, or something more up-to-date in the tissue line.

Now I absolutely flatly deny that I am a soul, or a body, or a mind, or an intelligence, or a brain, or a nervous system, or a bunch of glands, or any of the rest of these bits of me. The whole is greater than the part. And therefore, I, who am man alive, am greater than my soul, or spirit, or body, or mind, or consciousness, or anything else that is merely a part of me. I am a man, and alive. I am man alive, and as long as I can, I intend to go on being man alive.

For this reason I am a novelist. And being a novelist, I consider myself superior to the saint, the scientist, the philosopher, and the poet, who are all great masters of different bits of man alive, but never get the whole hog.

The novel is the one bright book of life. Books are not life. They are only tremulations on the ether. But the novel as a tremulation can make the whole man alive tremble. Which is more than poetry, philosophy, science, or any other book-tremulation can do.

The novel is the book of life. In this sense, the Bible is a great confused novel. You may say, it is about God. But it is really about man alive. Adam, Eve, Sarai, Abraham, Isaac, Jacob, Samuel, David, Bath-Sheba, Ruth, Esther, Solomon, Job, Isaiah, Jesus, Mark, Judas, Paul, Peter: what is it but man alive, from start to finish? Man alive, not mere bits. Even the Lord is another man alive, in a burning bush, throwing the tablets of stone at Moses's head.

I do hope you begin to get my idea, why the novel is supremely important, as a tremulation on the ether. Plato makes the perfect ideal being tremble in me. But that's only a bit of me. Perfection is only a bit, in the strange make-up of man alive. The Sermon on the Mount makes the selfless spirit of me quiver. But that, too, is only a bit of me. The Ten Commandments set the old Adam shivering in me, warning me that I am a thief and a murderer, unless I watch it. But even the old Adam is only a bit of me.

I very much like all these bits of me to be set trembling with life and the wisdom of life. But I do ask that the whole of me shall tremble in its wholeness, some time or other.

And this, of course, must happen in me, living.

But as far as it can happen from a communication, it can only happen when a whole novel communicates itself to me. The Bible—but *all* the Bible—and Homer, and Shakespeare: these are the supreme old novels. These are all things to all men. Which means that in their wholeness they affect the whole man alive, which is the man himself, beyond any part of him. They set the whole tree trembling with a new access of life, they do not just stimulate growth in one direction.

I don't want to grow in any one direction any more. And, if I can help it, I don't want to stimulate anybody else into some particular direction. A particular direction ends in a *cul-de-sac*. We're in a *cul-de-sac* at present.

I don't believe in any dazzling revelation, or in any supreme Word. "The grass withereth, the flower fadeth, but the Word of the Lord shall stand for ever." That's the kind of stuff we've drugged ourselves with. As a matter of fact, the grass withereth, but comes up all the greener for that reason, after the rains. The flower fadeth, and therefore the bud opens. But the Word of the Lord, being man-uttered and a mere vibration on the ether, becomes staler and staler, more and more boring, till at last we turn a deaf ear and it ceases to exist, far more finally than any withered grass. It is grass that renews its youth like the eagle, not any Word.

We should ask for no absolutes, or absolute. Once and for all and for ever, let us have done with the ugly imperialism of any absolute. There is no absolute good, there is nothing absolutely right. All things flow and change, and even change is not absolute. The whole is a strange assembly of apparently incongruous parts, slipping past one another.

Me, man alive, I am a very curious assembly of incongruous parts. My yea! of to-day is oddly different from my yea! of yesterday. My tears of to-morrow will have nothing to do with my tears of a year ago. If the one I love remains unchanged and unchanging, I shall cease to love her. It is only because she changes and startles me into change and defies my inertia, and is herself staggered in her inertia by my changing, that I can continue to love her. If she stayed put, I might as well love the pepper-pot.

In all this change, I maintain a certain integrity. But woe betide me if I try to put my finger on it. If I say of myself, I am this, I am that!—then, if I stick to it, I turn into a stupid fixed thing like a lamp-post. I shall never know wherein lies my integrity, my individuality, my me. I *can* never know it. It is useless to talk about my ego. That only means that I have made up an *idea* of myself, and that I am trying to cut myself out to pattern. Which is no good. You can cut your cloth to fit your coat, but you can't clip bits off your living body, to trim it down to your idea. True, you can put yourself into ideal corsets. But even in ideal corsets, fashions change.

Let us learn from the novel. In the novel, the characters can do nothing but *live*. If they keep on being good, according to pattern, or bad, according to pattern, or even volatile, according to pattern, they cease to live, and the novel falls dead. A character in a novel has got to live, or it is nothing.

We, likewise, in life have got to live, or we are nothing.

What we mean by living is, of course, just as indescribable as what we mean by *being*. Men get ideas into their heads, of what they mean by Life, and they proceed to cut life out to pattern. Sometimes they go into the desert to seek God, sometimes they go into the desert to seek cash, sometimes it is wine, woman, and song, and again it is water, political reform, and votes. You never know what it will be next: from killing your neighbor with hideous bombs and gas that tears the lungs, to supporting a Foundlings' Home and preaching infinite Love, and being co-respondent in a divorce.

In all this wild welter, we need some sort of guide. It's no good inventing Thou Shalt Nots!

What then? Turn truly, honorably to the novel, and see wherein you are man alive, and wherein you are dead man in life. You may love a woman as man alive, and you may be making love to a woman as sheer dead man in life. You may eat your dinner as man alive, or as a mere masticating corpse. As man alive you may have a shot at your enemy. But as a ghastly simulacrum of life you may be firing bombs into men who are neither your enemies nor your friends, but just things you are dead to. Which is criminal, when the things happen to be alive.

To be alive, to be man alive, to be whole man alive: that is the point. And at its best, the novel, and the novel supremely, can help you. It can help you not to be dead man in life. So much of a man walks about dead and a carcass in the street and house, to-day: so much of women is merely dead. Like a pianoforte with half the notes mute.

But in the novel you can see, plainly, when the man goes dead, the woman goes inert. You can develop an instinct of life, if you will, instead of a theory of right and wrong, good and bad.

In life, there is right and wrong, good and bad, all the time. But what is right in one case is wrong in another. And in the novel you see one man becoming a corpse, because of his so-called goodness, another going dead because of his so-called wickedness. Right and wrong is an instinct: but an instinct of the whole consciousness in a man, bodily, mental, spiritual at once. And only in the novel are *all* things given full play, or at least, they may be given full play, when we realize that life itself, and not inert safety, is the reason for living. For out of the full play of all things emerges the only thing that is anything, the wholeness of a man, the wholeness of a woman, man alive, and live woman.

✿

QUESTIONS FOR STUDY
AND TOPICS FOR DISCUSSION
on *Why the Novel Matters*

1. Observe how Lawrence presents his views in the first five paragraphs. He begins by using the pronoun "we" and (if we miss the raillery in his tone) this leads us to think that he shares our, the readers', beliefs. But he pulls us up short by declaring that the idea we have of ourselves, of the self, is "a funny sort of superstition." Using the actions of his own hand as an example, and changing from "we" to "I," he shows that our assumptions and habits of thought are foolish. Before we can protest, while we are sputtering on "buts," he drives home his contentions with drumfire intensity. He knows our objections, but he is grappling with us at close quarters, and he won't let up for an instant. The fifth paragraph is written as if he were saying: I know you believe, I know you will say . . . but that is just bunk. And he is off again on another flank, another assault on our beliefs.

He makes one reasonable point in this portion of the essay: Consciousness is better than inertia; a fully alive sense of being is all that keeps us from expiring into the inanimate universe. But he is deliberately unreasonable in the way he makes his point. He is abrasive, contentious, outrageous. He handles us roughly—but it is only for our own good. He wants to set us straight, to get us to see things truly and honestly, to inspire us with his own rage for life.

Continue this line of analysis through the rest of the essay. What is Lawrence's intention? What techniques of language and verbal devices does he use to express his purpose? How much of the *form* of the essay depends on the dramatic interplay of writer and reader? What is the effect of this interplay on the *content* of the work?

Begin by considering the style of the essay. The writing has the quality of exuberant talk. Admirers of Lawrence make much of this; they like to say that he writes as if he were talking. But there are many ways of talking. Sidney and Milton, not to mention Forster and Fitzgerald, write with the animation of speech. What is distinctive about Lawrence's talk?

Is it better to say that he writes like a man arguing? Even that is not enough, for there are many styles of argument. A man may harangue, hector, cajole, beguile, disarm his opponent— or he may reason with him. The range of manners is very wide, and the choice narrows according to whether the writer regards his reader as an adversary or as a partner in a dialogue. Does Lawrence regard the "dear reader" (see p. 235) sympathetically, or is he trying to provoke him? What is Lawrence's manner of argument? What are the devices of grammar, syntax, diction, rhythm, and typography by which Lawrence catches the inflections and gestures of argument?

And having established that, go further: What is the functional relationship between Lawrence's style of argument and the sense of the essay? If Lawrence is concerned with breaking down the reader's conventional casts of thought, his fixed beliefs about life and the novel, is this only the stratagem of his argument and the form of his rhetoric, or is it an essential part of the essay's content? Is the attack on the reader's beliefs only a trick of disputation, a kind of *argumentum ad hominem* (of the abusive variety), or is it a genuine issue?

2. How convincing is Lawrence's case in the first five paragraphs? What are some of the philosophical problems raised by his argument? Does he really mean that his hand has a life of its own and is just as much himself as his brain, his mind, or his soul? In what sense can his hand *know* a vast number of things? What would a philosopher—not the straw man Lawrence sets up, a feeble idealist, but a philosopher of a more realistic stamp— say about Lawrence's treatment of *knowing*? Would such a critique be relevant? What is Lawrence up to actually? Is he professing his own notion of knowing, or is he attacking some conventional sense of the concept? Why does Lawrence say that knowledge is nothing more than "all the things I know in the body" (p. 235)? Is he exaggerating?

3. What are the bases of Lawrence's objections to philosophers, parsons, scientists, and saints? Why are they "renegades" (p. 236)? How does he handle them? Does he pay due regard to the rules for valid argument, illustration, and proof? What religious doctrines and sacraments are alluded to and mocked in his treatment of St. Francis of Assisi (p. 236)? What other references does Lawrence make to religion? Why is he so exercised over "spirit"? Is he irreverent? Offensive? Funny? To what purpose?

4. Lawrence is nearly half-way through the essay before he gets around to stating a "proposition" as to why the novel matters. He claims it is because "the novel is the one bright book of life" that makes "the whole man alive tremble" (p. 237). Why didn't he begin the essay here? Why has he spent so much time on other matters? Has he only been laying the groundwork, the premises, of his case—showing what life is before attempting to show how the novel is the supreme expression of that sense of life? Is he a novelist because of what he has said up to now, or does he believe in what he has said because he is a novelist? In what ways is the novel superior to any other form of literature?

5. Some of Lawrence's critics have come down hard on his apparent worship of feeling. They are prepared to accept Lawrence's principle that "art provides an emotional experience," but they contend that he carries it to dangerous lengths. In support of this criticism they turn to such statements by Lawrence as the following: "My great religion is a belief in the blood, the flesh, as being wiser than the intellect. We can go wrong in our minds. But what our blood feels and believes and says, is always true."

Stylistically, these beliefs are supposed to account for the feverish pitch of his rhetoric. The charge has been made of Lawrence's poetry, and extended to all his work, that he commits the *fallacy of expressive form. Expressive form* (of the fallacious variety) is directly communicated feeling unmediated by formal order; it springs from the notion that if a thing is only intensely enough felt its mere expression in words will give it coherence and intelligibility.

Lawrence's defenders argue that his statements are merely polemical exaggerations, or perhaps metaphors, for what is basically a completely healthy moral position: that all the faculties are to be cultivated in order to achieve "spontaneous-creative fullness of being." And they argue further that his style is fragmented, repetitious, and disordered—but deliberately so, in order to express *felt* life, life as it is actually experienced with all the senses alive and pulsating.

What does Lawrence mean when he says in this essay that he wants literature to set the whole man trembling (p. 237)? Is his emphasis on trembling or on wholeness? Is "trembling" metaphoric? Of what exactly? Is Lawrence simply saying that he wants literature to provide a lively emotional experience? If more, what else exactly? Is he neglecting reason and other mental faculties altogether? Or is he placing them in a certain rank of importance? How much of Lawrence's argument on this point depends on a correction of the reader's assumptions? He knows that his readers will value reason. Is he advocating that feeling supplant reason? That it is the only thing of value? Or that feeling has an importance greater than the readers are prepared to acknowledge? Does the essay itself have a formal order, or is it guilty of the *fallacy of expressive form*?

6. What kinds of imagery does Lawrence use? The organic and biological figures are obvious enough. So are the images of dissection, direction, fixity, fluidity. Do these figures fall into coherent patterns? Do they inform the essay as, for example, the figure of sight informs Sidney's *An Apology for Poetry*, or are they used for local effect, as intensifying metaphors which are dropped as soon as the immediate identification is made? How much does Lawrence depend on tropes? Are his figures expressed by nouns, adjectives, or verbs? To what degree do Lawrence's expressive effects derive from other devices of style besides figurative language?

7. Analyze the sense and composition of the closing paragraph (p. 239). In what ways is the last sentence the epitome of the essay? What does Lawrence mean by the "full play of all things"? Analyze the balance in structure and the surprises in rhythm of the sentence. List all the grammatical forms of "life" and "being alive" in the essay. What are the effects of these variations? Does Lawrence try to make the reader *experience* the full play of ideas he is expressing? If he succeeds, what makes his essay, any essay, different from a novel? Has he changed his attitude toward the reader? Is he concerned now with correction? Is it necessary for the reader to realize that life itself is the reason for living *before* he can apprehend why the novel matters, or does Lawrence feel

that the novel will prove its value unaided? What is the relation of his arguments on absolutes, change, theories of right and wrong, divisions of body, mind, and spirit, this life and the after life, and all the rest, to the conviction that "the only thing that is anything" is the full play of everything?

8. Compare the manner and substance of Lawrence's argument with Milton's treatment of the statement "For books are not absolutely dead things, but do contain a potency of life in them to be as active as that soul was whose progeny they are" (p. 125).

THE CRACK-UP

BY *F. Scott Fitzgerald*

OF COURSE ALL LIFE is a process of breaking down, but the blows that do the dramatic side of the work—the big sudden blows that come, or seem to come, from outside—the ones you remember and blame things on and, in moments of weakness, tell your friends about, don't show their effect all at once. There is another sort of blow that comes from within—that you don't feel until it's too late to do anything about it, until you realize with finality that in some regard you will never be as good a man again. The first sort of breakage seems to happen quick—the second kind happens almost without your knowing it but is realized suddenly indeed.

Before I go on with this short history, let me make a general observation—the test of a first-rate intelligence is the ability to hold two opposed ideas in the mind at the same time, and still retain the ability to function. One should, for example, be able to see that things are hopeless and yet be determined to make them otherwise. This philosophy fitted on to my early adult life, when I saw the improbable, the implausible, often the "impossible," come true. Life was something you dominated if you were any good. Life yielded easily to intelligence and effort, or to what proportion could be mustered of both. It seemed a romantic business to be a successful literary man—you were not ever going to be as famous as a movie star but what note you had was probably longer-lived—you were never going to have the power of a man of strong political or religious convictions but you were certainly more independent. Of course within the practice of your trade you were forever unsatisfied—but I, for one, would not have chosen any other.

As the twenties passed, with my own twenties marching a little ahead of them, my two juvenile regrets—at not being big enough (or good enough) to play football in college, and at not getting overseas during the war—resolved themselves into childish waking dreams of imaginary heroism that were good enough to go to sleep on in restless nights. The big problems of life seemed to solve themselves, and if the business of fixing them was difficult, it made one too tired to think of more general problems.

Life, ten years ago, was largely a personal matter. I must hold in balance the sense of the futility of effort and the sense of the necessity to struggle; the conviction of the inevitability of failure and still the determination to "succeed"—and, more than these, the contradiction between the dead hand of the past and the high intentions of the future. If I could do this through the common ills—domestic, professional and personal—then the ego would continue as an arrow shot from nothingness to nothingness with such force that only gravity would bring it to earth at last.

For seventeen years, with a year of deliberate loafing and resting out in the center—things went on like that, with a new chore only a nice prospect for the next day. I was living hard, too, but: "Up to forty-nine it'll be all right," I said. "I can count on that. For a man who's lived as I have, that's all you could ask."

—And then, ten years this side of forty-nine, I suddenly realized that I had prematurely cracked.

(2)

Now a man can crack in many ways—can crack in the head—in which case the power of decision is taken from you by others! or in the body, when one can but submit to the white hospital world; or in the nerves. William Seabrook in an unsympathetic book tells, with some pride and a movie ending, of how he became a public charge. What led to his alcoholism or was bound up with it, was a collapse of his nervous system. Though the present writer was not so entangled—having at the time not tasted so much as a glass of beer for six months—it was his nervous reflexes that were giving way—too much anger and too many tears.

Moreover, to go back to my thesis that life has a varying offensive, the realization of having cracked was not simultaneous with a blow, but with a reprieve.

Not long before, I had sat in the office of a great doctor and listened to a grave sentence. With what, in retrospect, seems some equanimity, I had gone on about my affairs in the city where I was then living, not caring much, not thinking how much had been left undone, or what would become of this and that responsibility, like people do in books; I was well insured and anyhow I had been only a mediocre caretaker of most of the things left in my hands, even of my talent.

But I had a strong sudden instinct that I must be alone. I didn't want to see any people at all. I had seen so many people all my life—I was an average mixer, but more than average in a tendency to identify myself, my ideas, my destiny, with those of all classes that I came in contact with. I was always saving or being saved—in a single morning I would go through the emotions ascribable to Wellington at Waterloo. I lived in a world of inscrutable hostiles and inalienable friends and supporters.

But now I wanted to be absolutely alone and so arranged a certain insulation from ordinary cares.

It was not an unhappy time. I went away and there were fewer people. I found I was good-and-tired. I could lie around and was glad to, sleeping or dozing sometimes twenty hours a day and in the intervals trying resolutely not to think—instead I made lists—made lists and tore them up, hundreds of lists: of cavalry leaders and football players and cities, and popular tunes and pitchers, and happy times, and hobbies and houses lived in and how many suits since I left the army and how many pairs of shoes (I didn't count the suit I bought in Sorrento that shrunk, nor the pumps and dress shirt and collar that I carried around for years and never wore, because the pumps got damp and grainy and the shirt and collar got yellow and starch-rotted). And lists of women I'd liked, and of the times I had let myself be snubbed by people who had not been my betters in character or ability.

—And then suddenly, surprisingly, I got better.

—And cracked like an old plate as soon as I heard the news. That is the real end of this story. What was to be done about it will have to rest in what used to be called the "womb of time." Suffice it to say that after about an hour of solitary pillow-hugging, I began to realize that for two years my life had been a drawing on resources that I did not possess, that I had been mortgaging myself physically and spiritually up to the hilt. What was the small gift of life given back in comparison to that?— when there had once been a pride of direction and a confidence in enduring independence.

I realized that in those two years, in order to preserve something—an inner hush maybe, maybe not—I had weaned myself from all the things I used to love—that every act of life from the morning tooth-brush to the friend at dinner had become an effort. I saw that for a long time I had not liked people and things, but only followed the rickety old pretense of liking. I saw that even my love for those closest to me was become only an attempt to love, that my casual relations—with an editor, a tobacco seller, the child of a friend, were only what I remembered I *should* do, from other days. All in the same month I became bitter about such things as the sound of the radio, the advertisements in the magazines, the screech of tracks, the dead silence of the country—contemptuous at human softness, immediately (if secretively) quarrelsome toward hardness—hating the night when I couldn't sleep and hating the day because it went toward night. I slept on the heart side now because I knew that the sooner I could tire that out, even a little, the sooner would come that blessed hour of nightmare which, like a catharsis, would enable me to better meet the new day.

There were certain spots, certain faces I could look at. Like most Middle Westerners, I have never had any but the vaguest race prejudices—I always had a secret yen for the lovely Scandinavian blondes who sat on porches in St. Paul but hadn't emerged enough economically to be part of what was then society. They were too nice to be "chickens" and too quickly off the farmlands to seize a place in the sun, but I remember going round blocks to catch a single glimpse of shining hair—the bright shock of a girl I'd never know. This is urban, unpopular talk. It strays afield from the fact that in these latter days I couldn't stand the sight of Celts, English, Politicians, Strangers, Virginians, Negroes (light or dark), Hunting People, or retail clerks, and middlemen in general, all writers (I avoided writers very carefully because they can perpetuate trouble as no one else can)—and all the classes as classes and most of them as members of their class . . .

Trying to cling to something, I liked doctors and girl children up to the age of about thirteen and well-brought-up boy children from about eight years old on. I could have peace and happiness with these few categories of people. I forgot to add that I liked old men—men over seventy, sometimes over sixty if their faces looked seasoned. I liked Katharine Hepburn's face on the screen, no matter what was said about her pretentiousness, and Miriam Hopkins' face, and old friends if I only saw them once a year and could remember their ghosts.

All rather inhuman and undernourished, isn't it? Well, that, children, is the true sign of cracking up.

It is not a pretty picture. Inevitably it was carted here and there within its frame and exposed to various critics. One of them can only be described as a person whose life makes other people's lives seem like death—even this time when she was cast in the usually unappealing role of Job's comforter. In spite of the fact that this story is over, let me append our conversation as a sort of postscript:

"Instead of being so sorry for yourself, listen—" she said. (She always says "Listen," because she thinks while she talks—*really* thinks.) So she said: "Listen. Suppose this wasn't a crack in you —suppose it was a crack in the Grand Canyon."

"The crack's in me," I said heroically.

"Listen! The world only exists in your eyes—your conception of it. You can make it as big or as small as you want to. And you're trying to be a little puny individual. By God, if I ever cracked, I'd try to make the world crack with me. Listen! The world only exists through your apprehension of it, and so it's much better to say that it's not you that's cracked—it's the Grand Canyon."

"Baby et up all her Spinoza?"

"I don't know anything about Spinoza. I know—" She spoke, then, of old woes of her own, that seemed, in the telling, to have been more dolorous than mine, and how she had met them, over-ridden them, beaten them.

I felt a certain reaction to what she said, but I am a slow-thinking man, and it occurred to me simultaneously that of all natural forces, vitality is the incommunicable one. In days when juice came into one as an article without duty, one tried to distribute it—but always without success; to further mix metaphors, vitality never "takes." You have it or you haven't it, like health or brown eyes or honor or a baritone voice. I might have asked some of it from her, neatly wrapped and ready for home cooking and digestion, but I could never have got it—not if I'd waited around for a thousand hours with the tin cup of self-pity. I could walk from her door, holding myself very carefully like cracked crockery, and go away into the world of bitterness, where I was making a home with such materials as are found there—and quote to myself after I left her door:

"Ye are the salt of the earth. But if the salt hath lost its savour, wherewith shall it be salted?"

Matthew 5–13.

QUESTIONS FOR STUDY
AND TOPICS FOR DISCUSSION
ON *The Crack-Up*

1. This essay is one of three—the other two are entitled "Handle With Care" and "Pasting It Together"—which were published in *Esquire* magazine in February, March, and April of 1936. The essays treat one experience, and they are rightly considered by critics to form a dramatic whole, but they were not conceived as a unit.

"The Crack-Up" was written in October, 1935, in the little mountain town of Tryon, North Carolina. One day in February of that year, Fitzgerald, who was then living in Baltimore, hopped into his car alone and headed south. He wanted to escape the winter cold, and he needed a rest; a number of personal disappointments had left him feeling physically and creatively depleted. He drove as far as Tryon and, liking its climate and its air of quiet retreat, he stayed for a few weeks. He took a room at a hotel, stopped his notorious drinking, caught up on his sleep, and toured the surrounding countryside. When he returned to Baltimore in March, he came down with a case of influenza that sent him to a hospital. X-rays showed that he was also suffering from a recurrence of long-dormant tuberculosis. He was released in May with a warning from his doctor that if he didn't rest and take care of himself he would be dead within the year. He placed his daughter in the hands of friends, moved his wife from a mental hospital in New York State where she was a patient to another located near Tryon, and returned to North Carolina, where he spent a large part of the next two years trying to recuperate. Fitzgerald's life was at its bleakest when he wrote "The Crack-Up." After the essay was printed, the publisher of *Esquire* asked for more, and Fitzgerald responded by writing the other two essays which continued the account of his mental and physical crisis.

For some years before he wrote these essays Fitzgerald seemed to have reached a dead end in his career as a writer. He was dismissed by critics as a burnt-out case—a writer who had collapsed into mediocrity after a brilliant beginning. Fitzgerald himself, in a letter to his daughter just six months before his death in December, 1940, showed his awareness of the waste and the scattered triumphs of his last fifteen years:

> What little I've accomplished has been by the most laborious and uphill work, and I wish now I'd *never* relaxed or looked back—but said at the end of *The Great Gatsby*: "I've found my line—from now on this comes first. This is my immediate duty—without this I am nothing."

In the three essays which chronicle his crack-up Fitzgerald confronts directly and openly the decline of his powers as a writer, his creative bankruptcy, and he writes with, in that impressive phrase from his notebooks, "the authority of failure."

The confession of his failure, the openness of his self-exposure, distressed and embarrassed his acquaintances. Hemingway, for instance, was disgusted with the way Fitzgerald had "shamelessly" exposed himself in public. As Fitzgerald said in a letter to a friend:

> Ernest Hemingway wrote me an irritable letter in which he bawled me out for having been so public about what are essentially private affairs and should be written about in fiction or not at all.

Is this kind of criticism pertinent? Does Hemingway show an accurate understanding of the intention and sense of "The Crack-Up"? Admittedly, Fitzgerald portrays himself as falling apart. But is he abject in his collapse? Is he self-pitying and self-indulgent? In fronting the worst—the desolation of his dreams and the wreckage of his talent—doesn't Fitzgerald *transform* his opinions and character, and make, after the fall, a new and tougher self? Ostensibly, the essay is debasing and pathetic, but the total impression it makes is quite opposite.

What part does Fitzgerald's style play in creating this impression? "The Crack-Up" is distinctly different from the gushing, self-dramatizing sentimentality of so much of Fitzgerald's writing after *The Great Gatsby*. The very expression of "pasting it together" is a recovery of artistic mastery and strength of purpose.

Fitzgerald retains his old sensitivity, but he fortifies it with candor and irony. His style is a register of the transfiguration of the despair and bitterness of his crack-up. As Mark Schorer has said: *"The Crack-Up,* like almost everything else Fitzgerald wrote, is excellent to the degree by which it transcends mere pathos. This comes in part from his writing itself, which is marked by a colloquial ease that persistently achieves genuine poetic effects." If we say that Fitzgerald achieves in the writing of "The Crack-Up" a revitalization of the creative energies which are declared to have been dissipated and exhausted, is this "reading into" the essay, or is it part of the essay's intention and sense? Is the artistic triumph of the style an ironic reversal of the personal failure which is the ostensible subject of "The Crack-Up"? Is the essay "about" a failure or a recovery?

2. Why does Fitzgerald begin by describing, in general terms, two kinds of "blows" and two kinds of "breakage"? Why doesn't he begin at once with the account of what happened to him? What is the stylistic effect of "Of course"?

3. What is the sense and function of the general observation in the second paragraph? What is the relation of the observation to Fitzgerald's personal situation and condition? How does the thought of the paragraph govern all that follows in the chronicle of the author's crack-up? From what perspective in time is the observation made—before or after the crack-up? Why does Fitzgerald shift from first-person to second-person to third-person forms of address?

4. How substantial are the disappointments described in the third paragraph? Are they heroic setbacks—or deliberately trivial? One way of defining sentimentality is emotion which is mawkish because it is in excess of the facts. Is Fitzgerald being sentimental here? What is his tone?

5. Fitzgerald delivers the last sentence of the first section (p. 247) as if he were letting fly a surprising and swift punch. How is this effect achieved stylistically? To what purpose? Why does Fitzgerald suspend the main thought of the sentence? How does the casual manner of the material preceding the sentence prepare for its effect? Is the turn too sudden, too melodramatic? Which of the two kinds of blows specified in the first paragraph is he

about to describe? Why does he break the essay into two parts, and why the break here rather than at any other point?

6. Why does Fitzgerald say "I had prematurely cracked" rather than "I had prematurely broken down"? Is he describing a "breakdown" or a "crack-up"? How does he develop the metaphor of the crack-up? He says later in the essay that he cracked like an old plate; by this metaphor he seems to envision himself not in heroic, but in trivial and absurd terms. Is this the only sense of "cracked" which is described? How serious is Fitzgerald's "crack-up" really? Why does he seem deliberately to play it down by such metaphors as the cracked plate?

7. Why does he move again into general reflection at the start of the second section? Why doesn't he describe his emotions and his state of mind on suddenly realizing that he had prematurely cracked? What is the effect of his resuming the casual and "impersonal" manner of the beginning of the essay? Analyze the construction and effect of the dashes in this paragraph. What makes the end of the last sentence so impressive? Is this in the same key as the beginning of the paragraph?

8. Why does Fitzgerald say that his realization of having cracked was not simultaneous with a blow, but with a reprieve? What expectations is he crossing? The impression, of course, is that of an assault when one's guard is down, but an added suggestion is that of being robbed of the chance of making a heroic gesture. How is this sense of the muting of heroic assertion carried through the essay?

9. Why doesn't he bother to specify what the grave sentence was? Is his response to the sentence odd? Why does he emphasize that he didn't react "like people do in books"? What is the effect of the combination of "I was well insured" and "I had been only a mediocre caretaker . . ."? Why the word "anyhow"?

10. Why does Fitzgerald note that he had an abnormal tendency to identify with people and things? One of Fitzgerald's favorite poets was Keats. Keats's most famous single idea was his notion of *negative capability,* which he described in his letter of 21 December 1817 to George and Thomas Keats. Look up that passage—it is easily accessible—and try to determine the rele-

vance of the idea to Fitzgerald's essay. Consider especially the parallel between "negative capability" and Fitzgerald's general observation in the second paragraph of the essay.

11. Why does Fitzgerald describe the lists he kept while he was in retreat? Why does he change from generalized reflection to very particular description? What kind of mood and state of mind is conveyed by the description?

12. Analyze the construction and effect of the two sentences beginning "—And then suddenly . . ." (p. 248). How does Fitzgerald build towards this effect? Analyze the movement of the thought and the composition of the paragraphs from the beginning of the second section to this point. Trace the sequence of time and the progress of the tone. How does Fitzgerald keep these two sentences from sounding self-pitying?

13. If "that is the real end of this story," why does he go on? What direction does he follow from here to the end of the essay? What does he take up?

14. Consider the self-portrait drawn in the three paragraphs beginning "I realized that in those two years . . ." (p. 249). How does Fitzgerald depict himself? How is the reader meant to take this picture? Is the author being deliberately unpleasant and unappealing? How does he shock and surprise the reader? To what purpose?

In what way does the statement in the paragraph preceding this portion of the essay, "I began to realize that for two years my life had been a drawing on resources that I did not possess," govern the tenor and sense of the next three paragraphs? In what ways are these three paragraphs a contrast, in form and in substance, to the portion of the essay describing the author's too-easy sympathetic identification? Is the withdrawal recorded in the three paragraphs a permanent change in the author's person, or is it some new stage, an attempt at a toughness and hardness to balance his earlier sensitivity and flaccidity? Is he simply showing how sick he had become? Or is he trying out a new role engendered by his desperation? Why does he add the things he clung to during this period of his life? Just to soften the portrait? What is significant about the content of his crotchets?

What is the effect of the paragraph "All rather inhuman . . ." (p. 250) on the impression conveyed by the three paragraphs

preceding? What is the tone here? How does the ironic consciousness displayed here control the desperation of what is being
stated?

15. Analyze the composition and sense of Fitzgerald's conversation with the woman (p. 250). What does he mean when he
says she "was cast in the usually unappealing role of Job's comforter"? Is the author comparing himself to Job? Is the analogue
too heroic? What does Fitzgerald mean by the statement enclosed in parentheses—i.e., "(She always says . . .)"? What is its
tone? What is the difference in their responses to his condition?
What is the style, sense, and effect of the author's saying first,
" 'The crack's in me,' I said heroically," and then, " 'Baby et up
all her Spinoza?' "? Why does he reject her ministrations? Does
he refuse her attempt at comfort—or is it more that her "solution"
is too grand and heroic; that her courage is beyond his broken
powers? Does he mock her "vitality"? Does he flourish the tin
cup of his self-pity?

16. What is the effect of the Biblical quotation that ends the
essay? This is, of course, a bleak utterance; taken out of its Biblical context, it is bitter and despairing. Does Fitzgerald mean to
end on that note? Does the allusion have a local reference or
does it extend to the whole of his condition; that is, does he
mean that in his state he was unable to savor his friend's vitality
—or, more broadly, that he had hit bottom, unable or unwilling
to rise? Why does Fitzgerald say that he could walk from her
door "and go away into the world of bitterness, where I was
making a home with such materials as are found there"? What
does he mean? Has he cast out friendship along with his facility
for self-identification? Is he cracked beyond saving—or has he
salvaged something? Has Fitzgerald lost the ability to function
or has he in fact achieved some new balancing of opposed ideas?
Has he broken through to some equilibrium, different in composition from what existed before the crack-up, but paradoxically
sounder and more human, though less romantic and sentimental
—affirmative but not "heroic"? In what ways has the writing of
the essay *enacted* a balancing of bitterness and affirmation?

WHAT I BELIEVE

BY *E. M. Forster*

I DO NOT BELIEVE in Belief. But this is an age of faith, and there are so many militant creeds that, in self-defense, one has to formulate a creed of one's own. Tolerance, good temper and sympathy are no longer enough in a world which is rent by religious and racial persecution, in a world where ignorance rules, and science, who ought to have ruled, plays the subservient pimp. Tolerance, good temper and sympathy—they are what matter really, and if the human race is not to collapse they must come to the front before long. But for the moment they are not enough, their action is no stronger than a flower, battered beneath a military jack-boot. They want stiffening, even if the process coarsens them. Faith, to my mind, is a stiffening process, a sort of mental starch, which ought to be applied as sparingly as possible. I dislike the stuff. I do not believe in it, for its own sake, at all. Herein I probably differ from most people, who believe in Belief, and are only sorry they cannot swallow even more than they do. My lawgivers are Erasmus and Montaigne, not Moses and St. Paul. My temple stands not upon Mount Moriah but in that Elysian Field where even the immoral are admitted. My motto is: "Lord, I disbelieve—help thou my unbelief."

I have, however, to live in an Age of Faith—the sort of epoch I used to hear praised when I was a boy. It is extremely unpleasant

From *Two Cheers for Democracy* by E. M. Forster (New York: Harcourt, Brace & World, 1951), pp. 67–76. Copyright, 1939, by E. M. Forster. Reprinted by permission of Harcourt, Brace & World, Inc., and by permission of Edward Arnold (Publishers) Ltd.

really. It is bloody in every sense of the word. And I have to keep my end up in it. Where do I start?

With personal relationships. Here is something comparatively solid in a world full of violence and cruelty. Not absolutely solid, for Psychology has split and shattered the idea of a "Person," and has shown that there is something incalculable in each of us, which may at any moment rise to the surface and destroy our normal balance. We don't know what we are like. We can't know what other people are like. How, then, can we put any trust in personal relationships, or cling to them in the gathering political storm? In theory we cannot. But in practice we can and do. Though A is not unchangeably A or B unchangeably B, there can still be love and loyalty between the two. For the purpose of living one has to assume that the personality is solid, and the "self" is an entity, and to ignore all contrary evidence. And since to ignore evidence is one of the characteristics of faith, I certainly can proclaim that I believe in personal relationships.

Starting from them, I get a little order into the contemporary chaos. One must be fond of people and trust them if one is not to make a mess of life, and it is therefore essential that they should not let one down. They often do. The moral of which is that I must, myself, be as reliable as possible, and this I try to be. But reliability is not a matter of contract—that is the main difference between the world of personal relationships and the world of business relationships. It is a matter for the heart, which signs no documents. In other words, reliability is impossible unless there is a natural warmth. Most men possess this warmth, though they often have bad luck and get chilled. Most of them, even when they are politicians, *want* to keep faith. And one can, at all events, show one's own little light here, one's own poor little trembling flame, with the knowledge that it is not the only light that is shining in the darkness, and not the only one which the darkness does not comprehend. Personal relations are despised today. They are regarded as bourgeois luxuries, as products of a time of fair weather which is now past, and we are urged to get rid of them, and to dedicate ourselves to some movement or cause instead. I hate the idea of causes, and if I had to choose between betraying my country and betraying my friend, I hope I should have the guts to betray my country. Such a choice may scandalize the modern reader, and he may stretch out his patriotic hand to the telephone at once and ring up the police. It would not have shocked Dante, though. Dante places Brutus and Cassius in the lowest circle of Hell because they had chosen to betray their friend Julius Caesar rather than their country Rome. Probably one will not be asked to make such an agonizing choice. Still, there lies at the back of every creed something terrible and hard for which the worshipper may one day be required to suffer, and there is even a terror and a hardness in this creed of personal relationships, urbane and mild though it sounds. Love and loyalty to an individual can run counter to the claims of the State. When they do—down with the State, say I, which means that the State would down me.

This brings me along to Democracy, "even Love, the Beloved Republic, which feeds upon Freedom and lives." Democracy is not a Beloved Republic really, and never will be. But it is less hateful than other contemporary forms of government, and to that extent it deserves our support. It does start from the assumption that the individual is important, and that all types are needed to make a civilization. It does not divide its citizens into the bossers and the bossed—as an efficiency-regime tends to do. The people I admire most are those who are sensitive and want to create something or discover something, and do not see life in terms of power, and such people get more of a chance under a democracy than elsewhere. They found religions, great or small, or they produce literature and art, or they do disinterested scientific research, or they may be what is called "ordinary people," who are creative in their private lives, bring up their children decently, for instance, or help their neighbors. All these people need to express themselves; they cannot do so unless society allows them liberty to do so, and the society which allows them most liberty is a democracy.

Democracy has another merit. It allows criticism, and if there is not public criticism there are bound to be hushed-up scandals. That is why I believe in the Press, despite all its lies and vulgarity, and why I believe in Parliament. Parliament is often sneered at because it is a Talking Shop. I believe in it *because* it is a talking shop. I believe in the Private Member who makes himself a nuisance. He gets snubbed and is told that he is cranky or ill-informed, but he does expose abuses which would otherwise never have been mentioned, and very often an abuse gets put right just by being mentioned. Occasionally, too, a well-meaning public official starts losing his head in the cause of efficiency, and thinks himself God Almighty. Such officials are particularly frequent in the Home Office. Well, there will be questions about them in Parliament sooner or later, and then they will have to mind their steps. Whether Parliament is either a representative body or an efficient one is questionable, but I value it because it criticizes and talks, and because its chatter gets widely reported.

So Two Cheers for Democracy: one because it admits variety and two because it permits criticism. Two cheers are quite enough: there is no occasion to give three. Only Love the Beloved Republic deserves that.

What about Force, though? While we are trying to be sensitive and advanced and affectionate and tolerant, an unpleasant question pops up: does not all society rest upon force? If a government cannot count upon the police and the army, how can it hope to rule? And if an individual gets knocked on the head or sent to a labor camp, of what significance are his opinions?

This dilemma does not worry me as much as it does some. I realize that all society rests upon force. But all the great creative actions, all the decent human relations, occur during the intervals when force has not managed to come to the front. These intervals are what matter. I want them to be as frequent and as lengthy as possible, and I call them "civilization." Some people idealize force and pull it into the foreground and worship it, instead of keeping it in the background as long as possible. I think they make a mistake, and I think that their opposites, the mystics, err even more when they declare that force does not exist. I believe that it exists, and that one of our jobs is to prevent it from getting out of its box. It gets out sooner or later, and then it destroys us and all the lovely things which we have made. But it is not out all the time, for the fortunate reason that the strong are so stupid. Consider their conduct for a moment in the Niebelung's Ring. The giants there have the guns, or in other words the gold; but they do nothing with it, they do not realize that they are all-powerful, with the result that the catastrophe is delayed and the castle of Walhalla, insecure but glorious, fronts the storms. Fafnir, coiled round his hoard, grumbles and grunts; we can hear him under Europe today; the leaves of the wood already tremble, and the Bird calls its warnings uselessly. Fafnir will destroy us, but by a blessed dispensation he is stupid and slow, and creation goes on just outside the poisonous blast of his breath. The Nietzschean would hurry the monster up, the mystic would say he did not exist, but Wotan, wiser than either, hastens to create warriors before doom declares itself. The Valkyries are symbols not only of courage but of intelligence; they represent the human spirit snatching its opportunity while the going is good, and one of them even finds time to love. Brünnhilde's last song hymns the recurrence of love, and since it is the privilege of art to exaggerate, she goes even further, and proclaims the love which is eternally triumphant and feeds upon freedom, and lives.

So that is what I feel about force and violence. It is, alas! the ultimate reality on this earth, but it does not always get to the front. Some people call its absences "decadence"; I call them "civilization" and find in such interludes the chief justification for the human experiment. I look the other way until fate strikes me. Whether this is due to courage or to cowardice in my own case I cannot be sure. But I know that if men had not looked the other way in the past, nothing of any value would survive. The people I respect most behave as if they were immortal and as if society was eternal. Both assumptions are false; both of them must be accepted as true if we are to go on eating and working and loving, and are to keep open a few breathing holes for the human spirit. No millennium seems likely to descend upon humanity; no better and stronger League of Nations will be instituted; no form of Christianity and no alternative to Christianity will bring peace to the world or integrity to the individual; no "change of heart" will occur. And yet we need not despair, indeed, we cannot despair; the evidence of history shows us that men have always insisted on behaving creatively under the shadow of the sword; that they have done their artistic and scientific and domestic stuff for the sake of doing it, and that we had better follow their example under the shadow of the aeroplanes. Others, with more vision or courage than myself, see the salvation of humanity ahead, and will dismiss my conception of civilization as paltry, a sort of tip-and-run game. Certainly it is presumptuous to say that we *cannot* improve, and that Man, who has only been in power for a few thousand years, will never learn to make use of his power. All I mean is that, if people continue to kill one another as they do, the world cannot get better than it is, and that since there are more people than formerly, and their means for destroying one another superior, the world may well get worse. What is good in people—and consequently in the world—is their insistence on creation, their belief in friendship and loyalty for their own sakes; and though Violence remains and is, indeed, the major partner in this muddled establishment, I believe that creativeness remains too, and will always assume direction when violence sleeps. So, though I am not an optimist, I cannot agree with Sophocles that it were better never to have been born. And although, like Horace, I see no evidence that each batch of births is superior to the last, I leave the field open for the more complacent view. This is such a difficult moment to live in, one cannot help getting gloomy and also a bit rattled, and perhaps short-sighted.

In search of a refuge, we may perhaps turn to hero-worship. But here we shall get no help, in my opinion. Hero-worship is a dangerous vice, and one of the minor merits of a democracy is that it does not encourage it, or produce that unmanageable type of citizen known as the Great Man. It produces instead different kinds of small men—a much finer achievement. But people who cannot get interested in the variety of life, and cannot make up their own minds, get discontented over this, and they long for a hero to bow down before and to follow blindly. It is significant that a hero is an integral part of the authoritarian stock-in-trade today. An efficiency-regime cannot be run without a few heroes stuck about it to carry off the dullness—much as plums have to be put into a bad pudding to make it palatable. One hero at the top and a smaller one each side of him is a favorite arrangement, and the timid and the bored are comforted by the trinity, and, bowing down, feel exalted and strengthened.

No, I distrust Great Men. They produce a desert of uniformity around them and often a pool of blood too, and I always feel a little man's pleasure when they come a cropper. Every now and then one reads in the newspapers some such statement as: "The coup d'état appears to have failed, and Admiral Toma's whereabouts is at present unknown." Admiral Toma had probably every qualification for being a Great Man—an iron will, personal magnetism, dash, flair, sexlessness—but fate was against him, so he retires to unknown whereabouts instead of parading history with his peers. He fails with a completeness which no artist and no lover can experience, because with them the process of creation is itself an achievement, whereas with him the only possible achievement is success.

I believe in aristocracy, though—if that is the right word, and if a democrat may use it. Not an aristocracy of power, based upon rank and influence, but an aristocracy of the sensitive, the considerate and the plucky. Its members are to be found in all nations and classes, and all through the ages, and there is a secret understanding between them when they meet. They represent the true human tradition, the one permanent victory of our queer race over cruelty and chaos. Thousands of them perish in obscurity, a few are great names. They are sensitive for others as well as for themselves, they are considerate without being fussy, their pluck is not swankiness but the power to endure, and they can take a joke. I give no examples—it is risky to do that—but the reader may as well consider whether this is the type of person he would like to meet and to be, and whether (going farther with me) he would prefer that this type should *not* be an ascetic one. I am against asceticism myself. I am with the old Scotsman who wanted less chastity and more delicacy. I do not feel that my aristocrats are a real aristocracy if they thwart their bodies, since bodies are the instruments through which we register and enjoy the world. Still, I do not insist. This is not a major point. It is clearly possible to be sensitive, considerate and plucky and yet be an ascetic too; if anyone possesses the first three qualities, I will let him in! On they go—an invincible army, yet not a victorious one. The aristocrats, the elect, the chosen, the Best People—all the words that describe them are false, and all attempts to organize them fail. Again and again Authority, seeing their value, has tried to net them and to utilize them as the Egyptian Priesthood or the Christian Church or the Chinese Civil Service or the Group Movement, or some other worthy stunt. But they slip through the net and are gone; when the door is shut, they are no longer in the room; their temple, as one of them remarked, is the Holiness of the Heart's Affection, and their kingdom, though they never possess it, is the wide-open world.

With this type of person knocking about, and constantly crossing one's path if one has eyes to see or hands to feel, the experiment of earthly life cannot be dismissed as a failure. But it may well be hailed as a tragedy, the tragedy being that no device has been found by which these private decencies can be transmitted to public affairs. As soon as people have power they go crooked and sometimes dotty as well, because the possession of power lifts them into a region where normal honesty never pays. For instance, the man who is selling newspapers outside the Houses of Parliament can safely leave his papers to go for a drink and his cap beside them: anyone who takes a paper is sure to drop a copper into the cap. But the men who are inside the Houses of Parliament—they cannot trust one another like that, still less can the Government they compose trust other governments. No caps upon the pavement here, but suspicion, treachery and armaments. The more highly public life is organized the lower does its morality sink; the nations of today behave to each other worse than they ever did in the past, they cheat, rob, bully and bluff, make war without notice, and kill as many women and children as possible; whereas primitive tribes were at all events restrained by taboos. It is a humiliating outlook—though the greater the darkness, the brighter shine the little lights, reassuring one another, signalling: "Well, at all events, I'm still here. I don't like it very much, but how are you?" Unquenchable lights of my aristocracy! Signals of the invincible army! "Come along—anyway, let's have a good time while we can." I think they signal that too.

The Saviour of the future—if ever he comes—will not preach a new Gospel. He will merely utilize my aristocracy, he will make effective the good will and the good temper which are already existing. In other words, he will introduce a new technique. In economics, we are told that if there was a new technique of distribution, there need be no poverty, and people would not starve in one place while crops were being ploughed under in another. A similar change is needed in the sphere of morals and politics. The desire for it is by no means new; it was expressed, for example, in theological terms by Jacopone da Todi over six hundred years ago. "Ordina questo amore, O tu che m'ami," he said; "O thou who lovest me—set this love in order." His prayer was not granted, and I do not myself believe that it ever will be, but here, and not through a change of heart, is our probable route. Not by becoming better, but by ordering and distributing his native goodness, will Man shut up Force into its box, and so gain time to explore the universe and to set his mark upon it worthily. At present he only explores it at odd moments, when Force is looking the other way, and his divine creativeness appears as a trivial by-product, to be scrapped as soon as the drums beat and the bombers hum.

Such a change, claim the orthodox, can only be made by

Christianity, and will be made by it in God's good time: man always has failed and always will fail to organize his own goodness, and it is presumptuous of him to try. This claim—solemn as it is—leaves me cold. I cannot believe that Christianity will ever cope with the present world-wide mess, and I think that such influence as it retains in modern society is due to the money behind it, rather than to its spiritual appeal. It was a spiritual force once, but the indwelling spirit will have to be restated if it is to calm the waters again, and probably restated in a non-Christian form. Naturally a lot of people, and people who are not only good but able and intelligent, will disagree here; they will vehemently deny that Christianity has failed, or they will argue that its failure proceeds from the wickedness of men, and really proves its ultimate success. They have Faith, with a large F. My faith has a very small one, and I only intrude it because these are strenuous and serious days, and one likes to say what one thinks while speech is comparatively free: it may not be free much longer.

The above are the reflections of an individualist and a liberal who has found liberalism crumbling beneath him and at first felt ashamed. Then, looking around, he decided there was no special reason for shame, since other people, whatever they felt, were equally insecure. And as for individualism—there seems no way of getting off this, even if one wanted to. The dictator-hero can grind down his citizens till they are all alike, but he cannot melt them into a single man. That is beyond his power. He can order them to merge, he can incite them to mass-antics, but they are obliged to be born separately, and to die separately, and, owing to these unavoidable termini, will always be running off the totalitarian rails. The memory of birth and the expectation of death always lurk within the human being, making him separate from his fellows and consequently capable of intercourse with them. Naked I came into the world, naked I shall go out of it! And a very good thing too, for it reminds me that I am naked under my shirt, whatever its color.

QUESTIONS FOR STUDY
AND TOPICS FOR DISCUSSION
ON *What I Believe*

1. This essay appeared in the volume *I Believe: The Personal Philosophies of Certain Eminent Men and Women of Our Time* edited by Clifton Fadiman and published in 1939. In explaining the motive for the collection, Fadiman wrote: " . . . we felt, in the dark days amidst which we find ourselves, there might come from these distinguished men and women a profession of faith, a renewal of the covenant, a challenge to the anti-intellectual movement of our time." Most of the essays were published earlier in *The Nation* magazine under the title "Living Philosophies." Forster's contribution was the first in the series and was printed with the title "Two Cheers for Democracy" in the issue of July 16, 1938. His essay was published with the present title as a separate pamphlet in England in 1939.

What moved Forster to write a credo at this time? In what ways is the contemporary historical situation reflected in the argument of the essay? What challenges to his beliefs does Forster confront, and what is the manner of his response? What are the relations between the things he is defending and the style of his defense? He says that "one cannot help getting gloomy and also a bit rattled" (p. 263); does this show in his writing? Does he convey an air of crisis? Is he too urbane and soft-spoken for the dark days of 1939? Is he tougher than he seems? Forster fights shy of slogans, abstractions, heroic exhortations, doctrinaire commitments, and the whole noisy rhetoric of mobilization. What are the relations between these animadversions and the stands he takes on the issues in contention? What relationship does he establish with his audience? What modes of persuasion does he employ?

2. What tone does Forster establish in the first two sentences of the essay? How would they be delivered in actual speaking? The irony of his statement is transparent enough. He is obviously a man of strong beliefs. Why does he begin with a demurrer? Why does he risk sounding coy? Why does he give "Belief" an initial capital? He makes frequent use of the device. What are its implications for the tone and sense of the essay?

3. Analyze the rhetoric of Forster's argument in sentences 3–5. What does he assert? What does he admit? How does he qualify the admission? Does he grant too much? Does he take back what he seems to concede? What does he affirm? In what ways is this pattern of assertion, concession, and qualification characteristic of Forster's style and strategy in argument? How effective is the strategy?

4. "Pimp" coarsens the texture of the diction and would seem to be an odd choice for so genteel and delicate a temperament, and quite out of character with what has been called Forster's "tea-tabling" manner. Why does he use the word? Is he being fair to science? Is he trying to be fair? What is he up to?

5. Why does he say "come to the front"? What theme is declared in the metaphor, and how does it thread through the essay? What is the connection between the figure and the next sentence? Why does he compare the qualities of tolerance, good temper, and sympathy with the action of a flower? Why "battered" rather than "crushed" or "destroyed"?

6. What is the sense of "stiffening" in the next two sentences? What is the tone and meaning of: Faith is "a sort of mental starch"? Is the analogy an isolated figure used only for an intensifying effect, or is it part of some informing figurative design? Forster's writing seems to lack a pronounced metaphoric texture, but that may be deceiving. What other similes and metaphors convey something of the same idea expressed here? Think of the idea in other terms and say that "Faith" is an armor or a carapace. These words would signify some hard and confining encrustation. They would point to such congeries of contrasts as exterior rigidity and inner suppleness, repression and spontaneity, constraint and freedom—all of which, and more of the same, are very much a part of the plenary meaning of the essay. If one paraphrases Forster's argument at this point and says that dogmatical Belief hardens, stiffens, deforms, suffocates, re-

presses the spirit, one is using the *pattern* of Forster's words, and that pattern is as much figurative as it is denotative. In what ways, then, does Forster's argument on specific issues of politics, society, and philosophy fit into the larger design of his credo, and how is that design rendered in figurative language?

7. Lionel Trilling (*E. M. Forster,* 1943) has said of the argument in the first paragraph:

> An inadequate view of things, certainly—the questions and objections that would destroy it will be apparent at once. Here is a liberalism which seems to carry itself to the extreme of anarchy, a liberalism shot through with a sentimentally-literal Christian morality. It is *laissez faire* to the ultimate. In its casual anarchism it is an affront to the Western mind.
>
> But in the odd way that we have, we will feel better and more respectful of it if we understand that it is an entirely intentional affront. The laxness of the critical manner in which Forster sets forth his literary insights is no doubt the expression of a temperament—even of the fault of a temperament—but it is also the expression of an intention. It is *consciously* a contradiction of the Western tradition of intellect which believes that by making decisions, by choosing precisely, by evaluating correctly it can solve all difficulties.

What questions and objections are "apparent at once"? Does Forster know what he is doing? Is there any bite to his assertions? Why does he take the trouble to dissociate himself from "Moses and St. Paul," if, after all, the whole culture is embattled? Why should he bother to be nearly as hard upon orthodox religion as he is upon totalitarianism?

8. What is the tone in Forster's acknowledging that he has to live in an Age of Faith? *The Nation* version has "It is damned unpleasant, really;" why the change to "extremely unpleasant"? What are the several senses of "bloody"? How would you characterize the diction of this paragraph?

9. Analyze the rhetoric of Forster's argument in the third paragraph. Does he show an awareness of the voice of the Opposition? How convincing is his critique of Psychology? Is

his case the firmer and more persuasive for considering the qualifications and negations of his views? Is Forster claiming that we have to live a fiction—to live "as if" what theory tells us is not true? What are some of the philosophical problems involved in this position? Is he being naïve? What is the effect of the ironical turnabout of the last sentence of the paragraph upon the tenor of his case? Why is "faith" given without an initial capital?

10. How does Forster move from idea to idea in the fourth paragraph (p. 259)? If, as he says, it is essential that people should not let one down, and yet he concedes that in reality they do, has he undermined his position so drastically that what follows is more wistful desire than viable conviction? On what kind of appeal does he finally rest his case? Does he seem sentimental and indulgent? Analyze the images of warmth, light, and darkness. Are they trite?

11. How serious is Forster in saying that if he were forced to make a choice, he hopes he would have the guts to betray his country rather than his friend? Is he aware of the implications of his position? Is this one more instance of what Trilling called an "intentional affront"?

12. With what tone is the motto which begins Forster's defense of democracy (p. 260) meant to be delivered? Why is Democracy given an initial capital at the beginning and a lower-case letter at the end of the paragraph? His notions and sentiments about democracy are commonplace enough; they may even sound trite and simple-minded. What makes them unusual? Forster obviously avoids grandiose claims and affirms the most modest merits of democracy. What is the effect of the tactic? He uses similar tactics elsewhere in the essay. Why? What is the basis of his dislike of efficiency-regimes and power? Exactly why does Forster "believe in the Private Member who makes himself a nuisance" (p. 260)? What kind of talk does he value? What criticism of conformity is implied in this passage? What kills democracy and what keeps it alive?

13. The paragraph beginning "So Two Cheers for Democracy . . ." (p. 261) is often cited as an epitome of Forster's manner. Explain its tone and construction. What gives it bite

and point? What is its place in the rhetoric and argumentative design of the whole essay?

14. Why does Forster use questions in the paragraph introducing the matter of Force (p. 261) rather than the pattern of assertion, concession, and qualification? Does he face up to the difficulties of these questions in the ensuing argument? The aplomb of his manner—his unruffled poise in saying "this dilemma does not worry me as much as it does some"—might seem frivolous to the person who takes the questions earnestly and regards them as terrifying possibilities. Why doesn't Forster surrender to the impulse to cry havoc?

Forster's argument on this issue seems lucid enough, but it turns on several paradoxes that are hard to take. He concedes that force exists. When it gets out of hand, it destroys us and all the lovely things we have made. But force isn't always that powerful; it weakens its grip, tires, gets distracted, falls asleep. And in those intervals and intermissions, all the great creative actions, all the decent human relations, come to the front. Force and violence are the ultimate reality, but not the only reality. Creativity and decency are as much a fact of experience as their opposites. They, too, exist; they are real.

Now Forster is exasperating precisely because most of us cannot tolerate these contraries. We regard them as adversaries which live only if the others are extinguished. Forster can't have both, we say, for force must be countered by action if creativity, decency, and all those other values are to survive, and if he thinks that everything is going to come out all right just the same . . . well, he is only being, as Saul Bellow says of this sort of view in "The Sealed Treasure," "optimistic to the point of imbecility."

But Forster is no Pangloss. He is not happy with the way things are. He takes no cheer from future prospects. He isn't quite convinced that things will get better. He does not foresee the triumph of decency and creativity; these qualities are invincible but not victorious. He does not, to quote Bellow again, "raise the standard of pure Affirmation." If he must fight, it will be only a holding action—and his redoubt will be civilization. In its own way, this is no soft creed. It provides little solace; it offers no boisterous certainties; it gives neither the comfort of clean optimism nor the bracing vigor of straight pessimism; it is nothing to rally round;—but in its own terms, it is realistic.

If this is an accurate summary of Forster's views, what is the relation between his convictions and the style of the essay? How do these views shape the content? What is Forster's intention? What is his relationship to his audience? Does this paraphrase alter in any way the terms of your criticism of Forster's argument?

15. Why does Forster put "civilization" in quotation marks (p. 261)? Civilization is no less an abstraction than Belief, Faith, Democracy. Why should he value this over the others? How does he make it seem more appealing?

16. The statement that one of our jobs is to prevent force from getting out of its box (p. 261) may refer to the legend of Pandora's box, or to a jinni, or to a jack-in-the-box. Which allusion seems appropriate to the tone and tenor of the essay?

17. What is the effect of the ironical turnabout of the sentence beginning "Brünnhilde's last song . . ." (p. 262) upon the tone and content of the argument?

18. The two sentences beginning "The people I respect most . . ." (p. 262) are a rephrasing of a well-known and much-quoted passage from an essay by Forster on "Liberty in England" (1935). The original reads:

> I am worried by thoughts of a war oftener than by thoughts of my own death, yet the line to be adopted over both these nuisances is the same. One must behave as if one is immortal, and as if civilization is eternal. Both statements are false—I shall not survive, no more will the great globe itself—both of them must be assumed to be true if we are to go on eating and working and traveling, and keep open a few breathing holes for the human spirit.

What has been altered in the change of contexts? What effect would the rephrasing of the passage have upon a reader who knew the earlier work?

19. How does Forster treat heroes? What tricks does he use to cut them down to size? What is his motive? Does he display a small man's envy in his belittlement? Why does he include "sexlessness" among Admiral Toma's qualifications (p. 263)? Why "an iron will"? Is he being fair to Admiral Toma? Why do Great Men produce "uniformity"?

20. Why does Forster, a democrat, say he believes in "aristocracy"? What are the implications of Forster's tactic of crossing one's habitual response to words? Why does Forster say "plucky" rather than "heroic" or "courageous" (p. 264)? Pick out the colloquialisms in this paragraph. What other words could he have chosen? Why does he use these and not any others? To what purpose? With what effect? Why does he take up the matter of asceticism? Is it a digression? Has he dealt with the topic before in the essay? What are the connections among asceticism, chastity, and delicacy? What other arguments of the essay are reflected in his treatment of these notions? Why does he use initial capitals for certain phrases? Are all the words and phrases employing this device meant to be taken the same way? How do they differ among themselves and from the earlier instances? The "Holiness of the Heart's Affection" is an allusion to John Keats's letter to Benjamin Bailey of 22 November 1817. Is there any connection between the substance of the letter and Forster's argument? What makes Keats an exemplary figure for Forster? What is the play on temple and kingdom?

21. In what way does the theme of order and disorder inform the whole essay? Why does Forster recapitulate the argument of shutting up Force in its box (p. 265)? If, as he says, he does not believe that da Todi's prayer will ever be granted, why does he bother to mention the ordering and distributing of man's native goodness? Why does Forster spend so much time criticizing orthodox Christianity?

22. What is the rhetoric and tone of the last paragraph of the essay? Of what did Forster feel ashamed at first, and why? What is the point of the last two sentences? Is this the conclusion of the argument, in the sense of the logical implications of certain premises, or is it the conviction from which the credo springs? What *is* Forster's credo? What pattern of figures is reflected in "Naked I came into the world . . ."? What does he mean exactly?

THE NOBLE RIDER
AND THE
SOUND OF WORDS

BY *Wallace Stevens*

IN THE *Phaedrus*, Plato speaks of the soul in a figure. He says:

> Let our figure be of a composite nature—a pair of winged horses and a charioteer. Now the winged horses and the charioteer of the gods are all of them noble, and of noble breed, while ours are mixed; and we have a charioteer who drives them in a pair, and one of them is noble and of noble origin, and the other is ignoble and of ignoble origin; and, as might be expected, there is a great deal of trouble in managing them. I will endeavor to explain to you in what way the mortal differs from the immortal creature. The soul or animate being has the care of the inanimate, and traverses the whole heaven in divers forms appearing;—when perfect and fully winged she soars upward, and is the ruler of the universe; while the imperfect soul loses her feathers, and drooping in her flight at last settles on the solid ground.

We recognize at once, in this figure, Plato's pure poetry; and at the same time we recognize what Coleridge called Plato's dear, gorgeous nonsense. The truth is that we have scarcely read

From *The Necessary Angel: Essays on Reality and the Imagination* by Wallace Stevens (New York: Alfred A. Knopf, 1951), pp. 3–36. Copyright, 1942, by Wallace Stevens. Reprinted by permission of Alfred A. Knopf, Inc.

the passage before we have identified ourselves with the charioteer, have, in fact, taken his place and, driving his winged horses,
are traversing the whole heaven. Then suddenly we remember,
it may be, that the soul no longer exists and we droop in our
flight and at last settle on the solid ground. The figure becomes
antiquated and rustic.

(1)

What really happens in this brief experience? Why does this
figure, potent for so long, become merely the emblem of a
mythology, the rustic memorial of a belief in the soul and in a
distinction between good and evil? The answer to these questions
is, I think, a simple one.

I said that suddenly we remember that the soul no longer
exists and we droop in our flight. For that matter, neither charioteers nor chariots any longer exist. Consequently, the figure does
not become unreal because we are troubled about the soul. Besides, unreal things have a reality of their own, in poetry as elsewhere. We do not hesitate, in poetry, to yield ourselves to the
unreal, when it is possible to yield ourselves. The existence of
the soul, of charioteers and chariots and of winged horses is
immaterial. They did not exist for Plato, not even the charioteer
and chariot; for certainly a charioteer driving his chariot across
the whole heaven was for Plato precisely what he is for us. He
was unreal for Plato as he is for us. Plato, however, could yield
himself, was free to yield himself, to this gorgeous nonsense.
We cannot yield ourselves. We are not free to yield ourselves.

Just as the difficulty is not a difficulty about unreal things, since
the imagination accepts them, and since the poetry of the passage
is, for us, wholly the poetry of the unreal, so it is not an emotional
difficulty. Something else than the imagination is moved by the
statement that the horses of the gods are all of them noble, and
of noble breed or origin. The statement is a moving statement and
is intended to be so. It is insistent and its insistence moves us.
Its insistence is the insistence of a speaker, in this case Socrates,
who, for the moment, feels delight, even if a casual delight, in
the nobility and noble breed. Those images of nobility instantly
become nobility itself and determine the emotional level at which
the next page or two are to be read. The figure does not lose its
vitality because of any failure of feeling on Plato's part. He does

not communicate nobility coldly. His horses are not marble horses, the reference to their breed saves them from being that. The fact that the horses are not marble horses helps, moreover, to save the charioteer from being, say, a creature of cloud. The result is that we recognize, even if we cannot realize, the feelings of the robust poet clearly and fluently noting the images in his mind and by means of his robustness, clearness and fluency communicating much more than the images themselves. Yet we do not quite yield. We cannot. We do not feel free.

In trying to find out what it is that stands between Plato's figure and ourselves, we have to accept the idea that, however legendary it appears to be, it has had its vicissitudes. The history of a figure of speech or the history of an idea, such as the idea of nobility, cannot be very different from the history of anything else. It is the episodes that are of interest, and here the episode is that of our diffidence. By us and ourselves, I mean you and me; and yet not you and me as individuals but as representatives of a state of mind. Adams in his work on Vico makes the remark that the true history of the human race is a history of its progressive mental states. It is a remark of interest in this relation. We may assume that in the history of Plato's figure there have been incessant changes of response; that these changes have been psychological changes, and that our own diffidence is simply one more state of mind due to such a change.

The specific question is partly as to the nature of the change and partly as to the cause of it. In nature, the change is as follows: The imagination loses vitality as it ceases to adhere to what is real. When it adheres to the unreal and intensifies what is unreal, while its first effect may be extraordinary, that effect is the maximum effect that it will ever have. In Plato's figure, his imagination does not adhere to what is real. On the contrary, having created something unreal, it adheres to it and intensifies its unreality. Its first effect, its effect at first reading, is its maximum effect, when the imagination, being moved, puts us in the place of the charioteer, before the reason checks us. The case is, then, that we concede that the figure is all imagination. At the same time, we say that it has not the slightest meaning for us, except for its nobility. As to that, while we are moved by it, we are moved as observers. We recognize it perfectly. We do not realize it. We understand the feeling of it, the robust feeling, clearly and fluently communicated. Yet we understand it rather than participate in it.

As to the cause of the change, it is the loss of the figure's vitality. The reason why this particular figure has lost its vitality is that, in it, the imagination adheres to what is unreal. What happened, as we were traversing the whole heaven, is that the imagination lost its power to sustain us. It has the strength of reality or none at all.

(2)

What has just been said demonstrates that there are degrees of the imagination, as, for example, degrees of vitality and, therefore, of intensity. It is an implication that there are degrees of reality. The discourse about the two elements seems endless. For my own part, I intend merely to follow, in a very hasty way, the fortunes of the idea of nobility as a characteristic of the imagination, and even as its symbol or alter ego, through several of the episodes in its history, in order to determine, if possible, what its fate has been and what has determined its fate. This can be done only on the basis of the relation between the imagination and reality. What has been said in respect to the figure of the charioteer illustrates this.

I should like now to go on to other illustrations of the relation between the imagination and reality and particularly to illustrations that constitute episodes in the history of the idea of nobility. It would be agreeable to pass directly from the charioteer and his winged horses to Don Quixote. It would be like a return from what Plato calls "the back of heaven" to one's own spot. Nevertheless, there is Verrocchio (as one among others) with his statue of Bartolommeo Colleoni, in Venice, standing in the way. I have not selected him as a Neo-Platonist to relate us back from a modern time to Plato's time, although he does in fact so relate us, just as through Leonardo, his pupil, he strengthens the relationship. I have selected him because there, on the edge of the world in which we live today, he established a form of such nobility that it has never ceased to magnify us in our own eyes. It is like the form of an invincible man, who has come, slowly and boldly, through every warlike opposition of the past and who moves in our midst without dropping the bridle of the powerful horse from his hand, without taking off his helmet and without relaxing the attitude of a warrior of noble origin. What man on whose side the horseman fought could ever be anything but fearless, anything but indomitable? One feels the passion of rhetoric begin to stir and even to grow furious; and one thinks that, after all, the noble style, in whatever it creates, merely perpetuates the noble style. In this statue, the apposition between the imagination and reality is too favorable to the imagination. Our difficulty is not primarily with any detail. It is primarily with the whole. The point is not so much to analyze the difficulty as to determine whether we share it, to find out whether it exists, whether we regard this specimen of the genius of Verrocchio and of the Renaissance as a bit of uncommon panache, no longer quite the appropriate thing outdoors, or whether we regard it, in the language of Dr. Richards, as something inexhaustible to meditation or, to speak for myself, as a thing of a nobility responsive to the most minute demand. It seems, nowadays, what it may very well not have seemed a few years ago, a little overpowering, a little magnificent.

Undoubtedly, Don Quixote could be Bartolommeo Colleoni in Spain. The tradition of Italy is the tradition of the imagination. The tradition of Spain is the tradition of reality. There is no apparent reason why the reverse should not be true. If this is a just observation, it indicates that the relation between the imagination and reality is a question, more or less, of precise equilibrium. Thus it is not a question of the difference between grotesque extremes. My purpose is not to contrast Colleoni with Don Quixote. It is to say that one passed into the other, that one became and was the other. The difference between them is that Verrocchio believed in one kind of nobility and Cervantes, if he believed in any, believed in another kind. With Verrocchio it was an affair of the noble style, whatever his prepossession respecting the nobility of man as a real animal may have been. With Cervantes, nobility was not a thing of the imagination. It was a part of reality, it was something that exists in life, something so true to us that it is in danger of ceasing to exist, if we isolate it, something in the mind of a precarious tenure. These may be words. Certainly, however, Cervantes sought to set right the balance between the imagination and reality. As we come closer to our own times in Don Quixote and as we are drawn together by the intelligence common to the two periods, we may derive so much satisfaction from the restoration of reality as to become wholly prejudiced against the imagination. This is to reach a conclusion prematurely, let alone that it may be to reach a conclusion in respect to something as to which no conclusion is possible or desirable.

There is in Washington, in Lafayette Square, which is the square on which the White House faces, a statue of Andrew Jackson, riding a horse with one of the most beautiful tails in the world. General Jackson is raising his hat in a gay gesture, saluting the ladies of his generation. One looks at this work of Clark Mills and thinks of the remark of Bertrand Russell that to acquire immunity to eloquence is of the utmost importance to the citizens of a democracy. We are bound to think that Colleoni, as a mercenary, was a much less formidable man than General Jackson, that he meant less to fewer people and that, if Verrocchio could have applied his prodigious poetry to Jackson, the whole American outlook today might be imperial. This work is a work of fancy. Dr. Richards cites Coleridge's theory of fancy as opposed to imagination. Fancy is an activity of the mind which puts things together of choice, *not* the will, as a principle of the mind's being, striving to realize itself in knowing itself. Fancy, then, is an exercise of selection from among objects already supplied by association, a selection made for purposes which are not then and therein being shaped but have been already fixed. We are concerned then with an object occupying a position as remarkable as any that can be found in the United States in which there is not the slightest trace of the imagination. Treating this work as typical, it is obvious that the American will as a principle of the mind's being is easily satisfied in its efforts to realize itself in knowing itself. The statue may be dismissed, not without speaking of it again as a thing that at least makes us conscious of ourselves as we were, if not as we are. To that extent, it helps us to know ourselves. It helps us to know ourselves as we were and that helps us to know ourselves as we are. The statue is neither of the imagination nor of reality. That it is a work of fancy precludes it from being a work of the imagination. A glance at it shows it to be unreal. The bearing of this is that there can be works, and this includes poems, in which neither the imagination nor reality is present.

The other day I was reading a note about an American artist who was said to have "turned his back on the aesthetic whims and theories of the day, and established headquarters in lower Manhattan." Accompanying this note was a reproduction of a painting called *Wooden Horses*. It is a painting of a merry-go-round, possibly of several of them. One of the horses seems to be prancing. The others are going lickety-split, each one struggling to get the bit in his teeth. The horse in the center of the picture, painted yellow, has two riders, one a man, dressed in a carnival costume, who is seated in the saddle, the other a blonde, who is seated well up the horse's neck. The man has his arms under the girl's arms. He holds himself stiffly in order to keep his cigar out of the girl's hair. Her feet are in a second and shorter set of stirrups. She has the legs of a hammer-thrower. It is clear that the couple are accustomed to wooden horses and like them. A little behind them is a younger girl riding alone. She has a strong body and streaming hair. She wears a short-sleeved, red waist, a white skirt and an emphatic bracelet of pink coral. She has her eyes on the man's arms. Still farther behind, there is another girl. One does not see much more of her than her head. Her lips are painted bright red. It seems that it would be better if someone were to hold her on her horse. We, here, are not interested in any aspect of this picture except that it is a picture of ribald and hilarious reality. It is a picture wholly favorable to what is real. It is not without imagination and it is far from being without aesthetic theory.

(3)

These illustrations of the relation between the imagination and reality are an outline on the basis of which to indicate a tendency. Their usefulness is this: that they help to make clear, what no one may ever have doubted, that just as in this or that work the degrees of the imagination and of reality may vary, so this variation may exist as between the works of one age and the works of another. What I have said up to this point amounts to this: that the idea of nobility exists in art today only in degenerate forms or in a much diminished state, if, in fact, it exists at all or otherwise than on sufferance; that this is due to failure in the relation between the imagination and reality. I should now like to add that this failure is due, in turn, to the pressure of reality.

A variation between the sound of words in one age and the

sound of words in another age is an instance of the pressure of reality. Take the statement by Bateson that a language, considered semantically, evolves through a series of conflicts between the denotative and the connotative forces in words; between an asceticism tending to kill language by stripping words of all association and a hedonism tending to kill language by dissipating their sense in a multiplicity of associations. These conflicts are nothing more than changes in the relation between the imagination and reality. Bateson describes the seventeenth century in England as predominately a connotative period. The use of words in connotative senses was denounced by Locke and Hobbes, who desired a mathematical plainness; in short, perspicuous words. There followed in the eighteenth century an era of poetic diction. This was not the language of the age but a language of poetry peculiar to itself. In time, Wordsworth came to write the preface to the second edition of the *Lyrical Ballads* (1800), in which he said that the first volume had been published, "as an experiment, which, I hoped, might be of some use to ascertain how far, by fitting to metrical arrangement a selection of the real language of man in a state of vivid sensation, that sort of pleasure and that quantity of pleasure may be imparted, which a Poet may rationally endeavour to impart."

As the nineteenth century progressed, language once more became connotative. While there have been intermediate reactions, this tendency toward the connotative is the tendency today. The interest in semantics is evidence of this. In the case of some of our prose writers, as, for example, Joyce, the language, in quite different ways, is wholly connotative. When we say that Locke and Hobbes denounced the connotative use of words as an abuse, and when we speak of reactions and reforms, we are speaking, on the one hand, of a failure of the imagination to adhere to reality, and, on the other, of a use of language favorable to reality. The statement that the tendency toward the connotative is the tendency today is disputable. The general movement in the arts, that is to say, in painting and in music, has been the other way. It is hard to say that the tendency is toward the connotative in the use of words without also saying that the tendency is toward the imagination in other directions. The interest in the subconscious and in surrealism shows the tendency toward the imaginative. Boileau's remark that Descartes had cut poetry's throat is a remark that could have been made respecting a great many people during the last hundred years, and of no one more aptly than of Freud, who, as it happens, was familiar with it and repeats it in his *Future of an Illusion*. The object of that essay was to suggest a surrender to reality. His premise was that it is the unmistakable character of the present situation not that the promises of religion have become smaller but that they appear less credible to people. He notes the decline of religious belief and disagrees with the argument that man cannot in general do without the consolation of what he calls the religious illusion and that without it he would not endure the cruelty of reality. His conclusion is that man must venture at last into the hostile world and that this may be called education to reality. There is much more in that essay inimical to poetry and not least the observation in one of the final pages that "The voice of the intellect is a soft one, but it does not rest until it has gained a hearing." This, I fear, is intended to be the voice of the realist.

A tendency in language toward the connotative might very well parallel a tendency in other arts toward the denotative. We have just seen that that is in fact the situation. I suppose that the present always appears to be an illogical complication. The language of Joyce goes along with the dilapidations of Braque and Picasso and the music of the Austrians. To the extent that this painting and this music are the work of men who regard it as part of the science of painting and the science of music it is the work of realists. Actually its effect is that of the imagination, just as the effect of abstract painting is so often that of the imagination, although that may be different. Busoni said, in a letter to his wife, "I have made the painful discovery that nobody loves and feels music." Very likely, the reason there is a tendency in language toward the connotative today is that there are many who love it and feel it. It may be that Braque and Picasso love and feel painting and that Schönberg loves and feels music, although it seems that what they love and feel is something else.

A tendency toward the connotative, whether in language or elsewhere, cannot continue against the pressure of reality. If it is the pressure of reality that controls poetry, then the immediacy of various theories of poetry is not what it was. For instance, when Rostrevor Hamilton says, "The object of contemplation is the highly complex and unified content of consciousness, which comes into being through the developing subjective attitude of the percipient," he has in mind no such "content of consciousness" as every newspaper reader experiences today.

By way of further illustration, let me quote from Croce's Oxford lecture of 1933. He said: "If . . . poetry is intuition and expression, the fusion of sound and imagery, what is the material which takes on the form of sound and imagery? It is the whole man: the man who thinks and wills, and loves, and hates; who is strong and weak, sublime and pathetic, good and wicked; man in the exultation and agony of living; and together with the man, integral with him, it is all nature in its perpetual labour of evolution. . . . Poetry . . . is the triumph of contemplation. . . . Poetic genius chooses a strait path in which passion is calmed and calm is passionate."

Croce cannot have been thinking of a world in which all normal life is at least in suspense, or, if you like, under blockage. He was thinking of normal human experience.

Quite apart from the abnormal aspect of everyday life today, there is the normal aspect of it. The spirit of negation has been so active, so confident and so intolerant that the commonplaces about the romantic provoke us to wonder if our salvation, if the way out, is not the romantic. All the great things have been denied and we live in an intricacy of new and local mythologies, political, economic, poetic, which are asserted with an ever-enlarging incoherence. This is accompanied by an absence of any authority except force, operative or imminent. What has been called the disparagement of reason is an instance of the absence of authority. We pick up the radio and find that comedians regard the public use of words of more than two syllables as funny. We read of the opening of the National Gallery at Washington and we are convinced, in the end, that the pictures are counterfeit, that museums are impositions and that Mr. Mellon was a monster. We turn to a recent translation of Kierkegaard and we find him saying: "A great deal has been said about poetry reconciling one with existence; rather it might be said that it arouses one against existence; for poetry is unjust to men . . . it has use only for the elect, but that is a poor sort of reconciliation. I will take the case of sickness. Aesthetics replies proudly and quite consistently, 'That cannot be employed, poetry must not become a hospital.' Aesthetics culminates . . . by regarding sickness in accordance with the principle enunciated by Friedrich

Schlegel: 'Nur Gesundheit ist liebenswürdig.' (Health alone is lovable.)"

The enormous influence of education in giving everyone a little learning, and in giving large groups considerably more: something of history, something of philosophy, something of literature; the expansion of the middle class with its common preference for realistic satisfactions; the penetration of the masses of people by the ideas of liberal thinkers, even when that penetration is indirect, as by the reporting of the reasons why people oppose the ideas that they oppose,—these are normal aspects of everyday life. The way we live and the way we work alike cast us out on reality. If fifty private houses were to be built in New York this year, it would be a phenomenon. We no longer live in homes but in housing projects and this is so whether the project is literally a project or a club, a dormitory, a camp or an apartment in River House. It is not only that there are more of us and that we are actually close together. We are close together in every way. We lie in bed and listen to a broadcast from Cairo, and so on. There is no distance. We are intimate with people we have never seen and, unhappily, they are intimate with us. Democritus plucked his eye out because he could not look at a woman without thinking of her as a woman. If he had read a few of our novels, he would have torn himself to pieces. Dr. Richards has noted "the widespread increase in the aptitude of the average mind for self-dissolving introspection, the generally heightened awareness of the goings-on of our own minds, *merely as goings-on.*" This is nothing to the generally heightened awareness of the goings-on of other people's minds, *merely as goings-on.* The way we work is a good deal more difficult for the imagination than the highly civilized revolution that is occurring in respect to work indicates. It is, in the main, a revolution for more pay. We have been assured, by every visitor, that the American businessman is absorbed in his business and there is nothing to be gained by disputing it. As for the workers, it is enough to say that the word has grown to be literary. They have become, at their work, in the face of the machines, something approximating an abstraction, an energy. The time must be coming when, as they leave the factories, they will be passed through an air-chamber or a bar to revive them for riot and reading. I am sorry to have to add that to one that thinks, as Dr. Richards thinks, that poetry is the supreme use of language, some of the foreign universities in relation to our own appear to be, so far as the things of the imagination are concerned, as Verrocchio is to the sculptor of the statue of General Jackson.

These, nevertheless, are not the things that I had in mind when I spoke of the pressure of reality. These constitute the drift of incidents, to which we accustom ourselves as to the weather. Materialism is an old story and an indifferent one. Robert Wolseley said: "True genius . . . will enter into the hardest and dryest thing, enrich the most barren Soyl, and inform the meanest and most uncomely matter . . . the baser, the emptier, the obscurer, the fouler, and the less susceptible of Ornament the subject appears to be, the more is the Poet's Praise . . . who, as Horace says of Homer, can fetch Light out of Smoak, Roses out of Dunghills, and give a kind of Life to the Inanimate . . ." (Preface to Rochester's *Valentinian*, 1685, *English Association Essays and Studies* 1939). By the pressure of reality, I mean the pressure of an external event or events on the consciousness to the exclusion of any power of contemplation. The definition ought to be exact and, as it is, may be merely pretentious. But when one is trying to think of a whole generation and of a world at war, and trying at the same time to see what is happening to the imagination, particularly if one believes that that is what matters most, the plainest statement of what is happening can easily appear to be an affectation.

For more than ten years now, there has been an extraordinary pressure of news—let us say, news incomparably more pretentious than any description of it, news, at first, of the collapse of our system, or, call it, of life; then of news of a new world, but of a new world so uncertain that one did not know anything whatever of its nature, and does not know now, and could not tell whether it was to be all-English, all-German, all-Russian, all-Japanese, or all-American, and cannot tell now; and finally news of a war, which was a renewal of what, if it was not the greatest war, became such by this continuation. And for more than ten years, the consciousness of the world has concentrated on events which have made the ordinary movement of life seem to be the movement of people in the intervals of a storm. The disclosures of the impermanence of the past suggested, and suggest, an impermanence of the future. Little of what we have believed has been true. Only the prophecies are true. The present is an opportunity to repent. This is familiar enough. The war is only a part of a war-like whole. It is not possible to look backward and to see that the same thing was true in the past. It is a question of pressure, and pressure is incalculable and eludes the historian. The Napoleonic era is regarded as having had little or no effect on the poets and the novelists who lived in it. But Coleridge and Wordsworth and Sir Walter Scott and Jane Austen did not have to put up with Napoleon and Marx and Europe, Asia and Africa all at one time. It seems possible to say that they knew of the events of their day much as we know of the bombings in the interior of China and not at all as we know of the bombings of London, or, rather, as we should know of the bombings of Toronto or Montreal. Another part of the war-like whole to which we do not respond quite as we do to the news of war is the income tax. The blanks are specimens of mathematical prose. They titillate the instinct of self-preservation in a class in which that instinct has been forgotten. Virginia Woolf thought that the income tax, if it continued, would benefit poets by enlarging their vocabularies and I dare say that she was right.

If it is not possible to assert that the Napoleonic era was the end of one era in the history of the imagination and the beginning of another, one comes closer to the truth by making that assertion in respect to the French Revolution. The defeat or triumph of Hitler are parts of a war-like whole but the fate of an individual is different from the fate of a society. Rightly or wrongly, we feel that the fate of a society is involved in the orderly disorders of the present time. We are confronting, therefore, a set of events, not only beyond our power to tranquillize them in the mind, beyond our power to reduce them and metamorphose them, but events that stir the emotions to violence, that engage us in what is direct and immediate and real, and events that involve the concepts and sanctions that are the order of our lives and may involve our very lives; and these events are occurring persistently with increasing omen, in what may be called our presence. These are the things that I had in mind when I spoke of the pressure of reality, a pressure great enough and prolonged enough to bring about the end of one era in the history of the imagination and, if so, then great enough to bring about the beginning of another. It is one of the peculiarities of the imagination that it is always at the end of an era. What happens is that it is always attaching itself to a new reality, and adhering to it. It is not that there is a new imagination but that there is a new reality. The pressure of reality may, of course, be less than the general pressure that I have described. It exists for individuals according to the circumstances of their lives or according to the characteristics of their minds. To sum it up, the pressure of reality is, I think, the determining factor in the artistic character of an era and, as well, the determining factor in the artistic character of an individual. The resistance to this pressure or its evasion in the case of individuals of extraordinary imagination cancels the pressure so far as those individuals are concerned.

(4)

Suppose we try, now, to construct the figure of a poet, a possible poet. He cannot be a charioteer traversing vacant space, however ethereal. He must have lived all of the last two thousand years, and longer, and he must have instructed himself, as best he could, as he went along. He will have thought that Virgil, Dante, Shakespeare, Milton placed themselves in remote lands and in remote ages; that their men and women were the dead —and not the dead lying in the earth, but the dead still living in their remote lands and in their remote ages, and living in the earth or under it, or in the heavens—and he will wonder at those huge imaginations, in which what is remote becomes near, and what is dead lives with an intensity beyond any experience of life. He will consider that although he has himself witnessed, during the long period of his life, a general transition to reality, his own measure as a poet, in spite of all the passions of all the lovers of the truth, is the measure of his power to abstract himself, and to withdraw with him into his abstraction the reality on which the lovers of truth insist. He must be able to abstract himself and also to abstract reality, which he does by placing it in his imagination. He knows perfectly that he cannot be too noble a rider, that he cannot rise up loftily in helmet and armor on a horse of imposing bronze. He will think again of Milton and of what was said about him: that "the necessity of writing for one's living blunts the appreciation of writing when it bears the mark of perfection. Its quality disconcerts our hasty writers; they are ready to condemn it as preciosity and affectation. And if to them the musical and creative powers of words convey little pleasure, how out of date and irrelevant they must find the . . . music of Milton's verse." Don Quixote will make it imperative for him to make a choice, to come to a decision regarding the imagination and reality; and he will find that it is not a choice of one over the other and not a decision that divides them, but something subtler, a recognition that here, too, as between these poles, the universal interdependence exists, and hence his choice and his decision must be that they are equal and inseparable. To take a single instance: When Horatio says,

> Now cracks a noble heart. Good night, sweet prince,
> And flights of angels sing thee to thy rest!

are not the imagination and reality equal and inseparable? Above all, he will not forget General Jackson or the picture of the *Wooden Horses.*

I said of the picture that it was a work in which everything was favorable to reality. I hope that the use of that bare word has been enough. But without regard to its range of meaning in thought, it includes all its natural images, and its connotations are without limit. Bergson describes the visual perception of a motionless object as the most stable of internal states. He says: "The object may remain the same, I may look at it from the same side, at the same angle, in the same light; nevertheless, the vision I now have of it differs from that which I have just had, even if only because the one is an instant later than the other. My memory is there, which conveys something of the past into the present."

Dr. Joad's comment on this is: "Similarly with external things. Every body, every quality of a body resolves itself into an enormous number of vibrations, movements, changes. What is it that vibrates, moves, is changed? There is no answer. Philosophy has long dismissed the notion of substance and modern physics has endorsed the dismissal. . . . How, then, does the world come to appear to us as a collection of solid, static objects extended in space? Because of the intellect, which presents us with a false view of it."

The poet has his own meaning for reality, and the painter has, and the musician has; and besides what it means to the intelligence and to the senses, it means something to everyone, so to speak. Notwithstanding this, the word in its general sense, which is the sense in which I have used it, adapts itself instantly. The subject-matter of poetry is not that "collection of solid, static objects extended in space" but the life that is lived in the scene that it composes; and so reality is not that external scene but the life that is lived in it. Reality is things as they are. The general sense of the word proliferates its special senses. It is a jungle in itself. As in the case of a jungle, everything that makes it up is pretty much of one color. First, then, there is the reality that is taken for granted, that is latent and, on the whole, ignored. It is the comfortable American state of life of the eighties, the nineties and the first ten years of the present century. Next, there is the reality that has ceased to be indifferent, the years when the Victorians had been disposed of and intellectual minorities and social minorities began to take their place and to convert our state of life to something that might not be final. This much more vital reality made the life that had preceded it look like a volume of Ackermann's colored plates or one of Töpfer's books of sketches in Switzerland. I am trying to give the feel of it. It was the reality of twenty or thirty years ago. I say that it was a vital reality. The phrase gives a false impression. It was vital in the sense of being tense, of being instinct with the fatal or with what might be the fatal. The minorities began to convince us that the Victorians had left nothing behind. The Russians followed the Victorians, and the Germans, in their way, followed the Russians. The British Empire, directly or indirectly, was what was left and as to that one could not be sure whether it was a shield or a target. Reality then became violent and so remains. This much ought to be said to make it a little clearer that in speaking of the pressure of reality, I am thinking of life in a state of violence, not physically violent, as yet, for us in America, but physically violent for millions of our friends and for still more millions of our enemies and spiritually violent, it may be said, for everyone alive.

A possible poet must be a poet capable of resisting or evading the pressure of the reality of this last degree, with the knowledge that the degree of today may become a deadlier degree tomorrow. There is, however, no point to dramatizing the future in advance of the fact. I confine myself to the outline of a possible poet, with only the slightest sketch of his background.

(5)

Here I am, well-advanced in my paper, with everything of interest that I started out to say remaining to be said. I am interested in the nature of poetry and I have stated its nature, from one of the many points of view from which it is possible to state it. It is an interdependence of the imagination and reality as equals. This is not a definition, since it is incomplete. But it states the nature of poetry. Then I am interested in the role of the poet and this is paramount. In this area of my subject I might be expected to speak of the social, that is to say sociological or political, obligation of the poet. He has none. That he must be contemporaneous is as old as Longinus and I dare say older. But that he *is* contemporaneous is almost inevitable. How contemporaneous in the direct sense in which being contemporaneous is intended were the four great poets of whom I spoke a moment ago? I do not think that a poet owes any more as a social obligation than he owes as a moral obligation, and if there is anything concerning poetry about which people agree it is that the role of the poet is not to be found in morals. I cannot say what that wide agreement amounts to because the agreement (in which I do not join) that the poet is under a social obligation is equally wide. Reality is life and life is society and the imagination and reality; that is to say, the imagination and society are inseparable. That is pre-eminently true in the case of the poetic drama. The poetic drama needs a terrible genius before it is anything more than a literary relic. Besides the theater has forgotten that it could ever be terrible. It is not one of the instruments of fate, decidedly. Yes: the all-commanding subject-matter of poetry is life, the never-ceasing source. But it is not a social obligation. One does not love and go back to one's ancient mother as a social obligation. One goes back out of a suasion not to be denied. Unquestionably if a social movement moved one deeply enough, its moving poems would follow. No politician can command the imagination, directing it to do this or that. Stalin might grind his teeth the whole of a Russian winter and yet all the poets in the Soviets might remain silent the following spring. He might excite their imaginations by something he said or did. He would not command them. He is singularly free from that "cult of pomp," which is the comic side of the European disaster; and that means as much as anything to us. The truth is that the social obligation so closely urged is a phase of the pressure of reality which a poet (in the absence of dramatic poets) is bound to resist or evade today. Dante in Purgatory and Paradise was still the voice of the Middle Ages but not through fulfilling any social obligation. Since that is the role most frequently urged, if that role is eliminated, and if a possible poet is left facing life without any categorical exactions upon him, what then? What is his function? Certainly it is not to lead people out of the confusion in which they find themselves. Nor is it, I think, to comfort them while they follow their leaders to and fro. I think that his function is to make his imagination theirs and that he fulfills himself only as he sees his imagination become the light in the minds of others. His role, in short, is to help people to live their lives. Time and time again it has been said that he may not address himself to an élite. I think he may. There is not a poet whom we prize living today that does not address himself to an élite. The poet will continue to do this: to address himself to an élite even in a classless society, unless, perhaps, this exposes him to imprisonment or exile. In that event he is likely not to address himself to anyone at all. He may, like Shostakovich, content himself with pretence. He will, nevertheless, still be addressing himself to an élite, for all poets address themselves to someone and it is of the essence of that instinct, and it seems to amount to an instinct, that it should be to an élite, not to a drab but to a woman with the hair of a pythoness, not to a chamber of commerce but to a gallery of one's own, if there are enough of one's own to fill a gallery. And that élite, if it responds, not out of complaisance, but because the poet has quickened it, because he has educed from it that for which it was searching in itself and in the life around it and which it had not yet quite found, will thereafter do for the poet what he cannot do for himself, that is to say, receive his poetry.

I repeat that his role is to help people to live their lives. He has had immensely to do with giving life whatever savor it possesses. He has had to do with whatever the imagination and the senses have made of the world. He has, in fact, had to do with life except as the intellect has had to do with it and, as to that, no one is needed to tell us that poetry and philosophy are akin. I want to repeat for two reasons a number of observations made by Charles Mauron. The first reason is that these observations tell us what it is that a poet does to help people to live their lives and the second is that they prepare the way for a word concerning escapism. They are: that the artist transforms us into epicures; that he has to discover the possible work of art in the real world, then to extract it, when he does not himself compose it entirely; that he is *un amoureux perpétuel* of the world that he contemplates and thereby enriches; that art sets out to express the human soul; and finally that everything like a firm grasp of reality is eliminated from the aesthetic field. With these aphorisms in mind, how is it possible to condemn escapism? The poetic process is psychologically an escapist process. The chatter about escapism is, to my way of thinking, merely common cant. My own remarks about resisting or evading the pressure of reality mean escapism, if analyzed. Escapism has a pejorative sense, which it cannot be supposed that I include in the sense in which I use the word. The pejorative sense applies where the poet is not attached to reality, where the imagination does not adhere to reality, which, for my part, I regard as fundamental. If we go back to the collection of solid, static objects extended in space, which Dr. Joad posited, and if we say that the space is blank space, nowhere, without color, and that the objects, though solid, have no shadows and, though static, exert a mournful power, and, without elaborating this complete poverty, if suddenly we hear a different and familiar description of the place:

> This City now doth, like a garment, wear
> The beauty of the morning, silent bare,
> Ships, towers, domes, theatres, and temples lie
> Open unto the fields, and to the sky;
> All bright and glittering in the smokeless air;

if we have this experience, we know how poets help people to live their lives. This illustration must serve for all the rest. There is, in fact, a world of poetry indistinguishable from the world in which we live, or, I ought to say, no doubt, from the world in which we shall come to live, since what makes the poet the potent figure that he is, or was, or ought to be, is that he creates the world to which we turn incessantly and without knowing it and that he gives to life the supreme fictions without which we are unable to conceive of it.

And what about the sound of words? What about nobility, of which the fortunes were to be a kind of test of the value of the poet? I do not know of anything that will appear to have suffered more from the passage of time than the music of poetry and that has suffered less. The deepening need for words to express our thoughts and feelings which, we are sure, are all the truth that we shall ever experience, having no illusions, makes us listen to words when we hear them, loving them and feeling them, makes

us search the sound of them, for a finality, a perfection, an unalterable vibration, which it is only within the power of the
acutest poet to give them. Those of us who may have been thinking of the path of poetry, those who understand that words are
thoughts and not only our own thoughts but the thoughts of men
and women ignorant of what it is that they are thinking, must be
conscious of this: that, above everything else, poetry is words;
and that words, above everything else, are, in poetry, sounds.
This being so, my time and yours might have been better spent if
I had been less interested in trying to give our possible poet an
identity and less interested in trying to appoint him to his place.
But unless I had done these things, it might have been thought
that I was rhetorical, when I was speaking in the simplest way
about things of such importance that nothing is more so. A poet's
words are of things that do not exist without the words. Thus, the
image of the charioteer and of the winged horses, which has been
held to be precious for all of time that matters, was created by
words of things that never existed without the words. A description of Verrocchio's statue could be the integration of an illusion
equal to the statue itself. Poetry is a revelation in words by
means of the words. Croce was not speaking of poetry in particular when he said that language is perpetual creation. About
nobility I cannot be sure that the decline, not to say the disap-
pearance of nobility is anything more than a maladjustment between the imagination and reality. We have been a little insane
about the truth. We have had an obsession. In its ultimate extension, the truth about which we have been insane will lead us to
look beyond the truth to something in which the imagination
will be the dominant complement. It is not only that the imagination adheres to reality, but, also, that reality adheres to the
imagination and that the interdependence is essential. We may
emerge from our *bassesse* and, if we do, how would it happen if
not by the intervention of some fortune of the mind? And what
would that fortune of the mind happen to be? It might be only
commonsense but even that, a commonsense beyond the truth,
would be a nobility of long descent.

The poet refuses to allow his task to be set for him. He denies
that he has a task and considers that the organization of materia
poetica is a contradiction in terms. Yet the imagination gives to
everything that it touches a peculiarity, and it seems to me that
the peculiarity of the imagination is nobility, of which there are

many degrees. This inherent nobility is the natural source of another, which our extremely headstrong generation regards as false and decadent. I mean that nobility which is our spiritual height and depth; and while I know how difficult it is to express it, nevertheless I am bound to give a sense of it. Nothing could be more evasive and inaccessible. Nothing distorts itself and seeks disguise more quickly. There is a shame of disclosing it and in its definite presentations a horror of it. But there it is. The fact that it is there is what makes it possible to invite to the reading and writing of poetry men of intelligence and desire for life. I am not thinking of the ethical or the sonorous or at all of the manner of it. The manner of it is, in fact, its difficulty, which each man must feel each day differently, for himself. I am not thinking of the solemn, the portentous or demoded. On the other hand, I am evading a definition. If it is defined, it will be fixed and it must not be fixed. As in the case of an external thing, nobility resolves itself into an enormous number of vibrations, movements, changes. To fix it is to put an end to it. Let me show it to you unfixed.

Late last year Epstein exhibited some of his flower paintings at the Leicester Galleries in London. A commentator in *Apollo* said: "*How with this rage can beauty hold a plea* . . . The quotation from Shakespeare's 65th sonnet prefaces the catalogue. . . . It would be apropos to any other flower paintings than Mr. Epstein's. His make no pretence to fragility. They shout, explode all over the picture space and generally oppose the rage of the world with such a rage of form and colour as no flower in nature or pigment has done since Van Gogh."

What ferocious beauty the line from Shakespeare puts on when used under such circumstances! While it has its modulation of despair, it holds its plea and its plea is noble. There is no element more conspicuously absent from contemporary poetry than nobility. There is no element that poets have sought after, more curiously and more piously, certain of its obscure existence. Its voice is one of the inarticulate voices which it is their business to overhear and to record. The nobility of rhetoric is, of course, a lifeless nobility. Pareto's epigram that history is a cemetery of aristocracies easily becomes another: that poetry is a cemetery of nobilities. For the sensitive poet, conscious of negations, nothing is more difficult than the affirmations of nobility and yet there is nothing that he requires of himself more persistently, since in them and in their kind, alone, are to be found those sanctions that are the reasons for his being and for that occasional ecstasy, or ecstatic freedom of the mind, which is his special privilege.

It is hard to think of a thing more out of time than nobility. Looked at plainly it seems false and dead and ugly. To look at it at all makes us realize sharply that in our present, in the presence of our reality, the past looks false and is, therefore, dead and is, therefore, ugly; and we turn away from it as from something repulsive and particularly from the characteristic that it has a way of assuming: something that was noble in its day, grandeur that was, the rhetorical once. But as a wave is a force and not the water of which it is composed, which is never the same, so nobility is a force and not the manifestations of which it is composed, which are never the same. Possibly this description of it as a force will do more than anything else I can have said about it to reconcile you to it. It is not an artifice that the mind has added to human nature. The mind has added nothing to human nature. It is a violence from within that protects us from a violence without. It is the imagination pressing back against the pressure of reality. It seems, in the last analysis, to have something to do with our self-preservation; and that, no doubt, is why the expression of it, the sound of its words, helps us to live our lives.

QUESTIONS FOR STUDY
AND TOPICS FOR DISCUSSION
ON *The Noble Rider and the Sound of Words*

1. Stevens' essay was first read to an audience at Princeton University in the spring of 1941 as part of a symposium on "The Language of Poetry," and was included in the volume with the same title, edited by Allen Tate, published in 1942. Tate remarks that "the contributors were invited to prepare essays which should not sacrifice the difficult implications of the subject to the limited capacity of the ear of even the best audience." Does Stevens' essay have the air and manner of a speech? Does he employ any of the devices of spoken delivery and oral argument? How significant are these devices for the composition and effect of the work? Does Stevens make concessions to the limitations of the ear?

2. No one who attended the symposium, speakers and auditors alike, could ignore the fact of World War II. The contributors felt the pressure of this reality upon their deliberations; inevitably they had to consider the place of poetry in a world at war. What part does the occasion of the forum and the immediate historical context play in the argument of Stevens' essay? How does his response to the historical situation compare with that of E. M. Forster?

3. An apology for poetry would seem to have been unnecessary in a place where the audience was sympathetic, comprising as it did fellow poets, critics and teachers of literature, and, in general, people interested in the language of poetry,—but there is, for all that, a strong note of defense in Stevens' piece. Against what? Against whom and which parties? What is the difference between the apology Stevens makes and that which Sir Philip Sidney had to make?

4. One other aspect of the occasion is worth remarking. Although Stevens had been writing poetry for some time, he had only recently begun to receive widespread recognition as a major poet. During the thirties his poetry had been attacked as being impervious to life. He had been called a hedonist, an epicure, a dilettante, a dandy. He was accused of lacking high seriousness, social concern, and compassion for the human disaster of the age. The best that critics could find to say was that his poetry made "dear, gorgeous nonsense."

Stevens addresses himself to the question of the social obligation of the poet in Section 5 (pp. 290–292) of the essay, and it might appear, in view of the vicissitudes of his own career, that he is delivering a personal apology. He must have relished the irony of a man of his reputation making the very loftiest claims for poetry. To say that the purpose of poetry is to help people to live their lives . . . what could be more serious? Stevens turns the argument here into a lively contest. He is having his rounds, and he is very deft, very tough with his adversaries. Obviously, however, he is motivated by something more than petulance. He has more on his mind than a grudge match. As you watch his performance, you might ask yourself: Is Stevens justifying his own poetry merely, or is he defending some larger and less personal cause? What tricks does he play on his adversaries, what surprises does he work on his audience, and what purposes does his witty crosstalk serve? How does Stevens qualify his affirmations, and what does he affirm in the very act of making qualifications and seemingly outright denials? How does his mind work in argument? What is the language of his argument? How does his nimble play with words accommodate the solemnity of the occasion?

5. How does Stevens develop the passage from the *Phaedrus* in the introductory section of the essay? What words and figures does he pick up from the translation, and how does he play with them here and through the rest of the essay? How does he change Plato's sense in the repetition of "droop in flight" and "at last settle on the solid ground"? Why does Stevens call the figure "rustic"? Why does he say it "becomes" so? To what does the phrase "this brief experience" (p. 275) refer?

Why does Stevens begin the essay in this fashion rather than by taking up the argument, as he remarks later (p. 289), he "started out to say"? What "argument" does he advance by his reading of Plato's passage? Clearly, there is more at stake than the soul. Stevens seems to be taking issue with the conception of poetry as a winged horse, a Pegasus, which soars above the sensible actuality of the world into some ideal and universal realm. How does Stevens' position on this score compare with Sidney's in *An Apology for Poetry*?

Stevens' mediations between what is actual and what is ideal bear close watching as the essay unfolds, but it is clear from the outset that he means his illustrations, allusions, and examples to carry a substantial portion of his case. How is his treatment of the material in the introductory section typical of his "method" of argument? What is the discursive pattern of the essay—i.e., its movement from point to point in argument—and what is the relation between the discursive reasoning and the concrete illustrations?

6. Analyze the composition of Stevens' argument in Section 1 (pp. 275–277). He relies heavily on negations, reservations, and exceptions. Are these a trick of rhetoric, or are they necessary discriminations for sorting the intricate assumptions and implications of the question? What does he concede to the Platonic figure? With what does he take exception? What does he affirm? What is the relation between his affirmations and the distinctions he makes in his analysis of the figure?

How does Stevens repeat and vary, interweave and cross certain words, phrases, and concepts—e.g., "free to yield," "its insistence moves us," "adhere to reality"? How does each sentence collect a word from the sentences preceding, vary it, play with it, expand it, and employ it to move the argument from one point to the next? That is, how is an assertion developed by repetition and variation of the words which make it up? What is the connection between one paragraph and the next in this section?

In the last paragraph of the section (p. 277) Stevens returns to the question which initiated the excursion and he states his "simple answer." Why didn't he place this paragraph (and perhaps the paragraph just before) right after the first paragraph of the section? What is the form of the verbs in the sentence "What happened, as we were traversing . . ." (p. 277), and why does Stevens use it?

7. In Section 2 (pp. 277–280) Stevens says that he is going to

follow the fortunes of the idea of nobility as characteristic of the imagination. It is hard to think of two more amorphous and formidable abstractions than *imagination* and *reality*. Any precise sense of the terms would seem to call for an exhausting labor at definition and explanation. How does Stevens establish his sense of the terms? What procedures of definition and explanation does he employ? How much of the argument is carried by the illustrations? What guides Stevens' choice and treatment of the examples of equestrian figures and noble riders in this section of the essay? What is the progress from one example to the other? How does each reflect on the other?

8. Why does Stevens bother to say (p. 277) that it would be agreeable to go directly from Plato's figure to Don Quixote, but there is Verrocchio's statue of Colleoni, the famous fifteenth-century soldier of fortune, to consider? Why doesn't he go right to the point? Why does he say it would be a *return* from the "back of heaven" to *one's own spot*? What is the character of Stevens' writing in his description of Verrocchio's statue? How does the writing here compare with that which dominates Section 1? Since Stevens never traveled to Europe, he never saw the actual statue—the most he had to go on were copies or photographs—yet he makes its presence as palpable to the senses as if he and we were eyewitnesses. How does he work this feat? How does he make the act of reflection an *experience*? What does Stevens mean by remarking that the statue stirs "the passion of rhetoric"? What sense of "rhetoric" is implied in the essay? What is the effect of the word "furious"? Of the balanced construction of ". . . the noble style . . . merely perpetuates the noble style"? What is the meaning and effect of "panache"? Analyze the composition and sense of the last sentence of the paragraph (p. 278). Why does the statue seem different nowadays? Why the qualifications in "a little overpowering, a little magnificent"? What is the tone here?

9. Analyze the composition of the argument comparing Don Quixote and Colleoni (p. 278). What devices of parallelism and contrast does Stevens use? What devices of balanced structure does he employ in the syntax? What is being compared exactly? Does the comparison rely too much on how Stevens conceives Cervantes' creation? Does it need an explanation, as with the other figures, to carry conviction? What does Stevens concede in

the comparison? What differences does he treat casually? What does he insist upon? Would any other illustration besides that of Don Quixote have carried the point? How does Stevens move from point to point in the argument of this paragraph? Are there any surprises? Does he yield too much with "These may be words," and with the frequent use of the concessive auxiliary "may" in the ensuing sentences (pp. 278–279)? Is this the way debaters usually go about their business? Is it common for them to seem to yield so much, to follow an argument through so many apparent changes of mind and mood, through so many subtle qualifications of assertion? Why does Stevens write this way?

10. What is Stevens' tone in his description of Clark Mills's statue of Jackson? What sense of "poetry" is implied in the statement that "if Verrocchio could have applied his prodigious poetry to Jackson, the whole American outlook today might be imperial" (p. 279)? How important is the issue of "fancy"? Does it complicate the argument of the section? Was it prudent to introduce a third formidable abstraction—as if the two, imagination and reality, were not enough for one man to handle? How does Stevens make the term, which has a specific sense in literary criticism, reflect a principle of the American mind? What does Stevens think of the American principle typified by Mills's statue? Why does Stevens allow that the statue "at least makes us conscious of ourselves as we were"? How does he pick up the notion of art making consciousness later in the essay? How important is the notion to the argument of the whole?

11. What is Stevens' tone in his appreciation of *Wooden Horses*? What comparisons with the horses and riders in the other illustrations are implied? If this picture is "wholly favorable to what is real" (p. 280), does it have the *right* relation between the imagination and reality? How does the texture of Stevens' description of the figures in the picture differ from that of the previous examples? What does he make of the sharp particulars of color, clothes, physique, etc.? By what means does Stevens make the writing itself pulse with the "ribald and hilarious reality" the picture represents?

12. In Section 3 (pp. 280–287) Stevens turns to the part played by "the pressure of reality" in the failure of the relation between the imagination and reality. In considering the instance of this pressure on the sound of words, he makes a long excursion into the conflicts between "the denotative and connotative forces in words" (p. 281). Is this segment a digression, an essential part of the proof, or an extension of the main argument? Is there anything different about the writing? Is it more or less denotative? Is there any difference in the type and treatment of illustrations? Does the argument have the same savor and movement as before? Is it more or less terse and elliptical? Easier or harder to follow? Does Stevens seem as much at ease in this kind of discussion as he is with the material of the previous sections? Does he maintain the same relationship to an audience as in the earlier material?

13. In the middle of Section 3 Stevens considers the "normal aspect" of "everyday life today" (p. 283). He displays an asperity which appears to be quite at odds with the bemused irony of the earlier portions of the essay. Why has Stevens changed the tone and mood? What is the style and sense of the passage "We are close together in every way . . . he would have torn himself to pieces" (p. 284)? Of "As for the workers . . . to revive them for riot and reading" (p. 284)? Is this segment a digression? How does it follow upon the statement by Croce (p. 283)? What is its place in the larger design of the essay? If, as Stevens says on p. 285, the things discussed in this segment are not what he had in mind when he spoke of the pressure of reality, what purpose does the segment serve?

14. Stevens offers his definition of the "pressure of reality" on p. 285, and in making it he picks up the passage concerning "the content of consciousness" quoted from Rostrevor Hamilton on p. 282. In his view, what role does the imagination play in human consciousness? How has the content of consciousness been assaulted by the events of the time, the pressure of reality? What does this have to do with the normal aspect of everyday life today? With the sound of words? With the idea of nobility? How does Stevens knit together the separate strands of his argument in Section 3? What is the order of his case? How would this section, and the essay as a whole, have been changed if Stevens had placed the passage beginning "We are confronting . . ." (p. 286) immediately after the first paragraph (p. 280)?

15. In Section 4 (pp. 287-289) Stevens constructs his own figure of the poet. Why has he held off this long? How does he gather up words, phrases, and ideas from the earlier portions of the essay? Does Stevens make his figure simply by filling in what he has excluded as untenable in the other figures? What does he add? What qualities of the poet does he emphasize?

Why does Stevens give so much attention to the poet's relation to reality? How does he go about the task of establishing the "degrees" of reality? How does his procedure on this score compare with that on the degrees of imagination? How is the reader made to know which degrees of reality the poet must resist and which he must embrace?

Why does Stevens wait until the last paragraph (p. 289) to state the connection between the body of the section and the end of Section 3 (p. 287)? What does he repeat? What does he vary? What is the effect of the repetition with variations?

16. In Section 5 Stevens repeats what he has said earlier about the nature of poetry, that "it is an interdependence of the imagination and reality as equals" (p. 290), and turns to consider the role of the poet. He disputes a number of common notions; e.g., that the poet has a social obligation, that he may not address an élite, that poetry is escapist. Analyze the composition of his argument. How does he state the position against which he contends? In what fashion does he twist the words of the opposition to support his own stand? With each of these issues Stevens shifts the terms in contention. For example, he says that poetry *is* escapist (p. 292) in one sense, his sense, but not in the sense of the person who charges it to be a defect. How does Stevens achieve this turnabout exactly? How does he handle the other issues of the section? How does the give-and-take with an adversary in this section differ from the rest of the essay?

17. In the midst of parrying misconceptions Stevens advances his own idea about the role of the poet: "his role is to help people to live their lives" (p. 291). This may seem at once too simple and too grandiose. How does Stevens make the statement mean exactly what he says, and say exactly what he means? He quotes lines 4–8 from Wordsworth's famous sonnet "Composed Upon Westminster Bridge" and remarks: "if we have this experience, we know how poets help people to live their lives" (p. 292). He adds: "This illustration must serve for all the rest." But is that enough? Does it suffice to make his meaning clear? Or is

it rather that the whole of the essay, with all of its illustrations and reasoning, explains both the example and the statement it illustrates? In what fashion has Stevens already demonstrated the need for color, savor, heightened consciousness, truth of perception, gaiety, wonder, and all the other qualities he attributes to poetry—without which people cannot be said to live, really live, their lives? How does the whole of the essay fill out the denotative meanings in the climactic statement that the poet "creates the world to which we turn incessantly and without knowing it and . . . he gives to life the supreme fictions without which we are unable to conceive of it" (p. 292)? How has Stevens exploited the connotative force of words to make his case?

18. How does Stevens bring the argument around to rest on and illuminate the topic of the sound of words? He makes two key affirmations: "A poet's words are of things that do not exist without the words" (p. 293), and "Poetry is a revelation in words by means of the words" (p. 293). How does Stevens lead up to and clinch these assertions? What other aspects of his case are reflected in the treatment of this issue?

What does Stevens mean when he says "We have been a little insane about the truth" (p. 293)? How does he develop the statement? What words and ideas from the rest of the essay does he accommodate in its development? In saying that "It is not only that the imagination adheres to reality, but, also, that reality adheres to the imagination," Stevens rings a final and surprising variation on the relation between the imagination and reality. In what sense can it be said that Stevens has transformed this bare and abstract relation into a *figure*?

The word *bassesse* means "baseness" or "servility." How does poetry enable us to emerge from our *bassesse*? What words, images, and ideas from the rest of the essay are reflected in this point?

19. How does Stevens address himself to the matter of "that nobility which is our spiritual height and depth" (p. 294)? He is aware of the difficulties in expressing this nobility, but, as with almost all the issues in his case, he gives a sense of it, even if, as he says, he evades definition (p. 294). How genuine is Stevens being here? Is it just a trick to cover his inability to treat an idea with denotative rigor? How does the commentary on the line from Shakespeare help to prove his point? Why does Stevens

use the word "ferocious"? In what sense is the whole of his own essay mirrored in the remark "While it has its modulation of despair, it holds its plea and its plea is noble" (p. 294)? How does Stevens modulate from despair to some contrary of this mood? What senses of "nobility" is he at pains to exclude for poetry?

20. How does Stevens close the essay? What is the effect of the composition of the last five sentences? Three of these begin "It is . . ."; the last begins "It seems . . ." and includes what might appear to be weak qualifications: "in the last analysis," "have something to do," "no doubt" (p. 295). Is Stevens trailing off indecisively? Is he backing away from a final declaration too overpowering and magnificent? Or does he mean what he says in the last sentence very precisely? What is the exact sense of the sentence?

❦

"BUTTERFLIES"
FROM *Speak, Memory*

BY *Vladimir Nabokov*

(1)

ON A SUMMER MORNING, in the legendary Russia of my boyhood, my first glance upon awakening was for the chink between the shutters. If it disclosed a watery pallor, one had better not open the shutters at all, and so be spared the sight of a sullen day sitting for its picture in a puddle. How resentfully one would deduce, from a line of dull light, the leaden sky, the sodden sand, the gruel-like mess of broken brown blossoms under the lilacs—and that flat, fallow leaf (the first casualty of the season) pasted upon a wet garden bench!

But if the chink was a long glint of dewy brilliancy, then I made haste to have the window yield its treasure. With one blow, the room would be cleft into light and shade. The foliage of birches moving in the sun had the translucent green tone of grapes, and in contrast to this there was the dark velvet of fir trees against a blue of extraordinary intensity, the like of which I rediscovered only many years later, in the montane zone of Colorado.

From *Conclusive Evidence* by Vladimir Nabokov (New York: Harper & Brothers, 1951), pp. 79–92. Reprinted as *Speak, Memory* (New York: Grosset & Dunlap, 1960). This chapter originally appeared as "Butterflies" in the *New Yorker* (June 12, 1948), pp. 25–28. Copyright 1948, 1951, 1960, by Vladimir Nabokov. Reprinted by permission of the author.

From the age of six, everything I felt in connection with a rectangle of framed sunlight was dominated by a single passion. If my first glance of the morning was for the sun, my first thought was for the butterflies it would engender. The original event had been banal enough. On some honeysuckle near the veranda, I had happened to see a Swallowtail—a splendid, pale-yellow creature with black blotches and blue crenulations, and a cinnabar eyespot above each chrome-rimmed black tail. As it probed the inclined flower from which it hung, it kept restlessly jerking its great wings, and my desire for it was overwhelming. An agile footman caught it in my cap, after which it was transferred, cap and all, to a wardrobe, where the reek of naphthalene was fondly expected to kill it overnight. On the following morning, however, when my governess unlocked the wardrobe to take something out, the butterfly, with a mighty rustle, flew into her face, then made for the open window, and presently was but a golden fleck dipping and dodging and soaring eastward, over timber and tundra, to Vologda, Viatka and Perm, and beyond the gaunt Ural range to Yakutsk and Verkhne Kolymsk, and from Verkhne Kolymsk, where it lost a tail, to the fair Island of St. Lawrence, and across Alaska to Dawson, and southward along the Rocky Mountains—to be finally overtaken and captured, after a forty-year race, on a bright-yellow dandelion in a bright-green glade above Boulder.

Soon after the wardrobe affair I found a spectacular moth, and my mother dispatched it with ether. In later years, I used many killing agents, but the least contact with the initial stuff would always cause the door of the past to fly open; once, as a grown man, I was under ether during an operation, and with the vividness of a decalcomania picture I saw my own self in a sailor suit mounting a freshly emerged Emperor moth under the guidance of my smiling mother. It was all there, brilliantly reproduced in my dream, while my own vitals were being exposed: the soaking, ice-cold absorbent cotton pressed to the lemurian head of the moth; the subsiding spasms of its body; the satisfying crackle produced by the pin penetrating the hard crust of its thorax; the careful insertion of the point of the pin in the cork-bottomed groove of the spreading board; the symmetrical adjustment of the strong-veined, "windowed" wings under neatly affixed strips of semi-transparent paper.

(2)

I must have been eight or nine when, in a storeroom of our country house, among a medley of dusty objects, I discovered some wonderful books acquired in the days when my mother's mother had been interested in natural science and had had a famous university professor of zoology (Shimkevich) give private lessons to her daughter. Some of these books were mere curios, such as the four huge brown folios of Albertus Seba's work (*Locupletissimi Rerum Naturalium Thesauri Accurata Descriptio . . .*), printed in Amsterdam around 1750. On their coarse-grained pages I found woodcuts of serpents and butterflies and embryos. The fetus of an Ethiopian female child hanging by the neck in a glass jar, used to give me a nasty shock every time I came across it; nor did I much care for the stuffed hydra on plate CII, with its seven lion-toothed turtleheads on seven serpentine necks and its strange, bloated body which bore button-like tubercules along the sides and ended in a knotted tail.

Other books I found in that attic, among herbariums full of edelweiss flowers and crimson maple leaves, came closer to my subject. I took in my arms and carried downstairs glorious loads of fantastically attractive volumes: Maria Sibylla Merian's (1647–1717) lovely plates of Surinam insects, and Esper's noble *Die Schmetterlinge* (Erlangen, 1777), and Boisduval's *Icones Historiques de Lépidoptères Nouveaux ou Peu Connus* (Paris, begun in 1832). Still more exciting were the products of the latter half of the century—Newman's *Natural History of British Butterflies and Moths*, Hofmann's *Die Gross-Schmetterlinge Europas*, the Grand Duke Nikolai Mikhailovich's *Mémoires* on Asiatic lepidoptera (with incomparably beautiful figures painted by Kavrigin, Rybakov, Lang), Scudder's stupendous work on the *Butterflies of New England.*

By my early teens, I was voraciously reading entomological periodicals, especially English and Russian ones. Great upheavals were taking place in the development of systematics. Since the middle of the century, Continental lepidopterology had been, on the whole, a simple and stable affair, smoothly run by the Germans. Its high priest, Dr. Staudinger, was also the head of the largest firm of insect dealers. Even now, half a century after his death, German lepidopterists have not quite managed to shake off the hypnotic spell occasioned by his authority. He was still alive when his school began to lose ground as a scientific force in the world. While he and his followers stuck to specific and generic names sanctioned by long usage and were content to classify butterflies by characters visible to the naked eye, English-speaking authors were introducing nomenclatorial changes as a result of a strict application of the law of priority and taxonomic changes based on the microscopic study of organs. The Germans did their best to ignore the new trends and continued to cherish the philately-like side of entomology. Their solicitude for the "average collector who should not be made to dissect" is comparable to the way nervous publishers pamper the "average reader" —who should not be made to think.

There was another more general change, which coincided with my ardent adolescent interest in butterflies and moths. The Victorian and Staudingerian kind of species, hermetic and homogeneous, with sundry (alpine, polar, insular, etc.) "varieties" affixed to it from the outside, as it were, like incidental appendages, was replaced by a new, multiform and fluid kind of species, made up of geographical races or subspecies. The evolutional aspects of the case were thus brought out more clearly, by means of more flexible methods of classification, and further links between butterflies and the central problems of nature were provided by biological investigations.

The mysteries of mimicry had a special attraction for me. Its phenomena showed an artistic perfection usually associated with man-wrought things. Such was the imitation of oozing poison by bubble-like macules on a wing (complete with pseudo-refraction) or by glossy yellow knobs on a chrysalis ("Don't eat me—I have already been squashed, sampled and rejected"). When a certain moth resembled a certain wasp in shape and color, it also walked and moved its antennae in a waspish, un-mothlike manner. When a butterfly had to look like a leaf, not only were all the details of a leaf beautifully rendered but markings mimicking grub-bored holes were generously thrown in. "Natural selection," in the Darwinian sense, could not explain the miraculous coincidence of imitative aspect and imitative behavior nor could one appeal to the theory of "the struggle for life" when a protective device was carried to a point of mimetic subtlety, exuberance, and luxury far in excess of a predator's power of appreciation. I discovered in nature the nonutilitarian delights that I sought in art.

Both were a form of magic, both were a game of intricate enchantment and deception.

(3)

Few things indeed have I known in the way of emotion or appetite, ambition or achievement, that could surpass in richness and strength the excitement of entomological exploration. From the very first it had a great many intertwinkling facets. One of them was the acute desire to be alone, since any companion, no matter how quiet, interfered with the concentrated enjoyment of my mania. Its gratification admitted of no compromise or exception. Already when I was ten, tutors and governesses knew that the morning was mine and cautiously kept away.

In this connection, I remember the visit of a schoolmate, a boy of whom I was very fond and with whom I had excellent fun. He arrived one summer night from a town some fifty miles away. His father had recently perished in an accident, the family was ruined and the stout-hearted lad, not being able to afford the price of a railway ticket, had bicycled all those miles to spend a few days with me.

On the morning following his arrival, I did everything I could to get out of the house for my morning hike without his knowing where I had gone. Breakfastless, with hysterical haste, I gathered my net, pillboxes, sailor cap, and escaped through the window. Once in the forest, I was safe; but still I walked on, my calves quaking, my eyes full of scalding tears, the whole of me twitching with shame and self-disgust, as I visualized my poor friend, with his long pale face and black tie, moping in the hot garden—patting the panting dogs for want of something better to do, and trying hard to justify my absence to himself.

Let me look at my demon objectively. With the exception of my parents, no one really understood my obsession, and it was many years before I met a fellow-sufferer. One of the first things I learned was not to depend on others for the growth of my collection. Aunts, however, kept making me ridiculous presents—such as Denton mounts of resplendent but really quite ordinary insects. Our country doctor, with whom I had left the pupae of a rare moth when I went on a journey abroad, wrote me that everything had hatched finely; but in reality a mouse had got at the precious pupae, and upon my return the deceitful old man

produced some common Tortoise-shell butterflies, which, I presume, he had hurriedly caught in his garden and popped into
the breeding cage as plausible substitutes (so *he* thought). Better
than he, was an enthusiastic kitchen boy who would sometimes
borrow my equipment and come back two hours later in triumph
with a bagful of seething invertebrate life and several additional
items. Loosening the mouth of the net which he had tied up with
a string, he would pour out his cornucopian spoil—a mass of
grasshoppers, some sand, the two parts of a mushroom he had
thriftily plucked on the way home, more grasshoppers, more
sand, and one battered Cabbage butterfly.

I also found out very soon that an entomologist indulging in
his quiet quest was apt to provoke strange reactions in other
creatures. How often, when a picnic had been arranged, and I
would be self-consciously trying to get my humble implements
unnoticed into the tar-smelling charabanc (a tar preparation was
used to keep flies away from the horses) or the tea-smelling Opel
convertible (benzine forty years ago smelled that way), some
cousin or aunt of mine would remark: "Must you *really* take that
net with you? Can't you enjoy yourself like a normal boy? Don't
you think you are spoiling everybody's pleasure?" Near a sign
NACH BODENLAUBE, at Bad Kissingen, Bavaria, just as I was about
to join for a long walk my father and majestic old Muromtsev
(who, four years before, in 1906, had been President of the first
Russian Parliament), the latter turned his marble head toward
me, a vulnerable boy of eleven, and said with his famous solemnity: "Come with us by all means, but do not chase butterflies, child. It mars the rhythm of the walk." On a path above the
Black Sea, in the Crimea, among shrubs in waxy bloom, in March,
1919, a bow-legged Bolshevik sentry attempted to arrest me for
signaling (with my net, he said) to a British warship. In the summer of 1929, every time I walked through a village in the Eastern
Pyrenees, which I was exploring lepidopterologically, and happened to look back, I would see in my wake the villagers frozen
in the various attitudes my passage had caught them in, as if I
were Sodom and they Lot's wife. A decade later, in the Maritime
Alps, I once noticed the grass undulate in a serpentine way behind me because a fat rural policeman was wriggling after me on
his belly to find out if I were not trapping song birds. America
has shown even more of this morbid interest in my doings than
other countries have—perhaps because I was in my forties when I

came here to live, and the older the man, the queerer he looks
with a butterfly net in his hand. Stern farmers have drawn my
attention to NO FISHING signs; from cars passing me on the highway have come wild howls of derision; sleepy dogs, though unmindful of the worst bum, have perked up and come at me,
snarling; tiny tots have pointed me out to their puzzled mammas;
broadminded vacationists have asked me whether I was catching
bugs for bait; and one morning on a wasteland, lit by tall yuccas
in bloom, near Santa Fé, a big, black mare followed me for more
than a mile.

(4)

When, having shaken off all pursuers, I took the rough, red
road that ran from our house toward field and forest, the animation and luster of the day seemed like a tremor of sympathy
around me. Black *Erebia* butterflies ("Ringlets" as the old English
Aurelians used to call them), with a special gentle awkwardness
peculiar to their kind, danced among the firs. From a flower head
two male Coppers rose to a tremendous height, fighting all the
way up—and then, after a while came the downward flash of
one of them returning to his thistle. These were familiar insects,
but at any moment something better might cause me to stop
with a quick intake of breath. I remember one day when I warily
brought my net closer and closer to a little *Thecla* that had
daintily settled on a sprig. I could clearly see the White W on
its chocolate-brown underside. Its wings were closed and the
inferior ones were rubbing against each other in a curious circular
motion—possibly producing some small, blithe crepitation pitched
too high for a human ear to catch. I had long wanted that particular species, and, when near enough, I struck. You have heard
champion tennis-players moan after muffing an easy shot. You
have seen stunned golfers smile horrible, helpless smiles. But that
day nobody saw me shake out a piece of twig from an otherwise
empty net and stare at a hole in the tarlatan.

(5)

However, if the morning hunt had been a failure, one could
still look forward to mothing. Colors would die a long death on
June evenings. The lilac shrubs in full bloom before which I

stood, net in hand, displayed clusters of a fluffy grey in the dusk—
the ghost of purple. A moist young moon hung above the mist of
a neighboring meadow. In many a garden have I stood thus in
later years—in Athens, Antibes, Atlanta—but never have I waited
with such a keen desire as before those darkening lilacs. And
suddenly it would come, the low buzz passing from flower to
flower, the vibrational halo around the streamlined body of an
olive and pink Hummingbird moth poised in the air above the
corolla into which it had dipped its long tongue. Its handsome
black larva (resembling a diminutive cobra when it puffed out its
ocellated front segments) could be found on dank willow-herb
two months later. Thus every hour and season had its delights.
And, finally, on cold, or even frosty, autumn nights, one could
sugar for moths by painting tree trunks with a mixture of molas-
ses, beer, and rum. Through the gusty blackness, one's lantern
would illumine the stickily glistening furrows of the bark and two
or three large moths upon it imbibing the sweets, their nervous
wings half open butterfly fashion, the lower ones exhibiting their
incredible crimson silk from beneath the lichen-grey primaries.
"*Catocala adultera!*" I would triumphantly shriek in the direction
of the lighted windows of the house as I stumbled home to show
my captures to my father.

(6)

The "English" park that separated our house from the hay-
fields was an extensive and elaborate affair with labyrinthine
paths, Turgenevian benches, and imported oaks among the en-
demic firs and birches. The struggle that had gone on since my
grandfather's time to keep the park from reverting to the wild
state always fell short of complete success. No gardener could
cope with the hillocks of frizzly black earth that the pink hands
of moles kept heaping on the tidy sand of the main walk. Weeds
and fungi, and ridgelike tree roots crossed and recrossed the sun-
flecked trails. Bears had been eliminated in the eighties (two such
stuffed giants stood on their hind legs in our entrance hall), but
an occasional moose still visited the grounds. On a picturesque
boulder, a little mountain ash and a still smaller aspen had
climbed, holding hands, like two clumsy, shy children. Other,
more elusive trespassers—lost picnickers or merry villagers—
would drive our hoary gamekeeper Ivan crazy by scrawling ribald

words on the benches and gates. The disintegrating process continues still, in a different sense, for when, nowadays, I attempt to follow in memory the winding paths from one given point to another, I notice with alarm that there are many gaps, due to oblivion or ignorance, akin to the terra-incognita blanks mapmakers of old used to call "sleeping beauties."

Beyond the park, there were fields, with a continuous shimmer of butterfly wings over a shimmer of flowers—daisies, blue-bells, scabious, and others—which now rapidly pass by me in a kind of colored haze like those lovely, lush meadows, never to be explored, that one sees from the diner on a transcontinental journey. At the end of this grassy wonderland, the forest rose like a wall. There I roamed, scanning the tree trunks (the enchanted, the silent part of a tree) for certain tiny moths, called Pugs in England—delicate little creatures that cling in the daytime to speckled surfaces, with which their flat wings and turned-up abdomens blend. There, at the bottom of that sea of sunshot greenery, I slowly spun round the great boles. Nothing in the world would have seemed sweeter to me than to be able to add, by a stroke of luck, some remarkable new species to the long list of Pugs already named by others. And my pied imagination, ostensibly, and almost grotesquely, groveling to my desire (but all the time, in ghostly conspiracies behind the scenes, coolly planning the most distant events of my destiny), kept providing me with hallucinatory samples of small print: ". . . the only specimen so far known . . ." ". . . the only specimen known of *Eupithecia petropolitanata* was taken by a Russian schoolboy . . ." ". . . by a young Russian collector . . ." ". . . by myself in the Government of St. Petersburg, Czarskoe Selo District, in 1912 . . . 1913 . . . 1914 . . ."

Then came a June day when I felt the urge to push on still farther and explore the vast marshland beyond the Oredezh. After skirting the river for three or four miles, I found a rickety footbridge. While crossing over, I could see the huts of a hamlet on my left, apple trees, rows of tawny pine logs lying on a green bank, and the bright patches made on the turf by the scattered clothes of peasant girls, who, stark naked in shallow water, romped and yelled, heeding me as little as if I were the discarnate carrier of my present reminiscences.

On the other side of the river, a dense crowd of small, brightblue male butterflies that had been tippling on the rich, trampled mud and cow dung through which I had to trudge rose all together into the spangled air and settled again as soon as I had passed.

After making my way through some pine groves and alder scrub I came to the bog. No sooner had my ear caught the hum of diptera around me, the cry of a snipe overhead, the gulping sound of the morass under my foot, than I knew I would find here quite special arctic butterflies, whose pictures, or, still better, nonillustrated descriptions I had worshiped for several seasons. And the next moment I was among them. Over the bilberry shrubs, with fruit of a dim, dreamy blue, over the brown eye of stagnant water, over moss, over mire, over the intoxicating racemes of the lone and mysterious marsh-rocket, a dark little Fritillary, bearing the name of a Norse goddess, passed in a low, skimming flight. I pursued rose-margined Sulphurs, grey-marbled Satyrs. Unmindful of the mosquitoes that coated my forearms and neck, I stooped with a grunt of delight to snuff out the life of some silver-studded lepidopteron throbbing in the folds of my net. Through the smells of the bog, I caught the subtle perfume of butterfly wings on my fingers, a perfume which varies with the species—vanilla, or lemon, or musk, or a musty, sweetish odor difficult to define. Still unsated, I pressed forward. At last I saw I had come to the end of the marsh. The rising ground beyond was a paradise of lupines, columbines, and pentstemons. Mariposa lilies bloomed under Ponderosa pines. In the distance, fleeting cloud shadows dappled the dull green of slopes above timber line, and the grey and white of Longs Peak.

I confess I do not believe in time. I like to fold my magic carpet, after use, in such a way as to superimpose one part of the pattern upon another. Let visitors trip. And the highest enjoyment of timelessness—in a landscape selected at random—is when I stand among rare butterflies and their food plants. This is ecstasy, and behind the ecstasy is something else, which is hard to explain. It is like a momentary vacuum into which rushes all that I love. A sense of oneness with sun and stone. A thrill of gratitude to whom it may concern—to the contrapuntal genius of human fate or to tender ghosts humoring a lucky mortal.

❦

QUESTIONS FOR STUDY
AND TOPICS FOR DISCUSSION
ON *"Butterflies"*

1. "Butterflies" is a chapter from the autobiographical memoir, *Speak, Memory*. In his prefatory note Nabokov declares: "This account of the author's European past is as truthful as he could possibly make it. If there are any lapses, they are due to the frailty of memory, not to the trickery of art." He means what he says, but he plays an intricate game with words, and the reader must pick his way warily through many equivocations. The trickery of Nabokov's art is the passport of his voyage into the past; his art alone is the conclusive evidence of his testimony.

The grammatical mode of the title is significant. The author bids memory speak. Memory is an evocation, and clearly Nabokov's writing has a richly evocative tone and tenor, but the imperative suggests that evocation is less a quality of seeing and a capacity for recall than a mode of making. As the origin of the word reminds us, evocation is a summoning forward, a process of making things appear, as one might make a person, event, or object from the past, or even a ghost, appear in visible form, palpably *here*, present to the mind. Evocation shapes memory and gives it bodily form. The trick is, and it is something of that small miracle of conjuring all art performs, that Nabokov makes the reader see and feel the remembrances as if he himself had experienced the original happening. The reader enters into and shares Nabokov's memory.

What is especially intriguing about Nabokov's memoir is that he often writes as much about the process of remembering as about the thing remembered; as Sartre said of his novels: "He never writes without seeing himself write." It is this double consciousness that gives his work its peculiar density and allusiveness. Whatever his ostensible subject—his family and relations, his tutors, his first trials at writing, his life as an émigré, his hobbies of chess and butterfly collecting—he is always concerned with the relation of art and life, with his relation to time, with the *composition* of memory.

How does Nabokov make memory speak? What is the ostensible subject of this piece, and what is its relation to the author's profession and his consciousness of the act of composition? What relation between memory and imagination is implied or stated by the author in his treatment of "Butterflies"? Between art and memory? What convictions about time and nature underlie the treatment of the subject? How do they differ from your own conceptions of art, memory, nature, and time? How would you go about composing a memoir? Exactly what are the relations among the thing remembered, the faculty of remembering, and the power to put a remembrance into words? What makes a true portrait or chronicle, and what false?

2. Why does Nabokov call the Russia of his boyhood "legendary"? What other words in the piece suggest the same quality and tone? What would happen to the sense if any of the following words were substituted: "idyllic," "imaginary," "mythical," "fabled," "fabulous," "historical," "vanished," "romantic"?

3. What is the plain sense of the first two paragraphs of the piece? Why does Nabokov shape the content with such lushness of language? What are some of the devices of rhythm and diction? Why does he approach the topic in an oblique and periphrastic manner? From what stage of consciousness and expressive skill is the scene visualized and composed—the boy's, or the adult writer's? How would you characterize the writing? Is it "naturalistic"? "Impressionistic"? What does the writing reveal about the sensibility of the speaker? Does the window figure elsewhere in the piece? How, and to what purpose? What is the effect of "casualty"? Is the word proper for the immediate context? Is it picked up later?

Consider the passage elsewhere in the memoir where Nabokov comments upon the style of the author Sirin:

> Sirin's admirers made much, perhaps too much, of his unusual style, brilliant precision, functional imagery and that sort of thing. Russian readers who had been raised on the sturdy straightforwardness of Russian realism and had

called the bluff of decadent cheats, were impressed by the
mirror-like angles of his clear but weirdly misleading sentences and by the fact that the real life of his books flowed
in his figures of speech, which one critic compared to "windows giving upon a contiguous world . . . a rolling corollary, the shadow of a train of thought."

Nabokov does not divulge that V. K. Sirin was his own pen
name. He is describing his own fiction.

4. In recounting the origin of his passion for butterflies (p.
306), Nabokov writes as if forty years of his life were spent in
pursuit of the Swallowtail that was his first catch—and escaped.
The technique is that of splicing several disparate moments
ranging over vast stretches of terrain and time into one continuous action. What idea of time and space is implicit in the
technique? Where else is it used? To what purpose?

5. In the fourth paragraph (p. 306) the author combines his
memories of ether, his smiling mother, an operation, and the
mounting of a butterfly with strange effect. How would you
characterize this mode of construction? How is the passage meant
to be taken? What is the author up to?

6. In describing the second stage of the progress in his hobby
in Section 2 (pp. 307–308), what connections does the author suggest between his vocation as a writer and his approach to the
study of systematics, nomenclature, and classification in lepidopterology?

7. Why does Nabokov specify the books that fed his growing interest in the scholarship of butterflies (p. 307)? Is he
merely showing off his erudition? What pleasures does he seem
to take from scholarship and how are these related to "field
work"? What are his feelings about the illustrations and descriptive plates of these books? What other illustrations and
emblems are alluded to in the essay?

8. What is the tone of his critique of the Victorian and other
schemes of classification (p. 307)? How does this discussion
fit into the sense and design of the whole piece? What kinds of
evolution besides those of lepidopterology are implied in the
essay?

9. Consider the intention and sense of the last paragraph of Section 2 (p. 308). What is the meaning of "mimicry" in zoology? What is distinctive about Nabokov's idea of mimicry and protective coloration? Explain his association of the phenomenon of mimicry in nature with the nonutilitarian delights that he sought in art. What does the conjunction suggest about the subject and purpose of the whole essay? Why does he say both nature and art were a form of "deception"? How does this square with his remarks in the prefatory note? Are there any ways in which his own writing has an imitative aspect and imitative behavior? Protective coloration? Magic and enchantment? Deception?

10. What does the author take up in Section 3 (pp. 309–311), and why does he place the material here rather than elsewhere? What is the train of his thought? The mode of progression?

What is the word order of the first sentence? What other choices were possible?

11. What is the meaning and effect of "intertwinkling" facets (p. 309)? Why this rather than "interconnected" or "interlinking"? "Facets" has a zoological as well as the more common lapidary sense. Where else does the author employ zoological terms in a figurative manner? What effects are achieved by the interplay of literal and figurative meanings of zoological (and biological) words and concepts?

12. Nabokov refers to his hobby as an obsession and a mania (p. 309). What does he mean exactly? What is his tone? Apologetic? Self-critical? Ironically self-congratulatory? Why does he choose to recount the episode of his running off and leaving his pathetic friend behind? Does he try to justify his behavior? What made him act as he did? Is his remorse genuine? What is his attitude toward the efforts of relatives, friends, and servants to cater to his hobby? What kind of person does the speaker seem to make himself out to be? Peevish? Self-centered? Unfeeling? Ungrateful? If not these, what exactly? How conscious does the speaker appear to be of the full implications of what he is recounting? What is the real point of his self-exposures?

13. In the last paragraph of Section 3 (p. 310) the author relates the strange and amusing reactions his "quiet quest" provoked in other creatures. While his antics seem absurd in their

eyes, he makes their actions seem queerer and more laughable. What qualities of personality are revealed in this turning of tables? What kind of humor does the author use? Both here and in other places in the piece there are intimations of trespassing, of terrain hedged by barriers and broken into by interlopers and visitors, of open and closed gates, doors, and windows. Do these details form a thematic and figurative design or are they accidental? What do you make of them?

14. Why is Section 4 (p. 311) set off as a separate brief paragraph? What is its relation to what comes before and after? Having shaken off all pursuers and at last alone, the author continues his search, but oddly enough he ends on a note of failure. Why does he choose to chronicle a failure rather than boast of his successes? After all, Nabokov is an accredited expert in the field; he has written scholarly monographs on lepidopterology, and he has discovered and named several new species of butterflies. Are the delights of the pursuit and the elusiveness of the quarry more to his present purpose than the chronicling of his triumphs?

15. Section 5 (pp. 311–312) is, of course, a triumph of sorts, but is the catch the point of the section, or is it again the "excitement of entomological exploration"? What do you make of the contrast between the nocturnal setting of this section and the morning scene of the opening paragraphs of Section 1? Is it just a case of the author's turning his attention from the butterfly, which is diurnal in its habits, to the moth, which is nocturnal?

16. Section 6 (pp. 312–314) begins with a description of a park laid out in the manner of an English formal garden. Even when the author was a boy, the park was always in danger of "reverting to a wild state," and now that he is exiled from the place by time and the Russian Revolution, "the disintegrating process continues still, in a different sense." What sense? What is the relation of all this to the subject of butterflies? What is the mood of the first paragraph of the section?

17. The writing of the section has a resonance and scope of suggestion far exceeding its literal subject. A sense of generalized yearning and achievement surrounds the pursuit, and the pursuit itself is rendered in figurative terms—as a search for something beautiful and appealing which eludes capture but tantalizes and

beckons the "pied imagination" into aesthetic adventure and psychic exploration. The quarry flits and lights, and the exploration of memory is rendered in a manner very like, almost imitative of, the hunt for the butterfly. Why does Nabokov's writing invite such fanciful associations and correspondences? What enlarges the literal contours of the action?

18. Analyze the progress of the action in the windings of memory in paragraphs 2–5 of Section 6 (pp. 313–314). In what place does the action begin, and where does it end? Where is the river Oredezh? Where is Longs Peak? To what region are the flora of paragraph 5 indigenous? A series of events and moments of consciousness are displaced from their normal position and succession to form a continuous and synchronous action. Why does Nabokov use this technique? What are its implications for the sense of the piece? How does the technique embody the author's expressed purpose to try to achieve in imagination the "free world of timelessness"? Why should he think this worth achieving? In what sense has the author become a "discarnate" carrier of present reminiscences?

19. How does the last paragraph (p. 314) close the piece? What is the effect of the abrupt declaration of the first sentence? Analyze the phrasing, cadence, color, and tone of the paragraph and compare these aspects of its form with the paragraph preceding and with the prevailing character of the piece. Does it collapse the rhapsodic mood, or does it turn the flight in another direction? Why does he draw out the reflective implications of the technique of superimposition? Compared to the precise and sensuous evocations of the preceding paragraphs, this seems to treat large abstractions and loose generalities—time, timelessness, love, ecstasy. Are they that, or have these words taken on a graphic quality? Has he, for instance, *enacted* what he means by timelessness?

Why does he say "Let visitors trip"? How has he treated "vacuum" (and plenitude) elsewhere in the piece? What does he mean by "ecstasy"? Is the word fitting or extravagant? Exactly what is Nabokov grateful for? Why "to whom it may concern"? What does he mean by "a sense of oneness with sun and stone"? How has this been realized? Why "contrapuntal genius"? Why "tender" ghosts? Why does he regard himself as a "lucky mortal"?

THE SEALED
TREASURE

by *Saul Bellow*

A FEW YEARS AGO I traveled through the state of Illinois to gather material for an article. It was brilliant fall weather, the corn was high and it was intersected by straight, flat roads over which it was impossible not to drive at top speed. I went from Chicago to Galena and then south through the center of the state to Cairo and Shawneetown. Here and there, in some of the mining counties and in the depopulated towns along the Mississippi there were signs of depression and poverty, but these had the flavor of the far away and long ago, for the rest of the state was dizzily affluent. "Pig Heaven," some people said to me. "Never nothing like it." The shops were filled with goods and buyers. In the fields were the newest harvesting machines; in the houses washers, dryers, freezers and refrigerators, air conditioners, vacuum cleaners, Mixmasters, Waringblenders, television and stereophonic high-fi sets, electrical can openers, novels condensed by the *Reader's Digest* and slick magazines. In the yards, glossy cars in giddy colors, like ships from outer space.

Down in Egypt, as the narrow southern end of the state is called, a Negro woman, her head wrapped in an old-fashioned bandanna, flashed by in her blue Packard with a Boston bull terrier affectionately seated on her shoulder. Here at least was some instinct for the blending of old and new. For the most part, everything was as new as possible. Churches and super-markets had the same modern design. In the skies the rich farmers piloted their own planes. The workers bowled in alleys of choice hardwood where fouls were scored and pins reset by electronic devices. Fifty years ago the Illinois poet Vachel Lind-say had visited these towns preaching the Gospel of Beauty and calling on the people to build the New Jerusalem.

Except for the main stem, the streets were boringly empty, and at night even the main stem was almost deserted. Restless adolescents gathered in the ice-cream parlors or loitered before the chain saws, vibrators, outboard motors and garbage disposal units displayed in shop windows. These, like master spirits, ruled the night in silence.

Some important ingredients of life were conspicuously absent.

I had been asked to write about Illinois, but how was I to distinguish it from Indiana, Michigan, Iowa or Missouri? The houses were built and furnished in the same style, the cows were milked by the same machines, the programs broadcast by C.B.S. and N.B.C. were alike in Rockford, Illinois, and Danbury, Connecticut, and Salt Lake City, Utah. The magazines, the hair styles, the salad dressings, the film stars were not merely American but international. What but slight differences in the menu and the cut of the clothes distinguished the comfortable life of middle-class Illinois from that of Cologne or Frankfurt?

I asked, "What do people do, hereabouts?" "They work." "And when they don't work?" "They watch TV. They play a little poker or canasta or gin." "What else?" "They go to club meetings. Or to the drive-in movie. They pitch a little. They raise a little hell. They bowl. They drink some. They tinker around the place, fool with power-tools. They teach the kids baseball in the Little League. They're Den Mothers over at the Cub Scouts." "Yes, but what do they *do*?" "Well, mister, I'm telling you what they do. What are you getting at?" "You see, I'm writing an article on life here." "Is *that* so! Gosh, you're barking up the wrong tree. There ain't nothing here to write about. There's nothing doing here, or anywhere in Ellenois. It's boring." "You can't have millions of people and nothing doing." "I tell you, you want to write about Hollywood or Las Vegas or New York or Paris. That's where they've got excitement."

I had a score of conversations like this one.

Was the vitality of these people entirely absorbed by the new things? Had a superior inventive and productive power taken them over, paralyzing all the faculties it did not need? Or had the old understanding of reality been based on the threat of hunger and on the continual necessity for hard labor? Was it possible that what people complained of as boredom might in fact be an unbearable excitement caused by the greatness of the change?

I went to the libraries and was not surprised to learn that good books were very much in demand, and that there were people in central Illinois who read Plato, Tocqueville, Proust and Robert Frost. I had expected this. But what I did not understand was what use these isolated readers were making of the books they borrowed. With whom did they discuss them? At the country club, the bowling league, sorting mail at the post office or in the factory, over the back fence, how did they bring up Plato's Justice or Proust's Memory? Ordinary life gave them little opportunity for such conversation. "You can't have millions of people and nothing doing." I was dead sure of that. But the intelligence or cultivation of a woman in Moline, Illinois, would necessarily be her secret, almost her private vice. Her friends at the bridge club would think it very odd of her to think such things. She might not reveal them to her sister, nor perhaps even to her husband. They would be her discovery, her treasure ten times sealed, her private source of power.

"The language, the dress, and the daily actions of men in democracies are repugnant to ideal conceptions," said Tocqueville. He said more, but this is text enough for the moment. Let us set beside it the fact that these men, or some of them, will read *The Divine Comedy, The Tempest* and *Don Quixote*. What will they make of these works? They will, some of them, mix them up with television productions. Others will scale them down. Our understanding of them (it is time to drop the third person) will certainly be faulty. Nevertheless, they move us. That is to say, human greatness can still be seen by us. And it is not a question of the gnat who sees the elephant. We are not members of a different species. Without a certain innate sympathy we could not read Shakespeare and Cervantes. In our own contemporary novels this power to understand the greatest human qualities appears to be dispersed, transformed or altogether buried. A modern mass society has no open place for such qualities, no vocabulary for them and no ceremony (except in the churches) which makes them public. So they remain private and are mingled with other private things which vex us or of which we feel ashamed. But they are not lost. The saleswoman in Moline, Ill., *will* go to the library and borrow *Anna Karenina*. This society with its titanic products conditions but cannot absolutely denature us. It forces certain elements of the genius of our species to go into hiding. In America they take curiously personal, secret forms. Sometimes they corrupt people; sometimes they cause them to act with startling generosity. On the whole they are not to be found in what we call our Culture.

They are not in the streets, in the stores, at the movies. They are the missing ingredients.

The greatest danger, Dostoevsky warned in *The Brothers Karamazov*, was the universal ant-hill. D. H. Lawrence believed the common people of our industrial cities were like the great slave populations of the ancient empires. Joyce was apparently convinced that what happened to the ordinary modern man, his external life, was not interesting enough to chronicle. James Stephens in his preface to *Solitaria* by the Russian philosopher Rozanov said that novelists were trying to keep alive by artificial means feelings and states of being which had died out of the modern world, implying that we were only flattering the dwarfs by investing them with the passions of dead giants.

Mind manipulation, brainwashing and social engineering are only the newest developments in an evolution long understood by writers of the civilized world. When we read the best nineteenth and twentieth-century novelists we soon realize that they are trying in a variety of ways to establish a definition of human nature, to justify the continuation of life as well as the writing of novels. Like it or not, says Dostoevsky, it is our nature to be free, and under the sting of suffering to choose between good and evil. And Tolstoy says of human nature that it contains a need for truth which will never allow it to rest permanently in falsehood or unreality.

I think the novelists who take the bitterest view of our modern condition make the most of the art of the novel. "Do you think," Flaubert replies to a correspondent who has complained of *Madame Bovary*, that this ignoble reality, so disgusting to you in reproduction, does not oppress my heart as it does yours? If you knew me better you would know that I abhor ordinary existence. Personally, I have always held myself as aloof from it as I could. But aesthetically I desired this once—and only once—to plumb its very depths.

The writer's art appears to be a compensation for the hopelessness or meanness of existence. *He* by some method has retained the feelings and the ideal conceptions of which no sign remains in ordinary existence. Some novelists, the naturalists, have staked everything on ordinary existence in their desire to keep their connection with the surrounding world. Many of these have turned themselves into recording instruments at best, and at worst they have sucked up to the crowd, disgustingly. But the majority of modern novelists have followed the standard of Flaubert, the aesthetic standard. The shock caused by the loss of faith, says Professor Heller in *The Disinherited Mind,* made Burckhardt adopt an aesthetic view of history. If he is right, a sharp sense of disappointment and aestheticism go together. Flaubert complained that the exterior world was "disgusting, enervating, corruptive and brutalizing. . . . I am turning towards a kind of aesthetic mysticism," he wrote.

I am sticking to Flaubert because the connection between Yonville in Normandy and Galesburg, Illinois (and London and Chicago) is constantly growing closer; because Flaubert believed that the writer by means of imagery and style must supply the human qualities that the exterior world lacks; and because we have all been schooled in his method—we are like the isolated lady in Moline whose sensitivity is her ten times sealed treasure.

Disappointment with its human material is built into the contemporary novel. It is assumed that society cannot give the novelist suitable themes and characters. Therefore the important humanity of the novel must be the writer's own. His force, his virtuosity, his powers of poetry, his reading of fate are at the center of his book. The reader is invited to bring his sympathies to the writer rather than the characters, and this makes him something of a novelist too.

The insistent aesthetic purpose in novelists like Flaubert and Henry James and Virginia Woolf and James Joyce is tyrannical at times. It over-conditions the situation of the characters. We are greatly compensated with poetry and insight, but it often seems as though the writer were deprived of all power except the power to see and to despair. In reality, however, he has a very great power. Is it likely that Westerns, thrillers, movies, soap-operas and True Confessions can usurp that power and permanently replace it? Not unless human nature is malleable without limits and can be conditioned to do without its ancient bread and meat.

A work of fiction consists of a series of moments during which we are willingly engrossed in the experiences of others. Or, as a recent article in the *Hudson Review* puts it, "the exuberant conviction that the individual life of *somebody else* holds all human truth and human potentiality" must be shared by the novelist and his reader. Let us say, putting it as mildly as possible, that modern society does not often inspire this exuberant conviction. We must not lie to ourselves about this. We must not lie. The Americans are softly optimistic and do lie about the love they bear one another. My informant in Illinois was telling the truth when he said his life was boring, but he would have turned awfully pious if I had asked him whether he loved his neighbor. Then he would have stood on the creed and answered that he felt a boundless love for him.

The matter was put as strongly as possible by D. H. Lawrence. "The sympathetic heart is broken," he said. "We stink in each other's nostrils." That is, we cannot easily accept our own creaturely existence or that of others. And that is the fault of modern civilization, he tells us. We must in part agree, but the matter is so serious that we should be careful not to exaggerate. Our lives depend on it. Yes, there are good reasons for revulsion and fear. But revulsion and fear impair judgment. Anxiety destroys scale and suffering makes us lose perspective.

One would have to be optimistic to the point of imbecility to raise the standard of pure Affirmation and cry, "Yea, Yea," shrilly against the deep background of "Nays." But the sympathetic heart is sometimes broken, sometimes not. It is reckless to say "broken"; it is nonsense to say "whole and unimpaired." On either side we have the black and white of paranoia.

As for the novelist, it would become him to proceed with care and modesty. He should deplore no general evil on purely literary grounds. The world owes him nothing, and he has no business to be indignant with it on behalf of the novel. He must not expect life to bind itself to be stable for his sake or to accommodate his ambitions. If he must, let him, like Flaubert, "abhor ordinary existence." But he should not fall into despair over trifles. One of his legacies from Romanticism is a sensitivity to banality and ugliness in which originates much of the small change of modern fiction—the teeth that are crooked, the soiled underclothes, the clerk with carbuncles. From this comes a conventional unearned wretchedness, a bitterness about existence which is mere fashion. One of his legacies from Humanism is an idea of dignity which makes him think a great deal of what he sees about him absurd.

The enormous increases in population seem to have dwarfed the individual. So have modern physics and astronomy. But we may be somewhere between a false greatness and a false insignificance. At least we can stop misrepresenting ourselves to ourselves and realize that the only thing we can be in this world is human. We are temporarily miracle-sodden and feeling faint.

QUESTIONS FOR STUDY
AND TOPICS FOR DISCUSSION
ON *The Sealed Treasure*

1. Bellow's essay originally appeared in the *Times Literary Supplement* (London) as part of a symposium on "The Limits of Control." (The series ran in successive issues from May 3, 1960 to July 15, 1960, and later was collected in a volume entitled *The Writer's Dilemma,* published in 1961.) A group of "several representative authors," ten in all, were asked to consider "the position of the writer in an age which places greater value on the progress of technology than on the state of the individual." The question put to the authors was this: "What are the limits beyond his control that threaten the modern writer?"

How does Bellow order his response to the question posed for discussion? What is the form of his inquiry? What is his "position"? Why does he begin with a description of his trip in search of material for an article? Why not begin with his reflections on what he saw and heard during the trip—with the conclusions he reached? When does he get to the point of the argument? Where does the essay change from descriptive and narrative modes of writing to reflective and argumentative? How do these differences in mode of expression affect the sense of the piece? Why does Bellow divide the material into four sections? Why has he arranged the sections in their present order? How are they knit together? How is each section related to the whole? What other forms of arrangement and modes of expression were possible? Is the essay coherent? Unified? Is the impression of a mind thinking its way through the question and searching for answers, the impression of an inquiry in process, essential to the plenary meaning and effect of the essay?

2. What is the purpose and effect of the second sentence of the essay? Are the descriptive details functional or merely or-

namental? Why does Bellow bother with setting? What details of the argument of the essay are foreshadowed?

3. Why does Bellow say *dizzily* affluent (p. 321)? What other word or words might he have used? What image is suggested by the word? Compare the very last sentence of the essay (p. 327), and trace the pattern of figures which link these two points. What idea is embodied in this pattern of images, and how are idea and imagery related to the sense of the whole?

4. What is the tone of the portion of the first paragraph beginning with " 'Pig Heaven' . . ."? Is the speaker disgusted; admiring; indifferent; bemused? What is the construction of the last sentence of the paragraph? Its tone and imagery?

5. Explain the blendings and incongruities described in the second paragraph. How does Bellow regard the things he reports? As a novelist Bellow is noted for having a rich sense of humor. What evidences of humor, and what kinds of humor, are shown in this and other portions of the essay? How does this gift of humor enable Bellow to sustain the balance he argues a writer needs in order not to fall prey to the black and white of paranoia?

6. The third paragraph conveys an air of vacancy and stillness. How is this related to what comes before? What is the purpose and effect of the contrast between the restless adolescents and the implements of power and energy displayed in the shop windows and bedded down for the night? How is this contrast developed in the rest of the essay? What is the referent of "these"? Why do they rule the night in silence?

7. Why does Bellow set the last sentence of the first section (p. 322) as a separate paragraph? When does he take the statement up again? Why does he wait before specifying the missing ingredients?

8. What is the point of the first paragraph of the second section? What is its connection with the occasion? What are its implications for the form of the piece? How does Bellow move into the question of the discussion? As a writer in search of material, what is his connection with what he observes, and how does this anticipate the later discussion of the relation of the writer to the surrounding world?

9. What is the purpose and effect of the composite conversation (p. 322)? Why does Bellow make it up? In what ways does Bellow differ from his respondent? For example, how does each regard *doing*? Why don't they seem to be able to understand one another?

10. Why does Bellow use questions in the paragraph beginning "Was the vitality . . ." (p. 323) rather than declarative sentences? Are they genuine questions or rhetorical? What is their relation to what he has observed and experienced during his trip? Lifted out of context, the words "vitality," "power," "boredom," "paralysis" are abstractions. What overtones have they taken on in this essay? By what means have they been given graphic properties and a concrete texture?

11. In the next paragraph Bellow says that he was not surprised to find that good books were very much in demand, but he wonders "what use these isolated readers were making of the books they borrowed" (p. 323). In what sense are these readers isolated? What are the causes of their isolation? What does this have to do with the limits of control and the situation of the modern writer? Why does Bellow say that the intelligence or cultivation of the woman in Moline would necessarily be her *secret* and private *vice*? With what is the lady's private source of power contrasted? Why is the treasure sealed? How does Bellow play with the figures and meanings of the title of the essay?

12. How would you characterize the modes of argument and expression in the opening paragraph of the third section (p. 323)? How do these compare with the prevailing modes in the first two sections? Why does Bellow drop the interrogative form? Have the earlier questions been only a ploy to disarm the reader? Why does he say "it is time to drop the third person"?

What contrasts order the argument of the paragraph? The most obvious ones are those that turn on kinds and sources and manifestations of *power*. What are the several senses of the word here and throughout the essay? What is the relation of Bellow's argument to the issues and topics proposed in the question of the limits of control? How does he enlarge the province of the question? The notion that human qualities are dissipated in the pursuit of material wealth has been a commonplace since the Industrial Revolution. Wordsworth, for instance, said in a famous poem:

> The world is too much with us; late and soon,
> Getting and spending, we lay waste our powers.

Is this Bellow's complaint? Is he concerned only with affluence? What is his notion of the role played by technology in opening a schism between ordinary human existence and the "greatest human qualities," the "elements of the genius of our species"? Does Bellow define these qualities? Does he have to? What is his point? How does the general condition depicted in this paragraph affect the writer's task?

13. Bellow focuses on the writer's dilemma in the remaining paragraphs of the third section. What effect does everything that comes before have on his argument on this topic? How does he move from society to reader to writer? How are these interlaced? Bellow asserts: "The writer's art appears to be a compensation for the hopelessness or meanness of existence" (p. 325). Why *appears*? Does Bellow believe it *is*? Does this view accord with his observations and experiences during his trip through Illinois? Does Bellow agree with Flaubert's view of the modern condition? How modern is the condition to Bellow's mind? Does he follow the modern novelists who have taken up the aesthetic standard of Flaubert? Whose side is he on? What is the tone of the argument in this section of the essay, especially in the fifth and seventh paragraphs (pp. 324–325)? In what ways is the isolation of the reader, such as the lady in Moline, similar to or different from the isolation of the modern writer?

14. How does the fourth section (pp. 325–327) compare in subject, modes of argument, and character of expression with the preceding sections? Is Bellow being analytical; diagnostic; polemical; exhortative; asseverating? To whom is he directing his statements? What counsel and criticisms does he offer? What is the characteristic motion of his affirmations? Consider, for example, the rhetoric of his treatment of D. H. Lawrence's statement (p. 326). What does Bellow agree with, but from what does he dissociate himself? How does he expand the quotation? What is its relation to his own case? How does the paragraph immediately following anticipate a possible misunderstanding

of the implications of his position? What does Bellow end by affirming?

15. What is the plenary meaning and effect of the last paragraph (p. 327)? Its content is easy enough; it needs no paraphrase. But in what ways does it gather what has come before in the essay, not only in its ideas but in its pattern of imagery? What contraries does it reflect and how does it mediate between them? For example, what figures of scale and perspective are asserted? What is the tone of the passage, and how does this qualify what is affirmed? What saves the passage from the easy optimism Bellow has just castigated? We all like to think of ourselves as being on the side of humanity—the person he spoke to in Illinois would stand on that creed—but what gives Bellow's statement "the only thing we can be in this world is human" a fresh and distinctive authority? What is there about the style of the writing and the character of the speaker that makes his affirmation tough-minded and unsentimental? What patterns of thought and imagery are concluded in the last sentence? How does its rhythm contribute to the sense and effect of the statement?

NOTES OF
A NATIVE SON

BY *James Baldwin*

ON THE 29TH OF July, in 1943, my father died. On the same day, a few hours later, his last child was born. Over a month before this, while all our energies were concentrated in waiting for these events, there had been, in Detroit, one of the bloodiest race riots of the century. A few hours after my father's funeral, while he lay in state in the undertaker's chapel, a race riot broke out in Harlem. On the morning of the 3rd of August, we drove my father to the graveyard through a wilderness of smashed plate glass.

The day of my father's funeral had also been my nineteenth birthday. As we drove him to the graveyard, the spoils of injustice, anarchy, discontent, and hatred were all around us. It seemed to me that God himself had devised, to mark my father's end, the most sustained and brutally dissonant of codas. And it seemed to me, too, that the violence which rose all about us as my father left the world had been devised as a corrective for the pride of his eldest son. I had declined to believe in that apocalypse which had been central to my father's vision; very well, life seemed to be saying, here is something that will certainly pass for an apocalypse until the real thing comes along. I had inclined to be contemptuous of my father for the conditions of his life, for the conditions of our lives. When his life had ended I began to wonder about that life and also, in a new way, to be apprehensive about my own.

I had not known my father very well. We had got on badly, partly because we shared, in our different fashions, the vice of stubborn pride. When he was dead I realized that I had hardly ever spoken to him. When he had been dead a long time I began to wish I had. It seems to be typical of life in America where opportunities, real and fancied, are thicker than anywhere else on the globe, that the second generation has no time to talk to the first. No one, including my father, seems to have known exactly how old he was, but his mother had been born during slavery. He was of the first generation of free men. He, along with thousands of other Negroes, came North after 1919 and I was part of that generation which had never seen the landscape of what Negroes sometimes call the Old Country.

He had been born in New Orleans and had been a quite young man there during the time that Louis Armstrong, a boy, was running errands for the dives and honky-tonks of what was always presented to me as one of the most wicked of cities—to this day, whenever I think of New Orleans, I also helplessly think of Sodom and Gomorrah. My father never mentioned Louis Armstrong, except to forbid us to play his records; but there was a picture of him on our wall for a long time. One of my father's strong-willed female relatives had placed it there and forbade my father to take it down. He never did, but he eventually maneuvered her out of the house and when, some years later, she was in trouble and near death, he refused to do anything to help her.

He was, I think, very handsome. I gather this from photographs and from my own memories of him, dressed in his Sunday best and on his way to preach a sermon somewhere, when I was little. Handsome, proud, and ingrown, "like a toe-nail," somebody said. But he looked to me, as I grew older, like pictures I had seen of African tribal chieftains: he really should have been naked, with war-paint on and barbaric mementos, standing among spears. He could be chilling in the pulpit and indescribably cruel in his personal life and he was certainly the most bitter man I have ever met; yet it must be said that there was something else in him, buried in him, which lent him his tremendous power and, even, a rather crushing charm. It had something to do with his

blackness, I think—he was very black—with his blackness and his beauty, and with the fact that he knew that he was black but did not know that he was beautiful. He claimed to be proud of his blackness but it had also been the cause of much humiliation and it had fixed bleak boundaries to his life. He was not a young man when we were growing up and he had already suffered many kinds of ruin; in his outrageously demanding and protective way he loved his children, who were black like him and menaced, like him; and all these things sometimes showed in his face when he tried, never to my knowledge with any success, to establish contact with any of us. When he took one of his children on his knee to play, the child always became fretful and began to cry; when he tried to help one of us with our homework the absolutely unabating tension which emanated from him caused our minds and our tongues to become paralyzed, so that he, scarcely knowing why, flew into a rage and the child, not knowing why, was punished. If it ever entered his head to bring a surprise home for his children, it was, almost unfailingly, the wrong surprise and even the big watermelons he often brought home on his back in the summertime led to the most appalling scenes. I do not remember in all those years, that one of his children was ever glad to see him come home. From what I was able to gather of his early life, it seemed that this inability to establish contact with other people had always marked him and had been one of the things which had driven him out of New Orleans. There was something in him therefore, groping and tentative, which was never expressed and which was buried with him. One saw it most clearly when he was facing new people and hoping to impress them. But he never did, not for long. We went from church to smaller and more improbable church, he found himself in less and less demand as a minister, and by the time he died none of his friends had come to see him for a long time. He had lived and died in an intolerable bitterness of spirit and it frightened me, as we drove him to the graveyard through those unquiet, ruined streets, to see how powerful and overflowing this bitterness could be and to realize that this bitterness now was mine.

When he died I had been away from home for a little over a year. In that year I had had time to become aware of the meaning of all my father's bitter warnings, had discovered the secret of his proudly pursed lips and rigid carriage: I had discovered the weight of white people in the world. I saw that this had been for my ancestors and now would be for me an awful thing to live with and that the bitterness which had helped to kill my father could also kill me.

He had been ill a long time—in the mind, as we now realized, reliving instances of his fantastic intransigence in the new light of his affliction and endeavoring to feel a sorrow for him which never, quite, came true. We had not known that he was being eaten up by paranoia, and the discovery that his cruelty, to our bodies and our minds, had been one of the symptoms of his illness was not, then, enough to enable us to forgive him. The younger children felt, quite simply, relief that he would not be coming home anymore. My mother's observation that it was he, after all, who had kept them alive all these years meant nothing because the problems of keeping children alive are not real for children. The older children felt, with my father gone, that they could invite their friends to the house without fear that their friends would be insulted or, as had sometimes happened with me, being told that their friends were in league with the devil and intended to rob our family of everything we owned. (I didn't fail to wonder, and it made me hate him, what on earth we owned that anybody else would want.)

His illness was beyond all hope of healing before anyone realized that he was ill. He had always been so strange and had lived, like a prophet, in such unimaginably close communion with the Lord that his long silences which were punctuated by moans and hallelujahs and snatches of old songs while he sat at the living-room window never seemed odd to us. It was not until he refused to eat because, he said, his family was trying to poison him that my mother was forced to accept as a fact what had, until then, been only an unwilling suspicion. When he was committed, it was discovered that he had tuberculosis and, as it turned out, the disease of his mind allowed the disease of his body to destroy him. For the doctors could not force him to eat, either, and, though he was fed intravenously, it was clear from the beginning that there was no hope for him.

In my mind's eye I could see him, sitting at the window, locked up in his terrors; hating and fearing every living soul including his children who had betrayed him, too, by reaching towards the world which had despised him. There were nine of us. I began to wonder what it could have felt like for such a man to have had nine children whom he could barely feed. He used to make little jokes about our poverty, which never, of course, seemed very funny to us; they could not have seemed very funny to him, either, or else our all too feeble response to them would never have caused such rages. He spent great energy and achieved, to our chagrin, no small amount of success in keeping us away from the people who surrounded us, people who had all-night rent parties to which we listened when we should have been sleeping, people who cursed and drank and flashed razor blades on Lenox Avenue. He could not understand why, if they had so much energy to spare, they could not use it to make their lives better. He treated almost everybody on our block with a most uncharitable asperity and neither they, nor, of course, their children were slow to reciprocate.

The only white people who came to our house were welfare workers and bill collectors. It was almost always my mother who dealt with them, for my father's temper, which was at the mercy of his pride, was never to be trusted. It was clear that he felt their very presence in his home to be a violation: this was conveyed by his carriage, almost ludicrously stiff, and by his voice, harsh and vindictively polite. When I was around nine or ten I wrote a play which was directed by a young, white schoolteacher, a woman, who then took an interest in me, and gave me books to read and, in order to corroborate my theatrical bent, decided to take me to see what she somewhat tactlessly referred to as "real" plays. Theatergoing was forbidden in our house, but, with the really cruel intuitiveness of a child, I suspected that the color of this woman's skin would carry the day for me. When, at school, she suggested taking me to the theater, I did not, as I might have done if she had been a Negro, find a way of discouraging her, but agreed that she should pick me up at my house one evening. I then, very cleverly, left all the rest to my mother, who suggested to my father, as I knew she would, that it would not be very nice to let such a kind woman make the trip for nothing. Also, since it was a schoolteacher, I imagine that my mother countered the idea of sin with the idea of "education," which word, even with my father, carried a kind of bitter weight.

Before the teacher came my father took me aside to ask *why* she was coming, what *interest* she could possibly have in our house, in a boy like me. I said I didn't know but I, too, suggested that it had something to do with education. And I understood that my father was waiting for me to say something—I didn't quite know what; perhaps that I wanted his protection against this teacher and her "education." I said none of these things and the teacher came and we went out. It was clear, during the brief interview in our living room, that my father was agreeing very much against his will and that he would have refused permission if he had dared. The fact that he did not dare caused me to despise him: I had no way of knowing that he was facing in that living room a wholly unprecedented and frightening situation.

Later, when my father had been laid off from his job, this woman became very important to us. She was really a very sweet and generous woman and went to a great deal of trouble to be of help to us, particularly during one awful winter. My mother called her by the highest name she knew: she said she was a "christian." My father could scarcely disagree but during the four or five years of our relatively close association he never trusted her and was always trying to surprise in her open, Midwestern face the genuine, cunningly hidden, and hideous motivation. In later years, particularly when it began to be clear that this "education" of mine was going to lead me to perdition, he became more explicit and warned me that my white friends in high school were not really my friends and that I would see, when I was older, how white people would do anything to keep a Negro down. Some of them could be nice, he admitted, but none of them were to be trusted and most of them were not even nice. The best thing was to have as little to do with them as possible. I did not feel this way and I was certain, in my innocence, that I never would.

But the year which preceded my father's death had made a great change in my life. I had been living in New Jersey, working in defense plants, working and living among southerners, white and black. I knew about the south, of course, and about how southerners treated Negroes and how they expected them to behave, but it had never entered my mind that anyone would look at me and expect *me* to behave that way. I learned in New Jersey that to be a Negro meant, precisely, that one was never looked at but was simply at the mercy of the reflexes the color of one's skin caused in other people. I acted in New Jersey as I had always acted, that is as though I thought a great deal of myself—I had to *act* that way—with results that were, simply, unbelievable. I had scarcely arrived before I had earned the enmity, which was extraordinarily ingenious, of all my superiors and nearly all my co-workers. In the beginning, to make matters worse, I simply did not know what was happening. I did not know what I had done, and I shortly began to wonder what *anyone* could possibly do, to bring about such unanimous, active, and unbearably vocal hostility. I knew about jim-crow but I had never experienced it. I went to the same self-service restaurant three times and stood with all the Princeton boys before the counter, waiting for a hamburger and coffee; it was always an extraordinarily long time before anything was set before me; but it was not until the fourth visit that I learned that, in fact, nothing had ever been set before me: I had simply picked something up. Negroes were not served there, I was told, and they had been waiting for me to realize that I was always the only Negro present. Once I was told this, I determined to go there all the time. But now they were ready for me and, though some dreadful scenes were subsequently enacted in that restaurant, I never ate there again.

It was the same story all over New Jersey, in bars, bowling alleys, diners, places to live. I was always being forced to leave, silently, or with mutual imprecations. I very shortly became notorious and children giggled behind me when I passed and their elders whispered or shouted—they really believed that I was mad. And it did begin to work on my mind, of course; I began to be afraid to go anywhere and to compensate for this I went places to which I really should not have gone and where, God knows, I had no desire to be. My reputation in town naturally enhanced my reputation at work and my working day became one long series of acrobatics designed to keep me out of trouble. I cannot say that these acrobatics succeeded. It began to seem that the machinery of the organization I worked for was turning over, day and night, with but one aim: to eject me. I was fired once, and contrived, with the aid of a friend from New York, to get back on the payroll; was fired again, and bounced back again. It took a while to fire me for the third time, but the third time took. There were no loopholes anywhere. There was not even any way of getting back inside the gates.

That year in New Jersey lives in my mind as though it were

the year during which, having an unsuspected predilection for it, I first contracted some dread, chronic disease, the unfailing symptom of which is a kind of blind fever, a pounding in the skull and fire in the bowels. Once this disease is contracted, one can never be really carefree again, for the fever, without an instant's warning, can recur at any moment. It can wreck more important things than race relations. There is not a Negro alive who does not have this rage in his blood—one has the choice, merely, of living with it consciously or surrendering to it. As for me, this fever has recurred in me, and does, and will until the day I die.

My last night in New Jersey, a white friend from New York took me to the nearest big town, Trenton, to go to the movies and have a few drinks. As it turned out, he also saved me from, at the very least, a violent whipping. Almost every detail of that night stands out very clearly in my memory. I even remember the name of the movie we saw because its title impressed me as being so patly ironical. It was a movie about the German occupation of France, starring Maureen O'Hara and Charles Laughton and called *This Land Is Mine*. I remember the name of the diner we walked into when the movie ended: it was the "American Diner." When we walked in the counterman asked what we wanted and I remember answering with the casual sharpness which had become my habit: "We want a hamburger and a cup of coffee, what do you think we want?" I do not know why, after a year of such rebuffs, I so completely failed to anticipate his answer, which was, of course, "We don't serve Negroes here." This reply failed to discompose me, at least for the moment. I made some sardonic comment about the name of the diner and we walked out into the streets.

This was the time of what was called the "brown-out," when the lights in all American cities were very dim. When we re-entered the streets something happened to me which had the force of an optical illusion, or a nightmare. The streets were very crowded and I was facing north. People were moving in every direction but it seemed to me, in that instant, that all of the people I could see, and many more than that, were moving toward me, against me, and that everyone was white. I remember how their faces gleamed. And I felt, like a physical sensation, a *click* at the nape of my neck as though some interior string connecting my head to my body had been cut. I began to walk. I heard my friend call after me, but I ignored him. Heaven only knows what was going on in his mind, but he had the good sense not to touch me—I don't know what would have happened if he had—and to keep me in sight. I don't know what was going on in my mind, either; I certainly had no conscious plan. I wanted to do something to crush these white faces, which were crushing me. I walked for perhaps a block or two until I came to an enormous, glittering, and fashionable restaurant in which I knew not even the intercession of the Virgin would cause me to be served. I pushed through the doors and took the first vacant seat I saw, at a table for two, and waited.

I do not know how long I waited and I rather wonder, until today, what I could possibly have looked like. Whatever I looked like, I frightened the waitress who shortly appeared, and the moment she appeared all of my fury flowed towards her. I hated her for her white face, and for her great, astounded, frightened eyes. I felt that if she found a black man so frightening I would make her fright worthwhile.

She did not ask me what I wanted, but repeated, as though she had learned it somewhere, "We don't serve Negroes here." She did not say it with the blunt, derisive hostility to which I had grown so accustomed, but, rather, with a note of apology in her voice, and fear. This made me colder and more murderous than ever. I felt I had to do something with my hands. I wanted her to come close enough for me to get her neck between my hands.

So I pretended not to have understood her, hoping to draw her closer. And she did step a very short step closer, with her pencil poised incongruously over her pad, and repeated the formula: ". . . don't serve Negroes here."

Somehow, with the repetition of that phrase, which was already ringing in my head like a thousand bells of a nightmare, I realized that she would never come any closer and that I would have to strike from a distance. There was nothing on the table but an ordinary watermug half full of water, and I picked this up and hurled it with all my strength at her. She ducked and it missed her and shattered against the mirror behind the bar. And, with that sound, my frozen blood abruptly thawed, I returned from wherever I had been, I *saw*, for the first time, the restaurant, the people with their mouths open, already, as it seemed to me, rising as one man, and I realized what I had done, and where I was, and I was frightened. I rose and began running for the door. A round, potbellied man grabbed me by the nape of the neck just as I reached the doors and began to beat me about the face. I kicked him and got loose and ran into the streets. My friend whispered, *"Run!"* and I ran.

My friend stayed outside the restaurant long enough to misdirect my pursuers and the police, who arrived, he told me, at once. I do not know what I said to him when he came to my room that night. I could not have said much. I felt, in the oddest, most awful way, that I had somehow betrayed him. I lived it over and over and over again, the way one relives an automobile accident after it has happened and one finds oneself alone and safe. I could not get over two facts, both equally difficult for the imagination to grasp, and one was that I could have been murdered. But the other was that I had been ready to commit murder. I saw nothing very clearly but I did see this: that my life, my *real* life, was in danger, and not from anything other people might do but from the hatred I carried in my own heart.

(2)

I had returned home around the second week in June—in great haste because it seemed that my father's death and my mother's confinement were both but a matter of hours. In the case of my mother, it soon became clear that she had simply made a miscalculation. This had always been her tendency and I don't believe that a single one of us arrived in the world, or has since arrived anywhere else, on time. But none of us dawdled so intolerably about the business of being born as did my baby sister. We sometimes amused ourselves, during those endless, stifling weeks, by picturing the baby sitting within in the safe, warm dark, bitterly regretting the necessity of becoming a part of our chaos and stubbornly putting it off as long as possible. I understood her perfectly and congratulated her on showing such good sense so soon. Death, however, sat as purposefully at my father's bedside as life stirred within my mother's womb and it was harder to understand why he so lingered in that long shadow. It seemed that he had bent, and for a long time, too, all of his energies towards dying. Now death was ready for him but my father held back.

All of Harlem, indeed, seemed to be infected by waiting. I had never before known it to be so violently still. Racial tensions throughout this country were exacerbated during the early years of the war, partly because the labor market brought together hundreds of thousands of ill-prepared people and partly because Negro soldiers, regardless of where they were born, received their military training in the south. What happened in defense plants and army camps had repercussions, naturally, in every Negro ghetto. The situation in Harlem had grown bad enough for clergymen, policemen, educators, politicians, and social workers to assert in one breath that there was no "crime wave" and to offer, in the very next breath, suggestions as to how to combat it. These suggestions always seemed to involve playgrounds, despite the fact that racial skirmishes were occurring in the playgrounds, too. Playground or not, crime wave or not, the Harlem police force had been augmented in March, and the unrest grew—perhaps, in fact, partly as a result of the ghetto's instinctive hatred of policemen. Perhaps the most revealing news item, out of the steady parade of reports of muggings, stabbings, shootings, assaults, gang wars, and accusations of police brutality, is the item concerning six Negro girls who set upon a white girl in the subway because, as they all too accurately put it, she was stepping on their toes. Indeed she was, all over the nation.

I had never before been so aware of policemen, on foot, on horseback, on corners, everywhere, always two by two. Nor had I ever been so aware of small knots of people. They were on stoops and on corners and in doorways, and what was striking about them, I think, was that they did not seem to be talking. Never, when I passed these groups, did the usual sound of a curse or a laugh ring out and neither did there seem to be any hum of gossip. There was certainly, on the other hand, occurring between them communication extraordinarily intense. Another thing that was striking was the unexpected diversity of the people who made up these groups. Usually, for example, one would see a group of sharpies standing on the street corner, jiving the passing chicks; or a group of older men, usually, for some reason, in the vicinity of a barber shop, discussing baseball scores, or the numbers, or making rather chilling observations about women they had known. Women, in a general way, tended to be seen less often together—unless they were church women, or very young girls, or prostitutes met together for an unprofessional instant. But that summer I saw the strangest combinations: large, respectable, churchly matrons standing on the stoops or the corners with their hair tied up, together with a girl in sleazy satin whose face bore the marks of gin and the razor, or heavy-set, abrupt, no-nonsense older men, in company with the most disreputable and fanatical "race" men, or these same "race" men with the sharpies, or these sharpies with the churchly women. Seventh Day Adventists and Methodists and Spiritualists seemed to be hobnobbing with Holyrollers and they were all, alike, entangled with the most flagrant disbelievers; something heavy in their stance seemed to indicate that they had all, incredibly, seen a common vision, and on each face there seemed to be the same strange, bitter shadow.

The churchly women and the matter-of-fact, no-nonsense men had children in the Army. The sleazy girls they talked to had lovers there, the sharpies and the "race" men had friends and brothers there. It would have demanded an unquestioning patriotism, happily as uncommon in this country as it is undesirable, for these people not to have been disturbed by the bitter letters they received, by the newspaper stories they read, not to have been enraged by the posters, then to be found all over New York, which described the Japanese as "yellow-bellied Japs." It was only the "race" men, to be sure, who spoke ceaselessly of being revenged—how this vengeance was to be exacted was not clear—for the indignities and dangers suffered by Negro boys in uniform; but everybody felt a directionless, hopeless bitterness, as well as that panic which can scarcely be suppressed when one knows that a human being one loves is beyond one's reach, and in danger. This helplessness and this gnawing uneasiness does something, at length, to even the toughest mind. Perhaps the best way to sum all this up is to say that the people I knew felt, mainly, a peculiar kind of relief when they knew that their boys were being shipped out of the south, to do battle overseas. It was, perhaps, like feeling that the most dangerous part of a dangerous journey had been passed and that now, even if death should come, it would come with honor and without the complicity of their countrymen. Such a death would be, in short, a fact with which one could hope to live.

It was on the 28th of July, which I believe was a Wednesday, that I visited my father for the first time during his illness and for the last time in his life. The moment I saw him I knew why I had put off this visit so long. I had told my mother that I did not want to see him because I hated him. But this was not true. It was only that I *had* hated him and I wanted to hold on to this hatred. I did not want to look on him as a ruin: it was not a ruin I had hated. I imagine that one of the reasons people cling to their hates so stubbornly is because they sense, once hate is gone, that they will be forced to deal with pain.

We traveled out to him, his older sister and myself, to what seemed to be the very end of a very Long Island. It was hot and dusty and we wrangled, my aunt and I, all the way out, over the fact that I had recently begun to smoke and, as she said, to give myself airs. But I knew that she wrangled with me because she could not bear to face the fact of her brother's dying. Neither could I endure the reality of her despair, her unstated bafflement as to what had happened to her brother's life, and her own. So we wrangled and I smoked and from time to time she fell into a heavy reverie. Covertly, I watched her face, which was the face of an old woman; it had fallen in, the eyes were sunken and lightless; soon she would be dying, too.

In my childhood—it had not been so long ago—I had thought her beautiful. She had been quick-witted and quick-moving and very generous with all the children and each of her visits had been an event. At one time one of my brothers and myself had thought of running away to live with her. Now she could no longer produce out of her handbag some unexpected and yet familiar delight. She made me feel pity and revulsion and fear. It was awful to realize that she no longer caused me to feel affection. The closer we came to the hospital the more querulous she became and at the same time, naturally, grew more dependent on me. Between pity and guilt and fear I began to feel that there was another me trapped in my skull like a jack-in-the-box who might escape my control at any moment and fill the air with screaming.

She began to cry the moment we entered the room and she saw him lying there, all shriveled and still, like a little black monkey. The great, gleaming apparatus which fed him and would have compelled him to be still even if he had been able to move brought to mind, not beneficence, but torture; the tubes entering his arm made me think of pictures I had seen when a child, of Gulliver, tied down by the pygmies on that island. My aunt wept and wept, there was a whistling sound in my father's throat; nothing was said; he could not speak. I wanted to take his hand, to say something. But I do not know what I could have said, even if he could have heard me. He was not really in that room with us, he had at last really embarked on his journey; and though my aunt told me that he said he was going to meet Jesus, I did not hear anything except that whistling in his throat. The doctor came back and we left, into that unbearable train again, and home. In the morning came the telegram saying that he was dead. Then the house was suddenly full of relatives, friends, hysteria, and confusion and I quickly left my mother and the children to the care of those impressive women, who, in Negro communities at least, automatically appear at times of bereavement armed with lotions, proverbs, and patience, and an ability to cook. I went downtown. By the time I returned, later the same day, my mother had been carried to the hospital and the baby had been born.

(3)

For my father's funeral I had nothing black to wear and this posed a nagging problem all day long. It was one of those problems, simple, or impossible of solution, to which the mind insanely clings in order to avoid the mind's real trouble. I spent most of that day at the downtown apartment of a girl I knew, celebrating my birthday with whiskey and wondering what to wear that night. When planning a birthday celebration one naturally does not expect that it will be up against competition from a funeral and this girl had anticipated taking me out that night, for a big dinner and a night club afterwards. Sometime during the course of that long day we decided that we would go out anyway, when my father's funeral service was over. I imagine I decided it, since, as the funeral hour approached, it became clearer and clearer to me that I would not know what to do with myself when it was over. The girl, stifling her very lively concern as to the possible effects of the whiskey on one of my father's chief mourners, concentrated on being conciliatory and practically helpful. She found a black shirt for me somewhere and ironed it and, dressed in the darkest pants and jacket I owned, and slightly drunk, I made my way to my father's funeral.

The chapel was full, but not packed, and very quiet. There were, mainly, my father's relatives, and his children, and here and there I saw faces I had not seen since childhood, the faces of my father's one-time friends. They were very dark and solemn now, seeming somehow to suggest that they had known all along that something like this would happen. Chief among the mourners was my aunt, who had quarreled with my father all his life; by which I do not mean to suggest that her mourning was insincere or that she had not loved him. I suppose that she was one of the few people in the world who had, and their incessant quarreling proved precisely the strength of the tie that bound them. The only other person in the world, as far as I knew, whose relationship to my father rivaled my aunt's in depth was my mother, who was not there.

It seemed to me, of course, that it was a very long funeral. But it was, if anything, a rather shorter funeral than most, nor, since there were no overwhelming, uncontrollable expressions of grief, could it be called—if I dare to use the word—successful. The minister who preached my father's funeral sermon was one of the few my father had still been seeing as he neared his end. He presented to us in his sermon a man whom none of us had ever seen—a man thoughtful, patient, and forbearing, a Christian inspiration to all who knew him, and a model for his children. And no doubt the children, in their disturbed and guilty state, were almost ready to believe this; he had been remote enough to be anything and, anyway, the shock of the incontrovertible, that it was really our father lying up there in that casket, prepared the mind for anything. His sister moaned and this grief-stricken moaning was taken as corroboration. The other faces held a dark, non-committal thoughtfulness. This was not the man they had known, but they had scarcely expected to be confronted with *him;* this was, in a sense deeper than questions of fact, the man they had not known, and the man they had not known may have been the real one. The real man, whoever he had been, had suffered and now he was dead: this was all that was sure and all that mattered now. Every man in the chapel hoped that when his hour came he, too, would be eulogized, which is to say forgiven, and that all of his lapses, greeds, errors, and strayings from the truth would be invested with coherence and looked upon with charity. This was perhaps the last thing human beings could give each other and it was what they demanded, after all, of the Lord. Only the Lord saw the midnight tears, only He was present when one of His children, moaning and wringing hands, paced up and down the room. When one slapped one's child in anger the recoil in the heart reverberated through heaven and became part of the pain of the universe. And when the children were hungry and sullen and distrustful and one watched them, daily, growing wilder, and further away, and running headlong into danger, it was the Lord who knew what the charged heart endured as the strap was laid to the backside; the Lord alone who knew what one *would* have said if one had had, like the Lord, the gift of the living word. It was the Lord who knew of the impossibility every parent in that room faced: how to prepare the child for the day when the child would be despised and how to *create* in the child—by what means?—a stronger antidote to this poison than one had found for oneself. The avenues, side streets, bars, billiard halls, hospitals, police stations, and even the playgrounds of Harlem—not to mention the houses of correction, the jails, and the morgue—testified to the potency of the poison while remaining silent as to the efficacy of whatever antidote, irresistibly raising the question of whether or not such an antidote existed; raising, which was worse, the question of whether or not an antidote was desirable; perhaps poison should be fought with poison. With these several schisms in the mind and with more terrors in the heart than could be named, it was better not to judge the man who had gone down under an impossible burden. It was better to remember: *Thou knowest this man's fall; but thou knowest not his wrassling.*

While the preacher talked and I watched the children—years of changing their diapers, scrubbing them, slapping them, taking them to school, and scolding them had had the perhaps inevitable result of making me love them, though I am not sure I knew this then—my mind was busily breaking out with a rash of disconnected impressions. Snatches of popular songs, indecent jokes, bits of books I had read, movie sequences, faces, voices, political issues—I thought I was going mad; all these impressions suspended, as it were, in the solution of the faint nausea produced in me by the heat and liquor. For a moment I had the impression that my alcoholic breath, inefficiently disguised with chewing gum, filled the entire chapel. Then someone began singing one of my father's favorite songs and, abruptly, I was with him, sitting on his knee, in the hot, enormous, crowded church which was the

first church we attended. It was the Abyssinia Baptist Church on
138th Street. We had not gone there long. With this image, a
host of others came. I had forgotten, in the rage of my growing
up, how proud my father had been of me when I was little. Apparently, I had had a voice and my father had liked to show me
off before the members of the church. I had forgotten what he
had looked like when he was pleased but now I remembered that
he had always been grinning with pleasure when my solos ended.
I even remembered certain expressions on his face when he
teased my mother—had he loved her? I would never know. And
when had it all begun to change? For now it seemed that he
had not always been cruel. I remembered being taken for a hair-
cut and scraping my knee on the footrest of the barber's chair
and I remembered my father's face as he soothed my crying and
applied the stinging iodine. Then I remembered our fights, fights
which had been of the worst possible kind because my technique had been silence.

I remembered the one time in all our life together when we
had really spoken to each other.

It was on a Sunday and it must have been shortly before I left
home. We were walking, just the two of us, in our usual silence,
to or from church. I was in high school and had been doing a
lot of writing and I was, at about this time, the editor of the high
school magazine. But I had also been a Young Minister and had
been preaching from the pulpit. Lately, I had been taking fewer
engagements and preached as rarely as possible. It was said in
the church, quite truthfully, that I was "cooling off."

My father asked me abruptly, "You'd rather write than preach,
wouldn't you?"

I was astonished at his question—because it was a real question. I answered, "Yes."

That was all we said. It was awful to remember that that was
all we had *ever* said.

The casket now was opened and the mourners were being led
up the aisle to look for the last time on the deceased. The assumption was that the family was too overcome with grief to be
allowed to make this journey alone and I watched while my aunt
was led to the casket and, muffled in black, and shaking, led back
to her seat. I disapproved of forcing the children to look on their
dead father, considering that the shock of his death, or, more
truthfully, the shock of death as a reality, was already a little

more than a child could bear, but my judgment in this matter had been overruled and there they were, bewildered and frightened and very small, being led, one by one, to the casket. But there is also something very gallant about children at such moments. It has something to do with their silence and gravity and with the fact that one cannot help them. Their legs, somehow, seem *exposed,* so that it is at once incredible and terribly clear that their legs are all they have to hold them up.

I had not wanted to go to the casket myself and I certainly had not wished to be led there, but there was no way of avoiding either of these forms. One of the deacons led me up and I looked on my father's face. I cannot say that it looked like him at all. His blackness had been equivocated by powder and there was no suggestion in that casket of what his power had or could have been. He was simply an old man dead, and it was hard to believe that he had ever given anyone either joy or pain. Yet, his life filled that room. Further up the avenue his wife was holding his newborn child. Life and death so close together, and love and hatred, and right and wrong, said something to me which I did not want to hear concerning man, concerning the life of man.

After the funeral, while I was downtown desperately celebrating my birthday, a Negro soldier, in the lobby of the Hotel Braddock, got into a fight with a white policeman over a Negro girl. Negro girls, white policemen, in or out of uniform, and Negro males—in or out of uniform—were part of the furniture of the lobby of the Hotel Braddock and this was certainly not the first time such an incident had occurred. It was destined, however, to receive an unprecedented publicity, for the fight between the policeman and the soldier ended with the shooting of the soldier. Rumor, flowing immediately to the streets outside, stated that the soldier had been shot in the back, an instantaneous and revealing invention, and that the soldier had died protecting a Negro woman. The facts were somewhat different—for example, the soldier had not been shot in the back, and was not dead, and the girl seems to have been as dubious a symbol of womanhood as her white counterpart in Georgia usually is, but no one was interested in the facts. They preferred the invention because this invention expressed and corroborated their hates and fears so perfectly. It is just as well to remember that people are always doing this. Perhaps many of those legends, including

Christianity, to which the world clings began their conquest of the world with just some such concerted surrender to distortion. The effect, in Harlem, of this particular legend was like the effect of a lit match in a tin of gasoline. The mob gathered before the doors of the Hotel Braddock simply began to swell and to spread in every direction, and Harlem exploded.

The mob did not cross the ghetto lines. It would have been easy, for example, to have gone over Morningside Park on the west side or to have crossed the Grand Central railroad tracks at 125th Street on the east side, to wreak havoc in white neighborhoods. The mob seems to have been mainly interested in something more potent and real than the white face, that is, in white power, and the principal damage done during the riot of the summer of 1943 was to white business establishments in Harlem. It might have been a far bloodier story, of course, if, at the hour the riot began, these establishments had still been open. From the Hotel Braddock the mob fanned out, east and west along 125th Street, and for the entire length of Lenox, Seventh, and Eighth avenues. Along each of these avenues, and along each major side street—116th, 125th, 135th, and so on—bars, stores, pawnshops, restaurants, even little luncheonettes had been smashed open and entered and looted—looted, it might be added, with more haste than efficiency. The shelves really looked as though a bomb had struck them. Cans of beans and soup and dog food, along with toilet paper, corn flakes, sardines, and milk tumbled every which way, and abandoned cash registers and cases of beer leaned crazily out of the splintered windows and were strewn along the avenues. Sheets, blankets, and clothing of every description formed a kind of path, as though people had dropped them while running. I truly had not realized that Harlem *had* so many stores until I saw them all smashed open; the first time the word *wealth* ever entered my mind in relation to Harlem was when I saw it scattered in the streets. But one's first, incongruous impression of plenty was countered immediately by an impression of waste. None of this was doing anybody any good. It would have been better to have left the plate glass as it had been and the goods lying in the stores.

It would have been better, but it would also have been intolerable, for Harlem had needed something to smash. To smash something is the ghetto's chronic need. Most of the time it is the members of the ghetto who smash each other, and themselves.

But as long as the ghetto walls are standing there will always come a moment when these outlets do not work. That summer, for example, it was not enough to get into a fight on Lenox Avenue, or curse out one's cronies in the barber shops. If ever, indeed, the violence which fills Harlem's churches, pool halls, and bars erupts outward in a more direct fashion, Harlem and its citizens are likely to vanish in an apocalyptic flood. That this is not likely to happen is due to a great many reasons, most hidden and powerful among them the Negro's real relation to the white American. This relation prohibits, simply, anything as uncomplicated and satisfactory as pure hatred. In order really to hate white people, one has to blot so much out of the mind—and the heart—that this hatred itself becomes an exhausting and self-destructive pose. But this does not mean, on the other hand, that love comes easily: the white world is too powerful, too complacent, too ready with gratuitous humiliation, and, above all, too ignorant and too innocent for that. One is absolutely forced to make perpetual qualifications and one's own reactions are always canceling each other out. It is this, really, which has driven so many people mad, both white and black. One is always in the position of having to decide between amputation and gangrene. Amputation is swift but time may prove that the amputation was not necessary—or one may delay the amputation too long. Gangrene is slow, but it is impossible to be sure that one is reading one's symptoms right. The idea of going through life as a cripple is more than one can bear, and equally unbearable is the risk of swelling up slowly, in agony, with poison. And the trouble, finally, is that the risks are real even if the choices do not exist.

"But as for me and my house," my father had said, "we will serve the Lord." I wondered, as we drove him to his resting place, what this line had meant for him. I had heard him preach it many times. I had preached it once myself, proudly giving it an interpretation different from my father's. Now the whole thing came back to me, as though my father and I were on our way to Sunday school and I were memorizing the golden text: *And if it seem evil unto you to serve the Lord, choose you this day whom you will serve; whether the gods which your fathers served that were on the other side of the flood, or the gods of the Amorites, in which land ye dwell: but as for me and my house, we will serve the Lord.* I suspected in these familiar lines a meaning which had never been there for me before. All of my father's texts and songs, which I had decided were meaningless, were arranged before me at his death like empty bottles, waiting to hold the meaning which life would give them for me. This was his legacy: nothing is ever escaped. That bleakly memorable morning I hated the unbelievable streets and the Negroes and whites who had, equally, made them that way. But I knew that it was folly, as my father would have said, this bitterness was folly. It was necessary to hold on to the things that mattered. The dead man mattered, the new life mattered; blackness and whiteness did not matter; to believe that they did was to acquiesce in one's own destruction. Hatred, which could destroy so much, never failed to destroy the man who hated and this was an immutable law.

It began to seem that one would have to hold in the mind forever two ideas which seemed to be in opposition. The first idea was acceptance, the acceptance, totally without rancor, of life as it is, and men as they are: in the light of this idea, it goes without saying that injustice is a commonplace. But this did not mean that one could be complacent, for the second idea was of equal power: that one must never, in one's own life, accept these injustices as commonplace but must fight them with all one's strength. This fight begins, however, in the heart and it now had been laid to my charge to keep my own heart free of hatred and despair. This intimation made my heart heavy and, now that my father was irrecoverable, I wished that he had been beside me so that I could have searched his face for the answers which only the future would give me now.

❦

QUESTIONS FOR STUDY
AND TOPICS FOR DISCUSSION
ON *Notes of a Native Son*

1. What events are joined together in the first paragraph, and how do the terms which Baldwin uses to describe them inform the whole essay? With what tone are the facts set down? In what ways does the articulation of the themes declared in this paragraph shape and control the turbulent passions at the source of the essay?

Baldwin unravels the nexus of themes as he thinks his way through the piece, but they are felt to be entwined, even when he seems to be treating them one at a time; he plies the same strands, but in different orders of importance. In what ways are the themes interwoven, divided, and re-combined? What effect does the pattern of the whole have on the sense of a particular theme at any one point? What is the order of importance at the beginning of the essay, at the close, and at every significant point in between?

What relationship does Baldwin establish between episodes in his personal experience and events in the exterior world that have a public and general significance? He begins in a narrative mode, and one expects an autobiographical memoir, but he moves into reflective and argumentative modes engaging issues of a social and philosophical nature. How does each mode of expression function relative to the others, and how do they work together to achieve the author's intention? By what means does Baldwin make one man's testimony, one Negro writer's experience, speak for and to his group, his society, his particular country and time? To what audience is his testimony directed and to whom is it pertinent? What is the essay about exactly?

2. In the second paragraph Baldwin reports that the day of his father's funeral coincided with his nineteenth birthday. He

says: "When his life had ended I began to wonder about that life and also, in a new way, to be apprehensive about my own" (p. 334). The essay was written some twelve years after the funeral, and yet it is made to seem as if the author's wonderings and apprehensions were contiguous with the event. Indeed, the whole essay is shaped as if he were accompanying his father in the drive to the graveyard, his thoughts following in its train, and his reflections framed by its progress. The drive to the graveyard is more than an incidental narrative motif; it is a figure of composition which organizes the ideas and reflections of the piece and gives them direction and coherence.

However far we may wander with Baldwin into his remembrances, experiences, and beliefs, we follow with him the drive to his father's resting place, one life ended, one part of Baldwin's life closing, another beginning. This is an artifice, of course, for the reflections expressed may have occurred to the author at any time in the interval between the funeral and the writing of the essay, but the *form* of the work conveys the impression of a direct and immediate response to the occasion of his father's death. He considers the circumstances of his father's death, looks back to the origin of his sickness, traces the progress of his disease, reflects on the connections between his father's bitterness and that of himself and other Negroes, but the focus is always on the father and on those things of his life that are being buried with him, and those things that survive as a legacy to the son. The essay is an extended epitaph, a tribute—even, in its own way, a funeral eulogy, spoken by the author as if he were a mourner in the imaginary funeral procession of his own mind.

As such, the eulogy which emerges from the whole essay is in obvious contrast to the actual set-piece described in Section 3 (pp. 347–348). That eulogy is a fiction, a pathetic ritual, desperately believed in by the congregation in order that they might invest with coherence and dignity the broken and dishonored lives of their fallen brethren. Baldwin rejects the ritual and the customary obsequies, rejects the filial piety expected of him, so that he may set down his own bleak and terrible vision of the man and his life. He tries to see him steadily and to see him whole.

And in the end Baldwin wishes he could search his father's face for the questions he must bear in life. He has made his father an admonitory and exemplary presence. He looks to the deceased as a warning and as a guide to the perplexed living. The form of this transformation of his father by eulogy reaches deeply into analogues in classical literature and devotional conventions. Baldwin's treatment of his father in an extended epitaph has precedents in Greek and Latin works of literature, in English poetry, in many sixteenth- and seventeenth-century sermons. What, then, are the sources of the essay's power? The subject? The author's fierce candor? Or the art and form by which he shapes the content and enacts his outlook on experience? Has Donne's sermon *Death's Duel* any relevance to Baldwin's essay? What is the full significance of the title? It is an allusion to a famous novel by Richard Wright, and much of the essay concerns the bitter ironies of the position of the Negro in America, but the reference is multiple. In what way does the title refer to Baldwin's estrangement from his father and his progress from disaffection and alienation to an acceptance of parentage?

3. What kind of portrait of his father does Baldwin draw in paragraphs 3–5 (pp. 334–335)? From what perspectives in time and understanding does he view the subject? How does he compose the picture? What figures of speech does Baldwin use in his description, and how are these figures picked up and played upon later in the essay? What qualities of the man are depicted? How are these rendered? How much does Baldwin rely upon descriptive epithets, how much upon incident and illustration, how much upon "character analysis"? Is Baldwin's treatment of his father's "beauty" as affecting and convincing as that of his brooding and ingrown nature? What tone is conveyed by this detail, and how does it compare with the attitude that dominates the sketch?

4. In the sixth paragraph Baldwin declares: "I had discovered the weight of white people in the world" (p. 335). Does this strike a false note? Does it follow from the preceding description of his father? Can the paragraph be deleted? Why is it placed here rather than after the ninth paragraph (p. 337)? What effect does it have on Baldwin's ensuing account of his father's sickness?

5. Baldwin resumes his portrait by recounting two sicknesses: paranoia and tuberculosis—one mental, the other physical. How accurate is Baldwin's diagnosis? Does he distinguish between a

real illness and a figurative one? What relationship does he establish between his father's interior condition—the state of his mind—and the world about him? In what ways are the words and images Baldwin uses in rendering his father's afflictions picked up, embellished, and carried through the essay?

6. Baldwin is exceptionally candid in his account of the feelings of the family toward his father. What is his position in the family? From what vantage does he regard the feelings reported in the three paragraphs beginning "He had been ill a long time . . ." (pp. 336–337)? Where is Baldwin himself situated in the narrative? Why does he place the statement at the end of the paragraph in parentheses? Analyze the modes and functions of the pronouns and verbs of these paragraphs. Is Baldwin as much a part of the "we" as the other members of the family? Does he see things as they do (or did)? Is he detached? By what means does he establish involvement and distance? What role does his handling of verbs play in establishing difference between present reflection and past action?

7. In the paragraph beginning "The only white people . . ." (p. 337) Baldwin begins to shift the focus of his study from his father's temperament and afflictions to his own. The transition is slow, almost imperceptible, but he works by foreshadowings and associations that suggest rather than state causal connections. In what ways is the material of this and the following paragraphs dealing with race relations linked to what has come before? Is Baldwin concerned only, or even primarily, with tracing the origins and progress of his bitterness over race? Does he express any self-criticism? What other ways of arranging the material of the essay were possible? Could Baldwin have begun the essay here, stated explicitly the parallels between his father's bitterness and his own encounters with racial prejudice, and made the race riot in Harlem the climax and vindication of his outrage at the white man's treatment of the Negro in America? What effect would this rearrangement have upon the sense of the whole work? Why did Baldwin shape the content as it stands? What is the intention of the essay?

8. Consider the style and sense of Baldwin's account of his last night in Trenton (pp. 340–342). What caused him to act as he did? What images does Baldwin use in depicting his behavior?

How do these figure elsewhere in the essay? The images of feverishness and madness are obvious enough, but what images designate an eruption, a breaking out from confinements, a smashing of restraints? How are these related to similar figures and actions in the portrait of the father and the account of the riot in Harlem? Baldwin suggests that his composure cracked, his control snapped. Is the loss of control enacted in the writing? Why does he say that the episodes had the "force of an optical illusion, or a nightmare" (p. 340)? In what sense do the events seem *unreal*? Compare the statement toward the end of Section 2: "I began to feel that there was another me trapped in my skull like a jack-in-the-box who might escape my control at any moment and fill the air with screaming" (p. 345).

Analyze the syntax and rhythm of the sentences in the five paragraphs beginning "This was the time . . ." (pp. 340–342). What is the subject, verb, and predicate? Do the grammatical relationships fall into a consistent pattern? Are the sentences complex or simple? What is the relation of clause to clause? How are the clauses connected? What is the degree and kind of adjectival modification and parenthetical qualification? How much material intervenes between subject and predicate? What is the tempo and cadence?

Compare these sentences with those of some other portion of the essay (e.g., the paragraphs cited in Question 6). Are there any appreciable differences in composition? In what ways is each kind of composition appropriate to the sense and purpose of the respective portions?

In considering the narrative of the night in Trenton, think of modes of cinematic composition as an analogue and observe how Baldwin changes the focus of description and narration from panoramic shot to close-up, from broad impression to sharp and precise detail. In what ways are these alterations of focus suited to the content of the passage?

How does Baldwin end the sequence? Why does Baldwin say "my life, my *real* life, was in danger" (p. 342)? What does he mean exactly? What stage of his reflections is reached at the end of the section? From what has he escaped? What has he learned? What else does he have to learn? What is the connection between the close of this section and the concluding paragraph of the essay?

9. What part does Section 2 (pp. 342–346) play in the action of the whole? Baldwin begins by establishing two facts: His sister took a long time to be born, and his father a long time to die. How does he invest these facts with symbolic significance? By what means does Baldwin's writing extend and deepen the factual record? How do these symbolic expansions reflect the sense and design of the whole essay?

Why does Baldwin change the scene from his home to Harlem? How is Harlem personified (p. 343)? How does Baldwin characterize the situation there? How much of his account is factual reporting, and how much some other mode of writing? What kinds of figurative language does he use? Consider, for example, the following expressions: "a violent stillness," "an intensely communicative silence," "the strangest combinations of people." Why does Baldwin use a colloquial idiom in the third paragraph of the section?

An air of expectancy hovers over the narrative. Everyone on the stage is waiting: some for death, some for birth, the others for violence. Why does Baldwin make so much of this? Does it have something to do with the theme of apocalypse? What else?

10. Analyze the composition of the paragraph beginning "She began to cry . . ." (p. 345). What overtones and undertones sound in the passage? How are the facts and the literal details of the situation amplified and deepened? What kind of apparatus is Baldwin describing? What is it for? Why is it an instrument of torture? Why does Baldwin choose to render this last picture of his father as that of a man pinioned and silenced, virtually bound and gagged? Why does he use a paratactic construction in the sentence "My aunt wept and wept, there was a whistling sound in my father's throat; nothing was said; he could not speak"?

This is told with stunning force, but Baldwin has been a long time preparing for that effect. The strangling of the father's speech seems to be only a metaphor signifying the final violation of a man who has had to endure unbearable afflictions—but the power of that metaphor comes from the progress of his silences throughout the essay. Baldwin has depicted a man who shut himself in silence in defiance of and in retreat from the world, a man who cut himself off from his son, his family, and his people, and lost the capacity to distinguish his real and fancied enemies. The whistling in his throat is the last declension of a man who was strangled by the bitterness and madness outside and the bitterness and madness within his own mind.

To speak of "effect" in this connection might appear to cheapen the content of the experience. The facts speak for themselves, do they not? They do not require any embellishment or ornament. Yet, clearly, Baldwin uses much artifice in this essay. And just as clearly he uses artifice to tell rather than to hide truth. In this one passage he employs allusion, tropes, figures of thought, a variety of rhythms and syntax, a range of tones, and directing the whole, a deft control of intention and choice. By what means does Baldwin keep the stylistic devices mentioned from seeming artificial and fanciful?

What is the tone of the last four sentences of the section? Why does he go downtown? Why doesn't he elaborate his feelings about his father's death?

11. Why does Baldwin begin Section 3 (p. 346) by reporting that he had been drinking at a girl's apartment and that he had trouble finding the right clothes for the funeral? Is his behavior offensive? Is he disrespectful of the dead? What differentiates him from the other mourners? Does he feel out of place? Has he become a stranger to his people's customs? What is his attitude toward the observances? Does he mock the belief of the congregation in the ritual of the eulogy? What affinities and identities does he see between himself and the other people at the service? What makes him a "native son" in spite of their differences?

What is the style of Baldwin's reflections and memories during the eulogy (p. 348)? In what ways does the near-madness of his impressions differ in manner and mode of expression from the near-madness of his behavior during the Trenton restaurant episode?

What is the sense and style of the passage in which Baldwin recalls the one time he and his father had "really spoken to each other" (p. 349)? Why has he waited this long to tell it? Why does he place the reminiscence *after* the happy memories?

As in so many parts of the essay, Baldwin shifts rapidly and effortlessly from concrete detail to general statement, from close narrative to broad reflection. In the work of another writer the sentence "Life and death so close together . . ." (p. 350) might seem pretentious. So, as another instance, might the sentence "When one slapped one's child in anger the recoil in the heart reverberated through heaven and became part of the pain of the universe" (p. 348). How does Baldwin keep such statements honest?

Why is Baldwin so concerned with seeing his father as he *really* was in life and in death? How often does Baldwin use the word "reality," or the cognate forms, "real" and "really"? Compare the frequency of "bitterness." Which is more important at the end of the essay?

12. Analyze the composition of Baldwin's account of the riot in Harlem (p. 351). What figures of speech and thought does he employ? What is the tone? Gratified? Apologetic? Detached? Condemnatory? Sorrowful? What exactly? What is the connection between the events in Harlem and the death of his father? How does the author regard the implications of the riot for his own life? What is its place in the progress of his thought in the essay?

13. Does Baldwin make an "affirmation" in the last three paragraphs of the essay (beginning "It would have been better . . ." on p. 351)? Has he cast off hatred and embraced love? Has equanimity displaced bitterness; reasonableness, violence; tolerance, intolerance? Has he slaked his rage? Has the fever abated and the poison drained away? Is he cured of disease?

A certain kind of reader is likely to take an easy and undeserved comfort from these last paragraphs, believing that Baldwin is asking his people to forsake militancy and cast out bitterness. (And do what instead? Passively resist? Picket? Write petitions? Love his white brother? Endure? *Wait?* No wonder Baldwin has become more querulous and strident in his recent essays. He doesn't like the nostrums of Mister Charlie or the "white liberal" any more than he likes being called an Uncle Tom. He has armed his vision and hardened his sympathies, but he still has one object: to see "life as it is." He wants understanding, not compassion, but he is caught between two opacities and he has had to shout louder to be seen for what he is.) Exactly what is Baldwin affirming? With what and with whom has he made his peace?

14. In what ways is the adjectival modification of the sentence "That bleakly memorable morning I hated the unbelievable streets . . ." (p. 353) typical of Baldwin's style? He often uses the comparative and superlative degrees of adjectives and adverbs, and he often uses adjectives that express absolute states or qualities. Why? What effects are achieved? What are the risks of such constructions?

15. How does the last paragraph of the essay qualify the "affirmations" of the preceding two paragraphs? Baldwin's conclusion seems to have some affinities with the content of the essays by Fitzgerald, Forster, and Bellow. What are the differences both in style and sense? What opposites are pacified at the end of the essay? How stable is the balance? In what sense has the form of the essay composed the disorder and dissonances of its subject?